OXFORD BROOKES UNIVERSITY

BSc(Hons) IN APPLIED ACCOUNTING
TUTORIAL TEXT

Success in Your Research and Analysis Project

In this October 2005 edition

This Tutorial Text has been specially written around the detailed requirements of the Research and Analysis Project you need to complete to earn a BSc(Hons) in Applied Accounting from Oxford Brookes University.

It contains:

- The Guidelines (revised edition, updated 1 September 2005)
- A self-test questionnaire
- Overview of the project
- Advice on how to choose and define the project
- Step-by-step guidance on major project tasks on research and analysis
- Guidance on how to present your Report, what to do at mentor meetings, oral presentations and the Key Skills Statement
- Feedback from the examiner on projects submitted under the scheme and other issues.

This Tutorial Text is packed with checklists, exercises and examples

APPROVED BY OXFORD BROOKES UNIVERSITY AND THE ACCA

BPP Professional Education
October 2005

First edition 2000
Fifth edition October 2005

ISBN 0 7517 2392 4 (previous edition 0 7517 1761 4)

British Library Cataloguing-in-Publication Data
A catalogue record for this book is available from the British Library

Published by

BPP Professional Education
Aldine House, Aldine Place
London W12 8AW

www.bpp.com

Printed in Great Britain by W M Print
45-47 Frederick Street
Walsall, West Midlands
WS2 9NE

We are grateful to Oxford Brookes University for permission to reproduce in this text guidelines for this project. We would also like to thank the staff at Oxford Brookes University for their assistance in developing and updating this Tutorial Text.

Contents

Page

INTRODUCTION (v)

PART A: OFFICIAL MATERIAL AND SELF ASSESSMENT

PART B: THE RESEARCH AND ANALYSIS PROJECT

PART C: THE REPORT

PART D: MENTOR MEETINGS AND THE KEY SKILLS STATEMENT

APPENDICES

REVIEW FORM

ORDER FORM

PROJECT SUBMISSION FORM

INTRODUCTION

Under the ground-breaking partnership between the ACCA and Oxford Brookes University, students studying for ACCA exams are able, simultaneously, to study for a Bachelor of Science (Hons) degree in Applied Accounting. To be awarded this degree, students must pass relevant examinations in the ACCA's examination scheme and complete a Research and Analysis Project.

The Research and Analysis Project tests skills in independent research, practical analysis, IT and communication, written and oral. There is no 'syllabus' to study to, only a Project Topic to explore, define and complete.

Recognising that doing the Project will be a very different experience from study for professional exams, BPP has written this Tutorial Text specifically around the type of work you will have to do for the Project.

Only you can choose and complete a Project. However, because the BPP Tutorial Text is packed with advice, self-assessment exercises, checklists and examples, it provides an ideal roadmap.

BPP Seminars

BPP also offers a one-day seminar for students embarking on the Research and Analysis Project. It concentrates on focussing the student precisely on the requirements of the project and provides detailed guidance on choosing a topic, research and analysis techniques and the critical skills of report-writing and giving presentations. Please telephone our Customer Services department on 0845 0751 1000 (UK only) or 020 8740 2211 for further details and to make a booking.

Mentoring

Certain BPP tutors are qualified to act as mentors under the scheme. Please telephone our Customer Service department on 0845 0751 1000 (UK only) or 020 8740 2211 for further information.

BPP Professional Education
October 2005

Further study: the Oxford Institute MBA

As well as giving you a degree, the Project gives you a taster of what it is like to do research. If you enjoy it, you might feel encouraged, after you are ACCA-qualified, to try the MBA programme offered by the Oxford Institute of International Finance (a joint venture between ACCA and Oxford Brookes, and supported by BPP). Contact the Oxford Institute of International Finance for further information (telephone +44 (0) 1865 485800 or email info@oxfordinstitute.org).

Part A

Official material and self assessment

Chapter 1

THE GUIDELINES

Chapter topic list

Research and Analysis Project Guidelines

This chapter contains the official guidelines. The guidelines were updated by Oxford Brookes University in September 2005 and this text includes and refers to the updated version.

SECTION 1 INTRODUCTION

1.1 Requirements

ACCA and Oxford Brookes University have agreed to work in partnership to give students the opportunity to be awarded a BSc (Hons) in Applied Accounting. To obtain this degree you must:

(a) Pass the appropriate ACCA examination papers

(b) Demonstrate your ability to research, analyse, and use key skills, by undertaking a business related **Research and Analysis Report** and preparing a **Key Skills Statement**

In fulfilling requirement b) it will be necessary to work with a mentor and information regarding this relationship can be found on page 5 and in Appendix 3.

This document is intended to provide students with guidelines on how to carry out, complete and submit their Research and Analysis Project in order to qualify for the Oxford Brookes degree. These guidelines contain details of all tasks relating to both the Report and Key Skills Statement and are considered sufficient for those students who feel confident in their ability in each of the skills areas assessed, (see pages 7 and 8). An approved tutorial text is available to those who feel they require further support and guidance in developing these skills and in completing the Project, (see Appendix 2).

The preparation of your Research and Analysis Report and Key Skills Statement will be monitored and verified by your mentor before submission to Oxford Brookes University.

Your Research and Analysis Report and Key Skills Statement will be assessed as either pass or fail according to the University's regulations.

NB: It is essential that you read and understand the regulations contained in the Student Guide, (available on-line at http://www.accaglobal.com/students/professionalscheme/degreepartnership) and that you study Appendix 4 on page 18.

If you have any doubts over your eligibility and/or opt-in status in respect to the Oxford Brookes BSc degree, please contact ACCA Connect who will advise you. If you are not eligible and opted-in, then Oxford Brookes is not able to consider your Research and Analysis project and it will be returned to you unmarked.

1.2 Applying for the Degree

Students who have passed the appropriate examination papers required for the degree may submit their completed Research and Analysis Report and Key Skills Statement at any point in line with the Assessment Period Timetable published on the ACCA website (http://www.accaglobal.com/students/professionalscheme/degreepartnership.com). Students should send in their Research and Analysis Project together with their Submission Forms (see pages 23 and 24) and assessment fee to:

> The ACCA Office, The Business School
> Oxford Brookes University
> Wheatley Campus
> Oxford, OX33 1HX
> United Kingdom
>
> Email: acca@brookes.ac.uk

NB: The Research and Analysis Report and Key Skills Statement should be word processed on A4 paper and presented in a plastic folder/wallet and clipped together in some way. Students should note that if they fail to meet any particular submission deadline, for any reason, then they should delay submission until the next period.

1.3 ACCA Membership Requirements

This Project enables you to record evidence of experience for purposes of the Oxford Brookes degree only and does not count towards ACCA membership. Further training regulations apply for membership purposes.

SECTION 2: TASKS

You are required to:

- Write a business related Research and Analysis Report (up to 5,000 words)

- Participate in three meetings with your mentor, (see page 5), which will involve you in writing a progress update and delivering an oral presentation

- Reflect on your meetings with your mentor and write a Key Skills Statement (up to 1,500 words)

- Submit both the Research and Analysis Project report and the Key Skills Statement bound as one piece of work to Oxford Brookes. Do not submit the two documents separately.

2.1 Report

The Research and Analysis Report should be on a business-related topic (see page 11) which will demonstrate your ability to gather information, analyse the information you have collected and draw conclusions from your research. **Relevant spreadsheets must also be printed out and included within the project to show evidence of IT skills** (see page 8).

A sample printout of the formulae for part of the spreadsheet is the best evidence for this and is highly recommended.

Your Report must be in four sections as set out below:

INTRODUCTION

- Topic chosen and its context
- Your reasons for choosing the topic
- Aims and objectives of the report

INFORMATION GATHERING

- Sources used, and reasons for their use (these must be secondary and may be primary)
- Description of methods used to gather information

ANALYSIS

- Analysis of information
- Presentation of findings

CONCLUSIONS

- What the report has shown in relation to aims and objectives.

Guidance on the length of each section is given below. Please bear in mind that these are suggested word counts rather than requirements. However, the overall total of 5,000 words must not be exceeded. Oxford Brookes University reserves the right to fail any projects over 5,000 words.

The 5,000 word limit excludes the contents page, the appendices and the bibliography. However, your appendices should not consist of more than five sides of A4 including your spreadsheet data. There is no specific requirement on line spacing.

(a) Introduction +
(b) Information gathering   up to 1,500 words
(c) Analysis   up to 2,500 words
(d) Conclusions   up to 1,000 words

NB: Your total word count for the Report should be indicated on the title page of your Report for submission to Oxford Brookes University, and on your Submission Form.

2.2 Choosing Your Mentor

Your mentor will monitor your progress throughout this Project. He/she will be asked to verify your participation in the three meetings as set out on this page and confirm that the report has been carried out in accordance with the University's regulations.

It is your responsibility to find someone to act as your mentor and to arrange three meetings with him/her.

Ideally your mentor will be a line manager or partner in the firm or practice where you are or have been working, or your college/university tutor.

The person you choose **must** be one of the following:

- A qualified Chartered Certified Accountant
- Your employer/line manager (current or previous)
- Your tutor at College or University
- If the person you wish to choose as your mentor is not one of the above then you must contact the ACCA Office at Oxford Brookes University for approval.

5

2.3 Meetings with your Mentor

The three meetings with your mentor, each of which would normally be about half an hour long, should follow the framework set out below.

NB: A set of notes for your mentor can be found in Appendix 5, please pass these on to your chosen mentor as early as possible.

Meeting 1 – at the outset

To prepare for this you should have some idea on the choice of topic, (see page 10), and have embarked on preliminary investigation into the research areas and methods you may want to use. Following this meeting you should be able to set out a clear proposal of your choice of topic, research method and draft aims and objectives for your Report.

Meeting 2 – midway through your report

At this stage you should have completed the gathering of information for your Report and have some initial views as to your findings. An interim update on your progress in the form of a word-processed document should be presented to your mentor. This will then provide the framework for your discussion at this meeting.

Meeting 3 – towards completion of your report

You are required to prepare and deliver a fifteen minute presentation on your Report to your mentor, and if applicable your peer group (see option below). You should use appropriate presentation techniques in conjunction with your talk. You should be prepared to answer questions and provide explanations when requested.

Your mentor will be asked to provide confirmation that the three meetings took place in accordance with the given guidelines.

If it becomes necessary for whatever reason to change your mentor part way through the above framework, you will have to start again at Meeting 1 to allow your new mentor to verify your participation in all three meetings.

You may, if your mentor is happy to participate, arrange for further appointments in addition to the three compulsory meetings outlined in the above framework.

NB. It may be useful for you to keep a personal diary of reflections on your meetings to help you when writing up your Key Skills Statement.

2.4 Peer Group Presentation Option

Where your mentor is working with more than one student, presentations in Meeting 3 can take place in a group. However, Meetings 1 and 2 must only involve the mentor and individual student. This will enable you to deliver your presentation to an audience, receive feedback from your peers and in turn, critically review the work of others.

NB. The Research and Analysis Report must nevertheless be the work of the individual student and should not be carried out in a group. See Appendix 4 for further information on regulations regarding plagiarism, syndication and other forms of cheating.

2.5 Key Skills Statement

In the Key Skills Statement you should demonstrate personal learning arising from interaction with your mentor (and peer presentation group if applicable, see 2.4).

The Statement should concentrate on skills of communication and working with others and focus on your meetings with your mentor as the vehicle for your evidence. It should also clearly indicate where you have used IT skills, in particular word processing, spreadsheet and online database usage within your project.

PREPARING FOR MEETINGS

Describe how you prepared for the three meetings. Assess the importance of planning and organising in relation to the effectiveness of your meetings and of meetings in general.

QUESTIONING

Consider and explain the role of questioning in ensuring productive discussions with your mentor, in particular the use of appropriate questioning techniques.

LISTENING

Explain the importance of listening in ensuring that communication with your mentor was effective. Consider active listening techniques, sources of error and distortion in communication.

THE PRESENTATION

Assess the presentation identifying what went well and what could have been improved. You should attach 2 sides of A4 to your key skills statement showing an outline of your presentation.

SELF-ASSESSMENT OF INTERACTION

Using an appropriate model of communication, analyse and evaluate interaction with your mentor and if applicable with your peer discussion group, in relation to the key elements of successful communication.

Reflect on IT skills used.

For each of these areas illustrate your self-analysis with examples taken from the discussions and by referring to appropriate literature on communication, (see Appendix 2). Where appropriate consider what you would do differently in the future in similar

You should draw on the meetings with your mentor (and your peer presentation group if applicable), to analyse your ability to communicate and work with others. Present your findings using the framework shown.

For each of these areas illustrate your self-analysis with examples taken from the discussions and by referring to appropriate literature on communication, (see Appendix 2). Where appropriate consider what you would do differently in the future in similar circumstances.

As a guide each section of your Statement should be approx. 300 words. However, the overall total of 1,500 words, excluding your presentation outline, should not be exceeded for the Key Skills Statement.

NB. Your Key Skills word count should be indicated on the title page of your Statement and on the Submission Form.

2.6 Assessment

The following documents will be assessed:

- **Research and Analysis Report**
- **Key Skills Statement**

2.7 Criteria for Assessment of the Report

You must achieve a pass in each of the following areas.

Communication Skills

A pass in this area will be achieved by:

- A coherent and structured Report focused on the stated objectives and written in a lucid style

- Clear and accurate referencing (see Appendix 1). *Note that where you have quoted someone else's work and not referenced it, then this is plagiarism, which is a serious offence which will result in disciplinary action by Oxford Brookes University and possibly, also the ACCA. (See Appendix 4)*

Information gathering

A pass in this area will be achieved by:

- Evidence of an appropriate selection of methods of gathering information – these should relate to the topic/objectives of the Report

- Use of a range of information sources which must show evidence of wider reading and use of IT based sources

- Referencing of appropriate sources of information

Analysis and conclusions

A pass in this area will be achieved by:

- A relevant analysis of the information using an appropriate framework or tool

- A clear presentation of findings from the information gathered

- Appropriate conclusions from the analysis related to the objectives of the Report

IT skills

A pass in this area will be achieved by:

- Application of IT software to achieve a document with a clear layout and logical structure

- Use of a spreadsheet to analyse and present data in tabular and graphical form within the Report. A printout of relevant spreadsheets must be included, showing where ever possible the formulas used to make calculations.

2.8 Criteria for Assessment of the Key Skills Statement

A pass will be demonstrated by an analysis of your ability to communicate and work with others by providing:

- Reflection on the nature and structure of the meetings with your mentor through the identification of relevant and influencing factors

- Reflection on the meetings with your mentor examining the nature of the interactions which took place and showing an understanding of the key elements of successful face to face communication, in particular questioning and listening techniques

- A clear outline for the presentation made at Meeting 3 including identification of what went well and what could have been improved. This outline should include copies of PowerPoint/overhead slides or other visual aides that you used during your presentation.

- A self-assessment, drawing on evidence from meetings with your mentor, of your abilities to actively listen, ask appropriate questions, respond to others and achieve satisfactory outcomes

SECTION 3: THE REPORT PROCESS

3.1 Choosing a topic

The topic chosen for your Report should be linked to your organisation or to an organisation of your choice. This should be a real rather than fictitious organisation and consequently any data used should be actual data and fully referenced. If the identity of the company needs to be concealed for reasons of confidentiality, then this should be stated clearly in the project.

We strongly recommend that you choose a topic from the list on the following page. However, should you have an alternative topic which is of particular interest to you, we would advise you to put details in writing to the address on page 4 of these guidelines to confirm acceptability for this Project. You are advised to put your request in writing before starting work on the Report and to allow one month for consideration and response. Unapproved project titles will normally be failed automatically.

NB. In carrying out the research for your Report, if you intend to source any information not already in the public domain (i.e. from your employer or a client of your employer), then you are urged to bear in mind issues of confidentiality/data protection and to obtain clearance in writing from the relevant party.

3.2 Process Model

The following diagram shows how you might carry out the various processes involved in completing your report.

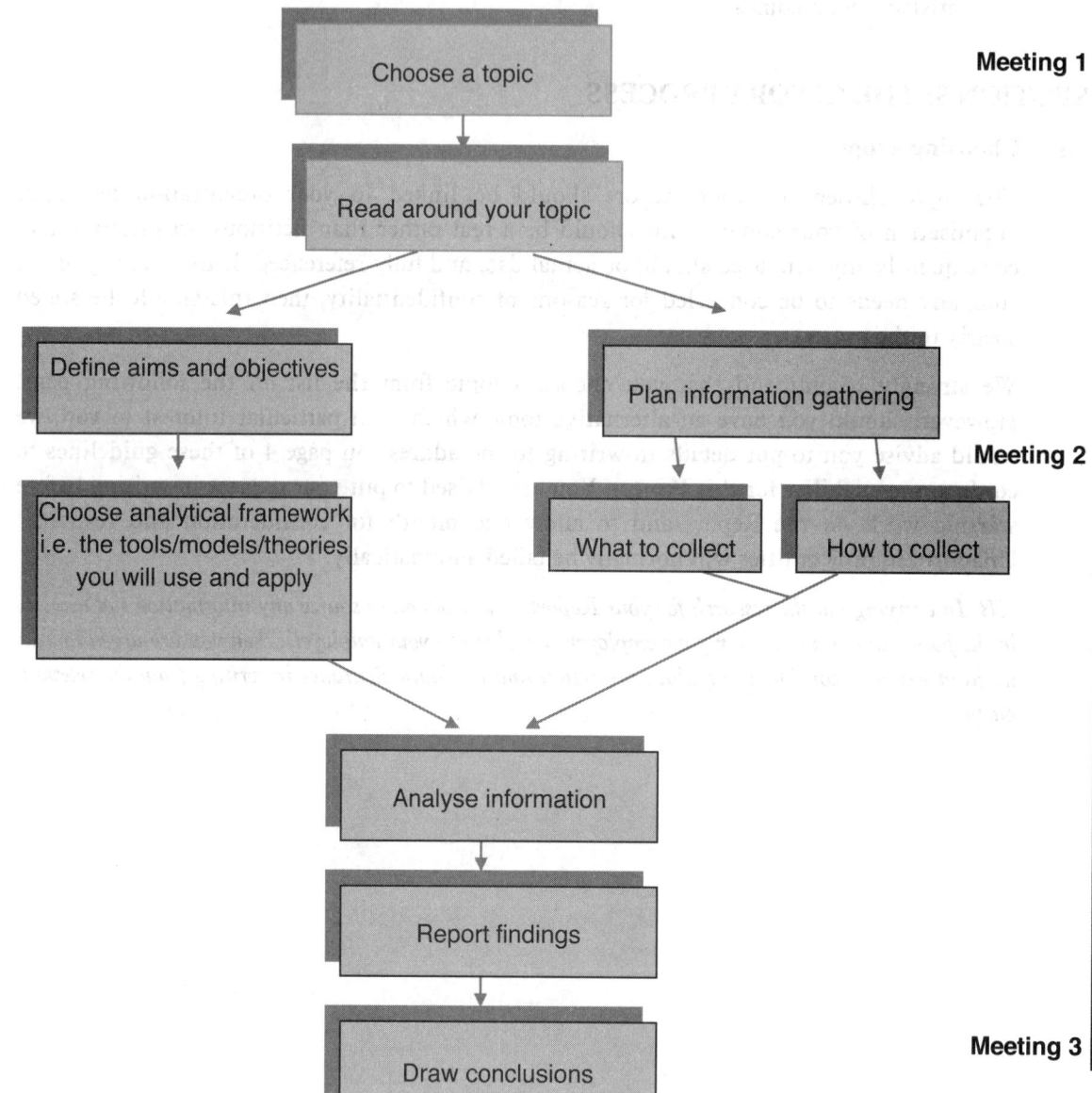

3.3 Recommended Topics for your Report

1. An analysis of the efficiency and/or effectiveness of a management accounting technique in an organisational setting.

2. An analysis of how the application of technology can contribute to an organisation's efficiency and/or effectiveness.

3. An examination of the impact of an aspect of existing or impending legislation on an organisation.

4. An analysis of the impact of e-business on an industry or organisation of your choice.

5. The identification of the effects of globalisation on an industry of your choice.

6. The identification of key factors or indicators in the motivation of employees in an organisation of your choice.

7. An analysis of the tax and profit implications of different company entities, changes in status or acquisitions or disposals of company assets.

8. An analysis of the financial situation of your choice of organisation

9. An examination of how to plan, develop and implement an appropriate information system in an organisation.

10. An analysis of how management accounting techniques are used to support decision-making in organisations.

11. An analysis of the costs and benefits of the internal audit/internal review activities within an organisation of your choice.

12. An analysis of the effect of any International Accounting standard on the accounts of any organisation in terms of profitability or financial stability or balance sheet value.

13. An analysis of future personnel requirements under conditions of change (including employee development).

14. An investigation of recent investment decisions by an organisation of your choice and how the use of different methods of risk and uncertainty analysis might affect such decisions.

15. An analysis of the role of working capital on the profitability and /or efficiency of an organisation of your choice.

16. An analysis of the effect of different sources of capital on investment decisions within an organisation of your choice.

17. An analysis of the effect of corporate governance on an organisation of your choice.

18. An examination of how to plan, develop and implement an appropriate PRP scheme in an organisation.

19. An analysis of the business and financial reasons and effects of creating a multinational merger company.

20. An analysis of the effects of IT failure and contingency plans within an organisation of your choice.

21. An analysis of the impact of the Euro on an organisation or industry of your choice.

22. Analyse the marketing strategy of an organisation of your choice, identifying the key success factors or indicators in the marketing mix and the activities of the organisation.

NB: Oxford Brookes University reserves the right to change the above titles from time to time. You must use the current titles unless you request special permission from Oxford Brookes University (see page 9). You will be given a project code to use when submitting your Research and Analysis Project.

3.4   Frequently Asked Questions

How do I get help in preparing for the project?

Several ACCA providers also offer tuition for this project. Premier Plus Centres will soon be offered the opportunity to become a Brookes recommended centre. Also there is an Oxford Brookes University approved Text published by BPP.

When do I submit the Project?

There are two opportunities each year to submit the project, each window of opportunity being six or seven weeks long immediately following the release of the professional examination results. The ACCA website gives the timetable for submission.

What is included in the Word Count?

Appendices, Contents pages and the Bibliography do not form part of the word count.

How important is the IT requirement?

Extremely important: If you do not show evidence of using a spreadsheet, for example, you are almost certain to fail.

How important is it to reference properly?

Along with IT, failure to reference properly is the most common reason for failing the project. The references must be both in the text, in the correct format, and in the Bibliography. One reason for this is to avoid plagiarism.

What is plagiarism?

Plagiarism occurs when you produce someone else's work within your report without acknowledging the fact. Clearly if you fail to provide a reference for a sentence or paragraph that you took from another text then that is Plagiarism. This is a serious disciplinary issue and may result in being permanently excluded from Oxford Brookes University.

If I want to do a different topic what do I do?

You must apply in writing to the ACCA office giving a broad outline of what you propose to do and the title of your project. You will only be successful in getting your title approved if it can be demonstrated that the project is applied to a particular organisation.

What happens after I submit the project?

You will receive an acknowledgment either by email or letter, normally within 1 month of submitting the project. The timetables for project submissions and despatch of results are given on the ACCA website.

What happens if I have passed?

You will receive a certificate, normally within 6 weeks of the results letter and you will be invited to a graduation ceremony at Oxford Brookes University in Oxford.

If I fail do I get told why?

You will get a limited amount of feedback on your mark sheet, which will also indicate which areas you passed and which areas you failed. If you wish to get a commentary, which gives you much more detail, then you may get one from the ACCA office at Oxford Brookes University on payment of £60 sterling.

What are the most common reasons for failure?

The most common reasons for failure are

- IT – in particular not including reasonable evidence that a spreadsheet has been used
- not referencing the work properly
- not including copies of the PowerPoint/overhead slides etc used in the presentation to the project mentor.
- insufficient analysis of the information that the student researches.

If I fail do I have to start with a completely new topic?

Not necessarily – it may be that you just have to remedy the deficiencies indicated in your mark sheet. In that case you may resubmit an amended report.

How many times can I submit the project?

You may submit the project as many times as you wish, provided each submission is within 10 years of your initial registration for the ACCA professional examinations. The standard fee (currently £50) must accompany every submission.

If I analyse some published financial statements, do I have to include them with my project?

No, not the complete publication but you should, include a copy of the key statements as an Appendix. Note that the Appendices do not form part of the word count.

I intend to analyse some questionnaires – do I have to include them all in my project?

No, but you must include a copy of the questionnaire and a summary of the responses as an Appendix.

3.5   Checklist prior to submission

Before you submit your project please use the following checklist to ensure that you have included all the relevant documents.

Are your section titles in line with the specified headings? ☐

Is there evidence of a spreadsheet and other IT and have you included a reflection in your Key Skills Statement? ☐

Have you included a Bibliography and correctly referenced it within the text? ☐

Are there word counts on the documents? ☐

Have you included a two page summary of your presentation? ☐

Has your mentor signed the Mark sheet? ☐

Have you attached both submission sheets? ☐

Is your payment attached giving details of your name and ACCA student number on the back of the cheque/bank draft? For visa payments we cannot accept American Express. ☐

Have you included an e-mail address so that we can give you your result by e-mail? ☐

Where appropriate, have you included key information from published financial statements in an Appendix? ☐

Have you included your questionnaire results and a sample of the questionnaire in an Appendix? ☐

Have you bound your project as one document using spiral bind, slide bind or comb bind? ☐

Have you signed the new submission forms (versions after September 2004), which have the new Oxford Brookes University regulations, without which we cannot mark your project? ☐

Results by email:

Please note when we are sending out your results your business email address will be more likely to have the capacity to receive the email and is less likely to be rejected or bounce back undelivered to us. We are only able to send out student's results once by email. Please make your email address very clear on the submission form.

Contact details:

If you move address before results are sent out please contact Oxford Brookes University, ACCA Office. The ACCA are unable to update us once you have submitted your project, which means you will need to contact both the ACCA

APPENDIX 1: HOW TO REFERENCE YOUR WORK

How to Reference Your Work and Construct a Bibliography

Referencing

Whenever you are directly quoting or referring to one of your sources of information, you should acknowledge this in the text as you go along. References should be clearly set out using the Harvard System. It is important to double check that all references in your text appear in the bibliography.

Bibliography

Your bibliography comes at the end of your Report. It is a list of all the sources you have used in compiling your Report eg books, articles, company publications, newspaper articles etc. The bibliography should be set out alphabetically using the Harvard System. It is not sufficient to merely include your sources of information in the Bibliography without including the proper reference in the text. Failure to do this will result in failure of the project.

How to reference your work and construct a bibliography

Correctly referencing your work is simple, and compulsory. You must reference all your sources of information. We do advise you to reference as you go along, rather than leaving it until the end of your assignment. There is nothing more time consuming than constructing a bibliography retrospectively.

References within your text

In the Harvard system references within the text are set out as follows:

EXAMPLE

In any organisation made up of different interest groups some conflict over goals is inevitable (Needle, 1994).

In the bibliography the reference shown above would appear in this way:

EXAMPLE OF A BOOK REFERENCE

Needle, D. (1994) <u>Business in Context</u>. 2nd Edition, London, Chapman & Hall

---

NB: You only cite the edition if it is not the first. Please note that the title of the book is either underlined or emboldened.

EXAMPLE OF A JOURNAL OR NEWSPAPER REFERENCE

Buxton, J. (1998) Management: The Growing Business: Co-operative's Wheels of Fortune. <u>The Financial Times</u>, February 24

NB: It's the title of the journal or newspaper that is either underlined or emboldened.

EXAMPLE OF A JOURNAL ARTICLE WHERE NO AUTHOR IS GIVEN

<u>The Economist</u> (1997) 'New technology is no snap', October 11, p125

Citing Electronic Sources

No standard agreed method has yet evolved for citing electronic sources. Electronic sources may include ftp sites, Telnet addresses, WWW and gopher pages, newsgroups and e-mail messages. The following book should help:

Li, Xia and Crane, Nancy B. (1996) **Electronic styles, a handbook for citing electronic information.** 2nd Edition, Medford, N.J., Information Today

There are also several guides you can view on the Internet.

A recommended example of a guide to citing Internet sources is accessible via:

http://www.bournemouth.ac.uk/library/using/citing_references.html

NB: This has a useful one-page summary as an appendix.

A simplified solution might be:

Author's last name, First name. Title of work. *Title of complete work if applicable in italics.* [protocol and address] [path] (date of message or visit).

EXAMPLE

Walker, Janice R. MLA-Style Citations of Electronic Sources.

http://www.columbia.edu/cu/cup/cgos/idx_basic.html

APPENDIX 2: APPROVED/RECOMMENDED READING

Oxford Brookes University/ACCA Approved Text

BPP (2005) Success in your Research & Analysis Project. 6th Edition, London, BPP

Additional Recommended Reading

Cameron, S. (2002) Business Students' Handbook: learning skills for study and employment. 2nd Edition, Harlow, Financial Times/Prentice Hall

Guirdham, M. (2002) Interpersonal Skills at Work. 2nd Edition, London, Prentice Hall

Hayes, J. (2002) Interpersonal Skills at work. 2nd Edition, Hove, Routledge

Honey, P. (1988) Face to Face: A Practical Guide to Interactive Skills. 2nd Edition, Aldershot, Gower

Honey, P. (2001) Improve your people skills. 2nd Edition, London CIPD

Hussey, J. Hussey, R. (1997) Business Research. Basingstoke, Macmillan

Northedge, A. (1990) The Good Study Guide. Milton Keynes, Open University

Pedler, M. Burgoyne, J. Boydell, T. (1994) A Manager's Guide to Self Development. Maidenhead, McGraw Hill

Saunders, M. Lewis, P. Thornhill, A. (2003) Research Methods for Business Students. 3rd Edition, Harlow, Financial Times/Prentice Hall

APPENDIX 3: MENTOR/STUDENT RELATIONSHIP

Mentor Guidelines

The mentor is primarily interested in the progress of your Project but is not your tutor. They will need to hear about your plans and will ask questions to help you reflect on the clarity of your thinking and the focus of your Report.

It is important to realise that your mentor is not your assessor but, as already stated, will be asked to provide confirmation that you participated in three meetings with him/her, provided a satisfactory progress update, and gave a presentation.

A mentor need not have expert knowledge of the field of your research or in research methods. You should not expect them to give you direction regarding the content, relevant references or design of your research for the Research and Analysis Report or Key Skills Statement.

Example questions for student/mentor meetings

MENTOR	STUDENT
Questions a mentor might want to ask a student as they progress through the research, preparation and presentation of their Research and Analysis Report and Key Skills Statement	Questions a student might want to ask their mentor as they progress through the research, preparation and presentation of their Research and Analysis Report and Key Skills Statement

1ST MEETING – PLANNING

What is your Report going to be about? How do you plan to do the Report? Why are you doing it in this way? What problems do you envisage? When will you do x, y and z?	I have considered the following alternatives; can I talk them through with you? This is my plan what do you think?

2ND MEETING – PROGRESS UPDATE

What difficulties have you had? How will you/have you overcome them? What are you going to do next? Are you on schedule/do you need to reschedule?	I have had this problem. Could you offer some advice?

3RD MEETING – REVIEW

What went well/badly? Does the Report meet its objectives? Does it make sense?	What went well/badly?

Questions a student should not expect their mentor to provide the answers to

What do I have to do to pass?
What do I do next?
What shall I read on this topic?
What do you know about this topic?
Will you structure my project for me?

APPENDIX 4: CHEATING

Students undertaking this project should be fully aware of the University regulations relating to cheating. Cheating may be defined as a deliberate and intended action, using trickery, practising deceit, or violating rules dishonestly. Students may be shocked by the use of the word 'cheating', but it is an indication of the seriousness with which the University takes these matters. Such cheating takes many forms in academic circumstances. The form most familiar to students is that of cheating in examinations. What may be less familiar are the ways in which students have attempted to cheat in the Research and Analysis Project – and have been found out and penalised.

These other ways of cheating are as follows:

- **Impersonation** – this means to undertake a piece of assessed work on behalf of, or to pretend to be, another student, or allowing another person to undertake an assessment on your behalf, or to pretend to be you.

- **Substitution** – this means submitting other people's work as though it were your own – either with, or without, their knowledge, and includes copying in examinations or in the submission of assessed work.

- **Duplication** – this means submitting work for assessment that is the same as, or broadly similar to, work submitted earlier for academic credit, without acknowledgement of the previous submission.

- **Falsification** – this includes the invention of data, their alteration, copying data from any other source, or otherwise obtaining them by unfair means, or inventing quotations and/or references.

- **Collusion** – this is a secret agreement or co-operation with others especially for a deceitful purpose, and includes copying or sharing another student's work, with his/her secret agreement that you can do so, or lending your work to another student in the reasonable knowledge that some or all of it will be copied, or secretly working with others jointly to produce a piece of work that is supposed to be your own work. Thus collusion is not collaboration, which is open co-operation with others, and which is used where it is considered to work in teams, and many university courses include assessments based on group work.

But, as far as the Research and Analysis Project is concerned, collusion and collaboration are unacceptable. The only person you will be working with is your Mentor, whose roles are clearly defined. Your mentor will encourage you to reflect upon your work, and will give friendly and expert guidance on the broad direction you should take. Your mentor is not in the same position as, for example, a project tutor at a university, and is not even expected to direct you to sources of information. The mentor may give constructive comments but would not be expected to write any part of the project.

There may be a group presentation and, no doubt, some feedback may be received jointly from a mentor to a group of students, but it is important that each individual student presents his or her own work and co-operative projects are not allowed.

- **Plagiarism** – this means taking or using another person's thoughts, writings or inventions and presenting them as though they were your own.

Plagiarism is probably the most common of these offences and perhaps a few additional words should be said about it. To acknowledge the work of others is more than a matter of good academic practice; it is the foundation stone of all academic practice. This is why so much attention is placed on correct referencing, and why students may find themselves unwittingly guilty of plagiarising because they have failed to follow the correct referencing procedures. As far as ACCA and Brookes are concerned, however, ignorance is no excuse, and plagiarism will be heavily penalised as it is viewed as a serious matter of cheating.

Plagiarism is not a complicated issue – if you quote/use the actual words of another author, or if you express the thoughts of an author in your own words, and you do not indicate (a) that you have done so and (b) where those words or thoughts can be found in published form, then you have plagiarised.

You will find more information and advice about plagiarism at the website given below, which gives a list of other useful websites on plagiarism.

www.mantex.co.uk/samples/plgrsm.htm

In particular, the website

http://sja.ucdavis.edu/SJA/plagiarism.html

gives a very readable set of examples of what is plagiarism and what is not – with a few tips on how to deal correctly with attributing of the work to others.

You may feel that there is too much emphasis on plagiarism but it has to be pointed out that if plagiarism is detected within a project, it is likely that you will not only fail the project but, as this is also a form of cheating, additional penalties may be applied.

The University takes all forms of cheating extremely seriously and has adopted a number of actions to detect cheating and in particular plagiarism. These include regular checks of certain websites that are known to assist students when attempting to cheat. The University also uses software to detect a change in writing style, which is a good indication that the work may be the result of several different writers.

APPENDIX 5: NOTES TO HELP YOUR MENTOR

PLEASE GIVE THESE THREE PAGES TO YOUR MENTOR

Thank you for agreeing to be a mentor for this programme. The notes below outline what the student will expect of you and what Oxford Brookes University would like you to do to help the student towards obtaining the Oxford Brookes University degree in Applied Accounting.

You should be interested in the progress of the Project but you are not expected to be a tutor. You would normally listen to the student's plans and may ask questions to help them reflect. If you can help the student think clearly about what they intend to do, then it will be an enormous help to them.

The student will need to have at least three meetings with you and what the student has to do in these three meetings is detailed on the next page.

Attached, also, is a page of suggested questions that you could ask – and some questions that you would not normally be expected to answer.

You do not need to have expert knowledge of the field of the student's research or in research methods. You should not expect to give the student direction on the content of the Project, relevant references or the design of the research.

You are not the student's assessor but Oxford Brookes would like confirmation that you participated in three meetings with him/her, that the student provided a satisfactory progress update, and gave a presentation that you observed. This confirmation, along with a statement of the capacity in which you qualify to act as a mentor, should be included on the second sheet of the student's Submission Form, that is whether you are employer, manager, tutor or ACCA member.

We would also like some confirmation that the Project is the student's own work and we ask you to certify this in Section D of the Research and Analysis Report form before the student sends their work to Oxford Brookes University.

Thank you again for participating in this Project.

Programme Director BSc (Hons) Applied Accounting
Oxford Brookes University

Information provided to students regarding their meetings with you

Meetings with your mentor

The three meetings with your mentor, each of which should normally be about half an hour long, should follow the framework set out below.

Meeting 1 – at the outset

To prepare for this you should have some proposals on the choice of topic, (see page 10), for your Research and Analysis Report and have embarked on preliminary investigation into the research areas and methods you may want to use. You should therefore take from this meeting a clear proposal of your choice of topic, research method and draft aims and objectives for your Report.

Meeting 2 – midway through your report

At this stage you should have completed the gathering of information for your Report and have some initial views as to your findings. An interim update on your progress in the form of a word-processed document should be presented to your mentor. This will then provide the framework for your discussion at this meeting.

Meeting 3 – towards completion of your report

You are required to prepare and deliver a fifteen minute presentation on your Report to your mentor, and if applicable your peer group (see option below). You should use appropriate presentation techniques in conjunction with your talk. You should be prepared to answer questions and provide explanations when requested.

Your mentor will be asked to provide confirmation that the three meetings took place in accordance with the guidelines above.

If it becomes necessary for whatever reason to change your mentor part way through the above framework, you will have to start again at Meeting 1 to allow your new mentor to verify your participation in all three meetings.

You may, if your mentor is happy to participate, arrange for further appointments in addition to the three compulsory meetings outlined in the above framework.

NB. It may be useful for you to keep a personal diary of reflections on your meetings to help you when writing up your Key Skills Statement.

Peer Group Presentation Option

Where your mentor is working with more than one student, presentations in Meeting 3 can take place in a group. However, Meetings 1 and 2 must only involve the mentor and individual student. This will enable you to deliver your presentation to an audience, receive feedback from your peers and in turn, critically review the work of others.

NB. The Research and Analysis Report must be the work of the individual student and should not be carried out in a group. See Appendix 4 of the Research and Analysis Project Guidelines for more information on regulations regarding plagiarism, syndication and other forms of cheating.

Example questions for student/mentor meetings

MENTOR	STUDENT
Questions a mentor might want to ask a student as they progress through the research, preparation and presentation of their Research and Analysis Report and Key Skills Statement	Questions a student might want to ask their mentor as they progress through the research, preparation and presentation of their Research and Analysis Report and Key Skills Statement

1ST MEETING – PLANNING

What is your Report going to be about? How do you plan to do the Report? Why are you doing it in this way? What problems do you envisage? When will you do x, y and z?	I have considered the following alternatives; can I talk them through with you? This is my plan what do you think?

2ND MEETING – PROGRESS UPDATE

What difficulties have you had? How will you/have you overcome them? What are you going to do next? Are you on schedule/do you need to reschedule?	I have had this problem. Could you offer some advice?

3RD MEETING – REVIEW

What went well/badly? Does the Report meet its objectives? Does it make sense?	What went well/badly?

Questions a student should not expect their mentor to provide the answers to

What do I have to do to pass?
What do I do next?
What shall I read on this topic?
What do you know about this topic?
Will you structure my project for me?

Submission Forms for Research and Analysis Project

INSTRUCTIONS:

Sections A, B and C of this form should be completed by the student and Section D by the Mentor and accompany your work which must be sent **by some secure recorded means of delivery** to:

The ACCA Office, Business School, Oxford Brookes University, Wheatley Campus, Wheatley, OXFORD, OX33 1HX, United Kingdom

SECTION A (Student to complete in Block Capitals)

Student Surname
Student First name
Student Address

Student Email Address – to receive project results via email. Please complete this only if you consent to receiving your results (and other correspondence) by email. Your business email is preferable.

ACCA Student Registration Number

Date of submission

Project topic number chosen

Alternative project topic '99' must be approved and signed by Oxford Brookes in advance of submission (acca@brookes.ac.uk)

I declare that the attached project is all my own work. I agree that I shall be bound by the regulations of Oxford Brookes University and the BSc (Applied Accounting Programme) regulations, which can be found on www.accaglobal.com/students/professionalscheme/degreepartnership/oxb_studyguide

Signature (for regulations) _____ date ....

Date on front of Research and Analysis Project Guidelines used _____

SECTION B (Payment Details)

A fee of £50 **sterling** must accompany this work, which should be in the form of cheque, credit or UK debit card payment or bank draft made **payable to Oxford Brookes University**. Cash is not acceptable.

Please tick **one** of the following options:

Option 1: Credit or UK Debit Card (We cannot accept American Express)

Card Number   Start Date   Expiry Date   Issue No

Signature (for payment) _____ date ....

Option 2 to tick:		Cheque		Bank Draft	

FOR OFFICE USE ONLY
DATE RECEIVED.......................................

Submission Forms for Research and Analysis Project

MARK SHEET

SECTION C (Student to complete in Block Capitals)

Student Surname

Student First name

ACCA Student Registration Number ☐☐☐☐☐☐☐ Date of submission ☐☐☐☐

Total Report word count:
Please note: this should not exceed 5000 words, otherwise you risk failure

Total Key Skills Statement word count:
Please note: this should not exceed 1500 words, otherwise you risk failure

SECTION D (Mentor to complete and sign)

Mentor's Certification:

I certify that to the best of my knowledge the project is the student's own work and that it has been carried out in accordance with the University's regulations, (see Student Guide available on-line at www.accaglobal.com), and that three meetings have been held with the student in accordance with the guidelines contained in Section 2.3 of the Research and Analysis Project Guidelines.

Mentor's Name	Address (Block capitals)

Capacity for acting as mentor: (tick choice) *(See 2.2 of the Research and Analysis Project Guidelines.)*	Employer Tutor/lecturer Qualified Chartered Certified Accountant	

Signature……………………………………………………….. Date…………………………….

SECTION E (For Office Use Only)

Markers sheet

PROJECT	PASS	FAIL	
Communication Skills	☐	☐	Please refer to the attached sheet for full feedback comments.
Information gathering	☐	☐	
Analysis and Conclusions	☐	☐	
IT Skills	☐	☐	

KEY SKILLS STATEMENT

	PASS	FAIL	
Preparing for meetings	☐	☐	You are required to undertake the mentoring again.(Moderator to delete as appropriate).
Questioning	☐	☐	Yes / No
Listening	☐	☐	
The presentation	☐	☐	
Self-Assessment of Interaction	☐	☐	
OVERALL RESULT	☐	☐	

Marker code		Date……………… …	Moderator code		Date ………………

Chapter 2

TEST YOUR SKILLS: SELF-ASSESSMENT QUESTIONNAIRE

Chapter topic list	
1	Eligibility for the degree
2	IT and word processing skills
3	Report writing and the structure of reports
4	Referencing material
5	Questioning techniques
6	Listening techniques
7	Communication models
8	Presentations

Introduction

The **Research and Analysis Project Guidelines** recognise that there are many students who will feel confident about tackling the project element of the Applied Accounting degree and will need to be guided only by the Guidelines themselves.

There will also be many students who have never undertaken a project like this before, and know that they will therefore need to learn and practise the techniques and skills involved. This book should prove to be invaluable for those students, as it is designed to provide further support and guidance in developing your skills and completing the Project.

There will also be a middle group: the students who are not sure whether or not they already have the necessary skills, and are not quite confident enough to launch into the research required for the production of the Project without doing some preparatory work. If you feel that you fall into that middle category, this chapter is for you. It will allow you to test your knowledge of some of the concepts and principles which you are expected to have in order to do the Project, and to assess whether you have the skills that you are expected to display.

This chapter contains a self-assessment questionnaire. Once completed, it will indicate to you which areas you can feel comfortable about and which areas you will need to work on, by reading the relevant sections of this book.

1 ELIGIBILITY FOR THE DEGREE

1.1 Under the current ACCA exam regime (effective from December 2001), you need to have sat and passed Papers 2.4, 2.5 and 2.6 and have completed or been exempted from the whole of Parts 1 and 2 of the qualification.

There are various provisions for students who started their studies under the old syllabus (effective until June 2001), and they should consult the ACCA for clarification of their position. There are regular articles about eligibility and the administration of the degree in the ACCA magazine *Student Accountant* and on the ACCA's website (http://www.acca.org.uk/students/oxb.html)

2 IT AND WORD PROCESSING SKILLS

2.1 Part of the assessment procedure will focus on your IT skills. It is a specific requirement of the Project that you produce some of your material in spreadsheet format, and the Guidelines advise you to provide a sample printout of the formulae you use in producing your spreadsheet. Additionally you are required to reflect on your usage of IT skills in your Key Skills Statement.

Exercise 1

(a) Can you produce a spreadsheet and show the formulae you have used?   **YES/NO**
(b) Can you present data in both tabular and graphical form?   **YES/NO**
(c) Can you use spelling and grammar checkers?   **YES/NO**
(d) Do you need to bring your word-processing skills up to date?   **YES/NO**
(e) Do you feel comfortable using the Internet for research purposes?   **YES/NO**

Self analysis

2.2 The tutorial text will provide some brief guidance on the use of spreadsheets but you should consider whether you are fully competent at other aspects of word processing. If not, you should attend a short course or perhaps buy one of the available manuals to teach you some of the basic skills.

3 REPORT WRITING AND THE STRUCTURE OF REPORTS

3.1 Your ability to write clearly and succinctly is of paramount importance here. Try these exercises to assess your skills.

Exercise 2

Put what follows into report format.

'The first criterion is whether this will be profitable over the estimated life cycle of product A. Another criterion which is related to the first criterion is that of estimated volume sales at the proposed price. A third criterion which needs to be considered when deciding whether or not to launch Product A is....'

Answer

(a) Decision criteria in rank order
    (i) Profit (ROI) over product life cycle
    (ii) Sales volume at proposed price
    (iii) ...

Exercise 3

Put these headings into the order in which you would expect to see them in a report.

Methods of research selected
Analysis of results
Conclusion
Terms of reference
Appendices
Observations
Bibliography
Executive summary

Answer

Terms of reference
Executive summary
Methods of research selected
Observations
Analysis of results
Conclusion
Appendices
Bibliography

Exercise 4

Use the information set out below to produce the heading of a report

Hugh Mountolive the Managing Director can see both sides of the arguments presented by Melissa and Clea regarding closing down the Alexandria factory and moving to Port Said, but is uncertain about how to evaluate such an important issue.

He has asked you, Justine Nessim the management accountant, to write a report covering all the major factors that need to be considered in relation to the closure and move, with a recommendation.

Answer

To: Hugh Mountolive, Managing Director
From: Justine Nessim, management accountant
Date:

Re: Analysis and recommendations of regarding the proposed closure of the factory in Alexandria and the move to Port Said

Exercise 5

You have a very tight word constraint in writing the Report and Key Skills Statement, which means that you will have to demonstrate the two skills of:

• prioritisation of issues arising from your research

• concise and succinct use of words

Test your ability here by attempting this exercise.

BMW pulled out of car manufacturing in the UK, by selling its investment in Rover Cars to another firm, although some parts of it were sold to Ford.

Here are some of the factors underlying the decision.

• Rover lost £750m in 1999.

• £150m of aid from the UK government to BMW was under threat from the European commission, given its concern over state subsidies.

• The pound was for some time very high compared to the euro, making exports from the UK to Europe very expensive.

27

- 10,000 jobs in Rover were at risk, as were 40,000 supplier jobs in the West Midlands. BMW had spent a lot of time and money on 'the English patient' since buying it.

- BMW had invested in Rover to enable BMW to become a volume car manufacturer as opposed to a niche maker of executive cars.

- BMW is the 14th largest motor manufacturer in an industry that has been consolidating recently.

- The UK is unlikely to join the euro for some time.

- Rover lost market share in the UK from 13.5% to 6% over 5 years. Not enough British buyers were buying Rover Cars.

- BMW could be vulnerable to a takeover.

- The main BMW brand is suffering.

What were BMW's priorities in reaching the decision? Show a rationale.

Answer (1)

Rationale

Survival of BMW. BMW's management wished to preserve BMW as a successful, independent company, and considered that future involvement with Rover would jeopardise this aim.

Key issues underlying the decision

	Priority – importance	Justification
1	Stem losses: no prospect of future profitability	**Future**. BMW had invested a lot in Rover, but what concerned them was the future – future incremental cash flows were negative. • Rover had been losing market share in the UK. • Exports had tailed off because of the high level of sterling. • New products had not been successful.
2	Concentrate on BMW brand	**External**. Too much management attention had been focused on Rover. No evidence existed that this had hit BMW brand yet, but managers were concerned about this.
3	Compete elsewhere: consolidation of motor industry	**External**. Motor firms are merging into larger groups – the reason why BMW bought Rover.

The answer above has a clear rationale and the relative importance of each item has been shown. It demonstrates good use of words and good prioritisation.

Answer (2)

- Rover lost £750m in 1999.
- The exchange rate is not favourable and so cars are expensive.
- Rover has been losing market share recently.
- BMW want to concentrate on building the BMW brand.

This sort of style would probably lead to a narrow fail because it does not clearly specify the **rationale** behind the decision, which is that Rover will be a **future** drain of cash for BMW, and that investing in Rover will prevent BMW from protecting its brand. In short, while the list is appropriate there is no underlying rationale.

Self analysis

3.2 It is up to you to judge your performance in the four exercises in the section of this questionnaire on report-writing skills, and you must be honest with yourself.

3.3　If you felt that the exercises were straightforward, you felt comfortable handling the material and your answers were roughly similar to ours, you have probably already got adequate report-writing skills.

3.4　However, if you felt that you were out of your depth in some of the exercises, or you did not fully understand what they required, you might find it helpful to practise, in order to improve your technique.

4　REFERENCING MATERIAL

4.1　The Research and Analysis Project Guidelines emphasise that you must reference your sources professionally and prepare a bibliography.

Exercise 6

(a)　George Franklin published a book in 1999, with a new edition in January 2003. The book was called 'Analysing the Retail Industry' and was published in Manchester by Business Publishers Ltd.

Show how you would acknowledge the most recent edition in the text of your Report and in the bibliography.

(b)　In the July 2003 issue of *Marketing Monthly* magazine there is an article by Sam Keller entitled 'Grasping the nettle: marketing the organic drinks phenomenon'.

Show how you would acknowledge the article in the text of your Report and in the bibliography.

(c)　The Sunday Times Business section contained a comment on the state of the British scheduled airline industry on page 3 of the issue of June 15th 2003. The comment had no attributable author name.

Show how you would acknowledge the comment in the text of your Report and in the bibliography.

(d)　On June 24th 2003, it was possible to read a comment by Anthea Rose on the ACCA's website (www.acca.co.uk) to the effect that the government is imposing too much red tape on small businesses. The comment was included in an article entitled 'Raising the audit threshold – raising the risk of fraud' which was originally posted on May 15th 2003.

Show how you would acknowledge this in the text of your Report and in the bibliography.

Answers

(a)　In the text:
(Franklin, 2003)
In the bibliography:
Franklin, G. (2003) <u>Analysing the Retail Industry</u>. 2nd edition, Manchester, Business Publishers.

(b)　In the text:
(Keller, 2003)
In the bibliography:
Keller, S. (2003) Grasping the nettle: marketing the organic drinks phenomenon. <u>Marketing Monthly</u>, July

(c)　In the text:
(The Sunday Times, 2003)
In the bibliography:
<u>The Sunday Times</u> (2003) Business section, June 15th, p.3

(d)　In the text:
(Rose, 2003)
In the bibliography:
Rose, A. Raising the audit threshold – raising the risk of fraud. <u>www.acca.co.uk</u> 15th May 2003. Accessed on 24th June 2003

Self analysis

4.2 If you are familiar with the Harvard system of referencing, you will be perfectly capable of referencing your Report in exactly the way specified by Oxford Brookes in the Project Guidelines.

4.3 If you were not familiar with the means of referencing shown above, you should either study the Project Guidelines in detail, or refer to the relevant section of this book.

5 QUESTIONING TECHNIQUES

5.1 In various sections of your Key Skills Statement, you are required to consider 'appropriate questioning techniques'.

Exercise 7

Which questioning techniques would you think are most likely to be relevant to your work?

Answer

You are most likely to employ (or at least discuss)

- Open
- Closed
- Leading
- Probing
- Multiple

Self analysis

5.2 If you are not familiar with these terms, you should do some work on questioning techniques. These are all covered in the Tutorial Text.

6 LISTENING TECHNIQUES

6.1 In various sections of your Key Skills Statement, you are required to consider 'appropriate listening techniques'.

Exercise 8

List the different methods (or styles) of listening which may be of significance when you are discussing listening techniques in your Key Skills Statement.

Answer

- Listening for content
- Critical listening
- Empathetic listening
- Attentive listening

Exercise 9

Do you think that listening is an active or a passive activity?

Answer

It is an active process. It is not the same as hearing, which is passive. Effective listening requires the deployment of specific skills.

Self analysis

6.2   If you are not familiar with the concept of active listening, or the terms used to describe different types of listening, you should do some work on listening techniques. These are covered in the Tutorial Text.

7   COMMUNICATION MODELS

7.1   In the Key Skills Statement, you are expected to refer to 'an appropriate model of communication' and assess and evaluate the extent to which you achieved good communication in the meetings which form part of the research Project.

Exercise 10

Draw a suitable diagram of a simple communication model.

Answer

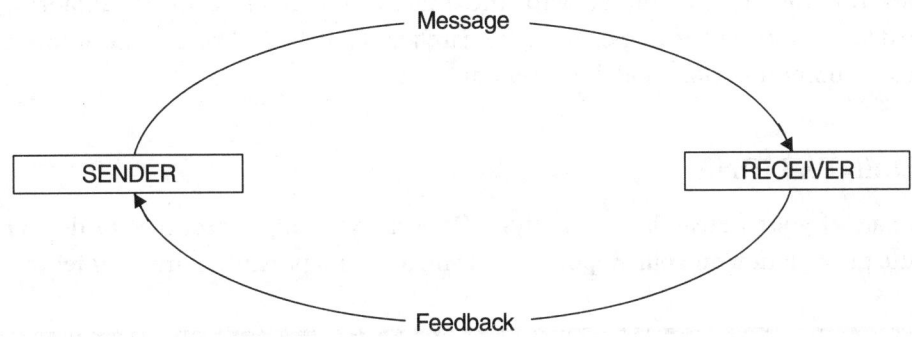

Exercise 11

Using the basic diagram set out above, fill in more detail to indicate what the sender is likely to send to the receiver, by what medium, and indicate how the message may be coded or decoded. Then add to your diagram any problems which can occur in communication.

Answer

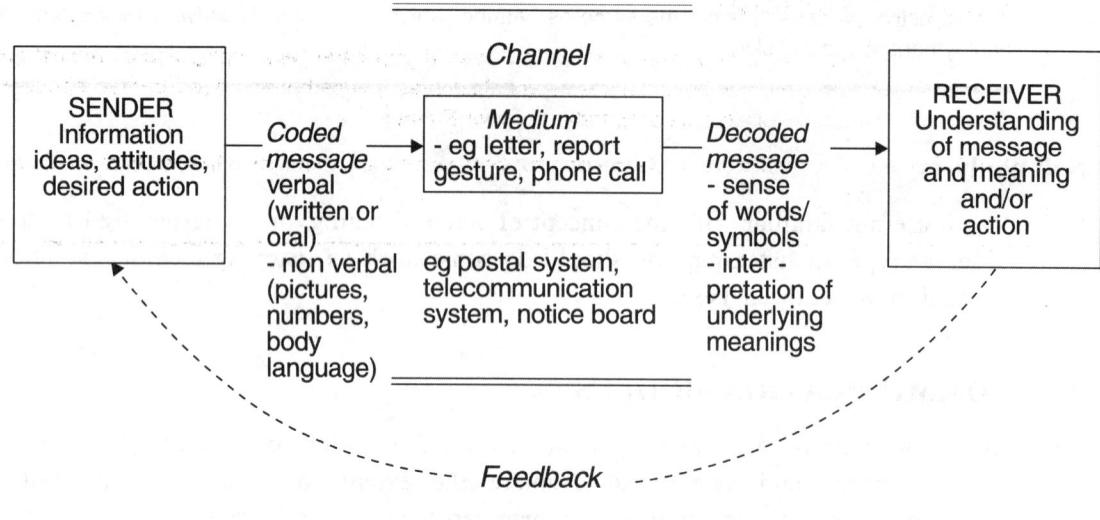

Self analysis

7.2 If you have studied models of communication before and are quite familiar with them, you should have had no problem drawing the diagrams and identifying the potential problems.

7.3 However, if you are not familiar with these ideas, you should consider exploring them in more detail before embarking on your Research and Analysis Project. The ability to use and discuss a communication model is essential.

8   PRESENTATIONS

8.1 As a part of your Research and Analysis Project, you will be required to deliver a fifteen minute presentation on your Report to your mentor and possibly a group of fellow students.

Exercise 12

Answer these questions:

(a) Have you delivered a formal presentation before?   **YES/NO**
(b) Do you feel confident about public speaking?   **YES/NO**
(c) Can you handle questions from an audience?   **YES/NO**
(d) Are you terrified at the thought of the presentation?   **YES/NO**

Self analysis

8.2 If you answered 'yes' to questions (a) to (c) and 'no' to question (d) you should feel confident about preparing for and delivering your presentation, and you need no coaching in techniques.

8.3 If you answered 'no' to questions (a) to (c) and 'yes' to question (d) you should read about presentation techniques before you reach that stage in the Research and Analysis Project.

Chapter roundup

You are the person who knows your skills the best. If you have been scrupulously honest with yourself, you should by now have come to a conclusion as to whether you need to read about and practise the required skills for the preparation of your Project.

If you feel that you need more guidance and support, you should find that in the relevant sections of this Tutorial Text.

Part B

The Research and Analysis Project

Chapter 3

THE PROJECT IN OUTLINE

Chapter topic list

---

1   The Research and Analysis Project: its role in your Degree

2   The abilities to be tested

3   Outline and overview of the work involved

4   What you are expected to produce at the end

5   Other people involved: your peer group and your mentor

Introduction

This chapter gives you a general overview of the project. Section 1 highlights the differences between the project (for a degree) and sitting exams for a professional qualification. You need only read this if you do not already have a degree – or if you feel you need to be reminded of the difference. Section 2 covers the skills covered, by linking it to the requirement of other accountancy-based degrees. Section 3 expands the overview of the work you will have to do; section 4 covers the issues involved in writing the Report and the Key Skills Statement.

1   THE RESEARCH AND ANALYSIS PROJECT: ITS ROLE IN YOUR DEGREE

What is so special about this project?

1.1   You are doing this Research and Analysis, the related Report and Key Skills Statement to obtain a **degree** from a respected UK awarding institution: a Bachelor of Science (Hons) in Applied Accounting from Oxford Brookes University.

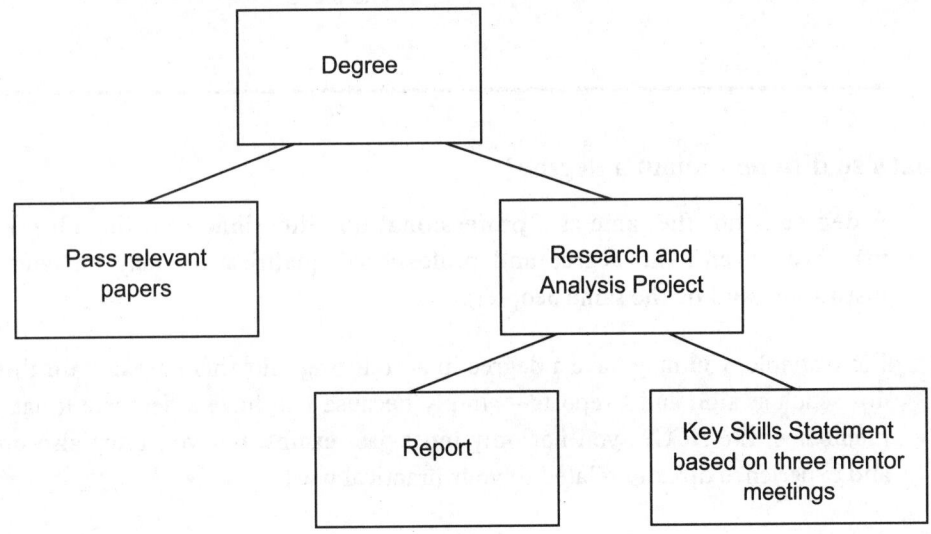

This is what you must do in the project.

Output	Process
A **Research and Analysis Project**	Choose a topic, research and analyse data, come to a conclusion.
A Report	Write a Report of 5,000 words based on your project.
A Key Skills Statement based around communication with a mentor and a presentation	Find a mentor; arrange and reflect upon three meetings; give a presentation; write a 1,500 word Key Skills Statement.

Think about the list above. This is very different from studying for ACCA exams, which are focused on satisfying the examiner in a three hour exam.

Exercise 1

Write down the key differences between the Research and Analysis project and studying for ACCA exams.

Answer

ACCA exams	Research and Analysis Project
Questions are precisely defined.	The topics chosen are very general and **you** must narrow them down to a Project objective.
Questions are precisely structured, with defined tasks clearly outlined and marks allocated.	You have to provide a structure and define what you are trying to discover.
You only have three hours.	You can take as long as you like.
Pen and paper.	You have to demonstrate familiarity with IT, such as use of word processing, spreadsheets etc: your report must be word processed.
You are working to a syllabus.	There is no syllabus.
Exam technique is your business only.	You have to reflect and report on the process of doing the Research and Analysis Project.
For many of the papers, the data is given. All you have to do is a read a question and answer it.	You will have to draw conclusions from reviewing your data, but this depends on:

- Identifying the right data in scope and depth
- Asking the right questions of the data

Your conclusion may not support what you set out to prove.

What's so different about a degree?

1.2 A **degree** is not the same as a **professional qualification,** even though the subject matter may overlap and the degree and professional qualification may be taught in the same institution (and by the same people!).

1.3 For example, you may have a degree in accounting, but there are certain things you cannot do – such as sign audit reports – simply because you have a degree. Or again, to become a member of the ACCA, you not only must pass exams, but you must also undergo training and experience directly related to your practical work.

1.4 A degree and a professional qualification are both stretching – but the **focus** is different.

(a) The **focus of a professional qualification** is working for others in a public role; the ACCA is checking – as part of its quality control procedures – that you are fit to be let loose on the fee-paying business community.

(b) The focus of a **degree is** not only the world of work. It offers you personal fulfilment, by stretching you to achieve a personal goal. The university is assisting you in this, but is also measuring you against your contemporaries: at college, in the country where you live, and around the world.

1.5 A degree typically involves testing certain abilities that may not be the focus of the examinations for your professional work. The context of a degree is the wider academic community.

(a) Degrees in one subject must in some respect be **comparable** with degrees in other subjects. A BSc in Applied Accounting should, all other things being equal, be worthy of the same esteem as a BSc in Engineering or a BA in Media Studies – a huge scope of subject matter. (It is insulting to suggest that some areas of study are 'easier' because they are different – but there has to be some common benchmark for achievement.)

(b) Degrees awarded by universities throughout the country should be of **comparable worth**. A first class honours should be a first class honours wherever this is earned.

(c) To be awarded a degree, you generally need to show that you have the knowledge and skills required by the degree programme.

(d) A BSc or BA is merely the first in a hierarchy of qualifications related to academic work. Therefore, **rigour** and **method** in approaching and understanding a topic are essential.

1.6 If you have acquired the necessary knowledge you are well on the way. However, knowledge is not really enough. Here is an extract from the draft **Benchmark Statement in Accountancy.** This is produced by the Quality Assurance Agency for Higher Education, a UK-based body whose role is to promote public confidence that the quality of provision and standards of awards in UK higher education is safeguarded and enhanced. All accountancy degrees awarded in the UK should follow this benchmark and your degree must deal with these issues.

Cognitive abilities and non-subject specific skills

On completion of a degree programme covered by this statement, a student should have acquired the following abilities and skills.

(a) A capacity for the critical evaluation of arguments and evidence.

(b) An ability to analyse and draw reasoned conclusions concerning structured and, to a more limited extent, unstructured problems from a given set of data and from data which must be acquired by the student.

(c) Ability to locate, extract and analyse data from multiple sources, including the acknowledgement and referencing of sources.

(d) Capacities for independent and self-managed learning.

(e) Numeracy skills, including the ability to manipulate financial and other numerical data and to appreciate statistical concepts at an appropriate level.

(f) Skills in the use of communications and information technology in acquiring, analysing and communicating information, including the use of spreadsheets and word processing software, the world-wide, web and e-mail.

> (g) Communication skills including the ability to present quantitative and qualitative information together with analysis, argument and commentary in a form appropriate to different intended audiences.
>
> (h) Normally, ability to work in groups, and other inter-personal skills including oral as well as written presentation skills.

1.7 The benchmark statement suggests a variety of **assessment activities** to test not only your **understanding** of conceptual and applied aspects of accountancy but also **'the cognitive abilities and non—subject specific skills they have developed as a consequence of** [your] studies'.

So this is what the Research and Analysis Project is for?

1.8 So now you know. The Research and Analysis Project is designed as an extra exercise to convert your hard-earned ACCA studies into a degree. Although it is advertised by Oxford Brookes University, there is an external examiner, appointed by the ACCA, who sits on the Examination Board.

What about the class of degree?

1.9 In the UK, undergraduate degrees fall typically into the following categories or classes 1st, 2:1, 2:2, 3rd.

1.10 The **class** of degree you receive in this case is determined by the average mark you receive in all of the relevant ACCA papers as moderated by Oxford Brookes University. These are all the papers in Parts 1 and 2. Once you have passed one of these papers, you **cannot** retake it simply to improve your class of degree by improving your average.

1.11 The **Research and Analysis Project** is either pass or fail. If you fail the Research and Analysis Project, you will not receive the degree, no matter how good your exam marks are. However, you can resubmit, having improved the Project as appropriate.

1.12 Here is a table summarising how marks in your professional exams will translate into class of degree.

Average mark	Degree classification
Below 50%	Fail
50% but less than 54%	Third class
54% but less than 58%	Second class, lower division
58% but less than 66%	Second class, upper division
66% or above	First class

(*Note.* The above averages are those within this degree programme only and are not the same as the averages used in other Oxford Brookes University degree classifications.)

Be a self-starter

1.13 Doing the Research and Analysis Project will be a very different **experience** from studying for ACCA exams. Hopefully, you will find it an interesting – if challenging – experience, one which will equip you with forensic skills in the world of work and which will broaden your horizons.

1.14   To some degree it is original work, not based on learning from Study Texts (no matter how good they are), nor is it based on rigorous and repeated question practice from Practice & Revision Kits (no matter how good they are).

1.15   Moreover, you will have to drive yourself. If you are used to a taught course, you may miss the structure of course exams, mocks and so forth – although you do have to conduct mentor meetings. It is **your** project, it is open-ended and, to an extent, you can follow your interests.

2   THE ABILITIES TO BE TESTED

2.1   For the Research and Analysis Project the **technical knowledge** you need is covered in the rigours of your ACCA exams. Let us examine the skills that the Research and Analysis Project is designed specifically to deal with.

Critical examination of arguments and evidence

2.2   Consider the following scenario.

Exercise 2

Let us say you are doing **Project Topic 6: The identification of key factors or indicators in the motivation of employees in an organisation of your choice**. As part of your research, you want to assess the relationship between reward schemes and motivation.

Four months ago, the sales manager at Saramago plc replaced a salary based scheme for 30 sales staff with a commission only scheme. He says: 'The new scheme has been a big success for the company and staff: they seem a lot happier. I mean, Bill came to see me last week and said he was really looking forward to his bonus, after all the work he'd put in. Money talks doesn't it?'.

How would you **critically examine** the arguments and evidence in this statement?

Answer

By **critical**, this does not mean saying to the sales manager 'That's rubbish, you're no good'. It means that, tactfully, you hold up the statement for review; you do not take it at face value. By **examine** it means that you have to inspect the data, tease out its meaning, test it and so on.

(a)   What does the sales manager mean by **'big success' for the company**? This is his argument. He has not presented you with any **evidence**.

   (i)   More **sales revenue** for the company? Is this quantified or measured? Are there sales reports? You'd need to see some figures.

   (ii)   Has this been accompanied by problems of credit control and bad debts?

   (iii)   Has the increase in revenue over the past four months **really** been affected by the bonus scheme?

   •   What about seasonal factors? Compared to a similar period last year, is the increase really so wonderful?

   •   Was revenue significantly up **before** the scheme was introduced?

(b)   **'Big success'** for staff? Are they earning more? In fact, is the company paying more than is really warranted by the increase? Are they happier?

(c)   His **argument** 'money talks' is that people are motivated mainly by money. Quite possibly, this is true in this case, but you need to put this in a context. His staff may be motivated by other factors, as suggested by a whole host of motivation theories.

(d)   His **evidence** about staff feelings is impressionistic: nothing wrong with that as such, but given he only mentions one person – Bill – this seems anecdotal. (Furthermore, Bill could have been complaining.)

(e)   The sales manager has every reason to praise a system he introduced himself.

If the sales manager were to unveil a detailed report with all the variances explained, proof that bad debts were not increasing and so on, you would see this in a different light.

Analyse and draw reasoned conclusions concerning structured and to a more limited extent unstructured problems from a given set of data and data which must be acquired by the student

2.3   There's quite a lot going on here. Let's look at what this means – from the end first.

Given data/data which must be acquired

2.4   As the Research and Analysis Project is not an exam, neither the ACCA nor Oxford Brookes will give you data. They suggest some Project Topics, but the data gathering work is yours. We cover this later – but it is for **you** to **define** what you need to know, to **plan** how to **obtain** data and to **implement** your plan.

Structured/unstructured problems

2.5   You will have already learnt about structured and unstructured problems elsewhere in your ACCA studies, but here is a recap.

(a)   A **structured problem** is one in which there is a defined number of elements, and it is possible to go about solving the problem in a systematic way.

(b)   An **unstructured problem**, on the other hand, is less easy to analyse as it appears to lack any obvious logic, underlying procedures or rules for solving it.

2.6   An example of a relatively **structured** problem might be as follows.

Example: sole trader

A sole trader decides to incorporate his/her business as a limited company and asks your advice as to whether this is a good idea and how to go about it.

(a)   Is it a good idea? It is relatively easy to model the effect of the change on:

- The legal position of the business
- The tax position

and so on, as there are defined rules as to how companies work.

(b)   How to go about it? Incorporating a company is a relatively routine procedure and the legal steps are easy to identify.

2.7   An example of a relatively unstructured problem is one which there are no simple steps to reach a result: it cannot simply be deconstructed into its components, if people disagree fundamentally as to the nature of the problem.

Example

Many organisations draw up a **mission statement**. This aims to describe what the organisation is 'for' and its aspirations. The mission statement is used as a communication tool to employees, shareholders and customers and so on.

Drawing up a mission statement is an 'unstructured' problem because:

(i)   There are no clear rules as to what a mission statement should be.

(ii)   Many 'stakeholders' have completely different perspectives on what organisations are for. These perspectives are not always easy to incorporate in one over-arching mission.

Ability to locate, extract and analyse data from multiple sources, including the acknowledgement and referencing of sources

2.8   This needs to be pulled apart.

Locate data

2.9   Where should you look to find what you want? Obviously, this depends on the type of data that you need to find.

Example

Let's say, for example, that you are interested in **Project Topic 12: An analysis of the effects of any International Accounting Standard (IAS) on the accounts of any organisation in terms of profitability, financial stability or balance sheet value**. Where would you find data?

(a)   Some of the data may be necessary **theoretical background**. You would need to find out where the standards are. You could for example, obtain them from a library or from the International Accounting Standards Committee. (You would also find ACCA-relevant explanations in the appropriate BPP Study Text.)

(b)   Some of the data may be specific to the entity under review. Some firms have shares listed on two stock exchanges (eg London and New York) and the reported financial performance may vary (eg according to US and UK GAAP). (International Accounting Standards may reduce this likelihood.) The Financial Director may have a particular view as to the value of IASs in this context (not least on the work involved in prepare two sets of accounts).

(c)   Some of the data would result from analysis and modelling. You could for example, try to see what would happen if you **re-stated** the accounts of a company originally prepared according to local GAAP according to IASs.

(d)   Some data could be provided by a review of relevant professional journals, such as Certified Accountant, the ACCA's Student Accountant, Accountancy – accounting standards are the subject of some debate, and even hit the business pages of some of the major newspapers on occasion.

(e)   Some data could be located by identifying and selecting a sample of respondents for a questionnaire.

Exercise 3

Jot down as many ways you can think of to **'extract'** data in relation to, the items (a) to (e) in the example above.

Answer

Just to give you an idea:

(a)   Taking notes (eg from a Study Text covering UK)
(b)   Making a tape recording of an interview with the Finance Director in which he/she describes her opinions in full and details in broad terms, the costs involved of preparing two sets of accounts.
(c)   Inputting data on to a spreadsheet for further analysis
(d)   Articles can be obtained by library visits or visits to relevant websites where a 'search' facility might enable you to review and print out certain articles
(e)   Designing a questionnaire, and getting answers to it

Analyse data

2.10 Here is an example of what we mean.

- Make sense of the data
- Apply theoretical concepts to it
- Compare it with other data for consistency

Exercise 4

Taking Exercise 3 and the example above, we can identify analytical tasks you could use.

Answer

Locate (Example)	Extract (Exercise 3)	Analyse
(a)	(a)	Determine principal differences between local GAAP and IASs
(b)	(b)	Need more detail as to costs. FD's response is likely to be personal and focused on his job and department
(c)	(c)	Provides numerical proof of effects on reported profits. Model effects on reported earnings
(d)	(d)	Identify current areas of controversy
(e)	(e)	Get a wider industry view

Exercise 5

You have a set of published financial accounts for the past three financial years and copies of relevant International Accounting Standards. What initially could you do to analyse the data?

Answer

The most obvious tool would be ratio analysis. From such data, you can easily calculate debtor, creditor and stock turnover, the total cash cycle and related trends, the proportion of working capital to total net assets, gearing and so on. You could then get an idea of the total performance of the company.

Of course the **significance** of your calculations will depend on other matters gleaned from other areas of your research. If, for example, local GAAP and IAS for goodwill differ, you would want to conduct your analysis with a purpose.

(a) Effect on reported profits and earnings per share.

(b) Your research must reveal industry peculiarities that lead to some treatments of goodwill being preferred over others.

Analyse and draw reasoned conclusions from

2.11 Effectively, this means that you have, as suggested earlier, to review your data, do things to it and come to a judgement about what the data may actually mean. A simple example may be correlation. But many examples are not so simple.

You are shown a graph showing sales of product X in the summer of 2004.

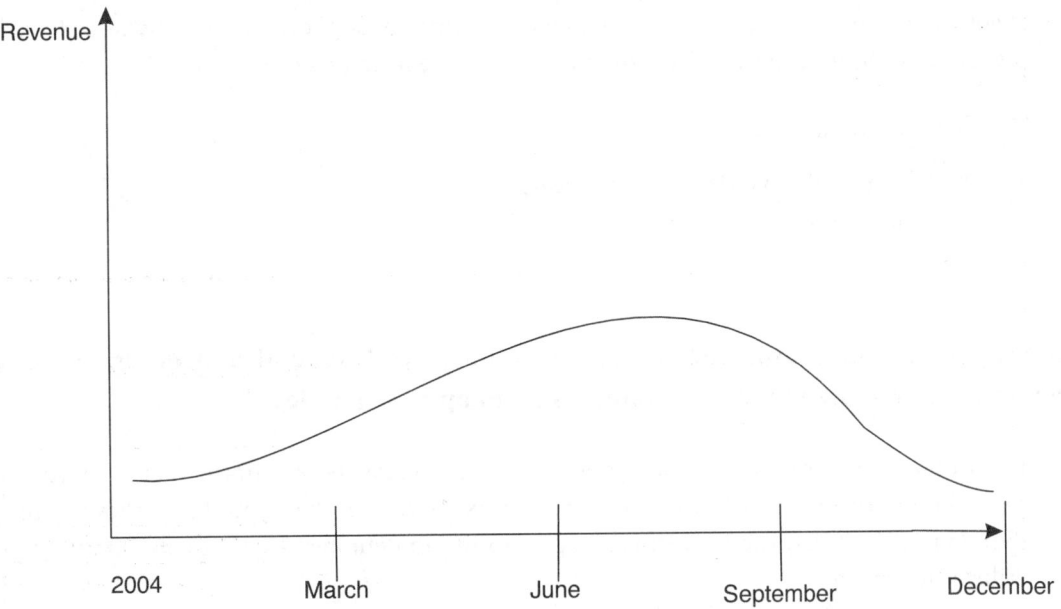

2.12 More of product X is sold in the summer of 2004 than in the winter. Without, for the time being, knowing what product X is you might **assume** that product X is sold when the temperature gets hotter.

   (a) If product X is ice-cream, then you can draw a reasoned analysis that high sales volumes relate to hot weather.

   (b) If product X is however, the Harry Potter books, their release will almost definitely not relate to the hot weather, more to the fact that there is huge demand for these anyway, and a new book was published in the late spring.

2.13 Other examples in a business context, are these.

   (a) If a company invests in new technology, and if labour productivity increases soon afterwards, you could reasonably conclude (all other things being equal), that the new technology enabled the workforce to become more productive.

   (b) One company's managers may invest in a high-risk project which offers a high reward if successful. In another company, managers are more cautious. A reasoned conclusion is that managers' attitude to risk depend on various different factors.

Example

This is directly related to **Project Topic 11: An analysis of the costs and benefits of the internal audit internal review activities within an organisation of your choice**. Managers might be reluctant to employ an internal audit team because of the salary cost. However, such a team may be able to identify improvements in the system, which will save money, and also will reduce internal audit costs.

A **reasoned conclusion** would be that an internal audit department should, for the sake of argument, be brought in, as it would have benefits (firmly derived from the data).

Capacity for independent and self managed learning

2.14 Independent and self-managed: this effectively means that you have to have the necessary skills to complete the project by yourself; in other words, you have the resources you need to learn without being spoon-fed by a tutor, and that you have to plan and manage your learning.

2.15   If you are one of the many students who have no tutorial support, you will by now, have had plenty of experience in this. We will cover some scheduling techniques in Chapter 5.

2.16   You should be able to show that:

- You can identify what you need to learn
- You can plan your learning time
- You will identify techniques to help you learn

Numeracy skills, including the ability to manipulate financial and other numerical data and to appreciate statistical concepts at an appropriate level

2.17   The Research and Analysis Project is **not** designed to **test** these skills as such: the work you have done sitting the ACCA exams so far is evidence that you have these skills in abundance. However, the Project is an opportunity to demonstrate that you can apply these skills or use them.

Look at the business situation below

Exercise 6

You are doing **Project Topic 16 'An analysis of different sources of capital on investment decisions within an organisation of your choice'**. The company is Iolinda Ltd, your employer, and you have a lot of data to use.

Iolinda Ltd is a biotechnology company about to be listed on a stock market. It has used genetic manipulation (GM) technology to generate a species of rose that is impervious to aphids. The company is very confident that the new rose will be a huge market success, but needs to conduct trials in plant nurseries. Of course, these trials may fail or have unintended consequences. There is a risk that the trials may fail and/or that environmentalists will disrupt them. Iolinda does have some other valuable patents, in GM technology for farmers, but this is the first time it will market directly to a consumer products industry (not food). Consumers and the gardening public will be propagating GM plants

The venture capital firms that have financed Iolinda want to recover their investment by selling shares. Other biotechnology companies have no difficulties in raising equity. However, the share prices of biotechnology firms have been quite volatile in relation to the market as a whole, with some spectacular successes and failures. Iolinda intends to float whether or not the rose project fails or succeeds.

Required

What **numerical analysis** could you do on data items (1) to (6) below?

(1)   Historic data on likely success/failure of trials of GM products (ie failure rate pre launch)

(2)   Cash flows required for the trials pre-launch

(3)   Proposed pricing strategy (eg penetration or skimming strategies) and sales forecast; distribution and marketing costs assuming launch is successful; comparative volumes in relation to other products

(4)   Projected earnings per share for the company as a whole, or similar information from the prospectus

(5)   Interest rates

(6)   Market values, dividend levels and yields, and betas of similar companies

Answer

Here are some ideas.

The **historic success rate** for GM product trials can be used to develop **probabilities** of the success of the trials, and so you can then calculate **expected values** of the future cash flows. These might give an idea of **risk**. However, you may also need to consider the risk that the **political climate** opposed to

GM products may significantly reduce the sales turnover. All this will be relevant to **investment appraisal**.

If significant cash flows are involved, you may be required to prepare **cash budgets** and to monitor **working capital.**

The proposed pricing strategy will give an idea of what cash flows might be expected and hence you could estimate the significance of the rose trial in the **overall product portfolio**.

With suitable information you might analyse the **risk** of the project, and use the **beta**, if it meets the relevant tests.

2.18　Note that there is a **limit** to the technical knowledge you need apply. (For example, you are unlikely to come across beta valuation in your ACCA exams until you have reached Part 3.)

Skills in the use of communications and information technology in acquiring, analysing and communicating information, including the use of spreadsheets, and word processing software, the world-wide web and email.

2.19　Here are some examples.

Acquiring	Conducting a web search using a search engine Visiting relevant websites
Analysing	Modelling using spreadsheets, such as 'what if?' analysis
Communicating	Emailing responses Communicating in a chat-room Joining a group Word processing your report Using graphics in spreadsheets

Communication skills including the ability to present quantitative and qualitative information together with analysis, argument and commentary in a form appropriate to different audiences

2.20　Communications skills are covered in Parts C and D of this Tutorial Text. The Research and Analysis Project tests your skills in:

- Report writing (the Report)
- Oral presentation (Key Skills Statement)

2.21　You have to present **analysis, argument and commentary**.

(a) **Analysis**: in the report, you need to be able to explain the analytical work you have done, and to describe your method. In fact, thinking how you would explain and justify your analytical work to an audience (eg friends) is a good way of testing whether you have done enough work.

(b) **Argument**: stating a case, and justifying it with reasoned argument.

(c) **Commentary**: a commentary could include adding detail, adding context and so on.

Exercise 7

The data below is taken from an unpublished undergraduate dissertation project.

Required

Each sentence is numbered. The ten sentences below contain a mix of **analysis**, **argument** and **commentary**.

Pick **one** example of each type of sentence

(1)   Sales people rarely consider a car as a perk; instead it is a pre-requisite for accepting a job. (2) However, the potential for a company car to motivate a sales force can be considerable if structured thoughtfully and is most powerful in satisfying higher social needs. (3) Within X plc cars are given to all salesman and better models are allocated according to the progress a salesman makes. (4) Some managers felt that a set of standards should be disclosed so that sales people know on what basis cars are allocated. (5) Survey results revealed that a car signifies financial status and social standing. (Packard, 1980). (6) Therefore, company cars have a significant motivational capacity, as well as being a cause of contention or jealousy especially taking Equity theory into account. (7) Hence this perk must be controlled with integrity and firmness. (8) A survey showed that for some sales people in London a car is of little practical usefulness in the selling task, as the London Underground is more practicable. (9) At present all X plc's sales staff are still issued with a car. (10) With reference to the Cafeteria reward system mentioned in Chapter 3, it may be more satisfactory for sales people to have a choice of a higher salary, a car or some other benefit.

Answer

(a)   **Argument**   Sentence (2): says why a car can motivate a sales force. Sentences (6) and (7): sentence (6) is based on facts described earlier.

(b)   **Commentary**   Sentences (3) and (4): descriptive about X plc

(c)   **Analysis**   There is little analysis in the extract given but it does confirm some of the data. Sentence 5 applies theory to reported results of a survey.

(*Note*. The reference to (Packard, 1980) would be fully described in the bibliography to this project. If you have not read through Appendix 1 of the Guidelines on referencing, do so now.)

Normally, ability to work in groups, and other interpersonal skills including oral communication skills

2.22   Finally, the Research Project and Analysis Project deals with your ability to put over a point in person. It is not an exercise in public speaking, but throughout your work you will have to be an effective oral communicator.

3   OUTLINE AND OVERVIEW OF THE WORK INVOLVED

3.1   Oxford Brookes University has provided useful guidelines. We will briefly go through each stage as outlined by Oxford Brookes University in the description of the project. This section is a **summary. Detailed coverage of research, mentor meetings etc is found in later chapters.**

Choosing a mentor

3.2   The suggested framework above offers a useful description of the key tasks involved in completing the project. If you already have a degree, you almost certainly have encountered these before but in outline there are two issues: **content** and **process**.

3.3   First of all, you should choose a mentor. This person can be your employer or line manager, a tutor or any member of the ACCA. You must do this first of all because you have to **report** on three meetings with your mentor in the Key Skills Statement. (See section 6 of this chapter for advice as to this.)

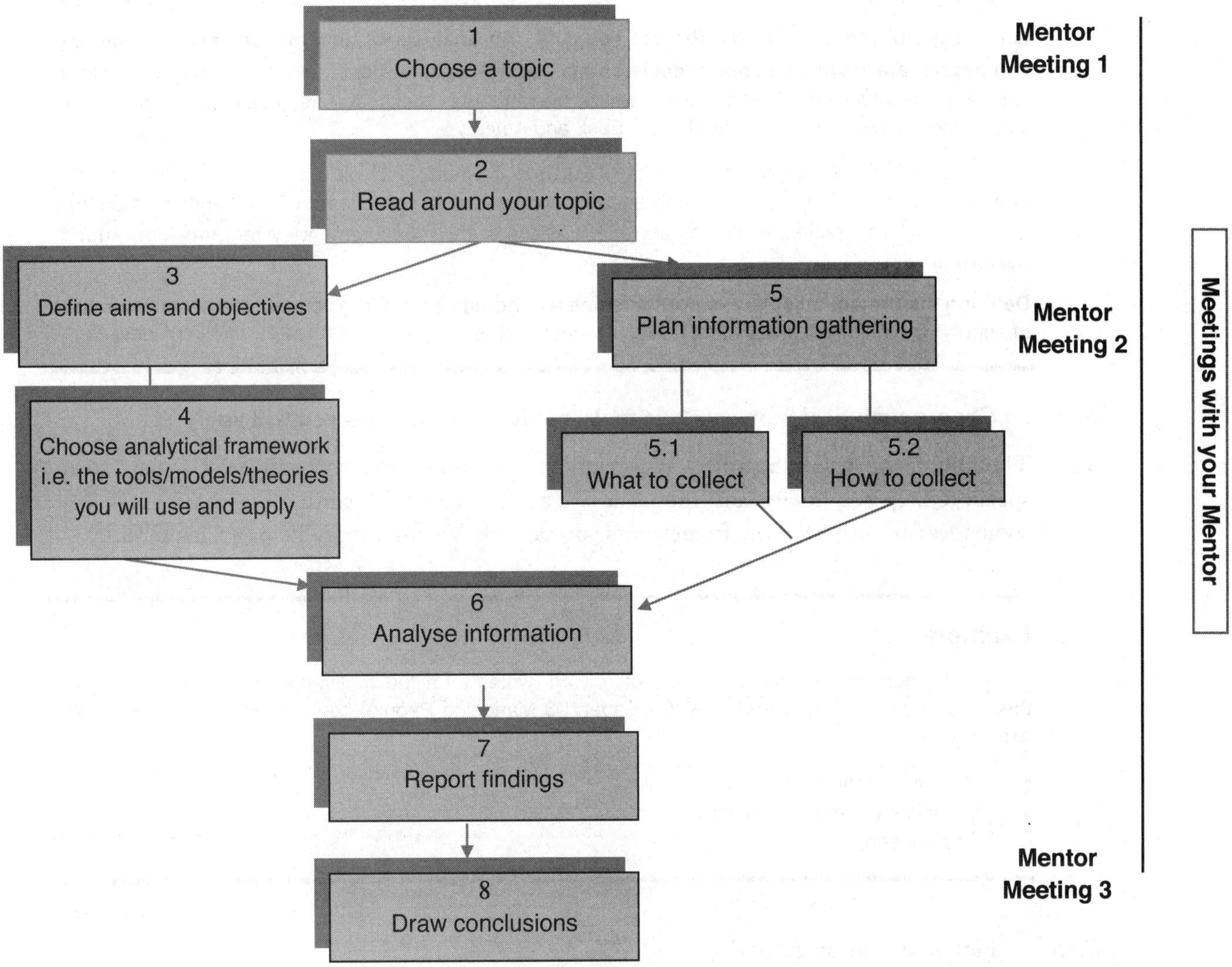

```
                              ┌──────────────────┐
                              │        1         │        Mentor
                              │  Choose a topic  │        Meeting 1
                              └──────────────────┘
                                       │
                                       ▼
                              ┌─────────────────────┐
                              │         2           │
                              │ Read around your topic │
                              └─────────────────────┘
```

3 Define aims and objectives	**5** Plan information gathering — **Mentor Meeting 2**
4 Choose analytical framework i.e. the tools/models/theories you will use and apply	**5.1** What to collect **5.2** How to collect

```
                    ┌──────────────────────┐
                    │          6           │
                    │  Analyse information  │
                    └──────────────────────┘
                               │
                               ▼
                    ┌──────────────────────┐
                    │          7           │
                    │   Report findings     │
                    └──────────────────────┘
                               │
                               ▼
                    ┌──────────────────────┐
                    │          8           │
                    │  Draw conclusions     │       Mentor
                    └──────────────────────┘       Meeting 3
```

Meetings with your Mentor

Steps 1 and 2. Choose a topic, read around the topic

3.4 Chapter 4 outlines the suggested topics in detail with some guidance notes as to how to go about this. There are **twenty two topics** in total. They are not like exam questions; they are very open, identifying the **broad area** of your research and analysis. They create a space, as it were, for you to fill.

3.5 You do not have to do a detailed literature review, but you may need to explore the issues. Some relevant knowledge may be found in BPP study material.

Step 3. Define aims and objectives of the project

3.6 We will cover this in more detail in Chapter 4 – but a project objective is very important.

3.7 Detailed guidance on defining the project objective is given in Chapter 4, but here is a taster. The project objective outlines **precisely** what you are going to do, the company involved and so on.

The first mentor meeting you have to report on covers the some outline proposals, how you intend to research them and your aims. The mentor will act as a sounding board, but does not take a directive role. More about this in Section 5.

Example

Let us say that you have chosen **Project Topic 10:** 'An analysis of how management accounting techniques are used to support decision-making in organisations'. Your employer is H plc, a company manufacturing forklift trucks, which markets the trucks and replacement parts through independent dealers in Europe, the Middle East, and Africa.

'The objective of this project is to evaluate the effectiveness of H plc's system for measuring the performance of its dealers and, through analysis and critique to put forward recommendations on how to improve it.' This project evaluates the effectiveness of the measurement system, **not operational performance**.

Defining the project objective is not the same as choosing a topic. The topic outlines a broad field of activity. The objective gives you a target to work towards.

Step 4. **Choose analytical framework, ie tools, models and theories you will apply**

3.8 The aim of the research project is to explore a situation and you will need a map, so to speak, to help you understand the terrain. Your earlier ACCA studies may have given you some ideas as to some of the frameworks you can use. We offer more help in Chapter 6.

Example

A project report investigated the effect of reward systems on the motivation of a sales force. The theoretical framework (covered in ACCA paper 1.3 Managing People) could be motivation theory, for example:

- Maslow's hierarchy of needs
- Expectancy theory and so on
- Equity theory

Step 5. **Plan information gathering**

3.9 We cover this in detail in Chapter 5. You have to **plan** for obtaining data: what you want and how you intend to collect it. You are likely to use a variety of research methods (covered in Chapter 6); these include **secondary research** (reading), and **primary research**.

Example

An Oxford Brookes University undergraduate did some research into whether, how and why companies communicate data about the impact of their operations on the physical environment.

- **What was needed**: a questionnaire to assess whether companies in the survey had a department specifically devoted to environmental issues, whether they had a stated policy, use of environmental schemes and so on.

- **How it was obtained**: the questionnaire had to be designed – not as straightforward as you think – mailed out and completed.

- A **sample** has to be selected.

- **What if it goes wrong**? Frequently, initial research plans go awry. You may need a contingency plan to meet your research objective.

3.10 Putting your well-made plans into effect will need skills of **time management, scheduling** and organisation. If you are sending out a questionnaire, you may not receive immediate

responses. You may have to book up meetings with other people. You may not be able to obtain all the books you need at one time.

Second meeting with your mentor

3.11 After you have gathered all the information you need, by whatever method, you should have some idea as to the progress of the project brief and the findings from your data. To gather your thoughts together, you will need to draft a **word processed** document **summarising your findings so far for discussion with the mentor**. This could be:

(a) A brief description of what you have done to date
(b) A brief summary of the information you have gathered
(c) Initial views

You should be about half way through the project. You may for example want to talk about how to interpret some of the data, if the results did not meet quite what you expected. You may feel it is necessary to do further research.

Step 6. Analysing the information

3.12 This is when a lot of the more difficult intellectual work takes place. You are in effect converting the data you have gathered into usable information, and you will be expected to show evidence of the use of IT at this stage. The analysis work involves interrogating the data, applying theory to it and so on, to obtain the information you need to satisfy the project objective.

Example

To do **Project Topic 6: 'The identification of key factors or indicators of motivation in an organisation of your choice'** your project objective is based on a stationery supplier.

In your data gathering exercise, you have obtained:

- Details of the company's sales figures, for each of the past 36 months, and of debtors ageing
- From a trade body, an index of prices for the industry as a whole

Your analysis phase could – depending on your project objective – start by adjusting the actual sales figures for general price changes in the industry as a whole. This would give you some idea as to the **underlying** performance of the company, to see whether it was doing better or worse than similar companies elsewhere. You could then obtain reports from other companies in the industry, such as key competitors. This suggests that one set of analytical work might generate more work.

Steps 7 and 8. Reporting findings and drawing conclusions

3.13 Here is an example of a conclusion from an undergraduate dissertation

---

Example

The aim of the project was to evaluate the effectiveness of a performance measurement system for dealers. Based on the study and evaluation of this report, the conclusion is that the performance measurement systems work reasonably well. This research aim has been met by meeting four project objectives.

1 Through secondary research, a standard for an effective performance measurement system was developed

2 The operations of the current system were investigated

3   The current system was evaluated in the light of the standard outlined in 1. This analysis showed that the system had been developed according to (1), but that there were some areas of dissatisfaction

4   Three recommendations were made to the company. One of these has already been adopted.

Third mentor meeting, presentation, report

3.14   To expand, the **final stage** of the project involves the following tasks.

(a)   The **intellectual labour** of drawing the data together into a **conclusion**, clearly based on the work done.

- You will need to assess what the information you have discerned actually means.
- You will have to describe your findings in terms of the project objective.

(b)   The **communication task of presenting your findings** in a 15 minute presentation to your mentor or peer group.

(c)   The **communication task of writing a 5,000 word Report** (with appendices).

(d)   The **communication task of writing a 1,500 Key Skills Statement** based on your communications.

These are covered in the next sections.

4   WHAT YOU ARE EXPECTED TO PRODUCE AT THE END

The Report

4.1   It is worth working through the requirements in some detail. Fortunately you are given quite specific guidance as to the length and weighting of the report. Details on Report writing are given in Chapter 9.

4.2   Word length: 5,000 words (plus NO MORE THAN 5 pages of appendices)

4.3   Your Report must be no longer than 5,000 words: if you write more Oxford Brookes University reserves the right to fail your project.

4.4   This is one of the key differences between the Research and Analysis Project and an undergraduate dissertation: a typical dissertation is often twice as long.

4.5   5,000 words sounds a lot – but this depends very much on how concisely you write. (We will be giving detailed hints and tips in Chapter 9 of the tutorial text.) And remember, you have to put the word count on the title page.

To put this in context:

At ten words a line, 5,000 words is = 500 lines.
At 50 lines a page, 5,000 words is ten pages.
If you double space your document it will be about 20 pages long.

> For your information, the **word count in this chapter so far, including headers** is:
>
> ## 6,573

This should give you some idea as to scale.

Recommended structure

4.6   The Guidelines also give a suggestion as to structure. This is not compulsory but you will be **taking no risks** by following this format.

Introduction	
• Topic chosen and its context	
• Your reasons for choosing the topic	
• Aims and objectives of the report	
Information gathering	Up to 1,500 words
• Sources used, and reasons for their use (these must be secondary and may be primary)	
• Description of methods used to gather information	
Analysis	
• Analysis of information	
• Presentation of findings	Up to 2,500 words
Conclusions	
• What the report has shown in relation to aims and objectives	Up to 1,000 words
Appendices	
• Up to 5 sides max	
Bibliography	

Getting a pass in the Report

4.7   Let us review Oxford Brookes University's criteria for **assessment** and pick out some key words.

1 Communication skills	Comment
1.1 **Coherent** and **structured** report **focused on the stated objectives** and **written in a lucid style**	
Coherent	This means logical, consistent and orderly. The different elements of the Report should fit together and relate with each other.
Structured	• Use of numbered paragraphs • Clear division into sections • Logical ordering of material for example • Argument followed by Evidence
Focused on the stated objectives	Your project must have an objective.
Written in a lucid style	You must pay attention to how you write. Your effective use of written business English is being tested here, as it is at work.

Communication skills continued	Comment
1.2 **Clear and accurate referencing**	Unlike ACCA exams, you must show where your information comes from. This is a requirement of much academic writing, so that your assertions can be verified, and it is clear that the work is your own and not plagiarised.
	In fact every reference must be identified. There are clear rules for this. Detailed guidance and examples follow in the Appendix.
2 Information gathering	
2.1 **Evidence of appropriate selection of methods of gathering information – these should relate to the topic/objectives of the project**	
• Evidence	You have to **show** what you have done. If you researched from an article, say, you should give full details of title, publication date etc.
	If you have conducted a questionnaire, you should show survey details.
• Appropriate selection of methods relate to the topic/objectives of the project	We will learn in Chapter 5 about selection of methods for gathering data
2.2 **Use of a range of information sources which must show evidence of wider reading and use of IT based sources**	
• Evidence	Again, you must describe what you have done to obtain your research data and this should be testable
• Wider reading	Again, very different from professional exams! You must **show** that you have read **around the topic area**, such as articles and relevant books. (In your degree studies, you cannot – sad to say! – rely on your BPP Study Text no matter how good it is.)
• IT based sources	You have to show how to use IT-based sources, surfing the net, CD-ROMs, on-line databases. You also have to reflect on your use of IT.
2.3 **Referencing of appropriate sources of information**	This is key to the credibility of your project. As an analogy, **referencing provides an audit trail of the research you have done** – if you are an auditor, not only must you check invoices, say, but take them as evidence that you have done so.
3 Analysis and conclusions	
3.1 A relevant analysis of the information using an appropriate framework or tool	
• Relevant	Your analysis must be focused to what you are trying to achieve; for example, if you are looking at working capital, a ratio analysis covering only profitability would not be relevant.
• Appropriate framework or tool	For example, when discussing motivation, you could use one of the recognised models of motivation as a framework.

3.2 Clear presentation of findings from the information gathered

Clear presentation	Remember your audience! You have to show the results of the analysis in your report in a way that others will understand. Do not assume that they are subject experts like the examiner in your normal ACCA exam.
	Use the graphics facility on the spreadsheet programme to aid presentation
Findings from the information gathered	You cannot simply make assertions; your analysis must come up with findings. For example, if you are discussing the effect of globalisation, say, on an industry of your choice, then you should be able to show evidence of the effect, or lack of it.
Appropriate conclusions	Your conclusion should be supported by the evidence, even if this is not what you expected to find.

IT skills	
(1) Application of IT skills to achieve a document with a clear layout and a logical structure	Your report must be word processed, and you may want to use some of the layout tools, such as automatic paragraph numbering, headers and footers, available in typical word processing packages
(2) Use of a spreadsheet to analyse and present data in a tabular and graphical form in the report	In Excel, it is a relatively easy exercise to turn numbers into graphs.
	Excel spreadsheets are ideal material for the appendices – no more than five pages. Show the formulae that you are using if you can; Oxford Brookes have said that it is very beneficial for you to do so, as you are then clearly demonstrating your ability to use IT.

The Key Skills Statement

4.8 The Key Skills Statement is a **record** (1,500 words) of three meetings you will have with your mentor. This will be supported by an outline of the presentation made to your mentor **or peer group. Although it is a written record it covers oral communication skills. Details are given in Chapter 12.**

4.9 The purpose of this is to enable you to show that you have considered your oral communication skills in the light of what is expected in the **benchmark statement mentioned in Section 1.** You are not expected to be a world-class public speaker, however, but there are techniques you can use to communicate effectively in a face-to-face context. You may have already acquired some of these techniques in other situations requiring communication, such as:

- Meetings with client staff
- Team briefings
- Interviews (both as interviewer and interviewee)
- Meetings with/presentation to other people in the organisation

4.10 The Guidelines helpfully offer you a structure for the Key Skills Statement. You are asked to:

- Communicate orally in meetings and in a 15 minute presentation

- Reflect on your oral communication

- Write down your reflections – including a judgement about your own performance – as to how you would do better

	Communication skills	Comments
(1)	**Preparing for meetings** Describe how you prepared for meetings Assess the importance of planning and organising in relation to the effectiveness of your meetings and meetings in general.	You must illustrate with examples, describing how you planned for the meeting
(2)	**Questioning** Consider and explain the role of questioning in ensuring productive discussions with your mentor in particular the use of appropriate questioning techniques.	A productive discussion is one you get results from. You must illustrate with examples of the types of questions you have asked: this means understanding the types of questions available.
(3)	**Listening** Explain the importance of listening in ensuring that communication with your mentor was effective. Consider active listening techniques, sources of error and distortion in communication.	You have to **listen actively** to what is being said, and be aware that you might be missing information or letting 'noise' impede your receptiveness to the communication. Were you distracted by extraneous factors or were there other issues that made the communication less effective (eg mutual misunderstanding).
(4)	**The presentation** Assess the presentation identifying what went well and what could have been improved. You should attach two sides of A4 to your Key Skills Statement showing an outline of the presentation.	You will have to speak for about 15 minutes, and reflect on how well it went.
(5)	**Self assessment of the interaction** Using an appropriate model of communication analyse and evaluate interaction with your mentor and if applicable with your peer discussion group, in relation to the key elements of successful communication.	You have to **apply a model** of communication to your interaction; using a model will force you to reflect on the communication process. • Give examples of what you did • Describe how you would go about it better • Refer to literature on communication

NO MORE THAN 1,500 WORDS PLUS THE PRESENTATION OUTLINE
The guidelines suggest 300 words approximately for each section above.
For guidance, this paragraph and box contain exactly 292 words.

5   OTHER PEOPLE INVOLVED: YOUR PEER GROUP AND YOUR MENTOR

Your peer group

5.1   First of all, the project is to be your own work. It is not a group project, and Oxford Brookes University **will FAIL projects that show evidence of syndication.**

Here is an extract from Oxford Brookes University guidance for undergraduate dissertations about 'syndication'.

> **Syndication**
>
> You must also take care that, unless you are specifically instructed that a piece of work for assessment is to be produced jointly with other students, the work you submit has been prepared by you alone. If you collude with other students to prepare a piece of work jointly, or copy each other's work, and pass it off as an individual effort, it is syndication and is against the University's regulations. It is also, obviously, against the rules to copy another student's work without his or her knowledge.

5.2 That said, if a number of people in your firm are doing the Research and Analysis Project, it would be a shame not to talk things over with them. Here are some suggestions as to how you can make **best** use of a peer group.

(a) **Choice of topics**. One way of ensuring that there is no syndication is to choose different topics from the list provided by Oxford Brookes University. As the list of topics is fairly broad, you may wish to brainstorm ideas.

(b) Colleagues at work might have a good idea as to **your strengths and weaknesses**. Given that written and oral communication are such an important part of the Research Project, it is sometimes good to be told that these are issues you have to work on.

(c) **Presentation**. Your third meeting with the mentor – at which you must give a 15 minute presentation – can take the form of a presentation to your peer group also.

(d) You may be able to share hints and tips about how to plan the project.

Your mentor's role

5.3 Firstly, you have to **find** a mentor. It will be worth your while doing this **before you start the project**.

5.4 There are two aspects to the role.

(a) **Formal**

- To be present at three meetings with you
- To verify to Oxford Brookes University that the meetings took place
- To confirm that the report has been carried out according to the Guidelines

(b) **Informal**

- Sounding board for ideas
- A champion for the degree project within the organisation; a mentor will appreciate that you have **other** demands on your time
- Give you unbiased constructive feedback about your presentation and communication skills
- Suggest fruitful avenues of enquiry
- Pull strings on your behalf with other managers

5.5 **A mentor's role is not**:

(a) To act as a tutor throughout the project
(b) To give detailed instructions on how to tackle the project
(c) To read and offer a detailed critique of your Report
(d) To act as a progress chaser on the project – you should be motivated enough

Who can be your mentor?

5.6 Your mentor can be:

(a) Your employer or line manager (current or previous) OR

(b) Your tutor at college or university OR

(c) A qualified Chartered Certified Accountant (sorry, but this excludes members of all other accountancy bodies unless they are also members of the ACCA). The qualification of your mentor to act will have to be certified on the Submission Form which accompanies your project.

Whoever you choose, you will have to reassure them that your project will not breach commercial confidentiality. More about this in a later chapter.

The external examiner commented in his first report on projects submitted that it is useful to have a mentor who has some research skills even if only at an 'introductory level'. Although the mentor will not be actively involved in your research, it would be helpful for them to understand the nature of research as an academic skill. The external examiner has also commented that in some cases students are not given particularly good advice by their mentor. A mentor will be far more effective if they have some idea of the criteria for a good piece of research and an appreciation of how to analyse findings. You should give some careful thought to your choice of mentor.

5.7 **If your mentor is 'your employer or line manager'**

(a) In theory it could be **anybody** – but you need someone who can give you constructive feedback and take a responsible, but not intrusive, interest in the project.

(b) You could ask your **immediate line manager** to assume this role – but remember that your line manager has an interest in keeping you working on what you are paid to do.

(c) You could ask your line manager to recommend someone else in the department or in another department.

(d) You could ask someone in the human resources department or, if you have a training department, in the training department to be your mentor.

5.8 **Briefing a mentor**

- Ask first of all – do not assume that your choice has the time or inclination to take this role.

- Explain carefully what the mentor has to do – in case he/she is frightened off.

- **Agree a timetable in advance if possible.** You know when the Report has to be submitted, and you may have to schedule your meetings and your own time with your mentor's other commitments.

- If you cannot make your appointments, give as much advance notice as possible.

- Make sure that you ask for feedback.

- Explain how important the degree is to you, and that a relatively limited use of mentor's time can help you get a degree.

- Explain how acquiring some of the skills in the project may make you a more effective worker (if this is indeed to be the case).

- You could also ask if the company would pay the £50 registration fee. After all, if they support your ACCA studies, this is not too much to ask.

Chapter roundup

- This chapter has given an overview of the different skills you need to adopt when doing the project, and a brief overview of what is involved.

- A degree has to satisfy other criteria than a professional qualification.

- The Research and Analysis Project enables Oxford Brookes University to test abilities required for all accountancy degrees.

- Research, analysis and communication skills are required.

- Nothing will be handed to you on a plate.

- You can set your own deadlines.

- We will go into more detail in later chapters

Chapter 4

CHOOSING AND DEFINING YOUR PROJECT

Chapter topic list

1   Oxford Brookes University's list of recommended project topics

2   Choosing your project

3   Project topics not on the list

4   Defining the project objective

5   Confidentiality

6   'Thought points' on each project topic

Introduction

This chapter discusses one of the most crucial decisions you will have to make: the choice of topic. Oxford Brookes University has indicated 22 broad topic outlines. However, you have to turn these into a project with a defined objective.

In Section 1 we outline the list of topics and the rationale for doing them. In Section 2 we give some hints as to how you can make your choice, following this up in Section 3 by discussing what to do if you have a burning desire to branch out on your own.

In Section 4, we offer some suggestions as to how to convert the choice of project into a genuine objective.

In Section 5 we discuss the complex issue of confidentiality and consider ways of solving potential problems.

In Section 6, we have jotted down some ideas about each topic to get you thinking.

---

1   OXFORD BROOKES UNIVERSITY'S LIST OF RECOMMENDED PROJECT TOPICS

1.1   The Guidelines offer you twenty two topic areas to choose from. Read them carefully.

Recommended topics for your Research and Analysis Report

1   An analysis of the efficiency and/or effectiveness of a management accounting technique in an organisational setting.

2   An analysis of how the application of technology can contribute to an organisation's efficiency and/or effectiveness.

3   An examination of the impact of an aspect of existing or impending legislation on an organisation.

4   An analysis of the impact of e-business on an industry or organisation of your choice.

5   The identification of the effects of globalisation on an industry of your choice.

6   The identification of key factors or indicators in the motivation of employees in an organisation of your choice.

7   An analysis of the tax and profit implications of different company entities, changes in status or acquisitions or disposals of company assets.

8   An analysis of the financial situation of your choice of organisation.

9   An examination of how to plan, develop and implement an appropriate information system in an organisation.

10 An analysis of how management accounting techniques are used to support decision-making in organisations.

11 An analysis of the costs and benefits of the internal audit/internal review activities within an organisation of your choice.

12 An analysis of the effect of any International Accounting Standard on the accounts of any organisation in terms of profitability or financial stability or balance sheet value.

13 An analysis of future personnel requirements under conditions of change (including employee development)

14 An investigation of recent investment decisions by an organisation of your choice and how the use of different methods of risk and uncertainty analysis might affect such decisions.

15 An analysis of the role of working capital on the profitability and /or efficiency of an organisation of your choice.

16 An analysis of the effect of different sources of capital on investment decisions within an organisation of your choice.

17 An analysis of the effect of corporate governance on an organisation of your choice.

18 An examination of how to plan, develop and implement an appropriate PRP system in an organisation.

19 An analysis of the business and financial reasons and effects of creating a multinational merger company.

20 An analysis of the effects of IT failure and contingency plans within an organisation of your choice.

21 An analysis of the impact of the Euro on an organisation or industry of your choice.

22 Analyse the marketing strategy of an organisation of your choice, identifying the key success factors or indicators in the marketing mix and the activities of the organisation.

The list of topics may occasionally be refreshed, (indeed topics 17 to 22 were additions to the original list) but the list above will remain current until December 2004. Oxford Brookes have said that any changes to the list after that date are only likely to be additions. Topics would only be deleted if they had ceased to be relevant, which is unlikely for any of the current list. If in doubt at the time of starting your project, consult the list of topics on the version of the Guidelines available on the ACCA's website as that will be completely up to date.

1.2   The **scope** of topics is very wide and would suggest **different treatments** and a **different scheme of work for each of them**. There are two ways of looking at this issue.

1.3   For example, contrast these two projects.

(a) **Project Topic 4: An analysis of the impact of e-business on an industry or organisation of your choice.**

   (i)   The scope of your **analysis of e-business** can be enormous, as you could cover marketing, its effect on sales volumes and revenues, raising finance, how you value e-businesses, information technology, effect on distribution, risks and costs.

   (ii)   An **industry of your choice** – almost any commercial concern, for example the music industry or a less 'fashionable' industry such as pulp and paper making – all have the potential to be changed by e-business. The scope of choice is wide.

   (iii)   **An organisation of your choice.** If you wish to focus on a **particular company**, you might find this easier to grasp; for example if you focus on food retailing, you might concentrate on a supermarket chain, such as Tesco in the UK or Walmart in the US.

(b) **Project Topic 12: An analysis of the effect of any International Accounting Standard on the accounts of any organisation in terms of profitability or financial stability or balance sheet value.**

   This alerts us to a different set of issues entirely.

   (i)   Firstly, you will be limited to **one** organisation (but you can use others for comparison).

   (ii)   You are restricted **to an organisation which has to prepare financial statements** according to local accounting standards (eg FRSs in the UK, MASB approved standards in Malaysia). You could thus exclude partnerships or sole traders, and much of the public sector. (Arguably, the transition to IASs involves a greater change in some jurisdictions, eg Germany, than others.)

   (iii)   For some companies IASs may not be relevant – if those companies have no intention of raising finance internationally.

   (iv)   Accounting using IASs is becoming a highly topical issue as we approach 2005, when all European Union listed companies (ie those quoted on a stock exchange) will be required to use them according to a European directive.

   You would need to provide further context of course, as the thinking on accounting standards evolves over time.

		Potential scope of research topic	
		Deep	**Broad**
Potential field of enquiry	Single organisation	Project 12?	
	Industry		Project 4?

1.4   So, on the topic grid above, Project 12 (IASs) would be in the top left hand corner (single company, deep), whereas Project Topic 4 (e-business) would be in the bottom right hand quadrant (industry, broad).

Exercise 1

Force yourself to read each Project Topic carefully and allocate it to one of the quadrants below. The purpose of this exercise is to get you to think carefully about your choice of project.

		Potential scope of research topic	
		Deep	Broad
Potential field of enquiry	Single organisation		
	Industry		

2 CHOOSING YOUR PROJECT

2.1 Your choice of topic is key in ensuring that the project is an interesting and enjoyable experience for you.

If you find a Project Topic you like strongly

2.2 With luck, you will see one straight away. If you are absolutely convinced of what you want to do, then read this section no further, ignore Section 3, and go straight to section 4 of this chapter. However, before you do that think carefully whether:

- you will be able to gain **access** to information (for example will there be issues of confidentiality if you are planning to base your research on your own company?)
- you will be able to obtain **enough** material: even if the topic interests you, you may not be able to find enough to say about it

If you like none of the Project Topics on the list

2.3 The list of topics has been **carefully** designed and developed by the academic staff at Oxford Brookes University. A great deal of thought has gone into this list, and it is appropriate for the BSc (Hons) in Applied Accounting and in the light of your ACCA studies to date. The Research and Analysis Project is not an undergraduate dissertation, but something unique to **this** degree. Therefore you are strongly advised to choose a topic from this list.

(a) **Firstly, look again more carefully**. You may find that with a little more thought, you can find a number of topics that interest you.

(b) Secondly, if you have difficulty making up your mind, then carry on reading this section.

If you cannot make up your mind, follow these steps

Step 1. Cross off the projects that definitely do not interest you

2.4 Even if you cannot find the topic you like, there may be a few that you would definitely want to avoid. This may narrow the field according to key criteria significantly, making it easier to choose from those remaining.

Step 2. Grade the remaining projects

2.5 In the example we suggest a number of **criteria by which you can grade the attractiveness** of a project. You can decide yourself what the most appropriate criteria are, and give each criterion a weighting (eg 3 marks max, 6 marks max etc). You can of course, change the weightings. (If relevance to your future career is more important than what your mentor thinks, then give it a higher weighting.) All we are suggesting is a technique **to help you prioritise**.

For each project you are grading, make a decision on each of the criteria, below.

(a) **How relevant is this topic to my experience to date**? (weighting 3 = very relevant; 0 = not relevant – make up your own weighting from now on.)

(b) **Can my employer benefit from the project topic**? Your employer may have issues worth investigating, which can be adapted for the Project. An advantage of taking this into account is that your employer may agree that at least some of the Project can be done in **working hours**, as the organisation will benefit.

(c) **How relevant is the topic to what I would be interested to pursue in my future career?**

   (i) If you want to work as an accountant for a bank, say, then some topics may be more relevant to the banking sector than others.

   (ii) You may not have a sector in mind, but may be interested in exploring management accounting issues in a strategic context.

(d) Some people are happier with a **broad brush**; others prefer a **forensic approach**.

(e) How far does the topic **build on technical or other knowledge I am confident of using**? The Research and Analysis Project covers particular skills, and most of the technical knowledge you have gleaned from your ACCA studies. But you may have other resources of your own you could bring to bear – for example you may have experience in developing an information system, or there has been an IS project in your department recently.

(f) Can I define **key issues** and **examples**?

   For example, if you are analysing the financial position of an organisation, you might identify cash flow as a major indicator of 'going concern' status.

(g) Can I **obtain data easily**? You may find that some topics are easier for you to research than others (for whatever reason). This will differ from person to person, but as you will be doing the Report while holding down a job, this is worth considering.

(h) From an informal chat with my **mentor**, how far do I think the project topic will enable me to get constructive **feedback** from him/her?

Step 3. Total the score

2.6 Add up the scores and you have a result. But then again, you might want to go back, and reweight the criteria. Or the result you arrive at may cause you to think seriously and

realise that you actually do not want to do this topic, in which case you can then focus on other topics.

Example

In the example below questions (c) and (e) are of more importance to the student than the other questions so they have a higher weighting. The student would be able to ignore projects 4 and 11 and should, strictly speaking, choose project 12, with the highest score. However as projects 12 and 15 are very close, the student might consider reviewing this assessment. The exercise at least narrows the choice down to two topics rather than the previous four.

Question		Project number and marks			
		No 4	No 11	No 12	No 15
(a)	How relevant/related is this topic to my experience to date?	3	0	2	1
(b)	Can my employer benefit from the Project Topic?	3	2	1	1
(c)	How relevant is the topic to what I would be interested in doing in my future career?	0	4	5	6
(d)	How does the topic reflect my preferences for breadth of scope over depth?	0	1	2	3
(e)	How far does the topic build on technical or other knowledge that I am confident using?	2	3	5	4
(e)	Can I define some key issues or examples?	0	0	1	2
(g)	Can I obtain data easily about this topic (eg background reading material, primary data)?	3	0	2	1
(h)	From an informal chat with my mentor, how far do I think the project topic will enable me to get constructive feedback from him/her?	4	3	2	1
Total		15	13	20	19

2.7 By now you have chosen your topic. Now you have to define your objective. Go to section 4.

Still unhappy?

2.8 If you really cannot make up your mind, read section 3 below.

3 PROJECT TOPICS NOT ON THE LIST

3.1 Below we reproduce what Oxford Brookes University has said about choosing topics. We still strongly advise you to reconsider doing your own thing, but here we go.

> We strongly recommend that you choose a topic from the list. However, should you have an alternative topic that is of particular interest to you, we would advise you to put details in writing to the address in these guidelines to confirm acceptability for this Project. You are advised to put your request in writing <u>before</u> starting work on the Report and to allow one month for consideration and response. Unapproved project titles will normally be failed automatically.

3.2 **To recap.**

Step 1. Write down your topic (so that it makes sense, as on the list). Then note in more detail what you intend to do, say half a page.

Step 2. Send your topic suggestion to Oxford Brookes University at the address given.

Step 3. Do not waste your or your mentor's time doing **any** work until you have received the go ahead in writing from Oxford Brookes University!

Oxford Brookes have said that almost all such requests are approved. Where a number of students seem to be asking to do the same sort of topic, it is then sometimes added to the formal list.

4 DEFINING THE PROJECT OBJECTIVE

4.1 Now we have selected a Project Topic, this is the next key issue for you to look at: **defining the project objective**. This will be the focus of the project and will direct your research and so it is worth spending a lot of time on this.

4.2 As an **analogy,** when choosing a holiday you may be looking for somewhere exciting to go. This is of course a matter of personal preference. You will need to translate 'somewhere exciting to go' into something concrete for you. If your definition of 'somewhere exciting to go' involves partying the night away, you might set yourself a definite objective of going to Ibiza. If 'somewhere exciting to go' means travelling to parts of the world you have never visited before, you might book a trip up the Amazon river.

4.3 So, your job is to turn the general nature of the Project Topic into something specific that you can latch on to, and design a research programme around. The external examiner has commented that the report must be business related and linked to an organisation. Some candidates have not linked their report to an organisation, but have instead written generally about the subject.

Analyse every word in the Project Topic

4.4 Each of the topics outlined is expressed as a brief sentence – which is why you have to read it carefully. For example, let's take Project Topic 6 and latch on to the **key words.**

Project Topic 6: The identification of key factors or indicators in the motivation of employees in an organisation of your choice.

Identification	This can lead to a number of questions. What does identification mean?
	(1) What are the key factors etc in this case?
	(2) The process of identifying the factors etc in this case.
	(3) The process of developing indicators to measure motivation.
	This can lead to discussions about whether people will give honest answers and so on.
Key factors	There is a lot of theory as to what motivates people. But in this **particular** organisation, what is important? **Key factors** are the underlying substance of motivation.
	You could take a theory of motivation and see how it works in practice.
Indicators	An **indicator** is something which shows something (eg a temperature gauge shows how hot it is). For motivation, the same **indicator** mean different things. A person working excessive overtime may be motivated to work late:
	• Because he/she loves the job
	• Out of a strong sense of responsibility to the customer or to other members of staff
	• Out of fear of looking less than committed if everybody else works late – an example of 'presenteeism'
	• Because he/she is inefficient
	• Because he/she needs the money
	• Because he/she has been bullied into it
	• Because he/she is using work as a substitute for dealing with personal problems
	and so on

Employees	Technically, '**employees**' means everybody employed by the company, and this includes the Board of Directors.
	Employees need not be taken just to mean 'non-managerial staff', even though this is how the word is often used.
	Are different levels of staff motivated in different ways?

4.5 You should now have a much richer appreciation of what could be covered by this Project Topic.

Categorisation

4.6 This is sometimes known as 'defining the research problem'. Here is an extract from an undergraduate dissertation to show what we mean. It is given in the introduction to a project report. Please note that it is **not** on the approved list of Project Topics. (We don't want to give too much away.)

Paragraph

1 This project evolved from a year's work in the Statistics and Finance Department in Q Ltd. During the year I spent much of my time analysing sales and contribution figures for individual areas and for the whole company. The other half of my job was to calculate commission payments each month and to authorise bonuses.

2 I was particularly interested in how the accounting and control systems within Q Ltd influenced behaviour and in turn what result these changes in behaviour had on the firm, At the same time as this it was clear that Q Ltd was experiencing deteriorating sales and declining contribution.

3 Therefore I set myself the aim to explore how effective different reward systems (which require accounting and control systems to operate) have been and could be used to motivate sales staff and sales performance, contribution and ultimately the profit of Q Ltd.

Conclusions are hard to prove but theory, opinion and logic can lead to some recommendations.

In a nutshell this encapsulates turning the Project Topic into a project objective.

(a) Paragraph 1 describes the context.

(b) Paragraph 2 describes the general area: equivalent to the 22 topics Oxford Brookes University provide. You could rephrase it. 'Describe how accounting and control systems influence behaviour in an organisation of your choice'.

(c) Paragraph 3 defines the aim of the project. There are other examples of accounting control systems but once you have identified the category the answer should slip in.

General category topic	Example of category example – project aim
Accounting control systems	• Reward systems
	• Costing systems etc
	• Budget systems
Behaviour	• Motivation of sales staff to perform better and thus improve **profitability**
	• Accurate budgets
	• Goal congruence
Organisation of your choice	Q Ltd, in this case

(d) You can now define the project aim by taking **examples** from the general category.

> Show the influence of accounting control systems on behaviour by describing how commission **reward systems** at Q Ltd contribute to **profitability** in the light of relevant **motivation** theory.

(i) You could, conceivably, have chosen how **budget** systems influence 'goal congruence', as both are specific examples of the category described.

(ii) Very sensibly, the author draws attention to **theory** and evidence, underscoring the possible limitations. For most of the Oxford Brookes University research topics, you will have to draw on theory.

4.7 If you read through the list of recommended Project Topics, you can probably find ways of applying this approach elsewhere. We give some pointers in section 5.

Still stuck for ideas? Mind maps, tree diagrams etc

4.8 You may still feel uncertain and you may wish to explore certain issues. Using a tree diagram or a mind map can help you explore a topic in some detail. On the next page is a chart covering some of the issues of **Project Topic 3: An analysis of the impact of an aspect of existing or impending legislation on an organisation.**

What you should do is start off with a key word say, and explore some of the issues from there. You may find that you can then link areas together.

Example

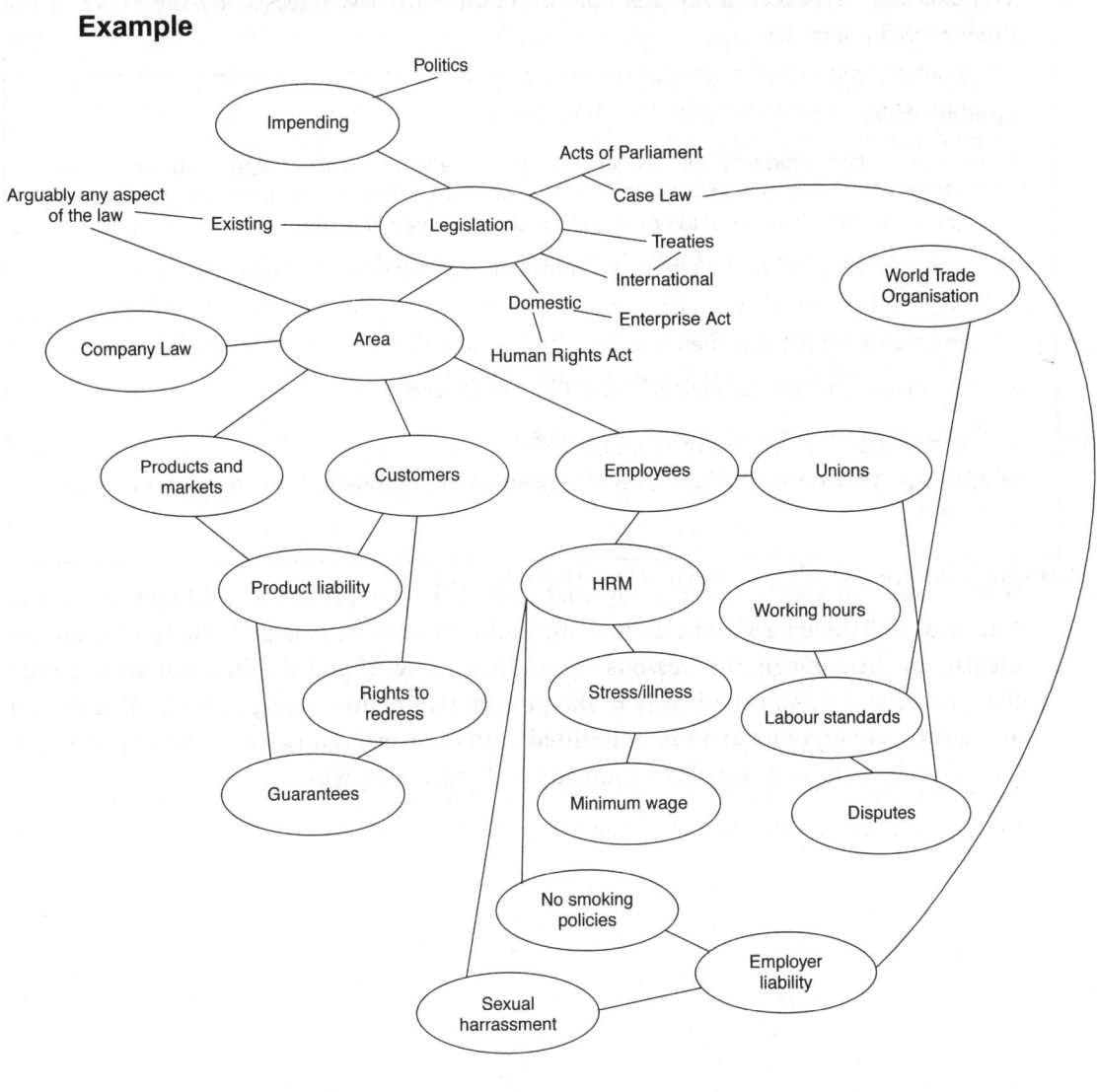

Testing the project objective: do a reality check

4.9 When you have formulated the project aim, you should test it; in other words you should show how it fits together. Here is what you should do.

Step 1. Identify what you would need to do to reach the aim. Is it feasible?

Step 2. Describe the project aim to a friend (this need not yet be one of the three mentor meetings). Does what you have said actually make sense?

4.10 You have a little more to do before your first mentor meeting, but for that you need a bit more about your proposed line of research, and the methods you will use.

4.11 Section 6 below aims to get you thinking about each of the project topics, to stimulate your creative juices.

5 CONFIDENTIALITY

5.1 You may be deterred from choosing a particular topic or defining your project objective in a particular way by concerns about the confidentiality of the material you will be dealing with, for example if writing about your own company.

5.2   You can take assurance from this note on confidentiality, released by the Head of the Business School in 2001.

Confidentiality

From time to time students will require that their Research and Analysis project be kept confidential. This may be because the conclusions are sensitive or perhaps the company information has commercial value or the organisation involved should be kept anonymous.

The following procedures contribute to confidentiality whenever the student requests that confidentiality is essential:

1   The projects are not published

2   The projects are held securely at Oxford Brookes University

3   The projects are disposed of after 12 months

4   Markers and External Examiners are advised of the confidential nature of the particular project.

5.3   Notice also that the Guidelines say that although your project should concern a real company and the data should be real and fully referenced, it is possible to conceal the identity of the company for reasons of confidentiality. If you do this, you should state that you have done so very clearly in the project. (Guidelines paragraph 3.1) You should also write a covering letter to be submitted with your project, again explaining that you have disguised the identity of the company and explaining why.

6 THOUGHT POINTS ON EACH PROJECT TOPIC

Project Topic 1

An analysis of the efficiency and/or effectiveness of a management accounting technique in an organisational setting.

Efficiency and effectiveness

- Meaning?
- Incompatibility between them
- Examples: overhead absorption rates and decision making
- Activity based costing

Efficiency

- Use of resources; financial, human, material
- Process management
- Business processes (and re-engineering)

Effectiveness

- Who defines what effectiveness is? Stakeholders
- Effectiveness of organisation in achieving its mission?
- Effectiveness of management accounting technique in doing what it is meant to

Management accounting technique

- Old technique
- New techniques
- Relevance to manufacturing system
- Service businesses
- Supposed benefits
- Actual benefits
- Costs/benefits of information

Use of technique

- Actual reporting
- Historical vs decision making uses
- Control systems
- Performance appraisal and reward
- Budgeting
- Dysfunctional decision making
- Goal congruence

Organisational setting

- Organisation as a whole
- One department
- As part of the management information systems
- Comparison with other organisations
- How are decisions really taken – management accounting information and mock bureaucracy
- Corporate culture – information and resource power

Project Topic 2

An analysis of how the application of technology can contribute to an organisation's efficiency and/or effectiveness

Application

- A software application
- The process of applying technology
- Installing technology
- Designing work around technology

Technology

- Equipment
- Techniques and work practices
- Work organisation (eg teams)

Type of technology

- Physical processes (eg manufacturing equipment)
- Communications processes (IT)
- Products
- Does not have to be 'high-tech' ; a low technology application can be as radical
- Information

Organisation

- Type
- Business
- Public sector
- Non profit orientated
- Size
- Management and departmental structure
- Compatibility of systems
- Technology and how the organisation works
- Location: centralised/decentralised
- People who use technology

Sector

- Manufacturing –high tech, or process
- Commodities etc (timber)
- Services (eg call centres, hospitals)
- Knowledge-based

Efficiency

- Output/input
- Resources: human, financial, material

Effectiveness

- Delivering results
- Satisfying stakeholders
- Help or hindrance
- Cost vs service
- Mass customisation

Project Topic 3

An examination of the impact of an aspect of existing or impending legislation on an organisation

We have used UK examples here, but many issues here may be reflected elsewhere.

Existing legislation

- Companies Act 1985 (most 'mainstream' company law)

- Companies Act 1989 (deals with objects clauses, registration of charges, elective and written resolutions)

- Insolvency Act 1986 (established licensed insolvency practitioners, administration procedures, creditors' voluntary arrangements)

- Company Securities (Insider Dealing) Act 1986

- Company Directors' Disqualification Act 1986

- Data Protection Acts 1984 and 1998

- Limited Partnerships Act 2000

- Employment Rights Act 1996 and Employment Relations Act 1999

- Competition Act 1998 (harmonisation of UK competition law with EC competition law; established Competition Commission in place of Monopolies and Mergers Commission)

- Electronic Communications Act 2000

- Human Rights Act 1998 (enacted in October 2000)

- Finance Acts each year

- Consider impact of international (eg European) legislation on the UK, or UK legislation on countries overseas

- Enterprise Act 2002, abolishing preferential status and administrative receiverships.

Impending legislation

- Forthcoming companies legislation

- Regulations against discrimination on grounds of disability, religious beliefs and sexual orientation (and in 2006, age)

Choice of organisation

- Depth of knowledge of the organisation
- Confidentiality an issue?
- Own experience?
- How easy to research?

Factors to consider

- State of play before the legislation (or the current situation if discussing impending legislation)
- Need for legislation: problems arising with the current situation
- Why was/is the legislation introduced?
- How effective has the legislation been?
- How can you quantify the impact of the legislation: statistics available/questionnaire appropriate?
- Need for further legislation
- Comparison of the chosen organisation with others
- Financial impact
- Social/environmental impact
- Effect on employees: if beneficial to employees, effect on company
- Ability to avoid legislation: loopholes

Project Topic 4

An analysis of the impact of e-business on an industry or organisation of your choice

Development of e-business

- Very rapid

- Types of business most affected (eg financial services, retail, travel)

- 'Boom or bust' scenario with dot com start-ups, but less impact with established businesses

- High public profile

- Highly topical: good availability of information likely

Features of e-business

- Big cash injections to start or to upgrade
- Need for sophisticated hardware and software: capital expenditure budget
- Highly-skilled, computer literate staff
- Ability to trade in international markets
- Fear among same-industry companies of being 'left behind' in e-commerce
- Risk of abandoning, ignoring or alienating traditional markets
- Well-publicised fears over computer security
- Move to centralised distribution

Industry or organisation of choice

- Organisation includes not just companies: consider charities, partnerships (the firm you work for?) pension funds, schools, universities, doctors' fundholding practices etc.

- Consider own experience

- Consider ease of access to information

- Consider confidentiality if dealing with a specific organisation

- Negative impact, eg effect on small independent booksellers of internet book-buying

- Could be an industry/organisation which is greatly affected

- Could be an industry/organisation which is not affected at all

- Could consider organisation as a whole or a specific department within it

- Could consider an organisation which is affected by other people's e-business, eg small local bookshop or travel agent

Analysis

- Financial: impact on income/expenditure/profits/losses

- Business valuations: difficulties

- Strategic: marketing, pricing, planning

- Social: impact on employees

- Compare what with what in the analysis? Eg current financial results with others over what period of time?

Project Topic 5

The identification of the effects of globalisation on an industry of your choice

Identification

- Not the same as analysis

- Identification means 'find out and state what they are'

- Analysis means 'work out the effects and differences'. Impliedly a greater emphasis on coming to a conclusion

Industry

- A wider brief than considering just one organisation

- Requires more of a broad brush approach

- Maybe entails comparison of different organisations

- Some industries are massively affected (eg oil, pharmaceuticals); others not at all (eg real ale)

- Consider your own experience, eg industries you have audited

Globalisation

- Move towards greater globalisation in late 20th century
- More likely due to ease of communications
- Desire for international representation, eg by accountancy firms
- Harmonisation of laws (within the EC)
- Harmonisation of accounting standards (worldwide)
- Impact of use or non-use of the euro
- Impact of exchange rates: strong dollar
- Issues of language and culture

Effects

- Need to consider both positive and negative
- Financial: impact on profits, sales
- Operational: need to start up elsewhere or close down some locations
- Marketing: need to cater to different types of market, and adjust advertising methods
- Social: impact of moving operations to another country, use of cheaper labour abroad
- Management: drawn from different international sources
- Areas of disparity: different attitudes to eg working practices
- Cyclical nature eg Far East's 'tiger economies' in decline
- Greater risk of merger/takeover to create global giants

Project Topic 6

The identification of key factors or indicators in the motivation of employees in an organisation of your choice

Choice of organisation

- 'Organisation' is a narrower brief than 'industry': greater requirement to be specific
- Might be difficult to obtain information
- Usually an area of confidentiality
- Your own organisation is relevant, but access to information still might be difficult
- Need to devise a questionnaire/survey; risk of low response rate
- Maybe conduct interviews with employees (guarantee their confidentiality)

Key factors

- The underlying substance of motivation
- Desire for recognition and reward
- Greed
- Fear of losing the job/job security
- Job satisfaction
- A way to pass the time/deflect attention from other problems
- Achievability of rewards

Indicators

- Indicators show you something or demonstrate it
- Rates of pay compared with industry averages
- Performance related pay
- Expected benefits
- Levels of overtime
- Levels of absenteeism
- Levels of morale
- Demands made in pay negotiations
- Working conditions
- Rates of staff turnover/ease of recruitment
- Levels of industrial unrest
- Degrees of productivity
- Public perception of the company

Motivation

- Motivation models or theories
- MacGregor's Theory X and Theory Y
- Maslow's hierarchy of needs
- Herzberg's two factor theory
- Vroom's Expectancy theory
- Handy's motivation calculus

Employees

- Everybody employed by the company, including managerial staff and directors (their motivation likely to be different from 'normal' employees)
- May be differences between part and full time

Project Topic 7

An analysis of the tax and profit implications of different company entities, changes in status or acquisition or disposals of company assets

Tax

- Corporate taxation
- Personal taxation (choice of remuneration packages for directors)
- Social security deductions
- Sector specific taxes
- Sales taxes
- Value added taxes
- Tax reliefs and incentives
- Trusts
- Withholding taxes

Profit

- Pre-tax
- Post-tax
- Deferred tax impact
- Dividends
- Different costs of different reporting structures (eg sole trader/partnership vs limited company)

Implications

- Planning issues
- Jurisdictions, domicile and so on
- Weighing up alternatives
- Avoidance vs evasion
- Different company entities

Company entities

- Listing on a stock exchange
- Multi-national structures
- Group structures
- Associates
- Subsidiaries
- Control issues

Changes in status

- Private to public status

- Mergers and acquisitions

- Financial implications of mergers and acquisitions

- Operational implications of mergers and acquisitions – change in underlying performance and its effect on profit; cultural problems; systems compatibility; redundancies

- Who benefits from mergers: shareholders in merged company? Shareholders in acquired company?

- Use of tax losses of acquired company

- Change of domicile

Project Topic 8

An analysis of the financial situation of your choice of organisation

Financial situation

Meaning

- Per financial statements
- Financial structure (eg debt/equity)
- Solvency

Current position

- Trends leading to current position
- Trends possibly for the future
- Financial position reflecting underlying operating performance
- Working capital
- Ratio calculations
- Industry comparisons
- Competitor comparisons

Reported financial results not reflecting 'true value'

- Fixed asset valuations: market vs historic cost
- Goodwill and intangible assets (eg brands)
- Off balance sheet finance
- Financial reporting vs decision making information

Fluctuations in performance

- Seasonal differences/trends
- Exchange rates

Financial engineering

- Off balance sheet finance
- Tax efficiency
- Financial restructuring
- Share issues, buy backs etc

Future position

- Going concern
- Profit vs cash flows
- Financial modelling

Project Topic 9

An examination of how to plan, develop and implement an appropriate information system in an organisation

Choice of organisation

- Needs not to have a suitable information system at the moment

- Could be your own organisation: suitable depth of knowledge

- Whole tone of answer depends on nature of organisation

- You will need to describe the organisation in some detail, explaining its IT needs and expectations, discussing its products and services, providing a profile of its users

Examination

- Implies a study of a topic, or looking at it in depth
- You will be expected to explain the procedures suggested in some detail
- Appropriate information system

Will depend on the type of business

- Consider the needs of the organisation

- Need for information management (identification of needs, sources and users of information)

- Identification of whether it is a support activity, a key operational activity, a turnround activity or a strategic activity

Systems theories

- Nolan's stage hypothesis
- Systems Development Lifecycle

Planning

- Expenditure and funding
- Centralisation or decentralisation
- Multi user and distributed systems
- LANs and WANs etc.
- Feasibility studies
- Cost-benefit analysis
- Acquisition procedures
- Financing methods
- Evaluation of proposals and tenders
- Software contracts
- Security, privacy and data protection

Development

- Methodologies (eg SSADM, SSM)

- Disaster recovery strategies

- Development techniques: data flow diagrams, entity relationship models, entity life histories, normalisation, Structured English, decision trees and decision tables

- Systems design techniques: dialogue design, file and database design, CASE tools, prototyping

Implementation

- Project management: network analysis, Gantt charts, project management software
- Installation and testing
- Staff training
- File conversion and changeover
- Post-implementation review

Project Topic 10

An analysis of how management accounting techniques are used to support decision making in organisations

Management accounting techniques

This could imply concentrating on or contrasting:

- One or more traditional techniques such as absorption costing

- One or more modern techniques such as ABC

This could also imply the whole management accounting system, ie all management accounting information in the context of the management information system.

- Is management accounting information incorporated within the organisation's information systems or separate?

- Who uses management accounting information?

- Future orientation? To what extent is it still reporting historic transactions?

- External orientation – competitor modelling, market modelling, sales forecasting

Decisions

- Investment decisions
- Divisional performance appraisal
- Pricing and other marketing decisions; advertising effectiveness
- Cost of quality
- Different performance measures

Decision making process

- Decision-making implies a management process (which people are involved, how management accounting information is obtained, who takes decisions) operating in an organisational setting

- Status of management accounting information within the overall information system of the organisation

- Are management accounting techniques used at all, or only notionally?

- Behavioural aspects of budgeting – do management accounting decisions influence behaviour?

How?

- General view of management information

- **Sample of decisions** and use of management accounting information in arriving at them

- You could review one important decision and see how management accounting was applied. You could see how critical it was or whether a different decision might have been taken had the management accounting information been different

- Availability of information – wide, narrow

- Information systems

Project Topic 11

An analysis of the costs and benefits of the internal audit/internal review activities within an organisation of your choice

An organisation of your choice

- Public sector
- Private sector
- Whole organisation or division/operating unit

Internal audit/internal review

- Different audit requirements

- Scope of audit vs review, from reporting to shareholders to value for money and operational effectiveness

- Integration of financial audit with review of operations

- Controls and processes

- Benefits of internal audit vs external audit

Costs

- Costs to whom?

- Stakeholders in the audit outcome – for example, public sector audits do not report to shareholders and may have different requirements

Types of cost

- Salaries and overheads of internal audit staff
- Costs of time spent by line management
- Costs of controls instituted

Benefits

- Benefits to whom?
- Reduced costs of external audit
- Value for money audit
- Identified savings
- Reduction of risk
- Management of the department

Project Topic 12

An analysis of the effect of any International Accounting Standard on the accounts of any organisation in terms of profitability or financial stability or balance sheet value

Effect on who or what?

- Results as reported in published statements
- Underlying classification of transactions data
- Format of accounts
- Distributable profits
- Asset valuations
- Performance ratios
- Management decision-making

Any International Accounting Standard

- See relevant FA texts for details

- Implies standards in issue as opposed to exposure drafts, but doubtless the latter could be used on a particular topic

- More interesting to choose an IAS very different from local practice

Accounts of any organisation

- Advantages of changing to IASs – only relevant to some companies

- Does not have to be one based in your home country. For example, could be a US corporation.

- Why do local and international standards differ?

- Are local standards better or worse? Why?

Profitability

- Pre tax
- Post tax
- Earnings per share
- Differences between IAS and local profits – for example in treatment of goodwill

Financial stability

- To what extent are reported financial statements relevant to the financial stability of any enterprise? Why would IASs make a difference?

- Use of information by investors

- Would IASs affect an organisation's credit rating and interest cost?

- Balance sheet value

- Asset valuation

- Intangible assets (eg goodwill)

- Impact on investors

- Liabilities, such as pensions and deferred tax

Project Topic 13

An analysis of future personnel requirements under conditions of change (including employee development)

Analysis

- Analysis means 'work out' and 'explain'
- Conditions of change probably need to be analysed as well

Analyse for what? (ie the subject)

- Does not specify whether for a specific organisation (actual or imaginary) or for an industry as a whole

- If for a 'live' organisation, data could be very sensitive, if not highly explosive

- Difficult to access information: most business organisations probably unwilling to supply it

- Need to disguise the identity of the subject 'organisation'

Personnel

- Various categories to consider depending on the organisation under consideration: one company could employ manual workers (skilled and unskilled), trainers, office staff, drivers, IT experts, accountants and managers, including directors

- Trade union factors to consider

- Employment legislation: Employment Rights Act 1996/Employment Relations Act 1999

- Costs of redundancies

- Exposure to unfair dismissal claims

Conditions of change

- Expansion, globalisation
- Changing markets, different products
- E-commerce
- Recession
- Company downsizing and reorganisation
- Effect on reputation of the organisation and public perception

Employee development

- Need to have suitably qualified staff at next upturn
- Employee training to keep abreast of developments (eg IT training)
- Need to keep employees motivated
- Greater emphasis on freedom of movement of workers
- Employees' expectations across the board are increasing, in the UK and overseas

How to predict future requirements

- Budgeting procedures
- Investment appraisal (eg in context of opening a new factory)
- Growth models
- Strategic planning
- Economy (domestic and international) generally and likely trends over the next few years

Project Topic 14

An investigation of recent investment decisions by an organisation of your choice and how the use of different methods of risk and uncertainty analysis might affect such decisions

An investigation

- An investigation is not an analysis, an identification or an analysis. It implies exploration and discovery rather than facts. It implies a systematic and perhaps detailed examination of a subject.

- An investigation could require that the same procedure be applied to a number of different examples of what you are looking into.

- This suggests a sample of investment decisions but these must be suitable for your research. Major investment decisions may be the most interesting.

Recent investment decisions

- Why recent? This indicates current management assumptions towards investment and current management assumptions as to risk

- However, recent investment decisions cannot be reviewed with the benefit of hindsight.

Types of investment decision

- Fixed asset expenditure
- Marketing campaigns
- New product launch
- R & D
- New information systems and IT
- Tangible/intangible benefits
- Acquiring a company

Decision making processes

- Programmed vs unprogrammed
- Structured vs unstructured
- Rational vs 'political'
- Strategic, tactical, operational

Risk and uncertainty

- Measurable or not measurable
- Probabilities
- Expected values
- Standard deviation and normal distribution
- Discount rates – adjust for risk
- Assessing risk – does the organisation systematise this?

Attitudes to risk

- Decision theory (eg maximax, maximin etc, regret) applied to the decisions managers took. Is there a consistent attitude to risk?

- How would you find out managers' attitudes to risk (eg questionnaire, review of how decisions were actually taken)?

- Risk/reward

- Do managers actually consider risk?

Project Topic 15

An analysis of the role of working capital on the profitability and/or efficiency of an organisation of your choice

Working capital

- Balance sheet definition, current assets and current liabilities
- Degrees of liquidity of current assets
- Current liabilities repayable on demand
- Operating cycle
- Cash cycle
- Working capital ratios such as stock turnover, debtor turnover, creditor turnover
- Stock levels

Role

- Obtain cash for use elsewhere

- Insolvency arises from lack of liquidity not lack of profitability

- Source of finance – it is sometimes alleged that many businesses rely on bank overdraft finance as a source of long term capital – not appropriate

Profitability

- Early payment discounts
- Bank overdraft and loan interest
- Cost of credit control
- Debt factoring (ie selling debts to a collector)
- Discounts
- Credit terms and sales force
- Bad debts
- Obsolete stock
- Relationships with suppliers and customers (eg trade discounts, credit periods)
- Volume vs profit
- Overtrading

Efficiency

Units of output/input – how to measure

- Supply chain management
- Just in time – minimise stocks
- Cost of capital tied up in stocks
- Efficient use of resources
- Earning money from current assets

Project Topic 16

An analysis of the effect of different sources of capital on investment decisions within an organisation of your choice

Note that this topic only refers to investment decisions in the abstract. It therefore gives you a fairly wide brief as to types of investment decision and source of capital.

Sources of capital

- Retained profits
- Types of debt, secured and unsecured
- Working capital
- Bonds
- Equity
- Tax impact?
- Cost of capital
- Equity markets
- Venture capital

Investment decisions

- Types of investment
- Size of investment
- Interest and discount rates
- Risk and investors' attitudes to financing risk
- Managers' objectives

Capital rationing

- What is meant by capital rationing?

- Why is capital so limited that it has to be rationed? Managers might like some projects from which there is no justifiable return

- Capital might be limited because of liquidity problems or if managers do not have easy access to capital markets?

- Government restrictions on use of capital

- Managers – eg owner managers – may prefer not to relinquish control of a business

- Explicit use of capital rationing as opposed to other means of appraisal.

Preferences for different sources

- Interest vs equity
- Retained profits are easy to control
- Transaction costs

Theoretical model of capital rationing as opposed to actual capital allocation decisions.

Project Topic 17

An analysis of the effect of corporate governance on an organisation of your choice

Corporate governance

- Increasingly important
- Cadbury report
- Hampel report
- Greenbury report
- Combined code (revised July 2003)
- Turnbull committee
- Reasons for its prominence: investor protection
                                public perception
                                good PR
- Contributes to 'openness'
- Impact depends on whether a private or public company or another type of organisation

Financial performance

- Directors' remuneration
- Share price movements
- Impact of corporate governance or practices such as off balance sheet finance and creative accounting
- Conflicts of interest between management and shareholders
- International comparisons

Other aspects of corporate governance

- Variety of directors required; executive, non executive etc

- Difficult to find people to act?

- Audit committee

- Reporting requirements; greater bureaucracy?

- Public relations: effect on company if seems to flout regulations with eg 'fat cat' payments to directors

Project Topic 18

An examination of how to plan, develop and implement an appropriate PRP scheme in an organisation

Choice of organisation

- no PRP in place at the moment

- could be your own organisation: suitable depth of knowledge

- you will need to describe the organisation in some detail, explaining needs and expectations of employees, discussing products and services and providing a profile of different roles.

Explanation

- implies a study of a topic, looking at in depth

- you will be expected to explain the procedures suggested in some detail

- identify an appropriate system

Depends of the type of business

- PRP for all employees?
- dependent on meeting personal targets, group targets or both?
- only applicable to some employees, eg managerial level?
- if so, is dissatisfaction likely in other grades?
- does it replace an existing bonus scheme? if so, how to justify to employees?

Appropriate systems of PRP

- build on to existing wage levels
- take a pay cut and then build up PRP
- company able to fund it adequately

How to set targets for performance

- must be feasible
- must not demotivate by being very difficult
- must not be too easy: scheme would be uneconomical

Planning

- expenditure and funding
- when to implement (after company year end? 1st January?)
- how to explain
- amendment to employee contracts
- evaluation of proposals
- feasibility study
- cost benefit analysis

Development
- employee relations
- budgets
- cash flow forecasts

Implementation

- project management
- staff explanations and counselling
- review and feedback after, say, six months

Project Topic 19

An analysis of the business and financial reasons and effects of creating a multinational merger company

Analysis

- Look at before and after situations to consider both reasons and effects
- Will require some form of conclusion

Business reasons

- Responds to increasing trend for globalisation
- Take advantage of ease of communications
- Desire for international representation
- Business synergy
- Need for expansion in different markets
- Ability to utilise an overseas (cheaper?) workforce
- Systems compatibility
- Change of domicile of group
- Remain competitive

Financial reasons

- To take advantage of or avoid pitfalls of exchange rates
- Economies of scale
- Accounting: sue of international accounting standards
- Tax implications
- Benefit to shareholders

Effects

- Consider both positive and negative
- Financial effects: turnover, profits
- Operational effects: redundancies, recruitment, production
- Marketing effects: cater for different markets, amend advertising methods
- Areas of conflict
- Areas of disparity: eg working practices
- Language issues: a barrier to communication?
- Merged entity may be too unwieldy and difficult to control
- Truly multinational or eg Just European
- Effect on share price
- Public perception to the merged entity

Project Topic 20

An analysis of the effects of IT failure and contingency plans within an organisation of your choice

Nature of task

- Not clear whether the requirement is analyse, examine or identify
- Therefore the choice is yours

IT failure

- Software: inappropriate, attacked by a virus, databases
- Hardware: hard drive
- Reasons: lack of training of staff outdated equipment
- Assessment of likelihood of IT failure

Effects of IT failure

- Loss of working time
- Loss of data
- Loss of records eg of debtors
- Delay in processing
- Threat to orders (people won't wait for you to fix it)
- Expensive to repair
- Could be catastrophic eg railway signalling, air traffic control, hospital systems
- Consider how to prevent a recurrence

Contingency plans

- Realistic

- Are they observed (eg nightly back-up of data?)
- Do they cater for all potential problems (eg back-up kept off site)
- Disaster recovery strategies
- Regular review and updating

Project Topic 21

An analysis of the impact of the Euro on an organisation or industry of your choice

Analysis of impact

- Must consider 'before' and 'after' scenarios
- Consider how long a period to include

Organisation or industry

- Could be your own organisation

- Think carefully about which industry: some industries not affected and therefore not much to say

Impact of the Euro

- When was it identified as an issue?

- Enough time given to prepare (eg change documentation)

- If dealing with other countries in Eurozone, processing accounts may be smoother

- If dealing with countries outside, more difficult

- Impact of movement in Euro exchange rate on a previously strong or weak national economy

- Impact on Euro of political events in other countries (eg Le Pen's election progress in France)

- UK companies may be increasingly expected to account in Euros with European partners

- Impact on prices and costs (evidence of rounding up)

- Possible volatility of other currencies in comparison

- Hedging etc less relevant in some companies

Project Topic 22

Analyse the marketing strategy of an organisation of your choice, identifying the key success factors or indicators in the marketing mix and the activities of the organisation.

Strategy

- A course of action to achieve a specific objective

Marketing

- Development of a marketing plan

- Company mission statement

- Statement of objectives

- Situation analysis

- Strategy development

- Implementation

Strategy formulation

- SWOT analysis

- Competitive strategy (eg Porter's Five Forces)

- Growth strategy: market penetration, market development, product development, diversification

Marketing mix

- Product: total product, product mix, product life-cycle

- Place: customer convenience and availability; distribution systems, franchising

- Price: perceived value, pricing process, strategy, demand elasticity, competition

- Promotion: image, communication, promotional mix, advertising

Chapter roundup

- This chapter has explored the twenty two project topics on the Oxford Brookes University list.

- By applying the techniques outlined, you should be able to narrow the possibilities down to one or two definite probabilities.

- If you choose a topic not on the list, ensure you get approval from Oxford Brookes before starting work.

Chapter 5

PLANNING AND MANAGING YOUR PROJECT

Chapter topic list

1   Project management skills and the Research and Analysis Project

2   Analysing the tasks

3   Estimating time

4   Building up a schedule

5   Using IT to help manage the Research and Analysis Project

6   Setting up your project file

7   Planning issues for each stage of the Research and Analysis Project

---

Introduction

In this chapter, we give you some hints and techniques for planning your Research and Analysis Project. You need to reflect on your **own** time management and organisational skills, **scheduling** the work, taking into account **lead times** for obtaining data. We also give hints on the use of IT. Finally, we give some brief suggestions as to the **planning** issues to consider at each stage of the project.

---

1   PROJECT MANAGEMENT SKILLS AND THE RESEARCH AND ANALYSIS PROJECT

The Research and Analysis Project

1.1   Any project – whether it is developing a new software package, or constructing a new building – is, in many ways, a unique, one-off task. But all **projects** have:

- A defined start. By choosing the project objective, you have started already.

- A defined project objective.

- A number of activities that need to be co-ordinated – some of them depend on earlier activities, some depend on other people.

- A budget (of money, hours, or whatever).

- A defined endpoint – in this case the **Report** and the **Key Skills Statement.**

1.2   In commercial projects, a project is successful if it is completed to the client's objectives, is on time and within budget. Even with commercial projects, this is often easier said than

done. A construction project might be delayed by unexpected problems, financing problems or just poor project management.

1.3 A research project, whether it be a PhD, an undergraduate dissertation, or the Research and Analysis Project is a special kind of project.

(a) **Issues of breadth** – you may find that the field is much broader than you thought, and you need to set up some clear boundaries (see below).

(b) **Issues of depth**. You may find that you need to go into more detail, if matters are not clear (see below)

(c) **Predictability**. You can research to ask a question; but you cannot predict at the outset what the result will be. The data obtained may not support what you are trying to prove (see Chapter 8).

(d) **Incomplete outcome**. Your 'result' may be a realisation that you need to do further research (see Chapter 8).

Example: breadth

Project Topic 4. 'An analysis of the impact of e-business on an industry or organisation of your choice.'

Let us assume you have defined your project objective as 'An analysis of the impact of the Internet on the distribution systems of the book trade industry'. Without giving too much away, you could find yourself covering two related but fundamentally distinct issues:

(a) **Retailing books** – on-line ordering, taking over from bookshops as a delivery mechanism – you might have scores of articles, price lists, website downloads and so on; you might find yourself drawn to wider issues of retailing.

(b) **Downloading books** – will paper disappear as a medium carrying intellectual property and will people download books from the Internet to PCs, mobile phones, or 'e-book' readers?

Are there different issues involved in different types of books – reference material, fiction and so on?

In practice, if you face this sort of problem, you may not have defined your project objective precisely enough.

Example: depth

Project Topic 10. 'An examination of how to plan, develop and implement an appropriate information system in an organisation.'

Let us say that your objective is 'An examination of how a Sage accounting software package was chosen and implemented in X Ltd.'

You may find yourself involved in the detail of how the programme works with certain types of hardware – does it use visual basic and so on? This might be relevant if dealing with implementation or changeover, or with functionality in the round – but not really the heart of what you should be doing, which should be about choice and implementation

In practice, if you face this sort of problem, it is because you are losing sight of the 'big picture', and are departing from the project objective.

The Research and Analysis Project is not an exam

1.4 We've made this point already in Chapters 3 and 4. But this difference is just as crucial for **how** you **plan** and **manage** your work as it is for choosing your project.

Deadlines and time pressure – how it differs

1.5 Here are some key contrasts about deadlines.

An ACCA exam	Research and Analysis Project
• Takes three hours, typically • You have to plan your time carefully in the exam room	You can take as little or as long as you like to do your research, and write the Report and Key Skills Statement
• Sat on one particular day • You have to plan your time carefully in the run up to this date: learning, practice and revision	You can submit it whenever you like – the date of submission may affect when it gets marked but if you miss one date, you will not be disqualified from the next one.
• Cannot be put off; if you miss one day, you have to resit.	You can put it off; the time it takes is up to you.
• Exam and studying are done outside the work environment	Depending on the topic you have chosen, some of the work **might** be done at work.

1.6 You ought to conclude from this that **your deadlines on the project are for you to manage**. You have to set them, especially when they involve others. You have to police them. This is – in part – what is meant by **independent and self managed learning**.

Realistically, how much time am I likely to need?

1.7 The answer to this question can – if you are not careful – be another question: 'How long is a piece of string?' But this is not good enough, is it? One important way of approaching this issue is by **analysing the work** involved and developing a realistic schedule based around it. There are a number of ways of doing this.

- Analysing the tasks
- Estimating the time you will need
- Developing schedules

2 ANALYSING THE TASKS

2.1 **Identify each task you have to do** and note it down.

2.2 For example, if you are cooking a meal, there are a number of different tasks, such as 'prepare vegetables' and 'make sauce'. Each of these tasks can be further subdivided. 'Prepare vegetables' can be subdivided into 'Prepare tomatoes', 'Prepare onions' and so on. 'Prepare onions' can be subdivided into 'Peel onions' and 'Chop onions'. Finally you will reach a point where you cannot subdivide the work any further. There is little point in going any further. This technique is called **Work Breakdown Structure**.

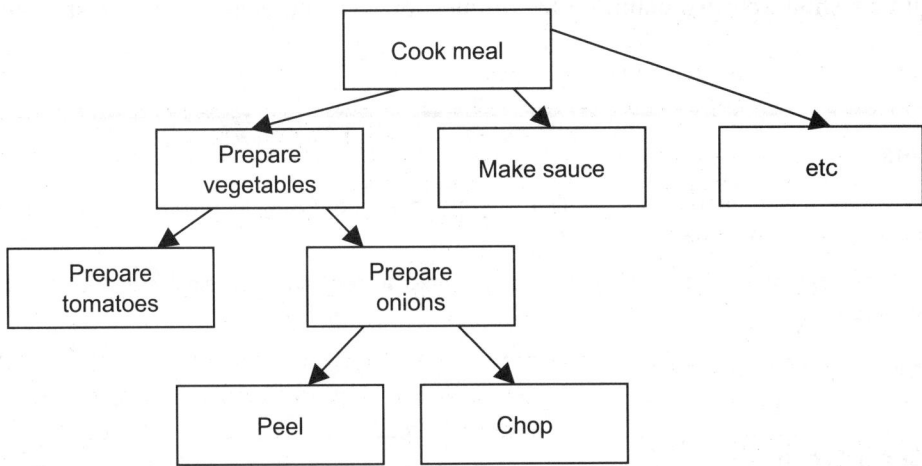

Below is an example from an unpublished undergraduate dissertation. This describes one part of the project, the research method. (We will cover this in the next chapter, but it is a good example of the variety of work that needs to be done.)

Example

Initially the work I carried out on the project was extremely informal in that whenever I met a salesman or spoke to a manager I would ask them about their feelings towards the present pay scheme or the method by which targets were allocated. When salesmen complained about errors in their commission payment due to faults in the payment scheme I was in an ideal position to suggest to managers changes and refinements in the pay scheme.

Secondary data

Following this initial exploration I decided to familiarise myself with the theory behind targeting specifically and, more generally, how information and control system influence behaviour. At the same time as this I spoke to people outside Q Ltd both from academic backgrounds, so as to develop ideas, and in other selling companies, so as to compare Q Ltd with other selling firms.

Primary data

Once I felt well briefed about the problem I sought permission from the Southern Sales Director, Mr X to interview his sales managers. He requested a questionnaire which I forwarded to him. Mr X made minor adjustments to this in form rather than content. For example, one question I asked was, 'Why do you think Q Ltd has higher turnover of salesmen than other similar companies?', this was changed to: 'Do you think Q Ltd has a higher turnover of salesmen than other similar companies? If so, why? (see appendix 1).

I developed the questionnaire with the background knowledge I had acquired and discussed some of the questions with Mr A, the Statistics and Finance Manager, my immediate superior.

Over a period of about a month I interviewed five sales managers, each interview lasting about one hour. I felt the questionnaire was a little restrictive, therefore I chose to approach the interviews informally using the questionnaire as a check that I had covered most of the points. This was specifically important as I felt that the psychological atmosphere of the interview would be at least as important as the mechanics of the interview. I realised that this would require me to be flexible, however, I didn't realise how flexible I would have to be. I organised one interview and found that this manager shared his room with another manager so I spent much of the interview making notes on discussion between the two of them, myself acting as a catalyst when discussion waned. This particular interview was especially useful since it uncovered issues such as the education and training of management that would otherwise have been overlooked. I decided to make written notes rather than a tape-recording because I though this might be offputting to the managers.

During the interviewing and recording process I tried to avoid personal bias and judgement and when incorporating findings into this text I tried to avoid jumping to simplistic conclusions without considering their implications.

2.3   We will now show you two planning techniques for you to use, and this is best done by an exercise.

Exercise

(a)   Identify the tasks involved in the first paragraph in the example above, and put them in a hierarchy.

(b)   Flesh out paragraph 2 in the example above into a tree diagram, similar to that given under paragraph 2.2.

Answer

(a)

Task breakdown		

1.1   Becoming familiar with the outlines at least of the scheme.
        1.1.1   Getting the details
        1.1.2 Reading them		

1.2   Arranging informal meetings with
        1.2.1   Salesmen
        1.2.2   Managers
                to discuss the issue and/or
                remembering to tag the issue on
                at the end of another meeting, ie
                12 meetings		

1.3   Within each meeting – say 12 meetings
        1.3.1   Asking how salesmen felt about the scheme
        1.3.2   Asking how the targets were allocated
        1.3.3 Taking notes of the response		

1.4 Developing refinements to the system		
1.5 Arranging meetings with managers to describe refinements developed.		

(b)

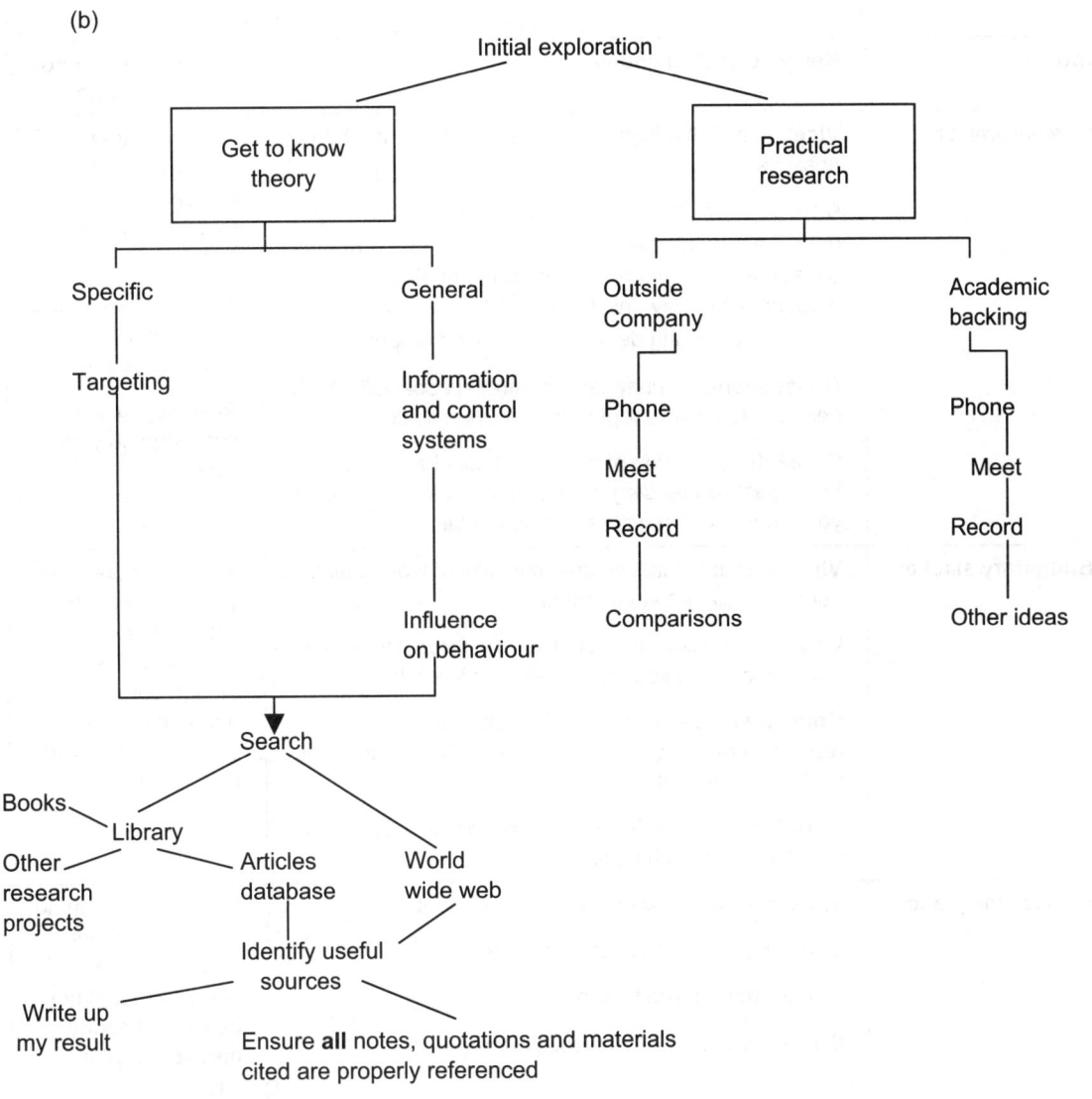

---

3   ESTIMATING TIME

3.1   The tasks in the example above all take time, especially phoning, e-mailing and paperwork. How good are you at estimating your use of time?

3.2   We suggest there are four types of estimators. How do you find out which you fall into?

Type	Key vice and its cause	How do you know it's you?
1 **Over-promiser**	**Vice**: promises things can be delivered sooner than is possible **Cause**? Unwillingness to sit down and plan hour by hour – 'a month' seems a long time ahead; 20 working days is, in fact, a lot less. Too willing to please a manager who may only be asking for information. Doesn't like asking people to wait for a response. **Consequence** – unnecessary stress, especially if other people rely on you; reputation for unreliability **Cure**? Keep records of how long tasks have taken you in the past (eg reading an article) and use these to plan your projects. Give yourself time to plan.	Your manager routinely makes allowances for the fact that you miss deadlines. You constantly fail to meet deadlines you have set yourself. At least you are consistent in your ways.
2 **Budgetary slacker**	**Vice**: over estimates volume/difficulty of work; builds in budgetary slack to everything **Cause**? Excessive fear of pressure; refusal to work at a faster pace than you are capable of; inefficiency **Consequence** – fewer learning opportunities; boredom; reputation of being slow or lazy, even though the only problem is estimation **Cure?** Set yourself targets to build confidence. Learn speed reading techniques?	Your manager gives you more work than you think you can cope with, even though you get it done and you are given no more work than others.
3 **All over the place**	**Vice**: over- or under-estimates time spent **Cause**? Cannot relate tasks to time. **Consequence**: frustration **Cure**? Try the over-promiser's cure	The most frustrating as others cannot predict a pattern of behaviour, and nor can you. Nobody believes anything you say
4 **Never gets it wrong**	The best position to be in. You're perfect	

(a) If you are an **over-promiser**, you will set yourself (and your mentor?) unrealistic deadlines for completing the Research and Analysis Project. Failing to meet them will depress you – you do not have other people to check your progress. If you do struggle to meet your self-imposed deadlines, you might rush or do inadequately your research or analysis.

(b) If you are a **budgetary slacker**, this is less of a problem, except that you might take longer on the Research and Analysis Project than you really need or you might be insufficiently ambitious.

(c) If you are completely **inconsistent** in your time estimation, you will face both problems at once. Arguably, you should not set yourself a time limit, but plan your work breakdown structure meticulously. Do not arrange meetings until you have finished this task and any preparation.

3.3   We have put some very approximate timings into the example in 2.4.

Task breakdown	Time guesstimate	Comment
1.1 Becoming familiar with the outlines at least of the scheme. 1.1.1 Getting the details 1.1.2 Reading them	1 hour	Could be longer
1.2 Arranging informal meetings with: 1.2.1 Salesmen to discuss the issue and/or remembering to tag the issue on at the end of another meeting, ie 12 meetings	5 minutes to fix up a meeting (phone, leave message etc) = 1 hour, approx Chase up if no response	Use IT? Email may be quicker. Microsoft Outlook allows you to book meetings by issuing a meeting request. Even so, with 12 private meetings, there are twelve different messages to be sent and responded to.
1.3 Within each meeting – say 12 meetings: 1.3.1 Asking how salesmen felt about the scheme 1.3.2 Asking how the targets were allocated 1.3.3 Taking notes of the response	45 minutes per meeting, around 9 hours	How about tape recording? **Note that 1 hour of tape recording takes about 6 hours of typing to transcribe it**. Note taking is probably quicker and should be sufficient.
1.4 Developing refinements to the system	2 hours	A lot of thought to go in to this; could well be longer.
1.5 Arranging meetings with two managers to describe refinements developed	10 mins	
1.6 Within each meeting	2 × 1 hour	

Total time – Over 15 hours? Almost certainly an underestimate. Only two days work? How about adding in interruptions, cancellations or postponements? If you are an over-promiser, **look carefully** at **task 1.2 Arranging informal meetings**: in the absence of email, arranging twelve meetings could take an hour to set up.

Dealing with your estimation problems – particularly for over-promisers

3.4   The best solution is to keep a **record**, on an experimental basis, of the time you spend on the activities below. They are related to the Research and Analysis Project.

Activity	Relevance	Note down how long you spent doing this
Read, absorb and **take notes** of an article in the ACCA *Student Accountant* on a subject that is unfamiliar to you – count the words first.	The Research and Analysis Project is about research, and you will have to do reading – skim reading may not be enough. Furthermore, the data you have to read and absorb may not be written or structured in a way you are familiar with. Directed to an academic or business audience, there may be new terminology to absorb	
Next time you **access the world wide web**, search for a business relevant website, and note how long it takes to access the information you want.	Some searches take a long time; you might have to use a number of different search engines to get what you want; you may want to download files – the speed of this depends on your internet connections. You are encouraged to use the internet in the Research and Analysis Project.	
Next time you set up a spreadsheet model at work or at home, time yourself – make the model reasonably complex, containing formulae and a graph.	The topic you have chosen may well require you to set up a spreadsheet and use it to model or manipulate data and present it an a form.	
Next time you **write a long letter or email** to someone, or a detailed report at work, time yourself and count the words. Note when you started and when you finished to account for distractions. Make sure that this is **word processed.**	Writing the Report will take a **lot** longer than this, as you will have to think about what you must do. If you **word process** a report, you may be surprised at the time you might spend formatting, printing out, editing what you have written and so on.	
In the **next meeting** you attend with your boss to discuss a substantive issue, time how long you spent: • Preparing for the meeting • In the meeting • Writing up any notes about what was said and decided	Note that guidance is given for meetings with your mentor but you may be meeting other people in the course of your project.	

3.5 We have chosen the activities above, because reading, surfing the net, spreadsheets, note taking, writing and meetings are typical activities you will do in the course of the Research and Analysis Project.

3.6 When you have identified the tasks you have to do, you might **classify** them as:

- Reading
- Web-searching

- Writing and word processing
- Data manipulation
- Spreadsheets
- Meetings: preparation, the meeting itself, notes afterwards

Combining tasks

3.7 In section 2, we suggested breaking down each task to get a realistic idea of what you have to do and the time available – so you know precisely what is involved.

3.8 Clearly, however, some jobs are best done in a **sequence or grouped together** in a batch.

(a) For example **attending a meeting** and **writing up your notes afterwards** are two different tasks. It does make sense, however, to write up your notes as soon as you can after the meeting, whilst it is fresh in your mind.

(b) **Sending out questionnaires**

(i) Response rates are typically low – 15% to 20%
(ii) So, to get resources you need to send over 130 questionnaires

If you are unlucky, you will have to photocopy, address and mail these yourself. Get it over in one hit, so you don't miss any out and you have a better idea as to when you should chase them.

3.9 **Other jobs are best done uninterrupted** or where concentration is needed. Creating a spreadsheet model of any sophistication is one of those jobs, given the need for formulae even in relatively simple models.

4 BUILDING UP A SCHEDULE

4.1 The Research and Analysis Project is a project with an end in view, a degree. You may have heard of people – perhaps friends (or friends of friends) from university – who have stayed on to do a further research qualification, such as a PhD, and whose research programme has drifted off.

4.2 Furthermore, unlike someone doing an undergraduate degree, you will almost certainly have to do your Research and Analysis Project work around your job and other social commitments – but you should already have experience of this in doing your ACCA exams to date.

Deadlines

4.3 Your deadlines and schedules are basically up to you. Again, you need a different mind-set to what you are used to for your normal ACCA exams. Studying for your ACCA exams, you made a decision to attend a particular exam sitting and then, perhaps, worked backwards from this, identifying that you had so many available hours to study for those papers

4.4 For the Research and Analysis Project, rather than working backwards from an exam date, you may be better advised to work **forwards** from a start date. This is because the Research and Analysis Project will involve work you are unfamiliar with. You will not know precisely the result you will come up with; you do not know exactly what the ramifications of the research will be.

Step 1. **Decide on a start date**

4.5 **Simple**? Yes, but have you briefed your partner, friends, family, and work colleagues that you are engaged on a final step to getting a degree from one of the UK's universities? They will support you if they know how important it is to you, and it will help them to be understanding – we hope – of long hours spent in the library, or even temporary increases in phone bills as a result of searching the net.

4.6 Your mentor will need to know too.

Step 2. **Review your programme of work**

4.7 The next section and chapters will describe in brief some of the typical tasks you will encounter in the Research and Analysis Project. You may already have some idea as to the number of hours needed.

Step 3. **Identify the learning resources you will need and when available**

4.8 Unlike ACCA studies, where you may have used the BPP Study Text, Practice & Revision Kits, and Passcards as your principal learning tools, the Research and Analysis Project requires you to hunt around and discover things. It may simply not be possible to do everything in the evenings – you might need to do some of this work during the week.

4.9 **Resources**

(a) **Library**: how far do you have to travel? Opening and closing times? Are there days when it is closed? Do you need a library pass? How will you get there? Walking distance? Bus and train times?

(b) **Local ACCA student society or centre**. You could enquire if there are facilities for you to use?

(c) **Computing power** – do you have access to a PC? If you do not have one at home, you may be able to use your office PC after hours or at weekends, for spreadsheet work and word processing your report. If you have to go into the office for this, this again affects the time you have available.

(d) **Internet.** If you have Internet access at home, all you need worry about is timing and cost. (Some useful hints and tips for Internet use in your research are given in Chapter 6.) Otherwise consider:

  (i) Are you close to a cyber-café? When is it busy or cheap? Can you print from it?

  (ii) Does a friend have net access?

  (iii) Could you obtain permission to use facilities at work to research via the net – always ask first!

Step 4. **Identify when the people you need to consult are available**

4.10 **People**

(a) Clearly, you need to find out when your **mentor** is available for the **three** mentor meetings you have to report on and other advice.

  (i) At work, you should be able to find out from your mentor when he/she is on holiday or is busy. Try to avoid busy periods – for example, if you mentor is the Financial Controller, it would be advisable to avoid the time between the year end cut-off and audit clearance.

(ii) If your mentor is a tutor at an academic institution, you will have to take into account teaching and marking commitments, and the fact that they may be unavailable in the holiday periods.

(iii) If your mentor is a member of the ACCA, in practice say, you will have to find out when he/she is free – it is wise to check and reconfirm meetings, as the urgent needs of a client will almost certainly come before the needs of your Research and Analysis Project.

Step 5. **Identifying other lead times**

4.11 Oxford Brookes' University timetable

Although you are under no pressure to attend a 'sitting', you should note that Oxford Brookes will mark the Report and Key Skills Statement only at particular times of year. You need not schedule your work around this, but you might have to wait a certain amount of time before submitting your Report and Key Skills Statement.

At the moment, you may submit your Project in the seven week period immediately after each set of ACCA exam results. You can do the work whenever you like, but you can only submit it at the specified times. This gives rise to deadlines each year of approximately half way through April and half way through October. Always check the final date on the ACCA website.

4.12 Lead times

Some of your research, as will be seen, may involve interviews and primary data as well as secondary data. With the possible exception of the World Wide Web, you must also build in lead times from when you ask something to when you receive it. Here are some indicative examples.

Example	
Reserving a book from the library if it is not stock	Two weeks? Perhaps longer if someone else is using it. You might have to wait until the weekend to collect it.
Ordering a book over the internet (eg from amazon.com, countrybooks.co.uk)	Amazon.com delivers worldwide, but a local internet book supplier might have better access to local materials. Depends on closeness to wholesalers.
Ordering a book from a bookshop	A quick phone call will establish if one is in stock.
Obtaining articles	Hopefully, your library will have relevant journals, or you have retained copies of the Students Newsletter.
Web searching	In theory, if material is downloadable you should be able to do immediately – a matter of minutes.
Postal questionnaire and other written requests for information to third parties	Remember that people are doing you a favour by filing in questionnaires. If you are unlucky, it may treated as junk mail! At certain times of year respondents may on holiday.
Meetings	Some people may be able to see you with no notice. For others, you may have to book some time in advance – weeks even.

Other planning aids

4.13 Useful planning tools are Gantt Charts (or Bar charts) and Network analysis.

4.14 You thus need to **schedule the activities** or tasks in the most efficient way given these two factors.

(a) The **dependency** of some activities on others. In other words, job B may need to be done before job C. For example, you may need to read articles before, say, designing a questionnaire.

(b) **Constraints on resources and their availability.** Some resources may not be available at the ideal time.

4.15 You will have a broad-brush time estimation for any activity. For this you need, in addition to the **duration** of each sub-unit of work:

(a) The **earliest time** work on a particular unit **can** be started

(b) The **latest time** it must be started – less of an issue unless you really are working to a deadline or around people's holidays

Gantt charts

4.16 A simple plan for a project is based on a **bar line chart**. This is sometimes called a **Gantt chart**.

(a) It can be used as a **progress control chart** with the lower section of each bar being completed as the activity is undertaken.

(b) A delay in a particular piece of work and its 'knock on' effect on other work can be shown in a **linked bar chart**. This shows the links between an activity and preceding activities which have to be completed before this particular activity can start.

4.17 Here is an example, from a construction project for a garage. We can see the delays to the foundations can then have a knock-on effect throughout the project.

No.	DESCRIPTION OF WORK OR ACTIVITY	TIME (DAYS)													
		1	2	3	4	5	6	7	8	9	10	11	12	13	14
1	Excavate for foundations and services (drainage)														
2	Concrete foundations														
3	Build walls and soakaways for drainage														
4	Construct roof														
5	Fit garage doors														
6	Provide services (electric)														
7	Plaster														
8	Decorate														

(a) **Advantages**

- Easy to understand

- **Flexible**: you can draw it on paper or on a spreadsheet – perhaps use colour coding for different jobs

- You can add other things, such as holidays or work commitments

- You can see at glance where you are, by showing 'actual' performance against plan

(b) **Disadvantages**: none, really, as far as the Research and Analysis Project is concerned, although for larger more complex projects its main drawback is that it does not specifically show how aspects of work are linked together.

Critical path analysis (CPA or network analysis)

4.18 To overcome this problem, there is a more sophisticated technique known as network analysis or critical path analysis. You are **unlikely** to need this, but you **may at work have access to project management software** and if, for some reason, you need to use it here is the underlying method.

4.19 Network analysis is a project planning technique which aims to map the activities in a particular project, and the relationship between them. CPA describes the **sequence** of activities, and how long they are going to take. These diagrams are drawn left to right.

(a) **Events** (1 and 2) are represented by circles. Activities (eg A) connect events.

(b) The **critical path** is represented by drawing an extra line or a thicker line between the activities on the path. It is the **minimum amount of time** that the project will take.

(c) It is the convention to note the earliest start date of any activity in the **top** right hand corner of the circle.

(d) We can then work **backwards** identifying the **latest** dates when activities have to start. These we insert in the bottom right quarter of the circle.

4.20 A completed network diagram would be as follows. The **critical path** is AEG. Note the **float time** of five days for Activity F. Activity F can begin any time between days 4 and 9, thus giving the project manager a degree of flexibility.

(a)

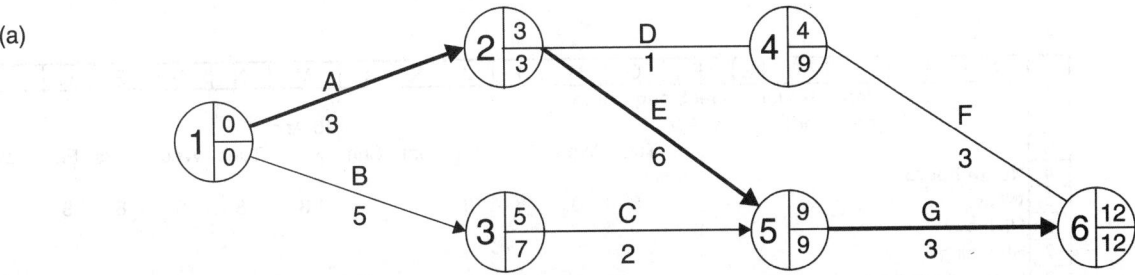

4.21 **Use of network analysis in the Research and Analysis Project**

(a) Use it if **lots** of activities **depend** on others and you can do things in parallel. For example, you can develop your spreadsheet model after you have, say, sent out a questionnaire (providing you know what you are looking for).

(b) It is less good at helping you **schedule** your Project Work with other areas of **your** life.

So what should my main planning aid be?

4.22 We strongly recommend that – whether on spreadsheet or paper – you draw up an overall schedule on a day-by-day basis, from the start until you intend to complete the project, analysing your time between:

(a) Work

      (b) Weekend/holiday

      (c) The Research and Analysis Project

4.23   Submit your plans to a **reality check.**

    (a) Your partner and/or family may feel that your plans to work 12 hours on Saturday and Sunday may not be conducive to personal happiness or family life; or that your plans to rise 2 hours earlier every morning are unlikely to meet fruition if you are a notoriously late sleeper.

    (b) Your **boss and work colleagues** may be able to advise you of busy times you have not already thought of, for example when you will be expected to provide cover for someone else on holiday.

    (c) Your **mentor** (at the first meeting) may have experience of other projects.

    (d) Lecturers at your college will have had years of experience dealing with undergraduate and postgraduate dissertations and research projects.

5   USING IT TO HELP MANAGE THE RESEARCH AND ANALYSIS PROJECT

5.1   Although it is not the purpose of this book to provide you with a guide to various IT software packages on the market, here are some hints and tips.

Using spreadsheets to plan your project

5.2   Although spreadsheets are designed for numerical analysis, they do offer a number of useful features that can be adapted for planning. Below is a simple example using Microsoft Excel. Let us assume that Task 1.1 is library research; you intend to spend 12 hours on this and you commence it on 8 April.

	A	B	C	D	E	F	G	H	I	J	K	L	M	N	O	P	Q	R	S
1			Plan	Actual		Week beginning													
2			(hrs)	(hrs)		08-Apr							15-Apr						
3						Mon	Tues	Wed	Thurs	Fri	Sat	Sun	Mon	Tues	Wed	Thurs	Fri	Sat	Sun
4	No. of hours																		
5	Work						8	8	8	8			8	8	8	8	8		
6	Holiday					8													
7	Shopping										2								
8	Cousin's wedding											6							
9																			
10																			
11	**Research & Analysis**																		
12	**Project**																		
13																			
14	**Task ref**																		
15																			
16	1.1	Library	12			5					5	2							
17				12		3					3	0						6	
18																			
19	1.2	Etc																	

Dates

5.3   You can easily **format cells** to show the **dates**, and you can do this automatically by using the **drag** command. If you are doing a Gantt chart, you can therefore set up the dates very easily. You could use the top cell of each column to signify dates.

Research and Analysis Project tasks and other commitments: time available

5.4 You can input your commitments down the side – as you see we have shown your work commitments at the top, as well as other calls on your time, and have given an hourly approximation.

5.5 You can use a **formula** to add up the total hours you plan to spend, and, in the row below, how many hours you have actually spent. You can use the Format/Cell/Pattern command to add colour or shades to each row of cells. You can see that you were over-optimistic in planning to do two hours work on the day of your cousin's wedding.

5.6 With time for experimentation and practice, you can do a lot more than this, for example flagging up if some tasks are overdue – but you will need to experiment yourself.

Scheduling and diary software

5.7 If your office operates a network system, such as **Microsoft Outlook** or Lotus Notes, it is quite possible to use this to plan your work.

   (a) Microsoft Outlook has a **calendar** facility. You can book up time in your calendar by clicking on the date and 'booking' the time as 'busy' or 'tentative' for your project work. You can print off your calendar by day, week or month.

   (b) When you are planning a meeting or activity, you can book **reminders** to yourself that something needs to be done.

   (c) Microsoft Outlook also has a 'task' list – this has the advantage of identifying automatically when something is overdue by turning it red.

5.8 Note that Microsoft Outlook is not designed to manage a project – but it can be a big help in managing your working life into which the Research and Analysis Project must fit.

Project management software

5.9 Specialised software is available to help you manage projects, for example Microsoft Project. This is almost certainly far too sophisticated and complex for the Research and Analysis Project, but if you are familiar with it anyhow, and, for example, it is available at work, you could use this to plan.

5.10 Here are some overall guidelines on using IT in planning and managing the Research and Analysis Project.

Subject	Comment
1 Garbage in, garbage out	No IT application is better than the data you put into it. If you do not think about **what** you have to do and **how long** it will take, and if your plan is fundamentally **flawed**, no amount of tinkering with IT will help you.
2 IT is a servant not master	If you feel that the project is taking shape in a different way from how you had planned, then you will need to change your plan; it will have to be flexible.
3 IT can waste time as well as save it	If your model is more complex or too sophisticated, and the stages in your project are quite simple, then maintaining the model may eat up time which you could more usefully spend on the project content.

6 SETTING UP YOUR PROJECT FILE

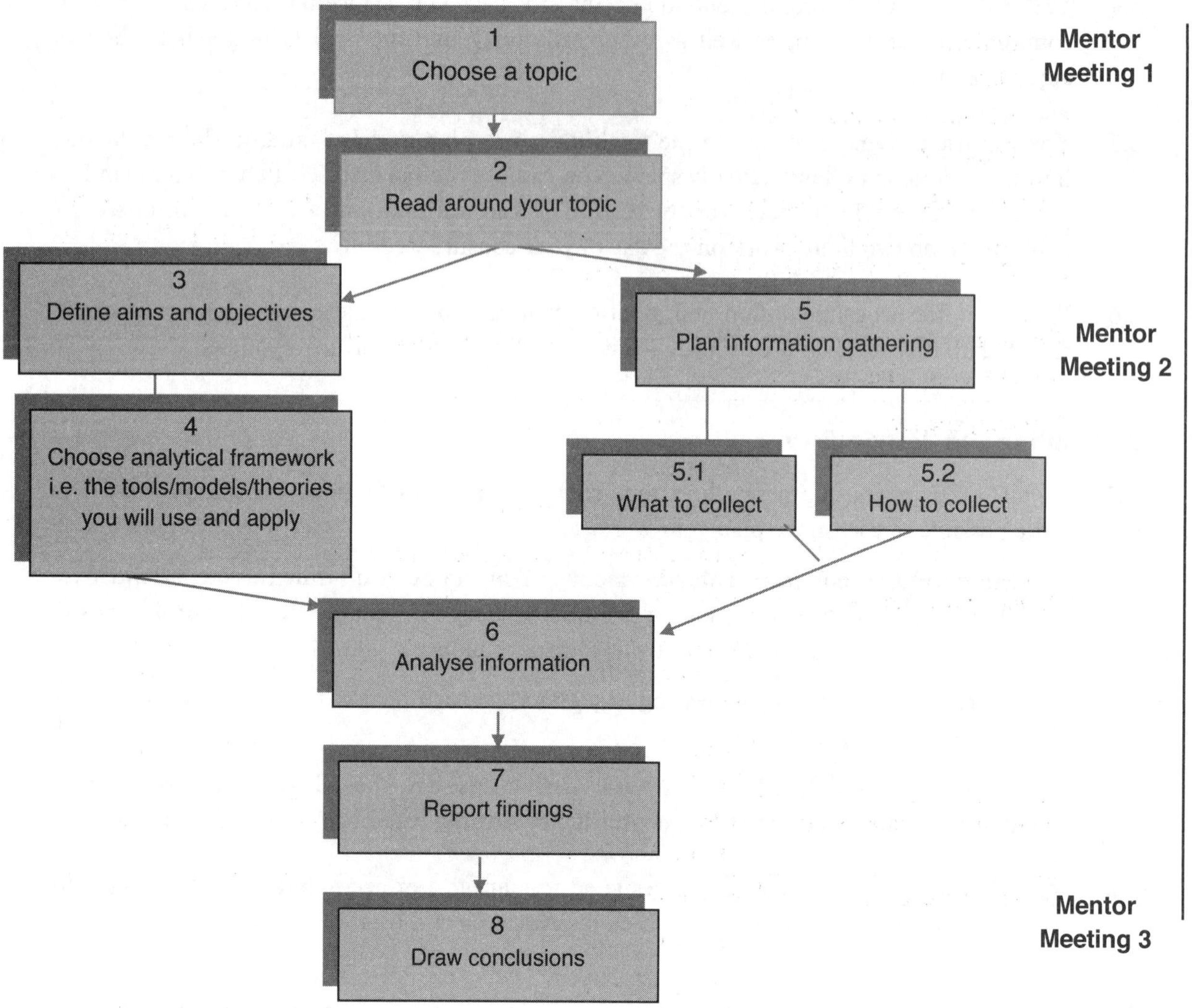

```
        ┌─────────────────────┐                              Mentor
        │         1           │                              Meeting 1
        │   Choose a topic    │
        └─────────────────────┘
                 │
        ┌─────────────────────┐
        │         2           │
        │ Read around your topic │
        └─────────────────────┘
          ╱                  ╲
┌─────────────────────┐    ┌─────────────────────────┐
│         3           │    │            5            │      Mentor
│ Define aims and     │    │ Plan information gathering│     Meeting 2
│ objectives          │    └─────────────────────────┘
└─────────────────────┘          │              │
┌─────────────────────┐   ┌──────────────┐ ┌──────────────┐
│         4           │   │     5.1      │ │     5.2      │
│ Choose analytical   │   │ What to collect │ │ How to collect │
│ framework i.e. the  │   └──────────────┘ └──────────────┘
│ tools/models/theories│         │              │
│ you will use and apply│        │              │
└─────────────────────┘         │              │
          ╲                     ╱
        ┌─────────────────────┐
        │         6           │
        │ Analyse information │
        └─────────────────────┘
                 │
        ┌─────────────────────┐
        │         7           │
        │   Report findings   │
        └─────────────────────┘
                 │
        ┌─────────────────────┐                              Mentor
        │         8           │                              Meeting 3
        │  Draw conclusions   │
        └─────────────────────┘
```

6.1 If you go back to the guidelines, you will note that Oxford Brookes University has already suggested a way of planning your project.

6.2 This is a useful framework for the Research and Analysis Project, but you do not have to adopt it of course. If you do, however, we strongly suggest that you break down the work into a work breakdown structure.

Setting up your file

6.3 One important planning task is **setting up a file for you to manage your data**. You may need two or more but if you start to order and record your paperwork from the outset, this will help you control and keep track. The abilities the Research and Analysis Project seeks to test are not only the content and thought but how you **organised** the process.

What you've read

6.4 Furthermore, you MUST keep a record of where you obtained your data as you MUST reference it in your Report. So, if you read an article about the logistics industry in the

Economist, say, or the business section of the **Middle Eastern Economic Digest** or the **Straits Times**, and if you have used this, then always note down:

- Article source
- Date
- Author, if attributed
- Page references

This is **evidence** of what you have done – as important for this Research and Analysis Project as your other work – DON'T RELY ON MEMORY. DON'T FORGET TO NOTE REFERENCES DOWN AS YOU USE THEM.

6.5   We suggest you obtain an A4 ring binder, with twice as many file dividers as you think can possibly need. Here are some subdivisions.

Planning section	Your schedules
	Meeting dates
	Any related correspondence
	Printouts of any emails regarding meetings
Project topic choice	Notes of why you chose the topic
	Copies of any articles you read to turn your topic into an objective: you may need this when writing your Report and discussing with mentor
	Notes with references: who wrote the article, who published it, when was it published, what journal published it
Notes of mentor meeting 1	Details of preparation, notes of meeting; everything you will need for the Key Skills Statement
Details of research	Research design
	What you did
	Notes and references
Analytical frameworks	Where you got them from
	Why you obtained them
Evidence	What data you decided to collect
	Rationale – why
	How you collected it (eg interview, questionnaire)
	You may need subsections for detailed working papers, questionnaires received
	Include copies of any authorisations you have had to reproduce material not in the public domain.
Analysis	What you did
	What tools you used
	Spreadsheet models you drew up – show the model first, and the formulae underneath it, in case the worst happens and you lose your more
Notes for mentor meeting 2	
...and so on	

7 PLANNING ISSUES FOR EACH STAGE OF THE RESEARCH AND ANALYSIS PROJECT

Step 1. Choose a topic

7.1 We have covered this in Chapter 4. The only **planning** issues are these, as discussed.

(a) A **reality check** to ensure that your choice of topic and the project objective are internally consistent and feasible. You may find, as you plan in detail what you want to do that you had not really appreciated the work involved. Creating a project plan will help you, here.

(b) Your first mentor meeting – see chapter 11 for details.

Step 2. Read around the subject matter

7.2 Unlike a fully fledged undergraduate dissertation, you are not required to complete a formal literature review; however, reading round the subject will help define the project objective. Planning issues are:

- Do only what you need to do to create a coherent project objective.

- Take notes of what you have read, as you may need to cite these in your Report and make sure you have kept a note of the source, so that it can be **referenced.**

- If possible, collect copies in your file.

Step 3. Define aims and objectives; choose analytical frameworks

7.3 The main planning issue is to make sure that your choice is feasible and sensible.

Step 4. Information gathering: getting permission

Getting permission

7.4 We must now highlight a key point. IF YOU ARE IN ANY DOUBT AS TO WHETHER YOU CAN REPRODUCE MATERIAL, GET PERMISSION TO DO SO.

Furthermore, if you work in an audit department, **unauthorised** use of client data is a BREACH OF PROFESSIONAL ETHICS.

7.5 You might therefore need to obtain permission **as part of the planning process**. Look at what the Guidelines state, as follows.

> **NB**: In carrying out the research for your report, if you intend to source any information not already in the public domain (i.e. from your employer or a client of your employer), then you are urged to bear in mind issues of confidentiality/data protection and to obtain clearance in writing from the relevant party.

7.6 Obtaining permission is something you must do at the start. Failure to do so may mean you will have to reconsider the whole project.

(a) If you are **an auditor,** you have access to client data on a confidential basis.

(i) The client is paying for the work to be done and may, quite reasonably and correctly, be concerned about breach of commercial confidentiality. Many clients might also object, as a matter of principle, that you are getting a benefit that the client has paid for.

    (ii)   On the other hand, some audit clients may welcome a project on a matter of commercial concern to them.

    (iii)   Do not assume that using the data and changing the name will be good enough.

    DO NOT approach the client directly. Instead speak to the **audit partner**.

(b)   If you are using data from your **own** employer, ask permission from your boss (or your mentor), who may have to get further clearance.

(c)   Finally, obtain these **permissions in writing**. Be quite precise in what you are asking.

Getting data

7.7   Data gathering is the area in which your planning and scheduling skills will come to the fore. We have already discussed the work breakdown structure, estimation and scheduling.

Example

Assume that you are to do **Project Topic 13: 'An analysis of personnel requirements under conditions of change (including employee development)'**.You are fortunate in that you have received permission from the human resources department of your own employer, X plc, to assess the personnel requirements of the sales administration, stock control, fulfilment (despatch) following the introduction of an on-line ordering system enabling customers to order directly via the web.

What to collect

You have decided that you want to gather data from all these departments covering:

- What managers perceive the human resources needs to be
- What employees consider the human resources needs are
- How they came to those views

To gather the information, you might plan to interview the managers and conduct a written anonymous survey of employees.

How to collect the data

- Design a list of questions to cover with managers in the interview – will have to be done outside of working hours

- Design questionnaire for employees to answer

- Ask human resources to agree to the questionnaire. Bearing in mind the sensitivity of the issues, this could take a few days.

- Set meeting dates with managers – this may have to be during working hours

- Distribute questionnaire

During this time, you could also be expanding your awareness by reading how other firms coped with technological change and motivation theory.

7.8   You may find, therefore, that you have to do some tasks in parallel with others, and that you have different types of data collection exercise in train at the same time.

Step 5. **Analyse information**

7.9   Order your work in a methodical way and, more importantly, the **allow yourself the time to be thorough. We strongly suggest that you do not carry out this stage only in a succession of lunch breaks. Use up** some holiday and devote a weekend to it.

7.10   Above all, record the work you have done.

Steps 6 and 7. **Report findings and conclusions**

7.11 We cover how to plan the mentor meetings, the Report and the Key Skills Statement in Parts C and D of this text

---

Chapter roundup

- This chapter has covered some of the basic planning issues.

- You will have to dovetail your work in line with the job and other commitments.

- There will be varying lead times according to the tasks you will do.

- Be realistic about your ability to set deadlines. Other people's needs also should be considered.

Chapter 6

CARRYING OUT RESEARCH

Chapter topic list

1   Types of research methods; a short, practical guide

2   Primary and secondary research

3   Identifying the information you need in the light of the project objectives

4   Secondary data, including the Internet

5   Using secondary data

6   Primary research

7   Surveys and questionnaires

8   Qualitative research

9   How good is your data?

10   Plagiarism

Introduction

This chapter covers the main area of the Research part of the Research and Analysis Project. This determines what data you obtain and the procedures you have to go through to find it. Although the content of the Research and Analysis Project might seem very different from, say, researching the behaviour of sub-atomic particles or researching into changing social attitudes, it is still **research**.

---

1   TYPES OF RESEARCH METHODS: A SHORT PRACTICAL GUIDE

1.1   Before launching into the practical detail, you might be as well to consider the **assumptions** upon which your choice of research methods is based. If you have certain prejudices as to what matters, then this might affect your review of the data or indeed the type of research you do.

1.2   The additional reading on the Reading List (Chapter 1) offers a variety of different approaches to research, but we will **illustrate** some contrasting approaches as used in **business to draw out some of the key issues.**

Exercise 1

What would you say are the key differences between the research methods below?

Situation 1

You have just been into a new fast food outlet. After your meal, a uniformed member of staff approaches you and says 'I am carrying out a survey into how customers view the quality and service we supply. By collecting a representative view of our customers' needs, we will be able to improve our

115

service. The results will be fed into a database and anonymity is guaranteed'. You are then asked a series of pre-scripted questions, to which you must choose an option for an answer. (For example, 'would you rate our food as poor, fair, good or excellent?') After answering the questions, the interviewer takes some of your personal details, thanks you and then proceeds to another table asking the same questions.

Situation 2

A pharmaceutical company is researching a new type of vaccine for influenza. Its scientists believe there could be a relationship between certain aspects of the virus's chemistry and the immune system.

It has given small doses of the vaccine to ten paid volunteers, who for the duration of the test are living in a special research facility. These volunteers are being monitored to see how the vaccine affects them when they are exposed to flu. At another research facility, the same number of volunteers is being given a 'placebo' and are also exposed to the virus.

Blood tests will be taken, so that scientists can see how the vaccine affects the body's response to the flu virus.

Situation 3

You have been asked to join a small group of five people for an evening to do some 'focus group research' on makes of car. The researcher introduces topics of conversation and asks people what they feel about motoring, what they feel about different brands of car, what their motoring habits are, and what frustrates them most about motoring and motor cars.

The researcher intervenes from time to time to steer the conversation to topics of interest or to clarify what people have said.

Situation 4

A researcher for an investment banking firm is reviewing companies engaged in e-commerce. She has obtained financial statements of twenty firms, and also details of movements in their respective share prices over the past four years. From this she compares data and compiles a report.

Answer

Situation 1

Seeks to find out **objective** facts that have some statistical relevance, from which inferences can be drawn. This sort of research is **quantitative** in that it aims to obtain a sample of data and generalise responses from it. It is **descriptive in that is describes the current state of affairs.** It might also seek to examine the relationships between two variables: rating of food and age of customer. Does a person's age correlate with their appreciation of the food?

Situation 2

Seeks to draw out **objective** facts, and is **testing a hypothesis** against empirical data (data derived from observation or experience). Of course, a small sample of ten may not be enough to get a general view, but it is strong evidence that further research could be useful.

Situation 3

Features quite often in the early stage of market research and, indeed, in other areas of research. It is called qualitative research.

Clearly the researcher is not trying to prove anything, nor is the researcher trying to find out objective facts from which statistical inferences can be made – the sample is obviously not meaningful and the questioning is not controlled. The researcher is trying to tease out ideas from what people say they feel about the situation.

What the researcher is probably doing is trying to come up with **ideas** for further research, no more. If, say, one of the people in the group was to say that 'car designers have no appreciation of the needs of parents carrying heavy shopping and looking after children', this would give them a lot to think about.

Situation 4

The data is easily obtained, and it is not new knowledge. The main purpose of the research is, however, to analyse and draw relationships between different areas of the data, to see if there might be common features which all the sample of companies share.

To summarise, here are some key words describing the type of research encountered in the situations.

Situation	Key words	Summary
1 Market research	Statistical Objective Descriptive Quantitative	Describing facts and relationships
2 Research into a vaccine	Objective Experimental Testing hypotheses Scientific	Testing hypotheses
3 Focus group	Qualitative Non-statistical Relationships Generate ideas	Exploring ideas
4 Investment banker	Relationships Analysis Factual	Analysis

1.3 Each of these types of research approach is legitimate in its own right, and you may use a combination of them in the Research and Analysis Project.

Example

For example, let us take **Project Topic 3: 'An analysis of the impact of existing or impending legislation on an organisation'.**

Let us assume that the organisation is your employer and the legislation relates to the relationships businesses have with their suppliers. One aspect of this is a proposal by the government to make it much easier for suppliers to sue for interest on bills that are paid late. Here are some research tasks.

1   **Exploring ideas** – are the people in the purchasing department aware? Do they care or know about the small print? What about the sales ledger department? Does the firm want to charge its own customers for late payment?

2   **Analysis** – review creditors and debtors ledger for payment periods. What is the maximum potential loss if this change is implemented? If the firm paid early, would it run up bank overdraft fees? If creditors are a source of finance, how expensive are they?

3   **Experimentation** – not really possible in this case.

4   **Describing facts** – if the firm has a large sales force, you may – if allowed – send a questionnaire to a sample (which can include all of them!) asking them if they know about the change and the terms and conditions they currently offer. The same could be sent to a buying department.

Clearly a lot of the work is going to be analysis – in fact, this work is cited in the topic title.

1.4 Below is how BPP would classify the Project Topics according to the main focus of the research – **however, your own choice of project objective will indicate the approach you should take.**

These are **only hints** – your own project objective may lead you on a quite different path.

	Project Topics	Main type of research activity?
1	An analysis of the efficiency and/or effectiveness of a management accounting technique in an organisational setting.	Analysis Describing Exploring
2	An analysis of how the application of technology can contribute to an organisation's efficiency and/or effectiveness.	Exploring Analysis Testing
3	An examination of the impact of an aspect of existing or impending legislation on an organisation.	Exploring Analysis
4	An analysis of the impact of e-business on an industry or organisation of your choice.	Exploring Analysis Describing
5	The identification of the effects of globalisation on an industry of your choice.	Exploring Describing
6	The identification of key factors or indicators in the motivation of employees in an organisation of your choice.	Exploring Describing Testing
7	An analysis of the tax and profit implications of different company entities, changes in status or acquisitions or disposals of company assets.	Analysis Describing Exploring
8	An analysis of the financial situation of your choice of organisation.	Analysis Exploring
9	An examination of how to plan, develop and implement an appropriate information system in an organisation.	Exploring Describing
10	An analysis of how management accounting techniques are used to support decision-making in organisations.	Analysis Exploring
11	An analysis of the costs and benefits of the internal audit/internal review activities within an organisation of your choice.	Analysis Exploring
12	An analysis of the effect of any International Accounting standard on the accounts of any organisation in terms of profitability or financial stability or balance sheet value.	Analysis Testing
13	An analysis of future personnel requirements under conditions of change (including employee development).	Exploring Analysis Describing
14	An investigation of recent investment decisions by an organisation of your choice and how the use of different methods of risk and uncertainty analysis might affect such decisions.	Exploring Analysis Describing
15	An analysis of the role of working capital on the profitability and /or efficiency of an organisation of your choice.	Analysis Describing
16	An analysis of the effect of different sources of capital on investment decisions possibly including capital rationing and its effects.	Analysis Describing Exploring

17	An analysis of the effect of corporate governance on financial performance of an organisation of your choice.	Analysis Testing Exploring
18	An examination of how to plan, develop and implement an appropriate PRP system in an organisation.	Exploring Describing
19	An analysis of the business and financial reasons and effects of creating a multinational merger company.	Analysis Exploring
20	An analysis of the effects of IT failure and contingency plans within an organisation of your choice.	Exploring Describing
21	An analysis of the impact of the Euro on an organisation or industry of your choice.	Analysis Describing
22	Analyse the marketing strategy of an organisation of your choice, identifying the key success factors or indicators in the marketing mix and the activities of the organisation.	Analysis Describing

1.5 This table only gives **tentative hints**.

(a) **Testing** appears rarely – you are not conducting a scientific experiment. The very fact that you – with management's endorsement – are asking questions, can make you a participant as well as an observer of the company you are researching. If you interview people, people may welcome the attention, and tell you what they think you – or senior managers – want to hear.

(b) **Exploring** appears everywhere. This is not to say that you should set up focus groups, but that you cannot dismiss the less certain, more tentative aspects of the enquiry.

(c) **Analysis appears in most topics.**

2 PRIMARY AND SECONDARY RESEARCH

What sort of research do I have to do?

2.1 As you read through the notes below, it will help if you keep the following in mind.

	Secondary data	Primary data
What it is	Data neither collected directly by the user nor specifically for the user, often under conditions unknown to the user – in other words, data collected not by YOU but by someone else for their own purposes or for general use	Data that is collected specifically by or for the user, at source, in other words by YOU in the Research and Analysis Project.
Quantitative, 'factual' or 'objective' example	**Government reports** – in the UK a good example is Social Trends, which contains government statistics about British society, employment in different industries, attitudes and so on. Such a report might be relevant to **Topic 13 Personnel requirements under conditions of change.** A company's **published financial statements** summarise and interpret company transactions data for the benefit of **shareholders**, not the needs of the Research and Analysis project.	A survey you conduct with a questionnaire you have designed, with regard to a sample. You aim to get a statistically significant result. An experiment

Qualitative example	An article in the ACCA Student Accountant magazine or in a book about theories of motivation.	A focus group you have conducted (in the manner of Situation 3 above) to talk about motivation
Role in Research and Analysis Project	You must make some use of secondary data.	Useful – perhaps even essential given some research objectives, but not compulsory for the Research and Analysis Project

2.2 Below is an example from an unpublished undergraduate dissertation. It should be familiar to you, because it featured in Chapter 5! Identify areas of primary and secondary research.

Example

1   Initially the work I carried out on the project was extremely informal in that whenever I met a salesman or spoke to a manager I would ask them about their feelings towards the present pay scheme or the method by which targets were allocated. When salesmen complained about errors in their commission payment due to faults in the payment scheme I was in an ideal position to suggest to managers changes and refinements in the pay scheme.

2   Following this initial exploration I decided to familiarise myself with the theory behind targeting specifically and, more generally, how information and control system influence behaviour. At the same time as this I spoke to people outside Q Ltd both from academic backgrounds, so as to develop ideas, and in other selling companies, so as to compare Q Ltd with other selling firms.

3   Once I felt well briefed about the problem I sought permission from the Southern Sales Director (Mr X) to interview his sales managers. He requested a questionnaire which I forwarded to him. Mr X made minor adjustments to this in form rather than content. For example, one question I asked was, 'Why do you think Q Ltd has higher turnover of salesmen than other similar companies?', this was changed to: 'Do you think Q Ltd has a higher turnover of salesmen than other similar companies? If so, why? (see appendix 1).

4   I developed the questionnaire with the background knowledge I had acquired and discussed some of the questions with Mr A, the Statistics and Finance Manager, my immediate superior.

5   Over a period of about a month I interviewed five sales managers, each interview lasting about one hour. I felt the questionnaire was a little restrictive, therefore I chose to approach the interviews informally using the questionnaire as a check that I had covered most of the points. This was specifically important as I felt that the psychological atmosphere of the interview would be at least as important as the mechanics of the interview. I realised that this would require me to be flexible, however, I didn't realise how flexible I would have to be. I organised one interview and found that this manager shared his room with another manager so I spent much of the interview making notes on discussion between the two of them, myself acting as a catalyst when discussion wained. This particular interview was especially useful since it uncovered issues such as the education and training of management that would otherwise have been overlooked. I decided to make written notes rather than a tape-recording because I though this might be offputting to the managers.

6   During the interviewing and recording process I tried to avoid personal bias and judgement and when incorporating findings into this text I tried to avoid jumping to simplistic conclusions without considering their implications.

Comment

The vast majority of this is primary research both quantitative and exploratory. Secondary research is only referred to in paragraph 2.

How much research do I have to do?

2.3 This is the crux of the matter. The project is testing skills in **Research and Analysis** and so you may want to know how much you should do.

READ THIS!	
A minimalist approach ...... In theory, you could only cite four sources which could be, for example: • An article in Student Accountant • A book – technical background from your BPP Study Text • Evidence of a website visit • A set of financial statements • The ACCA's model answer to an exam question	**Yes, but** .... • This will be **just** enough for Project Topic 8, say, but not for others. • You will need to use them very well indeed. • For many **Project Topics** you will **have** to read around the subject • **Using few sources is like not answering all the questions in an exam – you need to get top marks in order to pass.**
FEW SOURCES = HIGHER RISK OF FAILING	

2.4 The external examiner has made the point that some students' projects are too superficial. The research that you undertake must have some depth and must be accompanied by analysis of your findings. If the work you do is described by the examiner as 'shallow' (which it will be if all you do is read a few articles and cobble them all together into an essay) your project will fail.

3 IDENTIFYING THE INFORMATION YOU NEED IN THE LIGHT OF THE PROJECT OBJECTIVES

3.1 You have a choice of twenty two topics, but each has to be whittled down to a project objective, as described in chapter 4. Once you have done so, you will have a fair idea of what you want. Here are two questions you might ask to clarify your thinking.

1 What am I trying to prove or disprove?
2 What am I trying to show?

	Implication	Example
1. What am I trying to prove or disprove?	Weighing up a statement in the light of collected evidence	**Project Topic 6: the identification of key factors or indicators in the motivation of employees in an organisation of your choice** **Example objective**: to demonstrate that the white collar employees of XX2 Ltd are motivated principally by salary levels **What am I trying to prove?** That salary is the main motivating factor for this group of employees and that they are not influenced by other factors **Information that could disprove this** You actually find that a sizeable minority of the employees are not motivated primarily by salary. On closer analysis you find that these are the older members of staff, and further analysis of the results of your questionnaire indicate that they are motivated more by working conditions and job satisfaction

	Implication	Example
2. What am I trying to show?	Reveal the results of your discoveries in a particular area. You are not trying to prove or disprove a point but come to some conclusions from certain types of data.	**Project Topic 7: An analysis of the tax and profit implications of different company entities, changes in status or acquisitions or disposals of company assets** **Example objective**: B Partners is a consultancy firm with offices worldwide. Its senior partners have decided to incorporate its overseas branches as separate limited companies. The information you need to illustrate this: • Tax and profit figures under the old scheme • Effect of the new scheme • Attempt to isolate effect of change of status at other times • Profit implications – not only reported profits, but changes in attitude to risk?

3.2 In practice, your research is likely to involve both sorts of question. It is not our job here to give a detailed blow-by-blow breakdown of what you should do. **Each project has to be unique.**

Generating information requirements

3.3 Here you really need the detail project objective and you have to work logically and ruthlessly from this. You need to define – and report – the following.

- Scope
- Focus
- Contexts

Define scope

3.4 **Scope of your enquiries** – the boundaries of what you are doing.

  (a) **Over time** – a time period for your data

  (i) **Frequency.** Review of financial statements – these are produced annually.

  (ii) **Start and end dates of the event you are describing,** for example when was it decided to buy a new information system (Project Topic 9)

  (iii) **Sensible time period for the subject in question** – for example, the costs and benefits of internal audit (Project Topic 11) need a reasonably long time horizon – two or three years, not just one month – to be assessed.

  (b) **Geography** – global, international, regional, local businesses, industries or environment

  (c) **Industry** etc

  (d) **Size of a transaction** – for example, auditors look at 'material' or representative items, not everything.

3.5 You **may need to justify your scope** in your report – for example, if you have chosen an unusual time period, there may be a good reason (eg before and after adoption of International Accounting Standards).

Define focus

3.6   Focus of analysis – what are you collecting data about? **Here are some examples.**

- Individuals, for example on a project dealing with motivation issues

- Groups of people (eg a department, such as 'the sales force', suppliers)

- Procedures and processes within an organisation, for example how investment decisions are made

- Events, actions or decisions, for example the adoption of an International Accounting Standard, or the decision to buy a subsidiary

- Inputs (eg material, informational) or outputs

- An organisation as a whole

You may, of course, collect data about a number of the above.

Define contexts

3.7   By context, we mean factors in the **immediate environment** of the Project, such as the unique characteristics of the company, which will affect:

- The data collection methods employed, perhaps

- The content of what you need to define

For example, **motivational issues** for managers in a company that has just been **taken over** and, perhaps, has seen a round of redundancies and dismissals, may be quite different from a successful firm which is taking people on and needs to integrate them into the organisation.

Example

		Information
Project objective	**Project Topic 16: analysis of different sources of capital on investment decisions, in an organisation of your choice** **Example objective**: Assess how managers in X plc invest in projects according to strictly rational, financial criteria	What evidence do I need to show of background reading to ensure I make sensible judgements?
To prove	Investment decisions are made strictly as a result of rational criteria and follow what would be suggested by capital rationing techniques	
Scope • Time period? • Organisational	18 months to January 2005. X plc – compare practice in offices in London and Malaysia office	Self explanatory
Focus	Capital expenditure decisions over £20,000/RM100,000	But how big is this sample? You may have to reduce this scope.

		Information
Context	X plc is decentralised company with two main offices, in London, UK and in Kuala Lumpur, Malaysia. In the late 1990s, the Malaysian government introduced control on the import and export of foreign currency.	Each office may have different formal procedures and authorisation limits. Obtain procedures manuals from both offices. Ask accounts department to give you details of capex decisions, eg a list for you to review. You may take a sample.

3.8 We suggest that in your **project file** you set up a separate section for this issue. You **may** need to use a number of free flowing techniques to define the information you need, perhaps in a tree diagram.

Define what each item of information is for

3.9 Once you have decided what information you need, we advise you to keep a record of why you collected it. Here is an example. You could have a set up such as this, with even a brief summary as to the eventual usefulness of the data – the 'result'.

Information source	Reasons	Result
Procedures manual for capex of Kuala Lumpur office	• To identify formal systems for approving capital expenditure • To compare with actual decisions taken • To see whether capital rationing is mentioned in procedural criteria	Obtained Procedures manual only describes procedures for authorisation, rather than the business decision underlying it
Conversation – phone or email with relevant managers	• To ask how capex decisions are taken • To ask permission for recent examples (NB Follow up in writing)	

Detailed advice

3.10 Detailed advice on primary and secondary data is given in the next sections of this chapter

4 SECONDARY DATA, INCLUDING THE INTERNET

4.1 The following is a guide to the use of secondary data. It can only be couched in the most general terms, as each project is unique and has its own data requirements.

Where should you look

4.2 As this is a Research and Analysis Project, you are expected to think for yourself in this respect – we have already given some hints as to possible sources in the Thought Points section of Chapter 4, Choosing a Project.

Internal sources of secondary data

4.3   Your employer probably has large amounts of information, not designed for your research, but useful to you, and this will be held on a departmental basis. Do not limit your interest to the accounts department! Monthly management accounts are only part of what is available for your research. And remember, the accounts department is rarely the **driver** of a business.

4.4   **Accounts department**

- Procedures manual
- Management accounts – balance sheets
- Financial data
- Accounting policies
- Tax details
- Working capital

4.5   **Sales and marketing department**

- Sales reports by region
- Sales by customer
- Sales by product
- Competitor intelligence
- Market prospects and reports
- Customer complaints
- Marketing research reports
- Brand strategy and values
- Distribution chains

4.6   **Production and operations**

- Operations data
- Efficiency and capacity detail
- Process flow charts
- Detailed product costings
- Input prices
- Supply chain

4.7   **Human resources**

- Number of employees
- Recruitment procedures
- Training programmes
- Staff turnover details
- Details of pay

External secondary data

4.8   It is hard to give detailed rules about where you should look, except that you should search for **relevant** data, and try to make use of the Internet. Clearly, the use of **secondary** data is going to be more crucial for some topics than others – such as **Project Topic 5: 'The identification of the effects of globalisation on an industry of your choice'**.

Books

4.9 You need to take care here. For the technical knowledge covered by the other syllabuses in the ACCA qualification, you might consult (in addition to the BPP Study Text) the other books on the **ACCA's reading list** if they are relevant to your project.

4.10 Articles in the ACCA's **Student Accountant** magazine often refer to books that have been published recently – if there is an article relevant to your project than it might have **references**. (This is also true of other journals.)

4.11 **Your college or public library**. Even if you do not know what you are looking for, you may find some time spent browsing is quite useful. Many libraries use the Dewey Decimal System – there is no need to go into this here, but this is a well-established means of classifying books.

4.12 Bookshops which sell over the internet (or a site such as Amazon.com) sometimes enable you to type in a Key Word, which might generate some titles about a topic – even if you do not buy them, you may find them in your local library.

Journals and articles

4.13 Your obvious first choice should be the ACCA's **Student Accountant**. This contains a wealth of articles relevant to the ACCA qualification. Otherwise, no list can be prescriptive.

4.14 A college library is likely to have other **academic journals**, such as the **Harvard Business Review**. Again, rather than list them here, you may be able to find a list from your own college library of what is published – perhaps an article may be obtained or copied for you.

4.15 Other business or current affairs journals and newspapers, such as the **Economist**, Straits Times, **Asian Wall Street Journal** etc, may have surveys relevant to different business areas.

4.16 **Trade journals** are also useful – most countries have journals produced by relevant trade bodies, detailing developments in the industry. You can use the Internet to access the websites of **trade associations**. Increasingly, businesses in an industry are setting up electronic markets

---

Example

The UK has a large and developed printing and publishing industry. The trade body, PIRA, aims to promote best practice and has an extensive publication programme. Two examples – of many industry publications – are:

- The Bookseller – for the retail book trade
- Paper focus – for paper buyers

4.17 The **Internet** is an excellent source of secondary data if used with care.

(a) For example, you can use a **search engine** which will bring up websites of interest. Some websites will allow you to download articles. Some of these websites – the **Economist Intelligence Unit** is one – offer articles for download. Another is www.ft.com, (the Financial Times). Many of these will be in PDF (portable document file) format. You will need to download **Adobe Acrobat Reader** for this – fortunately

Acrobat Reader is **free** and it is possible that the site will have a link to Adobe to enable you to download the software yourself.

(b) Your internet service provider may also refer you to magazines and on-line newspapers.

Government ministries and agencies

4.18 Government agencies are good sources of economic and other statistical information. Most countries have an agency that provides national statistics. This varies significantly from country to country in terms of what is produced and the format, but you should be able to find:

(a) Economic data (eg UK Annual Abstract of Statistics)
(b) Social data (eg on population size and structure)
(c) Market data (eg export promotion)

A lot of government statistics previously only available in print, such as Social Trends, Economic Trends and Regional Trends, are now available free online in PDF format at www.statistics.gov.uk, the website of the Office of National Statistics (ONS). However, it is not always easy to find them direct from the ONS home page. Searching for (eg) Social Trends on a site such as www.google.co.uk can be a quicker way of getting to the relevant part of the ONS website.

Regulatory bodies and industry associations

4.19 There are many quasi-government and other public sector bodies which can provide data on a particular industry sector.

Other sources

4.20 There are some sources of data which you may not be able to access in a personal capacity, but which your employer might have access to, by virtue of being in a particular industry or dealing with clients from a particular industry. These include:

- A business directory (eg Kompass)
- Market research data (eg Nielson consumer surveys)

5 USING SECONDARY DATA

5.1 Secondary data is used in many business situations, not just in academic research. Secondary data:

- Can provide a backdrop to primary research
- Can act as a substitute for field research
- Can be used as a technique in itself

Backdrop to primary research

5.2 Secondary data may also be used to set the **parameters** for primary research. In an **unfamiliar field**, it is natural that the researcher will carry out some **basic research** in the area, using journals, existing reports, the press and any contacts with relevant knowledge. Such investigations will provide guidance on a number of areas.

- Possible data sources
- Data collection
- Methods of collection (relevant populations, sampling methods and so on)

Substitute for primary research

5.3   The (often substantial) **cost** of primary research **might be avoided** should existing secondary data be sufficient. Given the low response rate available for questionnaires, secondary research might do the job just as well. There are some situations however, in which secondary data is bound to be **insufficient**.

A technique in itself

5.4   Some types of information can **only be acquired through secondary data**, in particular **trends** over time. The **historical data** published on, say, trends in the behaviour of an industry over time, cannot realistically be replaced by a one-off study.

How reliable is secondary data?

5.5   The quality of the secondary data

(a)   Preparers may have an axe to grind; trade associations may not include data which runs counter to the interest of its members.

(b)   Why was **the data** being collected in the first place? Random samples with a poor response rate are particularly questionable). Government statistics and information based on them are often relatively dated, though information technology has speeded up the process).

(c)   **How were parameters defined**. This is directly related to '**focus**' in 3.6 above. What do you mean by '**employees**'.

5.6   Advantages arising from the use of secondary data.

(a)   Secondary data may solve the problem **without** the need for any primary research: **time and money is thereby saved.**

(b)   Secondary data sources are a great deal **cheaper** than those for primary research.

(c)   Secondary data, while not necessarily fulfilling your information needs, can be of great use by:

(i)   **Setting the parameters**, defining a hypothesis, highlighting variables, in other words, helping to focus on the central problem

(ii)   **Providing guidance**, by showing past methods of research and so on, for primary data collection

(iii)   **Helping to assimilate the primary research** with past research, highlighting trends and the like

(d)   **You have to use this data source for the Research and Analysis Project.**

5.7   **Issues to bear in mind in secondary data**

Topic	Comment
Relevance	The data may not be relevant to the research objectives in terms of the data content itself, classifications used or units of measurement.
Cost	Although secondary data is usually cheaper than primary data, some specialist reports can cost large amounts of money.
Availability	Secondary data may not exist in the specific product or market area.
Bias	The secondary data may be biased, depending on who originally carried it out and for what purpose. Attempts should be made to obtain the most original source of the data, to assess it for such bias.

Topic	Comment
Statistical accuracy	Was the sample representative?
	Was the questionnaire or other measurement instrument(s) properly constructed?
	Were possible biases in response or in non-response dealt with and accounted for?
	Was the data properly analysed using appropriate statistical techniques?
	Was a sufficiently large sample used?
	Does the report include the raw data?
	In addition, was any raw data omitted from the final report, and why?
Sufficiency	Even after fulfilling all the above criteria, the secondary data may be insufficient and primary research would therefore be necessary.

5.8   The golden rule when using secondary data is **use only meaningful data.**

(a)   **Begin with internal sources** and a firm with a good management information system should be able to provide a great deal of data.

(b)   External information should be consulted in order of ease and speed of access: directories, catalogues and indexes before books, abstracts and periodicals.

(c)   **Do not accept it at face value. The Internet, for example, is a mine of misinformation.**

5.9   For the Research and Analysis Project, follow the **key rules** below to keep control of your use of secondary data.

KEY RULES

Reference

Record

Review

Relate

5.10   We suggest that for each item of secondary data you use, you prepare a **sheet** as follows.

Data item	Fill in
Reference	
• Source	
• Author	
• When and how obtained	
• Citation details: Note down all you need to do to reference according to the Harvard system	
Record	
Attach photocopy/print out or take notes – see Reference above if you want to rely on them	
Review	
• What is the data saying?	
Relate	
• How does this tie in with the project objectives?	
• How does it relate to other areas of the project, eg primary research?	
• Do I intend to use it – if so, how?	

6 PRIMARY RESEARCH

6.1 Primary research obtains the data particularly relevant to the project you have. Read the following extract from an unpublished undergraduate dissertation.

Example

The **aim** was to find out what environmental information companies make available to external parties and how useful this is. I decided that the best **method** to gather this information was to become an external party myself and write to them asking for their annual reports and any published environmental information. This way, my research would **not be subject to individual company bias** concerning what they publish, as a survey or interview may be.

Comparisons were only made on the information that I received. This may have had its limitations in that more information could exist, but this was **a representative sample of what an average external reader** would receive – the objective in question.

I **selected** seven companies to request such information from, this small number would allow a more detailed focus on issues. Companies were selected from those mentioned in past ACCA environmental reporting towards together with two randomly selected companies of my own (Dixons and Allied Domeqc).

The dimensions of performance that I concentrated my analysis on were based upon the main points that the first chapter of the literature review discovered. This would enable me to discover if what writers believed was actually being communicated and if what I found was disclosed in reality, matched.

The **annual reports** were requested, to see what **environmental disclosure** they contained and also to discover if any financial environmental information was present in anticipation of the future environmental accounting chapter.

I feel this chapter was a very effective use of primary research. However, one **weakness** was the narrow range of companies considered. A study of companies not recommended by ACCA and operating in several differing industries, may provide more issues. Although this may prove difficult if not enough environmental data is disclosed to make comparisons. To question the companies via telephone rather than an 'official' letter may result in a more relaxed attitude reaping more open responses.

Environmental questionnaire

Next, I wanted to discover how the **internal background of the firms can affect the external environmental communication** they may or may not produce.

I thought a **questionnaire** was appropriate to reach the large amount of companies that I wanted to involve. I chose thirty companies from the catalogue of annual reports at Wheatley library (see appendix twelve), consciously trying to include a range of industries. Measures were implemented to increase the chances of companies replying.

- I obtained contact names by telephoning the companies beforehand.

- A stamped addressed envelope was enclosed for replies.

- Anonymity was ensured.

- The questions took a closed category format, meaning all respondents had to do was tick relevant boxes.

- Only fourteen questions were asked.

I also structured the questions to start general before getting more specific to ease respondents into the correct way of thinking. The questionnaire can be seen in appendix eleven.

My approach was successful, indicated by the 73% response rate of which 18% were unwilling to take part. This left me with 18 completed questionnaires, split equally over service and manufacturing industries.

To conduct my analysis I first **identified the main categories** of environmental disclosure methods and issues that the majority of the companies portrayed. I then **formed questions** from these categories, seen in table 6.1, which I used for testing. These were answered in a basic 'yes' or 'no' manner but supplemented with detailed information within the appendices. I only based observations upon the companies I was studying and so they became each others benchmarks for my comments.

Points to note

6.2   Some matters to note – from the words in the text highlighted in **bold**.

(a)   The research had a purpose or aim.

(b)   The method was developed from the aim.

(c)   The author is concerned about the reliability of the data.

(d)   The author described the analysis done.

(e)   The questionnaire required quite a lot of work in designing and getting them completed.

6.3   Also, note that primary research can be **quantitative** and **qualitative**.

Sampling

6.4   In most practical situations the population will be too large to carry out a complete survey and only a sample will be examined. Your research project is not necessarily a statistical market research exercise but your sample should be **meaningful in terms of the Project objective** – which could be to suggest further research.

The choice of a sample

6.5   If your project **does aim at statistical meaningfulness**, one of the most important requirements of sample data is that they should be **complete**. Sampling methods fall into three main groups.

- Random sampling
- Quasi-random sampling
- Non-random sampling

Random sampling

6.6   **To ensure that the sample selected is free from bias, random sampling must be used. Inferences about the population being sampled can then be made validly.**

6.7   **A simple random sample is a sample selected in such a way that every item in the population has an equal chance of being included.**

6.8   For example, if you wanted to take a random sample of library books, it would not be good enough to pick them off the shelves, even if you picked them at random. This is because the books which were out on loan would stand no chance of being chosen. You would either have to make sure that all the books were on the shelves before taking your sample, or find some other way of sampling (for example, using the library index cards).

Sampling frames

6.9   If random sampling is used then it is necessary to construct a **sampling frame**. A **sampling frame** is a numbered list of all items in a population.

Once a numbered list of all items in the population has been made, it is easy to select a random sample, simply by generating a list of random numbers.

6.10 For instance, if you wanted to select a random sample of companies in any industry, it would be useful to have a list of names:

0   Ashford
1   Da Costa
2   WM Print

...

Now the numbers 0, 1, 2 and so on can be used to select the random sample. It is normal to start the numbering at 0, so that when 0 appears in a list of random numbers it can be used.

6.11   A sampling frame should have the following characteristics.

- **Completeness**. Are all members of the population included on the list?
- **Accuracy**. Is the information correct?
- **Adequacy**. Does it cover the entire population?
- **Up to dateness**. Is the list up to date?
- **Convenience**. Is the sampling frame readily accessible?
- **Non-duplication**. Does each member of the population appear on the list only once?

6.12   Drawbacks of random sampling

(a)   Selected items are subject to the full range of variation inherent in the population.
(b)   An unrepresentative sample may result.
(c)   An adequate sampling frame might not exist.
(d)   The numbering of the population might be laborious.
(e)   It might be difficult to obtain the data if the selected items cover a wide area.
(f)   It might be costly to obtain the data if the selected items cover a wide area.

Quasi-random sampling

6.13   When it is too difficult or too costly to obtain a random sample, **quasi-random sampling** is necessary. **Quasi-random sampling** is a sampling method which provides a good approximation to random sampling. As with random sampling, it necessitates the existence of a sampling frame. The main methods of quasi-random sampling are as follows.

- Systematic sampling
- Stratified sampling
- Multistage sampling

6.14   Systematic sampling

Systematic sampling is a sampling method which works by selecting every nth item after a random start. If it were decided to select a sample of 20 from a population of 800, then every 40th ($800 \div 20$) item after a random start in the first 40 should be selected. The starting point could be found using the lottery method or random number tables. If (say) 23 was chosen, then the sample would include the 23rd, 63rd, 103rd, 143rd ... 783rd items. The gap of 40 is known as the **sampling interval**. This approach may be familiar to you from audit work, if a sample of invoices is selected for checking.

6.15   Stratified sampling

Stratified sampling is a method of sampling which involves dividing the population into strata or categories. Random samples are then taken from each stratum or category.

In many situations, stratified sampling is the best method of choosing a sample. Stratified sampling is best demonstrated by means of an example.

Example

In **Project Topic 13: An analysis of future personnel requirements under conditions of change**, you are carrying out an employee attitude survey on their training needs. The firm you work for is a large retail firm with many small outlets distributed all over the country. The Human Resource Manager says that 5% of the total employees are senior executive or professional staff, 30% are managerial and supervisory staff and the remaining 65% work as sales assistants. If a sample of 200 was required:

Senior executives 5% × 200 =	10
Managerial and supervisory 30% × 200 =	60
Sales assistants 65% × 200 =	130
	200

You would then select 10 executives at random, and so on.

6.16 The main **disadvantage** of stratification is that it requires **prior knowledge of each item in the population**.

6.17 **Multistage sampling** is a non-random sampling method which involves dividing the population into a number of sub-populations and then selecting a small sample of these sub-populations at random. Each sub-population is then divided further, and then a small sample is again selected at random. This process is repeated as many times as is necessary.

Example

You are doing **Project Topic 13: An analysis of personnel requirements under conditions of change**. You work for a large retail organisation with many branches.

A survey of spending habits is being planned to cover the whole of your firm.

The country is divided into a number of regions and a small sample of these is selected at random. Each of the regions selected is subdivided into smaller units. This process is repeated as many times as necessary and finally, a random sample of the relevant employees working in each of the smallest units is taken. A fair approximation to a random sample can be obtained.

Thus, we might choose a random sample of four regions, and from each of these areas, select a random sample of ten outlets. From each outlet, a random sample of five people might be selected so that the total sample size is 4 × 510 × 5 = 200 people.

Non-random sampling

6.18 When a sampling frame cannot be established, **non-random sampling** is necessary. There are two main methods of non-random sampling.

- Quota sampling
- Cluster sampling

6.19 **Quota sampling.** In **quota sampling**, randomness is forfeited in the interests of cheapness and administrative simplicity. Investigators are told to interview all the people they meet up to a certain quota. For example, going back to paragraph 6.15, you would not select a random sample but would interview the first people you came across. (The sample would not be random because not all the population in each unit has an equal chance of being selected.)

6.20 **Cluster sampling** is a non-random sampling method that involves selecting one definable subsection of the population as the sample, that subsection assumed to be representative of the population in question.

6.21 For example, all the employees of one region might be taken as a cluster sample of all employees in the company.

6.22 **Advantages** of cluster sampling

- It is a good alternative to multistage sampling if a satisfactory sampling frame does not exist.

- It is inexpensive to operate.

6.23 The main **disadvantage** of cluster sampling is the potential for considerable bias.

7 SURVEYS AND QUESTIONNAIRES

7.1 The data used in a statistical survey, whether variables or attributes, can be either **primary data** or **secondary data**.

7.2 Primary and secondary data both have their advantages and limitations.

Primary data	Secondary data
Advantage	**Advantage**
The investigator knows where the data came from and is aware of any inadequacies or limitations in the data.	Cheaply available.
Disadvantage	**Disadvantages**
It is expensive to collect primary data.	The investigator did not collect the data and is therefore unaware of any inadequacies or limitations in the data.

Survey methods of collecting data

7.3 There are two basic methods of collecting primary data from individuals.

(a) They can be **asked questions.**
(b) **Their behaviour can be observed**.

This involves the collection of data using **surveys**, for example structured interviews, postal questionnaires or, possibly, e-mailed questionnaires.

Errors in survey methods of collecting data

7.4 There are three main types of error that can appear in survey methods of collecting data.

(a) **Sampling error**. It is quite usual for a sample of the population to be surveyed, rather than the entire population. If the sample surveyed is **not representative** of the population from which it is drawn, a sampling error will arise.

(b) **Response error** arises because respondents are either **unable** or **unwilling** to **respond**.

Interviews

7.5 There are basically two types of interview that can be used to collect quantitative data, the **personal (face to face) interview** and the **telephone interview**.

Advantages of personal interviews

7.6 (a) The interviewer is able to **reduce respondent anxiety** and **allay potential embarrassment**, thereby increasing the response rate and decreasing the potential for error.

(b) The routing ('if yes go to question 7, if no go to question 10') of questions is made easier due to the experience of the interviewer.

(c) Interviewers can ask, within narrow limits, for a respondent's answer to be clarified.

(d) The questions can be given in a **fixed order** with a **fixed wording** and the answers can be recorded in a **standard manner**. If there is more than one interviewer involved in the survey this will reduce variability.

(e) **Standardised questions** and ways of recording the responses mean that less skilled interviewers may be used, thereby reducing the cost of the survey.

(f) **Pictures, signs** and **objects** can be used.

Disadvantages of personal interviews

7.7 (a) They can be **time consuming**.

(b) They can be **costly** to complete.

(c) Questionnaires can be **difficult to design**.

(d) Questions must often be kept relatively simple, thus restricting the depth of data collected.

(e) Questions must normally be **closed** because of the difficulties of recording answers to open questions.

(f) Interviewers cannot probe vague or ambiguous replies.

Arranging interviews and meetings

7.8 (a) If the matter is at all sensitive, you may need to get authorisation from a senior member of the organisation.

(b) If you are interviewing people you do not know, give them advance warning.

(c) **Do not just turn up**. Always book a time in advance. If the interviewee works in an open plan office, you may want to **book a place**. (You can book meetings via e-mail or use Microsoft Outlook.)

Telephone surveys

7.9 *Advantages*

(a) The response is **rapid**.

(b) There is a **standard sampling frame** – the **telephone directory**, which can be systematically or randomly sampled.

(c) A **wide geographical area** can be covered fairly cheaply.

(d) It may be **easier to ask sensitive or embarrassing questions**.

(e) In the Research and Analysis Project, you may need to let people know in advance that you are going to call them.

7.10 **Disadvantages**

(a) A **biased sample** may result from the fact that a large proportion (about 10%) of people do not have telephones (representing certain portions of the population such as old people or students) and many of those who do are ex-directory.

(b) It is **not possible to use 'showcards'** or pictures.

(c) The **refusal rate is much higher** than with face-to-face interviews, and the interview often cut short.

(d) It is **not possible to see the interviewee's expressions** or to develop the rapport that is possible with personal interviews.

(e) The interview **must be short**.

Postal surveys

7.11 We are using the term 'postal' survey to cover all methods in which the questionnaire is given to the respondent and returned to the investigator without personal contact. Such questionnaires could be posted but might also be left in pigeonholes or on desks.

7.12 Postal questionnaires have the following **advantages** over personal interviews.

(a) The **cost per person** is likely **to be less**, so more people can be sampled, and central control is facilitated.

(b) It is usually possible to **ask more questions** because the people completing the forms (the respondents) can do so in their own time.

(c) **All respondents are presented with questions in the same way**. There is no opportunity for an interviewer to influence responses (interviewer bias) or to misrecord them.

(d) It may be **easier to ask personal or embarrassing questions** in a postal questionnaire than in a personal interview.

(e) Respondents **may need to look up information for the questionnaire**. This will be easier if the questionnaire is sent to their homes or places of work.

E-mail survey

7.13 Surveys can be done via e-mail, even though 'spamming' people with unwanted email is not likely to win you any friends.

(a) If you are conducting an e-mail survey at work, you can **attach** a document or spreadsheet to the email, asking the respondent to open the document or spreadsheet, complete it, save it and return.

(b) You may be able to ask your questions in the e-mail itself, asking the respondent to reply and return the e-mail.

Quantitative research questionnaire design

It is worth noting that the external examiner has commented that 'candidates who used questionnaires in their analysis generally did quite well, as they had a ready source of data for their analysis'.

Designing the questionnaire

7.14 **The sampling process can be an important contributor to the quality and value of the survey process.** Where survey findings are technically suspect, this is most commonly because there are **flaws in the design of the questionnaire.**

7.15 **Core principles of questionnaire design**

- **Decide precisely what information** you wish to obtain from each individual question

- **Ensure that the question gives you this information** as precisely as possible

- Ensure that there is **no possibility of misunderstanding or ambiguity** about the question or its answer

7.16 **Common pitfalls**

(a) **Ambiguity and uncertainty about language or terminology.** Don't assume people will understand what you mean.

(b) **Lack of clarity about the information required.** You should always stop and ask yourself some fundamental questions. Why am I asking this question? What is it intended to find out? What exactly do I want to know? **Will this question give me the information I need?** These questions are often not explicitly addressed, with the result that the wrong question (or only part of the right question) is asked. In an employee survey, for example, the questionnaire could ask:

> Which of the following do you feel are barriers to your undertaking further training or development in your own time?
>
> - Lack of spare time
> - Lack of motivation
> - Personal/domestic commitments
> - Cost

The respondents could tick most **if not all** of these options. The survey designer really wanted to ask not **whether** these factors were seen as barriers, but **which** were the most significant barriers and **how** significant they were.

(c) **Conflation of multiple questions into one.** In a survey, for example, respondents could be asked, 'How often does your workgroup meet to discuss performance, quality and safety issues?' The assumption behind this question – is that managers called workgroups together to discuss all three of these issues. Some workgroups may not meet at all, some may meet infrequently and some could meet relatively often but may only discuss performance issues.

(d) **Making unjustified assumptions.** For example, 'In reviewing your performance, which of the following methods does your manager use?' The assumption here, of course, is that the manager reviews the respondent's performance at all.

Leading questions

7.17 The question may still provide misleading data if it appears to be **leading the respondent towards a particular answer.** People may still feel **uncertain** about its outcomes and they may still feel **suspicious of your motives** for conducting it. In such cases, some may feel very keen to give the 'right' answer – the answer that they believe you or the organisation would like to hear.

'Agree/disagree' and other formats

7.18 This problem occurs most commonly when respondents are asked to **indicate their level of agreement or disagreement** with a particular statement. It is prudent, therefore, to include a **mixture of positive and negative statements**, which do not suggest any intrinsic preference.

7.19 In some cases, the choice of statement can **significantly undermine the value of the information obtained**. 'The quality of work in my department is generally excellent'. If the respondent agrees with this statement the meaning was clear – that he or she thought the quality of work in the department was generally excellent. However, if the respondent **disagreed** with the statement, the meaning was less clear. Did they think the quality was moderate or even poor?

7.20 In general, the questions in a written questionnaire should be of the **multiple choice** type, so providing the basis for quantitative analysis.

7.21 **Survey questions** can be divided into two broad categories; those **exploring attitudes** or opinions and those **seeking some form of factual information**.

    (a) In the former category would generally fall, for example, the 'agree/disagree' format, such as 'Safety is always a paramount concern for the organisation. Do you:

- Agree strongly?
- Agree slightly?
- Disagree slightly?
- Disagree strongly'?

    (b) In the latter category might fall questions about, say, the frequency of workgroup meetings or about recent experience of training.

7.22 Respondents **are commonly reluctant to give extreme responses** and prefer to hover around the middle ground. If you have an odd number of items in your scale, you may find that respondents disproportionately opt for the neutral option. There are benefits in forcing respondents off the fence by **offering only an even number of options**, so that the respondent has to choose between, say, 'agree slightly' and 'disagree slightly'. In this way, you gain a clearer perspective on the **true direction of opinion**.

7.23 Where you are asking to identify preferences from among a number of options, you may ask respondents to **rank the options against a given criterion**, such as 'Which of the following do you think are the most important contributors to high workgroup performance? (Please rank in order of importance.)'

    (a) If you use this format, you should remember to indicate **how the ranking should be applied**. Is number 1 the **most** or the **least** important factor? Ranking questions can seem **confusing** to respondents and are best used sparingly. In any cases, it is rarely worth asking respondents to rank more than the first three or four items. Beyond that, rankings usually become fairly arbitrary.

    (b) A more straightforward approach is to ask respondents simply to **select one item** – 'Which of the following do you think is the single most important contributor to high workgroup performance? (Please tick one only.)' Although slightly less detailed, this question is easier both to complete and to analyse.

7.24 In collecting **factual** information, you may again wish to **use scales** where the required information lies on a continuum. For example, 'How many days have you spent training in the past 12 months? Fewer than 3 days/4 – 6 days/6 – 10 days/more than 10 days.'

7.25 Where you are exploring more discrete items of information, you may simply ask respondents to **select the most relevant items**. For example, you might ask, 'Which of the following types of training have you undertaken in the last year? (Please tick any that apply.)' In this case, you are not asking respondents to evaluate the options against one another, but simply to make a choice between those that are and those that are not significant. This format can also be applied in cases of **opinions and attitudes**.

Building the questionnaire

7.26 The overall structure of the questionnaire can take a number of forms, depending on the purpose and nature of the survey. As a general rule, when you are exploring a given topic, you should aim to be as systematic as possible in **progressing from the general to the specific**.

(a) **Context.** Typically, your initial aim should be to gain an understanding of the **broad context** within which opinions are held.

(b) You can then progress to gaining an understanding of the **nature and strength of opinion** in a given area.

(c) **Detail.** Finally, you can move, step by step, towards identifying the **detail that underpins these**.

Context

7.27 To illustrate this, let us take an example – a questionnaire designed to explore the issues of reward and recognition. The questionnaire might begin, for example, by asking a question about perceptions of reward and recognition in the organisation generally.

> How satisfied are you with the level of recognition and reward you receive for your achievements at work?
>
> - Very satisfied
> - Fairly satisfied
> - Fairly dissatisfied
> - Very dissatisfied?

7.28 The **responses** to this question will help provide you with a **context** within which you can interpret the more detailed information you will obtain from subsequent questions.

Perceptions

7.29 Having defined the broad organisational context, you can begin to focus more precisely on the detail of the specific topic. The next question might be:

> If you feel that your work achievements are recognised, what form does this recognition generally take? (Please tick any that apply.)
>
> - Increased basic pay
> - Bonus payment
> - Other financial reward
> - Promotion
> - Verbal congratulations
> - Non-financial reward
> - Other (please specify)

7.30 This will provide you with an understanding of the **current perceptions of the topic –** what respondents' perceptions of the rewards they typically receive for work achievements are.

7.31 If you are researching your current employer, you may feel **tempted to omit** this kind of 'state of play' question on the basis that **you already know** enough about what happens currently in the organisation. It is easy to assume that **your** perceptions and perspective reflect those of others. But you should not assume this. Someone approaching retirement may have an entirely different view on life from someone just starting work.

Preferences

7.32 Having identified people's perceptions of the current state of play in the specific area, you can then move to the next level of detail and begin to explore, for example, their **preferences** for reward and recognition. You might ask:

> Which of the following forms of recognition for work achievements do you find most motivating? (Please tick one only.)
>
> - Increased basic pay
> - Bonus payment
> - Other financial reward
> - Promotion
> - Verbal congratulations
> - Non-financial reward
> - Other (please specify)

7.33 Mapping these expressed preferences against the current perceived position should indicate very clearly **if or where there is gap between the current and the desired positions.**

Ensuring accurate responses

7.34 This general process of moving from the general to the specific is sometimes known as '**funnelling**'.

(a) It is an important device for **ensuring precision in interpretation.**

(b) It may also help you to provide a meaningful interpretation of responses that may be influenced by extraneous factors, such as **self-interest.**

(c) **The use of broad, contextual questions, however, will help you to interpret such responses** against a range of other issues and concerns. You might, for instance, ask respondents, initially, to rank areas of potential dissatisfaction in order of significance. This will then provide you with a basis on which to evaluate any specific expression of dissatisfaction with the really important issue.

7.35 **Other questionnaire structures** can also be used to **minimise the influence of external factors.** If you are exploring a range of issues, for example, it can be helpful to distribute questions about each respective issue throughout the questionnaire, **rather than bunching them in discrete sections.** This can help reduce what is sometimes known as the 'halo effect', which is when overall positive or negative feelings about a given issue influence responses to individual questions.

Questionnaire length and layout

7.36 There is generally a trade-off between questionnaire length and the level of response. The **longer and more detailed** the questionnaire, the **more likely** you are to encounter **resistance** from potential respondents.

7.37 Despite these caveats, the following crude guidelines for different forms of questionnaire administration may be helpful.

(a) **Cold surveys.** Where the questionnaire is being sent out with no preparation and where respondents have no particular incentive to respond, you should aim for an absolute maximum of 4 sides of paper and no more than 15 to 20 questions (including sub-questions), but in many cases, it will be preferable to aim for just 1 or 2 sides of paper and even fewer questions. The key issue here is likely to be one of presentation. You will want to suggest that the survey is easy to complete and will involve comparatively little of the respondent's time. Therefore, simple, 'user-friendly' layout is likely to be an even more significant issue than the overall length.

(b) **Postal questionnaires.** Where respondents have been briefed and prepared, but are nevertheless expected to complete the questionnaire entirely in their own time, you should generally aim for a questionnaire of some 6 to 8 sides of paper, ideally with no more than 30 to 40 questions. If potential respondents put the questionnaire to one side, the chances are that a substantial proportion will not get around to completing it at all.

(c) **Questionnaires completed in work time.** Where the **organisation** allocates some work time to completing the questionnaire, you can generally risk a rather longer questionnaire – probably up to 10 to 12 pages and 50 to 60 questions.

7.38 Some other general points about questionnaire design are also worth stressing. First, make sure that you provide **clear instructions** throughout, indicating precisely how the questionnaire should be completed. These should be simply phrased and as concise as possible. It is also a good idea to **provide some examples** of specific question types and how they should be completed. As always, one good example is worth several dozen words of explanation.

Laying out the questionnaire

7.39 (a) If respondents have to complete the questionnaire themselves, it must be approachable and as short as possible. Consider the use of **lines, boxes, different type faces and print sizes and small pictures**. Use plenty of space.

(b) Consider the use of **tick boxes**. Is it clear where ticks go or how to respond in each case? For analysis, will it be easy to transfer responses from the forms to a summary sheet or a computer? Consider pre-coding the answers.

(c) Explain the **purpose of the survey** at the beginning of the questionnaire and where possible guarantee confidentiality. Emphasise the date by which it must be returned.

(d) At the end of the questionnaire, **thank the respondent** and make it clear what they should do with the completed questionnaire.

Pilot tests

7.40 It is vital to **pilot test questionnaires** since mistakes, ambiguities and embarrassments in a questionnaire can be expensive once the main data collection phase has been entered. Do

not send any questionnaire out 'cold' without getting someone else to work through it in detail.

The Likert scale

7.41 This approach can be summarised in three steps – (a), (b) and (c).

(a) A list of statements is prepared about the topic being researched, and a test group of respondents is asked to rate each statement on a scale from strong agreement to strong disagreement.

(b) A numerical value is given to each response:

5 Strongly agree
4 Agree
3 Don't know
2 Disagree
1 Strongly disagree

(c) Each respondent's scores for all the statements are added up to give a total score for the topic, which may reflect overall positive or negative attitudes: responses to individual statements can also be analysed to get more meaningful information about the pattern of responses.

7.42 Likert scales are simple to prepare and administer. You may have been asked to complete such an inventory test over the telephone, or seen one in a magazine. However, again you should be aware that scale values have no absolute meaning, and are limited in their statistical uses, on an 'interval' scale.

7.43 An example of a questionnaire using a variety of techniques can be found on the next page.

Part B: The Research and Analysis Project

Name	Description	Example

CLOSED-END QUESTIONS

Dichotomous — A question with two possible answers.

'In arranging this trip, did you personally phone British Airways?'

Yes ☐   No ☐

Multiple choice — A question with three or more answers.

'With whom are you travelling on this flight?'

No one	☐	Children only	☐
Spouse	☐	Business associates/	
Spouse and		friends/relatives	☐
children	☐	An organised tour group	☐

Likert scale — A statement with which the respondent shows the amount of agreement/disagreement.

'Small airlines generally give better service

Strongly disagree 1	Disagree 2	Neither agree nor disagree 3	Agree 4	Strongly agree 5
☐	☐	☐	☐	☐

Semantic differential — A scale connecting two bipolar words, where the respondent selects the point that represents his or her opinion.

British Airways

Large ------------------- Small
Experienced ------------ Inexperienced
Modern   Old-fashioned

Importance scale — A scale that rates the importance of some attribute.

Extremely important 1	Very important 2	Somewhat important 3	Not very important 4	Not at all important 5
☐	☐	☐	☐	☐

Rating scale — A scale that rates some attribute from 'poor' to 'excellent'.

Excellent	Very good	Good	Fair	Poor

Intention-to-buy scale — A scale that describes the respondent's intention to buy.

'If an inflight telephone was available on a long flight, I would'

Definitely buy 1	Probably buy 2	Not sure 3	Probably not buy 4	Definitely not buy 5
☐	☐	☐	☐	☐

OPEN-END QUESTIONS

Completely unstructured — A question that respondents can answer in an almost unlimited number of ways.

'What is your opinion of British Airways?'

Word association — Words are presented, one at a time, and respondents mention the first word that comes to mind.

'What is the first word that comes to mind when you hear the following'
Airline _____
British _____
Travel _____

Sentence completion — An incomplete sentence is presented and respondents complete the sentence.

'When I choose an airline, the most important consideration in my decision is _____ '

Story completion — An incomplete story is presented, and respondents are asked to complete it.

'I flew B.A. a few days ago. I noticed that the exterior and interior of the plane had bright colours. This aroused in me the following thoughts and feelings.' Now complete the story.

Picture completion — A picture of two characters is presented, with one making a statement. Respondents are asked to identify with the other and fill in the empty balloon.

The inflight entertainment's good

Thematic Apperception Test (TAT) — A picture is presented and respondents are asked to make up a story about what they think is happening or may happen in the picture.

The Semantic Differential scale

7.44 (a) Scales are constructed on a number of **'dimensions'** – pairs of opposite attributes or qualities, expressed as adjectives – valued on a continuum from +3 to –3.

Profile of Car Model X

	+3	+2	+1	0	-1	-2	-3	
Modern								Old-fashioned
Fast								Slow
Attractive								Unattractive
Powerful								Weak
Responsive								Unresponsive
Glamorous								Ordinary

(b) Respondents are asked to **select the position of the object** being researched (in this case the car) on each continuum, according to the degree to which they think the adjective describes the object. (If the car is very powerful but not terribly responsive, say, it might rate +3 on the powerful-weak dimension, and +1 on the responsive-unresponsive scale.)

(c) A **'profile'** is thus built up by each respondent.

7.45 The main problem with Semantic Differential scales is the **subjectivity attached to language**. Words are mean different things to different people. (The word 'old-fashioned' in our car profile above may mean 'old-hat' to some and 'classic' to others.)

7.46 The other problem of measuring responses to, and perceptions of, different attributes of the same thing is that **one attribute can influence our perception of other attributes** and some attributes bring clusters of other assumed attributes with them (stereotypes). Think, for example, about our model X car: if it looks sleek and attractive, we may perceive it as a fast car – whether it is or not – and if we think of old-fashioned cars as glamorous (because of stereotypes of 'classic' cars and the people who drive them) we might distort our glamour rating.

Example

Here is an example from an unpublished undergraduate dissertation about how firms report on the environment.

ENVIRONMENTAL QUESTIONNAIRE

> ### Environmental questionnaire
>
> **Please answer as many questions as applicable ticking the relevant boxes. All answers will be treated as anonymous.**
>
> **Thank you**
>
> Q1. Is your company predominantly operating in a service or manufacturing industry?
>
> Service ....
> Manufacturing ....
>
> Q2. What is your company's average annual turnover?
>
> Service £..........
>
> Q3. (a) Does your company have a separate environmental department or manager?
>
> • Environmental department ....
> • Environmental manager ....
> • Neither ....

(b) If you do have an environmental department or manager how long has this been

- Length of time ....

Q4. Does your company have separate environmental policy?

- Yes ....
- No ....

If Yes, are all employees made aware of this?
- Yes ....
- No ....
Some are, some are not ....

Q5. Does your company utilise any of the following environmental initiatives? (Please tick all that are applicable.)

- Energy conservation ....
- Control of emissions ....
- Recycling ....
- Reusing ....
- Buying from environmentally friendly suppliers ....
- Monitoring and controlling waste ....
- Using recycled stationery ....
- Tree Planting ....
- Other ....
Please state...

Q6. Is your company aware of any environmental impacts it may have?

- Yes – and we are controlling them ....
- Yes – and we are investigating them ....
- Yes – but other organisational matters are our priority at the moment ....
- No – we do not affect our environment ....
- No ....
Don't know ....

Q7. Does your company publish any environmental information:

- Yes ....
- No (if no go to question 12) ....

Q8. If environmental information is published, what was the motivation behind it?

- Shareholder pressure ....
- Government legislation ....
- Competitive advantage ....
- Concern for the environment ....
- Other ....
Please state ....

Q9. Who is your intended audience for published environmental information?

- Shareholders ....
- Government ....
- Employees ....
- Competitors ....
- Suppliers ....
- General public ....
- Other
Please state ....

Q10. Is this published information:

- Included in your Annual Report? ....
- Published separately but distributed at the same time as your
  Annual Report? ....
- Distributed at a time other than that when annual Report
  is published? ....

Q11. What form does this published information take?

- Narrative disclosure ....
- Statistical indicators ....
- Mixture of narrative and statistical ....
- Financial data ....
- Environmental achievements ....
- Environmental targets ....

Q12. Does your company have separate environmental information that it uses for internal management decisions?

- Yes ....
- No – we use the published environmental data ....
- No – we do not incorporate environmental data in management
  decisions ....

Q13. If you do have environmental information is this part of an environmental management system?

- Yes ....
- No ....

If no, are there any plans to introduce such a system?

- Yes ....
- No ....

Q14. Does your company believe environmental impacts are going to be an increasing business issue as we approach and enter the millennium?

- Yes ....
- No ....

Thank you very much for your time and help.
Please return completed questionnaires in the stamped addressed envelope provided.

8 QUALITATIVE RESEARCH

Qualitative research is another process which aims to collect primary data. Its main methods are the open-ended interview, whether this be a depth interview (one-to-one) or a group discussion (focus group), and projective techniques. The form of the data collected is narrative rather than isolated statements reduceable to numbers. **Its main purpose is to understand people's behaviour and perceptions rather than to measure them.**

8.1 The key to qualitative research is to allow the respondents to say what they feel and think in response to flexible, 'prompting' questioning, rather than to give their responses to set questions and often set answers in a questionnaire.

Unstructured interviews

8.2 Neither interviewer or respondent is bound by the structure of a questionnaire in an **unstructured interview**. Interviewers may have a checklist of topics to cover in questioning, but they are free to word such questions as they wish. The order in which questions are covered may also be varied. This will allow the respondent to control the data flow and for the interviewer to explore more thoroughly particular views of the respondent and why they are held. Unstructured interviews are a very useful way of capturing data which is qualitative in nature. Such interviews may also provide the researcher with relevant questions which could be put to a wider audience of respondents using structured or semi-structured interview techniques, especially if quantitative data is required.

Depth interviews

8.3 Motivational research often uses the psychoanalytic method of **depth interviews**. The pattern of questioning should assist the respondent to explore deeper levels of thought. Motives and explanations of behaviour often lie well **below the surface**. It is a **time-consuming** and **expensive** process. Taped interviews and analysis of transcripts are often used. A single individual or a small team may conduct depth interviewing. Depth interviews may have fewer than ten respondents.

8.4 **Strengths of depth interviews**

   (a) **Longitudinal information** (such as information on decision-making processes) can be gathered from one respondent at a time, thereby aiding clarity of interpretation and analysis.

   (b) Intimate and **personal material** can be more easily accessed and discussed.

   (c) Respondents are **less likely to confine themselves** simply to reiterating socially acceptable attitudes.

8.5 **Disadvantages**

   (a) They are **time consuming** to conduct and to analyse. **Each depth interview needs to be written up shortly afterwards and reflected on.** If each interview lasts between one and two hours, a maximum of two per day is often all that is possible.

   (b) They are more **costly** than group discussions.

   (c) There is a temptation to begin treating depth interviews as if they were simply another form of questionnaire survey, thinking in terms of quantitative questions like 'how many' rather than qualitative issues like 'how', 'why' or 'what'.

   (d) A certain amount of expertise is needed in depth interviews.

8.6 In a depth interview the key line of communication is between the interviewer and the respondent. They have an **open-ended conversation**, not constrained by a formal questionnaire, and the qualitative data are captured as narrative by means of an audio or video tape.

Focus groups

8.7 **Focus groups** are useful in providing the researcher with **qualitative data**. Qualitative data can often provide greater insight than quantitative data and does not lend itself to the simple application of standard statistical methods.

8.8 Focus groups usually consist of 8 to 10 respondents and an interviewer taking the role of group moderator. The group moderator introduces topics for discussion and intervenes as necessary to encourage respondents or to direct discussions if they threaten to wander too far off the point. The moderator will also need to control any powerful personalities and prevent them from dominating the group.

8.9 Group discussions may be **audio or video tape recorded** for later analysis and interpretation. The researcher must be careful not to generalise too much from such small scale qualitative research. **Group discussion is very dependent on the skill of the group moderator.** It is inexpensive to conduct, it can be done quickly and it can provide useful, timely, qualitative data.

8.10 Focus groups are often used at the early stage of research to get a feel for the subject matter under discussion and to create possibilities for more structured research. Four to eight groups may be assembled and each group interviewed for one, two or three hours.

8.11 **Advantages of focus groups**

(a) The group environment with 'everybody in the same boat' can be **less intimidating** than other techniques of research which rely on one-to-one contact (such as depth interviews).

(b) What respondents say in a group often **sparks off experiences** or ideas on the part of others.

(c) **Differences between consumers** are highlighted, making it possible to understand a range of attitudes in a short space of time.

(d) It is **easier to observe groups** and there is more to observe simply because of the intricate behaviour patterns within a collection of people.

(e) **Social and cultural influences** are highlighted.

(f) Groups provide a **social context** that is a 'hot-house' reflection of the real world.

(g) Groups are **cheaper and faster** than depth interviews.

8.12 **Disadvantages of focus groups**

(a) Group processes may **inhibit some people from making a full contribution** and may encourage others to become exhibitionistic.

(b) Group processes **may stall** to the point where they cannot be retrieved by the moderator.

(c) Some groups may **take a life of their own,** so that what is said has validity only in the short-lived context of the group.

(d) It is not usually possible to identify **which group members said what,** unless the proceedings have been video recorded.

(e) It is **not easy to find a common time** when all can participate.

8.13 When planning qualitative research using focus groups, a number of factors need to be considered.

Type	Comment
Type of group	A standard group is of 7-9 respondents, but other types may also be used.
Membership	Who takes part in the discussion depends on who the researcher wants to talk to (users or non-users, for instance) and whether they all need to be similar (homogenous).
Number of groups	Having more than 12 groups in a research project would be very unusual, mainly because nothing new would come out of a thirteenth one!
Recruitment	Usually on the basis of a quota sample: respondents are screened by a short questionnaire to see whether they are suitable. In order to persuade them to join in, the members are usually given an incentive plus expenses.
Discussion topics	These will be decided by the researcher with regard to the purpose of the group discussion, that is the data that are required. There should be a number of topics since the interviewer needs to be able to restart discussion once a topic has been fully discussed.
Involvement	The researcher is asking for a deep level of involvement and commitment.

9 HOW GOOD IS YOUR DATA?

9.1 Once you have done the research you **intended** to do, you should draw your data together and take a hard look at it as a whole, the secondary data and primary data.

9.2 Remember that the Research and Analysis Project is not **deadline driven**, nor is there a syllabus. You will be marked on your ability to do some research, analysis and communication.

9.3 **Ask yourself these questions.**

	Question	Yes/No
1	Have I done all that I set out to do?	
2	Does the data I have obtained give me a chance to conduct an analysis on the lines of the project objective?	
3	If the answer to (1) or (2) is no, have I obtained data by another adequate route?	
4	Is my use of sources sufficient to fulfil the criteria for use of references in the marking scheme for this project?	
5	Have I made sure I have referenced and recorded my data?	
6	ACID TEST Does the data I have collected put me on the right path for fulfilling the project objective?	

10 PLAGIARISM

10.1 As a committed professional, you should not have to read this section.

10.2 Your research project is original work. Do not pretend that others' work is your own – always cite your sources, and give credit where it is due.

10.3 Sadly, some students seem to ignore the strictures against syndication and plagiarism. It is equivalent, perhaps, to cheating in a exam. Academic staff the world over are wise to all the ploys – you will get caught, so don't try. Reproduced below are Oxford Brookes University's guidelines for their own undergraduate students. Take note.

> The University has strict rules to ensure that students' work for assessment is actually the result of their individual effort, skills and knowledge and has not been produced by means that will give an unfair advantage over the students.
>
> **Plagiarism**
>
> Under the University's regulations students must ensure that any work submitted for assessment is genuinely their own and is not plagiarised (borrowed or copied, without specific acknowledgement, or stolen from other published or unpublished work). If you are quoting actual words from a published or unpublished source in the text of your course work, there are correct academic conventions for how you should do this which you must follow. The Library has a good leaflet on the subject and your tutor can also help you. It is not good enough just to list sources in a bibliography at the end of your essay or dissertation if you do not acknowledge the actual quotes in the text. Neither is it acceptable to change some of the words or the order of sentences if, by failing to acknowledge the source properly, you give the impression that it is your own work.

You should also read with care Appendix 4 of the Research and Analysis Project Guidelines, on Cheating, as this helps to explain what actions can be defined as plagiarism and forms of collusion.

The external examiner has commented that cases of plagiarism have been detected in Research and Analysis Projects submitted. In all cases, the project is failed by Oxford Brookes (so you don't get the degree) and disciplinary action is taken by the ACCA which can include being expelled from membership.

Refer back to the guidelines in Chapter 1 for advice on how to avoid plagiarism and for some suggestions of good websites which help you to avoid plagiarising inadvertently. Remember, if you **reference** everything, you cannot be accused of plagiarising another person's work.

Referencing

10.4 It should be obvious from the above that you need to reference your material very thoroughly, given the requirements of the Guidelines. If you are at all uncertain as to how you should reference material, you are strongly advised to try the exercises in the Appendix.

Chapter roundup

- This chapter has covered research.

- The **type of research** you adopt will vary according to the project objective.

- The research you do should be **determined** by the project objective.

- There are many sources of secondary data. You may need to do some primary research also.

- Not all research is looking for statistically accurate information.

Chapter 7

ANALYSIS

Chapter topic list

1   Analysing data in the light of the project objective

2   Choosing analytical tools

3   Looking at the data

4   Organising the data

5   Modelling the data

Introduction

Once you have obtained the data through your research programme, you will then need to analyse this in order to draw conclusions from it. The type of analysis you will do will be determined by the project objective – as we have seen some project topics are more descriptive and exploratory than others.

As the Research and Analysis Project aims to test your use of IT, it is perhaps appropriate that you use a spreadsheet in your analysis – the precise use of it will depend on what you intend to do – the spreadsheet can also be used to enhance the graphical presentation of your results.

---

1   ANALYSING DATA IN THE LIGHT OF THE PROJECT OBJECTIVE

1.1   As indicated in the previous chapter, the type of information and data you obtain will be determined by the project:

- Topic
- Objective
- Scope, Focus and Context of your data search

1.2   You might have done a mix of quantitative and qualitative research, using a variety of methods.

(a)   You could have conducted a survey of companies or people in an industry by sending out a questionnaire, as we illustrated. This technique is useful even if it is not attempting to select a statistically valid sample – you may be trying to find things out for which statistical analysis is not relevant.

(b)   Interviews can be used to obtain quantitative and qualitative data.

1.3   The previous chapter suggested that you **categorise** the secondary data that you obtain. We will now go on to reviewing its content, as this will form the scope of your analysis.

The CLOM model

1.4 You are likely to succeed in your analysis task if you go about it in a systematic way. Don't just rush into creating a spreadsheet and thinking this will be enough – you may be ignoring other ways of looking at the data. We therefore propose the CLOM framework to **structure your approach to this task.**

The CLOM model

CHOOSE
LOOK
ORGANISE
MODEL

You will do each of these tasks to a greater or lesser extent depending on the project objective.

---

2 CHOOSING ANALTYICAL TOOLS

2.1 One of the steps in the Oxford Brookes University model suggests choosing a theoretical **framework** or ideas with which to review or assess your data.

2.2 Bear in mind that the Research and Analysis Project is testing specific research and communication skills. You should have obtained the theory while studying for your ACCA qualification. However, there is nothing to stop you going above that level, and you would be well advised to read around to demonstrate your research abilities. (Note that you can choose to do the Research and Analysis Project at various points in your studies.)

2.3 A good way of getting to know the theories and ideas you might want to use might be to **read the ACCA's syllabuses.**

2.4 If you wait to do the degree until after you have completed Part 3 of the ACCA's syllabus, you will, through your work on paper 3.3 Performance Management and 3.7 Strategic Financial Management, have plenty to go on at undergraduate level. These papers will be useful particularly for wider issues of business strategy. (Needless to say, the targeted BPP Study Text covers these at an appropriate level.) In fact the ACCA recommend that students only do the project once they have completed the whole of the ACCA qualification as it is only in the Part 3 papers that you acquire some of the business acumen and analytical skills that you will need. However plenty of students who have only reached Part 2 of ACCA have been successful in their projects.

Example

For example, you may choose **Project Topic 5: The identification of the effects of globalisation on an organisation of your choice.** Paper 3.5 Strategic Business Planning and Development covers two relevant theoretical models: Porter's theory of competitive forces and his theory of the competitive advantage of nations.

2.5 If you decide to do the Research and Analysis Project before the remaining papers at Part 3, you still have a lot to go on.

2.6 Below we have listed what we believe to be the most relevant current exam syllabuses to each of the Project Topics. However this depends very much on **your detailed project objective.**

Part B: The Research and Analysis Project

	Project Topic:	Current syllabus	Relevant papers in ACCA old syllabus
1	An analysis of the efficiency and/or effectiveness of a management accounting technique in an organisational setting.	3.3	9
2	An analysis of how the application of technology can contribute to an organisation's efficiency and/or effectiveness.	1.3, 2.1, 3.5	4, 5, 12
3	An examination of the impact of an aspect of existing or impending legislation on an organisation.	1.3, 2.2, 3.5	2, 4, 12
4	An analysis of the impact of e-business on an industry or organisation of your choice.	1.3, 2.1, 3.5, 3.7	3,4,5, 12
5	The identification of the effects of globalisation on an industry of your choice.	1.3	3,4,12,14
6	The identification of key factors or indicators in the motivation of employees in an organisation of your choice.	1.3, 3.5	4,12
7	An analysis of the tax and profit implications of different company entities, changes in status or acquisitions or disposals of company assets.	1.1, 2.2, 2.3, 3.2, 3.3, 3.6	1, 2, 7, 10, 11, 13
8	An analysis of the financial situation of your choice of organisation.	1.1, 2.4, 2.5, 3.3, 3.6, 3.7	1, 8, 9, 10, 13, 14
9	An examination of how to plan, develop and implement an appropriate information system in an organisation.	2.1, 3.4	5, 12
10	An analysis of how management accounting techniques are used to support decision-making in organisations.	1.2, 2.4, 3.3, 3.7	3, 8, 9, 14
11	An analysis of the costs and benefits of the internal audit/internal review activities within an organisation of your choice.	2.1, 2.6, 3.3	5, 6, 8, 10
12	An analysis of the effect of any International Accounting Standard on the accounts of any organisation in terms of profitability or financial stability or balance sheet value.	1.1, 2.5, 3.6	Papers 1, 10, 13 (local and international variants) 14
13	An analysis of future personnel requirements under conditions of change (including employee development).	1.3	4, 5, 8, 9, 12
14	An investigation of recent investment decisions by an organisation of your choice and how the use of different methods of risk and uncertainty analysis might affect such decisions.	2.4, 3.3, 3.7	8, 9 , 14
15	An analysis of the role of working capital on the profitability and/or efficiency of an organisation of your choice.	1.2, 2.4, 3.7	3, 8, 14
16	An analysis of the effect of different sources of capital on investment decisions in an organisation of your choice.	2.4, 3.7	8, 14
17	An analysis of the effect of corporate governance on an organisation of your choice.	2.2, 3.3, 3.7	12, 13, 14
18	An examination of how to plan, develop and implement an appropriate PRP system in an organisation.	1.3, 3.5	4, 12
19	An analysis of the business and financial reasons and effects of creating a multinational merger company.	3.5, 3.6, 3.7	13, 14
20	An analysis of the effects of IT failure and contingency plans within an organisation of your choice.	2.1, 3.4	5
21	An analysis of the impact of the Euro on an organisation or industry of your choice.	3.7	13
22	Analyse the marketing mix of your choice of organisation, identifying the key success factors or indicators in the marketing mix and the activities of the organisation.	3.5	12

Other sources

2.7 However, there is no need to restrict yourself to this. Your reading – particularly the **secondary research** you have done – may have included theoretical models and frameworks which you can use to interpret or apply to your data.

3 LOOKING AT THE DATA

3.1 In the Research section, you went into some detail about reviewing your data, as to whether it is suitable to satisfy the project objective. You want to take a **broad overview** of what you have found.

Secondary data

3.2 We suggest that you set up a schedule listing the data down the side with the project objective across the top and noting the analytical work you can do on each.

Example

Let us say that you are doing **Project Topic 8: An analysis of the financial situation of your choice of organisation**. You have focused on the financial situation of a mobile phone company which has recently spent a significant amount of money in bidding for a licence to run 'third generation' **mobile phone** services in the UK.

Your **project objective** is a review of the financial position of X plc to assess the impact of licence expenditure on the financial position of the company, with regard to reported and forecast profits and the company's investment decisions.

All your information has come from the public domain – you do not have privileged access to the firm's accounts and plans. When you have contacted the firm, you have been given copies of marketing literature and press releases.

This is what you may have obtained.

Project objective: assess impact of licence expenditure on X plc's financial position with regard to forecast profits and the company's investment decisions	
Item	**What does it tell me? How can I use it?**
Published financial statements for the past three years of the firm and its competitors. You have obtained these by writing to the firms concerned (note that financial statements can also often be downloaded from the company's website).	• **Source data:** trends in financial position • **Accounts:** relevant ratios can be calculated • **Key issues** 'before and after' comparisons • **Chairman's report:** contains operational information and assumptions for the future growth and development of the business • **Segmental reporting**
Press releases by X plc and its competitors justifying the expenditure on the licence	• **Public justification** as to why investment decisions were taken; may be supported by estimates of future demand
A special supplement from the *Economist* about the mobile telecommunications industry	A general contextual study written by expert journalists. Can be used to provide a framework for X plc in the light of other companies. A useful 'reality check'.
Downloads from the company's website and that of its competitors	

Item	What does it tell me? How can I use it?
Current consumer advertising material regarding wireless application protocol (WAP) phones	What is currently promised
Relevant BPP Study Texts dealing with ratio analysis and decision making	Provide analytical tools to be applied to any company
An article from Student Accountant about decision making	Analytical tools to be applied to any company
A report by Oftel (the UK's regulatory body for the telecommunications industry) on Consumers' Use of Mobile Telephony, downloaded from Oftel's website.	Contextual study about the industry. Current consumer usage and concerns. Could be used to assess X plc's statements about its strategy

You need to **integrate** these items of data, a mix of quantitative and qualitative data. Hence, you can apply ratio analysis techniques in the BPP Study Text to the financial statements. You can use the Oftel study to assess the realism of the forecasts.

You may find you need more information than that suggested above.

Example

Here is an example from an unpublished undergraduate dissertation into environmental reporting by companies, cited in the last chapter.

ANALYSIS OF COMPANY ENVIRONMENTAL INFORMATION
AVAILABLE TO EXTERNAL PARTIES

A PLC

THE ENVIRONMENTAL INFORMATION AVAILABLE	
WHAT ENVIRONMENTAL INFORMATION WAS RECEIVED IN ADDITION TO THE FINANCIAL ANNUAL REPORTS AND ACCOUNTS?	A joint Health, Safety and Environment Report 1997.
THE FINANCIAL ANNUAL REPORT AND ACCOUNTS	
ANY ENVIRONMENTAL INFORMATION GIVEN IN FINANCIAL ANNUAL REPORT AND ACCOUNTS?	Environmental costs are 'considered to be an ordinary part of business and as such these amounts are not accounted for separately'. Estimates of environmental costs and liabilities are given. Notes to the accounts give policies regarding environmental expenditure recognition and measurement. Chairman's foreword; 'Shell companies are increasingly working with community and environmental groups'.
THE ADDITIONAL ENVIRONMENTAL INFORMATION	
NARRATIVE ENVIRONMENTAL INFORMATION?	Detailed on environmental issues such as sustainable development and renewable resources along with sections entitled 'Shell's view' – although lengthy and slightly shallow.
VISUAL CHART ENVIRONMENTAL INFORMATION?	Seven pages of performance charts with both direct and relative data concerning emissions etc, together with a commentary.
ENVIRONMENTAL TARGETS?	Projections of performance are given but not specific targets.
ENVIRONMENTAL POLICY?	
ENVIRONMENTAL DATA EXTERNALLY VERIFIED?	Yes, by their independent auditors.
OTHER COMMENTS?	General commitment statements. Glossary of terms included.

Primary data

3.3   Your data collection exercise may include a survey or records of interviews or conversations. You should do a brief summary of this to cover what it should tell you, as you will want to do further analysis. (Numerical analysis is still useful even if it not statistically perfect.)

Data health check

3.4   It is worth your while carrying out a health check on some of the data obtained, particularly secondary data.

Is the data up to date?	
Who is the data intended for?	
Why has the data been produced and what are the interests of the producer of the data?	
What does the data leave out?	

3.5   If this is **too** specific, use the following guidelines.

Guideline	Comment
Common sense	Clearly data which is 'dated', which emanates from dubious sources or which is based on unrepresentative samples should be treated with caution.
Statistical approaches	There are a variety of sampling methods for survey data as already described, which are appropriate to different situations. All of them involve some degree of risk (some probability of error). The degree of risk of statistical error can, however, be computed.
Expert judgement	The same data can be interpreted differently by different people The following array – 98.7, 98.6, 98.6, 98.4, 98.1, 98.1- might be regarded by a statistician as a declining trend but to a business manager the figures may represent a very steady state.
The intuitive approach	Some people have a better feel for figures than others and seem able to judge the value and validity of data intuitively. However, this requires specific knowledge and experience.
The questioning approach	Always question the origin and the basis of the data. Recognise that human errors occur when manipulating data, that bias can occur in questionnaire design: ask to see the questionnaire, check the figures. Furthermore, for information released to the public domain, bear in mind that: (a) Governments and political parties tend to be very selective in the data they choose to use (b) Many newspapers follow a 'political' line and are likely to be selective or even biased (c) Most journalists are not trained statisticians and may interpret data incorrectly

4 ORGANISING THE DATA

4.1 Once you have reviewed your data, you should now be in a position to extract information from it. This process can take a variety of forms, depending on the volume and variety of the data collected. The starting point is going to be **organisation**. Key tools are:

- Your **project file** organised in the most suitable way to structure the data to meet the project objective

- A **spreadsheet** perhaps to collect and arrange data you may have collected

- A **photocopier** so that data relevant to different areas of your report can be duplicated, so that you do not have to go back and forth in your files for key results

- **Highlighter pens** to mark up key words and key points

4.2 You will need to organise your data and your analytical work in the light of the objective of the project.

(a) We have drawn on the distinction between structured and unstructured data in an earlier chapter.

(b) Structured data may be primary or secondary, but you need to incorporate it into a model for further analysis.

(c) Unstructured data needs to be organised in your mind so that you can draw lessons from it and relate it to other areas of data.

Example

The data below is taken from an unpublished undergraduate dissertation.

'My approach was successful, indicated by the 73% response rate of which 18% were unwilling to take part (see note below). This left me with 18 completed questionnaires, spilt equally over service and manufacturing industries.

I analysed the data by dividing it into three groups.

- Company's internal environmental background
- Company's environmental information available for external parties
- Environmental information used for internal management decisions

The questions asked were designed to fit these categories enabling linkages and hypotheses between them to be made in answering the original objective of the chapter.

Obviously there are certain limitations such as a lack of knowledge by the respondent or differing interpretations of the questions. This may be improved by using a telephone survey, however, this would be a lengthy process, meaning that I would have to reduce the questionnaire and so may harm data in this way.

Note

A 73% response rate is truly amazing, but may have been achieved by detailed preparation, choice of sample, or pre-arrangement. Do not be surprised if response rates are between 15 – 20%.

4.3 A good place to start is an **example**. Here, the author has written to a number of companies and has obtained data in a **variety of formats**, but wants to extract relevant information for purposes of comparability. This is the start of a thorough review to see how companies report environmental data.

Example

Analysis of a company environmental data

COMPANIES	QUESTION							
	1	2	3	4	5	6	7	8
A plc	Y	Y	Y	Y	Y	?	N	Y
B plc	N	N	Y	-	-	-	-	-
C plc	Y	N	Y	Y	Y	Y	Y	?
D plc	Y	N	Y	Y	Y	N	N	Y
E plc	N	N	Y	-	-	-	-	-
F plc	Y	Y	N	Y	Y	Y	Y	Y
G plc	Y	Y	Y	Y	Y	Y	Y	Y

Key:

About the Environmental Information Available

Question 1: Is separate environmental information published other than that included within the financial annual report and accounts?

About the Financial Annual Report and Accounts

Question 2: Is any environmental financial[1] information given?
Question 3: Is any narrative environmental information given?

About the Separately Published Environmental Information

Question 4: Is any narrative environmental information given?
Question 5: Are visual environmental performance charts given?
Question 6: Are environmental targets detailed?
Question 7: Do they give an environmental policy?
Question 8: Is the environmental data externally verified?

Y = yes
N = No
? = To some extent
- = Not applicable

[1] Includes both figures and financial policies regarding environmental issues.

4.4 By 'organising' your data you are beginning to identify connections and relationships.

Organising structured data

4.5 In the last chapter we illustrated, in some detail, a questionnaire sent to respondents to discuss data about companies' responses to the environment. Already, part of the 'organisation' work had been done in the data design. The questionnaire is relatively structured; it may or may not produce results of statistical validity from the population from which it is drawn in total, but you will be able to do a lot of work on your sample. At the very least, this will suggest further work for you to do.

4.6 What you need to do, therefore, is **collate** the available data in a means susceptible to **manipulation**. This obviously depends on the size of your sample, but even if you have only obtained twenty interviews, you can find it quite useful to manipulate the data in a model.

Example

If you review the 14-question questionnaire in Chapter 6, you will note that the format of the required response differs from question to question.

Q1   Is your company predominantly operating in a service or manufacturing industry?

Service ....
Manufacturing ....

Does your company utilise any of the following environmental initiatives? (Please tick all that are applicable.)

Energy conservation ....
Control of emissions ....
Recycling ....
Reusing ....
Buying from environmentally friendly suppliers ....
Monitoring and controlling waste ....
Using recycled stationery ....
Tree Planting ....
Other ....
Please state...

4.7   **You could prepare a spreadsheet in order to capture the data** of a spreadsheet application. Spreadsheets offer a variety of tools from simple arithmetic – still very useful – to more complicated statistical analysis as revealed by the formula keys.

Remember that it is a specific requirement of the Guidelines that you submit a spreadsheet as part of your report. Failure to demonstrate your spreadsheet skills will result in failure of your project. Since you will have to produce a spreadsheet in any event, you can start to prepare the ground by using one to organise your data.

A very simple application of Excel to collect data

4.8   If you use Microsoft Excel, look at the manual or try the help keys. Even with quite simple spreadsheet operations, you can generate a lot of information. Here is an example.

(a)   **Head up the columns of the spreadsheet** with the names of the five companies. Indicate the date you received the responses, if at all. Alternatively, you might set up a separate spreadsheet schedule for this planning aspect.

(b)   Head up further columns: total, percentage and so on, for some work to do on the data.

(c)   The questions are on the rows. Each response has a row to itself.

(d)   Now, you want to turn these responses into data. Not all will be susceptible to manipulation, but for some responses you could give a YES the value of 1. By adding across you can get the total number of companies answering YES to a question and you can carry out a percentage calculation.

	A	B	C	D	E	F	G	H	I	J	K	L	M	N
1	Version 1													
2				A	B	C	D	E					Total	%
3	Is your company													
4	predominantly in													
5														
6	Services		Yes = 1	1			1						2	40%
7	Manufacturing		Yes = 1		1	1		1					3	60%
8														
9	Does your company													
10	utilise													
11	Energy conservation		Yes = 1	0	0	1	0	0					1	20%
12	Emission control		Yes = 1	0	0	1	0	0					1	20%
13	Recycling		Yes = 1	0	1	1	1	0					3	60%
14	Reuse		Yes = 1	0	1	1	0	0					2	40%
15	Eco-friendly suppliers		Yes = 1	1	1	0	0	0					2	40%
16	Waste monitoring		Yes = 1	0	1	0	0	0					1	20%
17	Recycled stationery		Yes = 1	1	1	0	1	0					3	60%
18	Tree planting		Yes = 1	0	0	0	0	0					0	0%
19	Other		Yes = 1	0	0	1	0	0					1	20%

4.9 You could organise your data further. Before you input it, you could identify which companies are in **services** and which are in **manufacturing**, thereby enabling you to calculate percentages for each. Of course, **you can use formulae and modelling tools** to do this – but if you think a key difference will be between services and manufacturing companies, simply organising your data into these columns can provide you with more information. You can see for example that whereas 60% of all the sample use recycled stationery, 100% of service companies do so.

	A	B	C	D	E	F	G	H	I	J	K	L	M	N
23				Services				Manufacturers					ALL	
24	Version 2			A	D	Total	%	C	B	E	Total	%	Total	%
25														
26	Is your company													
27	predominantly in													
28														
29	Services		Yes = 1	1	1								2	40%
30	Manufacturing		Yes = 1					1	1	1			3	60%
31														
32	Does your company													
33	utilise													
34	Energy conservation		Yes = 1	0	0	0	0%	1	0	0	1	33%	1	20%
35	Emission control		Yes = 1	0	0	0	0%	1	0	0	1	33%	1	20%
36	Recycling		Yes = 1	0	1	1	50%	1	1	0	2	67%	3	60%
37	Reuse		Yes = 1	0	0	0	0%	1	1	0	2	67%	2	40%
38	Eco-friendly suppliers		Yes = 1	1	0	1	50%	0	1	0	1	33%	2	40%
39	Waste monitoring		Yes = 1	0	0	0	0%	0	1	0	1	33%	1	20%
40	Recycled stationery		Yes = 1	1	1	2	100%	0	1	0	1	33%	3	60%
41	Tree planting		Yes = 1	0	0	0	0%	0	0	0	0	0%	0	0%
42	Other		Yes = 1	0	0	0	0%	1	0	0	1	33%	1	20%

More sophisticated uses

4.10 We will cover the use of Excel to analyse and model data in the next section. Some universities have access to a statistical package called SPSS. SPSS enables you to do a much wider variety of statistical tests then Excel, but you may not have access to it.

Organising other data in your file

4.11 The other data you have obtained may appear in a variety of formats: newspaper articles, extracts from textbooks, website download, notes you have taken of interviews. Doubtless you have read them in some detail, but you want to start thinking of the story that you are going to tell about them.

4.12 We have already suggested various different tasks in setting up your filing system.

Organising quantitative secondary data

4.13 Again, the best way of looking at this is by use of **examples**. You want to ensure that the data is organised in a form that can support your project objective.

Example

This time we shall have a look at **Project Topic 13: 'An analysis of future personnel requirements under conditions of change.'**

For the sake of argument, your project is based around an information technology service firm. This firm, as part of its global expansion, needs to operate on a 24 hour basis to serve overseas markets, and your project is based on the personnel needs generated by this change.

The firm is based in the UK, and as part of your secondary data collection you have obtained government statistics as follows (Social Trends, ONS).

(a) At the end of June 1998 there were 116,000 young people on the Modern Apprenticeship scheme, over four times more than the figure for 1996. There are considerable differences in the choice of Modern Apprenticeships undertaken by men and women. The most popular MA, with 15 per cent of all apprenticeships, was engineering manufacturing, although only 4 per cent of these were undertaken by women (chart). Men also form the majority of those taking apprenticeships in the motor industry, construction and electrical installation engineering. Women, on the other hand, predominate in business administration (the second most popular MA with 14 per cent of all apprentices), health and social care, hairdressing and retailing. Overall the ten most popular MA sectors shown in the chart account for more than three-quarters of all apprenticeships; in all there are 77 MA sectors.

Among employees, training and development in the workplace are increasingly important aspects of working life. The Investors in People (IIP) provides a national standard which helps employers to look critically at their training needs, and links investment in training directly to the achievement of their business goals.

People in training on Modern Apprenticeships: by sector and gender, 1998[1]

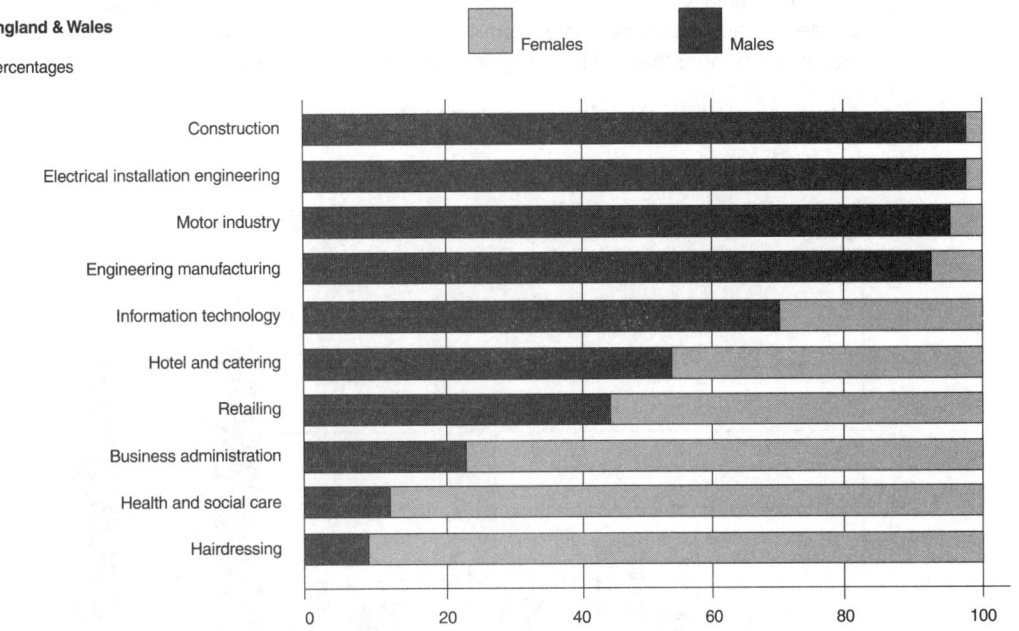

1 At 30 June 1998

Source: Department for Education and Employment

(b) In Spring 1998, around half of all UK employees in temporary jobs were on fixed period contracts, around one in five were engaged in casual work, and one in seven worked for agencies. Gender differences were apparent when employees gave reasons for taking on temporary work. A higher proportion of women than men stated that they did not want a permanent job, whereas a higher proportion of men than women stated that they could not find a permanent job.

The number of people holding second jobs rose steadily from 1992, reaching a highpoint in 1995 and 1996 (chart 4.11). More women than men have second jobs. Almost half of those with a second job worked part time in their main job. In Spring 1998 the average actual weekly hours worked by full-time employees with a second job was 47, compared with an average of 39 hours a week worked by full-time employees without a second job.

People in employment with a second job[1]: by gender

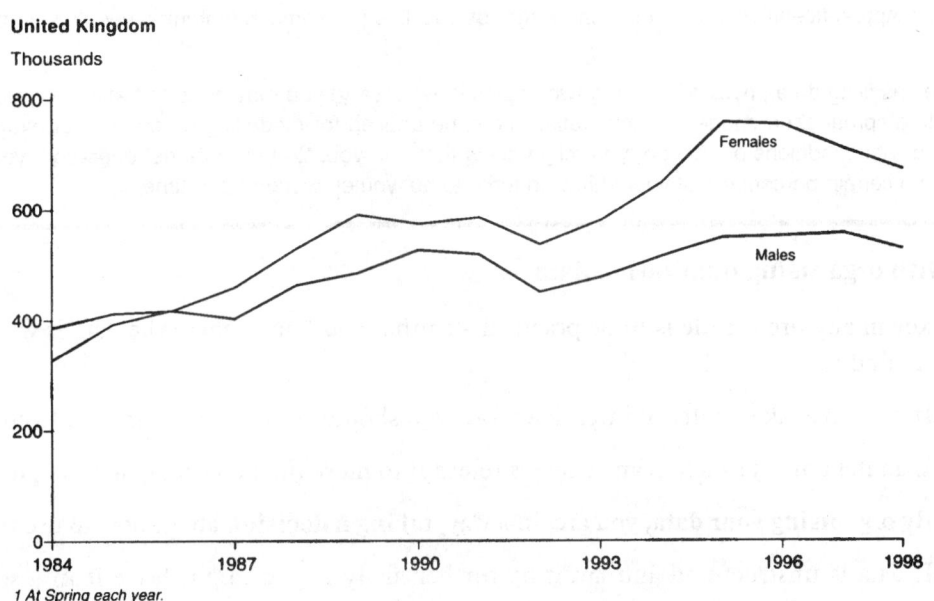

1 At Spring each year.

Source: Labour Force Survey, Office for National Statistics

Time at work

In Spring 1998 more than 5 million people, around a fifth of all those in work in the United Kingdom, usually worked more than 48 hours a week in their main job (Chart 4.12). About a quarter of those working more than 48 hours a week were self-employed. About 30 per cent of men worked more than 48 hours a week compared with 7 per cent of all women.

Total usual weekly hours of work¹: by gender, Spring 1998

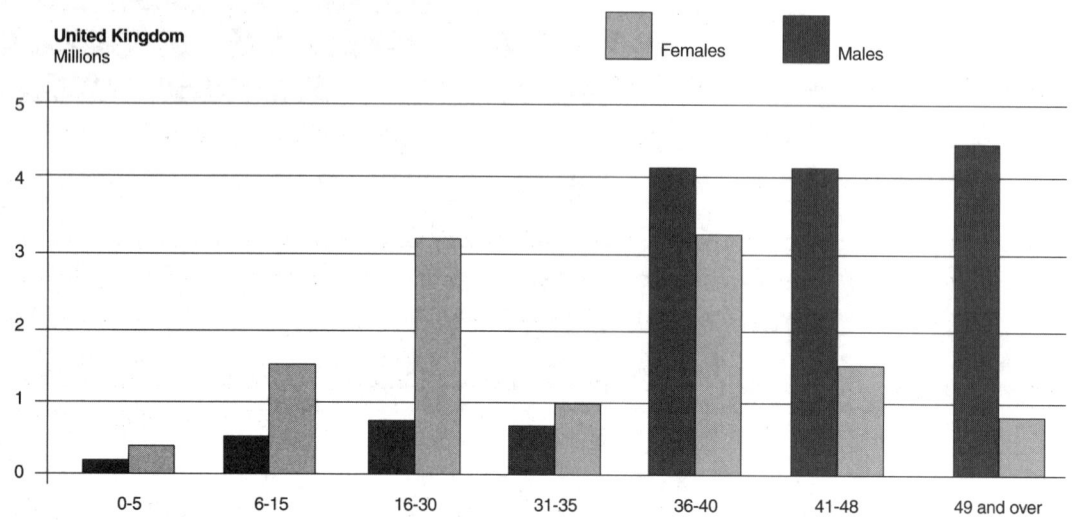

1 At Spring for all of working age in employment: males aged 16 to 64; females aged 16 to 59.

Source: Labour Force Survey, Office for National Statistics

What is each piece of data telling you?

Problems with the data are that it is more impressionistic than you might like, and you will have to make some effort to glean out what you want.

Item (a) tells you about training needs in general and the balance between the sexes. You could **file this under the 'employee development'** as it addresses training and modern apprenticeships. You could also **file this under 'recruitment'** if, for example, you want to relate this to catchment groups of employees.

Item (b) provides you with details of the working population. Combined with (a) you could surmise that employing part time workers is going to mean employing more women; however, fewer of them do Modern Apprenticeships in IT, which can **suggest** possible problems in obtaining people with the right skills.

As well as filing data physically (taking two copies if necessary) you may need to transfer or recast the data to a spreadsheet model, if such statistics can be applied for modelling purposes. For example, in dealing with conditions of change, you might show that – in your 24 hour internet operation, you might expect a certain percentage of your shift workforce to be women working part time.

Dealing with organising qualitative data

4.14 The key in any project file is to be practical – so that you know where the data is when you want to find it.

(a) If you have taken notes of interviews, say, you should summarise them on a front sheet.

(b) If an item of data such as an article is relevant to more than one area, make copies.

(c) By **organising your data,** you are, in a way, **taking a decision** about how to use it.

(d) If data is unstructured and awaiting further analysis you might leave it in a separate 'unprocessed' section.

5 MODELLING THE DATA

5.1 In a **model**, you are, effectively, seeking to set up relationships to allow further analysis. You can do this in a number of ways.

(a) Spreadsheet modelling. As well as using a spreadsheet as a glorified calculator, it does offer a variety of statistical tools – not as good as SPSS, but sufficient for the Research and Analysis Project.

(b) There are various techniques of modelling and analysing **qualitative** data.

Spreadsheet models – an example

5.2 In section 3, we described the use of a spreadsheet as a means of capturing and organising data in a very simple way.

5.3 Constructing a spreadsheet model is something you might do as a matter of course in your work, in preparing budgets or analysing performance. We do not intend to provide a guide to working with spreadsheets but here is a possible application.

5.4 **Any spreadsheet model is constructed using formulae.** You will find a simple guide in the **help facility** of your spreadsheet package – print this out, if you want a manual record. Here are examples.

(a) =C4*5. This formula **multiplies** the value in C4 by 5. The result will appear in the cell holding the formula.

(b) =C4*B10. This **multiplies** the value in C4 by the value in B10. In general this is better than option (a). Why? Because the result is in a separate cell and if '5' is a variable that can change, you can first enter the new number to the cell.

(c) =C4/E5. This **divides** the value in C4 by the value in E5. (Note that * means multiply and / means divide by.)

(d) =(C4*B10)–D1. This **multiplies** the value in C4 by that in B10 and then subtracts the value in D1 from the result. Note that generally the computer will perform multiplication and division before addition or subtraction.

(e) =C4*117.5%. This **adds** 17.5% to the value in C4. It could be used to calculate a price including 17.5% VAT. When you enter 17.5%, it may be displayed on screen as 0.175, depending on how the spreadsheet is set up.

(f) =(C4+C5+C6)/3. This, in effect, calculates the **average** of the values in C4, C5 and C6. Note that the brackets tell the computer to perform the addition first. Without the brackets the computer would first divide the value in C6 by 3 and then add the result to the total of the values in C4 and C5.

(g) $= 2\wedge 2$ gives you 2 **to the power** of 2, in other words 2^2. Likewise $= 2\wedge 3$ gives you 2 cubed and so on.

(h) $= 4 \wedge (1/2)$ gives you the **square root** of 4. Likewise $27 \wedge (1/3)$ gives you the cube root of 27 and so on. Do not forget the brackets.

5.5 To **display all the underlying formulae** in your spreadsheet, instead of the numbers, click on Tools, then on Options, then on View and put an X in the box next to Formulas to display them or remove it to display numbers. You could usefully do this to display a sample of your formulae for your spreadsheet, as suggested by Oxford Brookes. Include the sample as one of your appendices.

Example

The following four insurance salesmen each earn a basic salary of £14,000 pa. They also earn a commission of 2% of sales. The following spreadsheet has been created to process their commission and total earnings.

	A	B	C	D	E
1	*Sales team salaries and commissions - 19XX*				
2	Name	Sales	Salary	Commission	Total earnings
3		£	£	£	£
4	Northington	284,000	14,000	5,680	19,680
5	Souther	193,000	14,000	3,860	17,860
6	Weston	12,000	14,000	240	14,240
7	Easterman	152,000	14,000	3,040	17,040
8					
9	Total	641,000	56,000	12,820	68,820
10					
11					
12	*Variables*				
13	Basic Salary	14,000			
14	Commission rate	0.02			
15					
16					
17					
18					
19					
20					

Possible formulae are as follows.

(a) =B4*B14, for cell D4.

(b) =C6+D6, for cell E6.

(c) =SUM(D4:D7), for cell D9.

(d) For cell E9, there is a **variety of possibilities** here, depending on whether you set the cell as the total of the earnings of each salesman (cells E4 to E7) or as the total of the different elements of remuneration (cells C9 and D9). Of course, it would be nice to **know that the calculation works in both directions.** This would give added assurance that there are no errors. A suitable formulae for this purpose would be:

=IF(SUM(E4:E7)=SUM(C9:D9),SUM(E4:E7),"ERROR")

5.6 You may want to compare actual results with budgets or targets to see how far it has exceeded, or fallen short of, its expectations. It is useful to express **variations as a percentage of the original budget**, for example sales may be 10% higher than predicted.

Conditions in formulae

5.7 Suppose the company employing the salesmen in the above example awards a bonus (in addition to the commission) to those salesmen who exceed their target by more than £1,000. It is possible to **get the spreadsheet to work out who is entitled to the bonus**. (In our example you can see this for yourself easily enough, but if there were 100 salesmen it would be tedious to have to look down a long list.)

5.8 Look at the first section of the spreadsheet. We are trying to determine whether Northington would be shown as entitled to a bonus. The formula used may vary slightly from one spreadsheet program to the next. We will enter the following:

=IF(B4>1000,"BONUS"," ").

The formula could be entered in column F.

5.9 This formula has three parts inside the brackets.

IF (**condition**, result if **true**, result if **false**).

The **inverted commas** (") mean that **text** is to appear in the cell. Here the text will either be the word '**bonus**' or, if the target was not exceeded, a **blank space**. The contents of the cell could equally well be a number (as in paragraph 1.4(d)).

> Note the following symbols which can be used in formulae with conditions:
>
> | < | less than |
> |---|-----------|
> | <= | less than or equal to |
> | = | equal to |
> | >= | greater than or equal to |
> | > | greater than |
> | <> | not equal to |

5.10 There is nothing very difficult about conditions in formulae, but great care must be taken to put **brackets** and **commas** in the right places.

Examples of formulae with conditions

Discounts

5.11 A company offers a discount of 5% to customers who order more than £1,000 worth of goods. A spreadsheet showing what customers will pay might look like this.

	A	B	C	D	E	F
1	**Discount Traders Ltd**					
2	*Sales analysis - April 19XX*					
3	Customer	Sales	5% discount	Sales (net)		
4		£	£	£		
5	Arthur	956.00	0.00	956.00		
6	Dent	1423.00	71.15	1351.85		
7	Ford	2894.00	144.70	2749.30		
8	Prefect	842.00	0.00	842.00		
9						
10						

5.12 The formula in cell C5 is: =IF(B5>1,000,(0.05*B5),0). This means, if the value in B5 is greater than £1,000 multiply it by 0.05, otherwise the discount will be zero. Cell D5 will calculate the amount net of discount, using the formula: =B5-C5. The same conditional formula with the cell references changed will be found in cells C6, C7 and C8. **Strictly**, the variables £1,000 and 5% should be entered in a **different part** of the spreadsheet.

Examination results

5.13 Suppose the pass mark for an examination is 50% and you want to see easily from a long list who has passed and who has failed. If a candidate's score is in cell B2, an appropriate formula for cell C2 would be: =IF(B2<50,"FAILED","PASSED").

As you may have noticed from an earlier example, the placing of text in inverted commas in a conditional function will cause the text to be printed out or displayed as appropriate.

Oxford Brookes strongly recommend that if possible you include a sample printout of the formulae for part of the spreadsheet as evidence of your IT skills.

Graphics

5.14 It is usually possible to convert tabulated data in a spreadsheet into a variety of bar chart or graphical formats. We will look again at the Discount Traders Ltd example from paragraph 5.11.

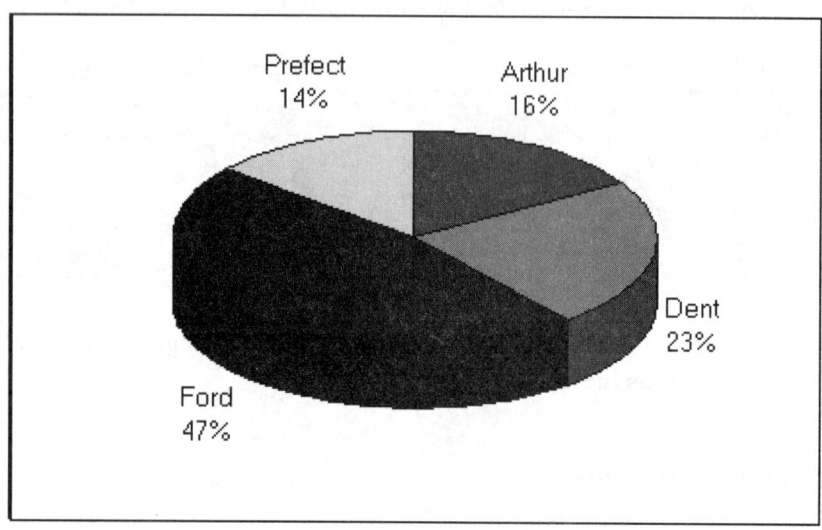

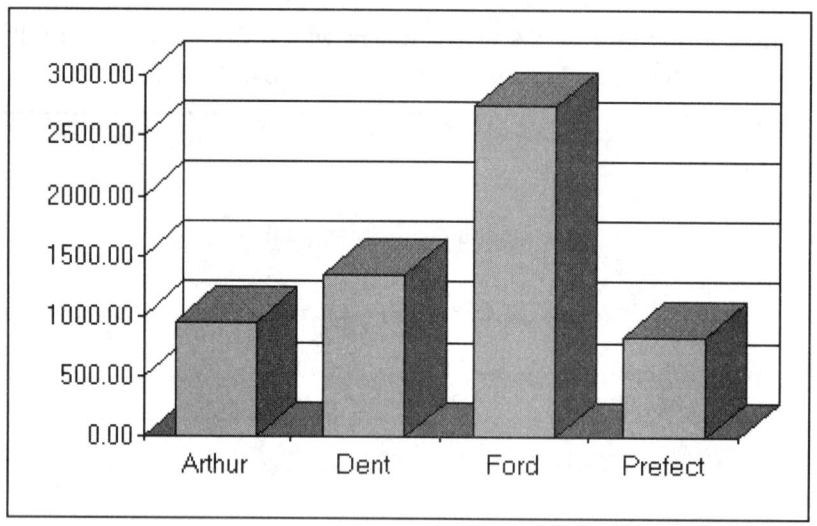

Other spreadsheet features

5.15 Excel offers many more facilities for analysing data.

   (a) If you go to the **formula bar** in Excel, and click on the = sign you will get a list of options such as SUM, AND and so on, including Averages and NPV analysis, correlation and regression and so on.

   (b) The help facility also lists everything you can do.

Avoiding over-complex models

5.16 When building a spreadsheet model to analyse your data, be sure to remember the following key points.

(a) **Do not make your spreadsheet more complex** than it needs to be – for some calculations, a pocket calculator will be just as good.

(b) Use **the auditing tool to check your formulae are correct.**

(c) Check your formulae are correct by doing some manual calculations

(d) Do a trial run. If you are not quite sure what you want to do, experiment with a small number of data items before applying them wholesale.

5.17 Here are examples as to how you could use Excel in the Research and Analysis Project.

Examples

Project Topic 8: An analysis of the financial situation of your choice of organisation.

Ratio Analysis

Project Topic 12: An analysis of the effect of any International Accounting Standard on the accounts of any organisation in terms of profitability or financial stability or balance sheet value.

You could model the effect, say, of differences in the treatment of taxation or pension benefits on the financial statements. You could even go further by using the spreadsheet to help you re-cast the financial statements drawn up under local accounting rules (eg FRSs in the UK, MAS and MASB approved accounting standards in Malaysia).

Project Topic 15: An analysis of the role of working capital on the profitability and/or efficiency of an organisation of your choice.

You could use what if? analysis to assess the impact of different payment periods and means of finance

Project Topic 16: An analysis of the effect of different sources of capital on investment decisions in an organisation of your choice.

You could use spreadsheets to analyse capital needs. Excel has useful functions for calculating net present values and internal rates of return.

Project Topic 4: An analysis of the impact of e-business on an industry or organisation of your choice.

This is less obvious as the spreadsheet would depend very much on the data collected but if you wanted to use the graphic facilities to interpret data collected you could do so.

Project Topic 13: An analysis of future personnel requirements under conditions of change (including employee development).

Depending on market data, you could use spreadsheets to calculate relationships. For example, major mobile phone groups have, effectively, paid £630 per UK customer for the licences for 'next generation' mobile phones. You could calculate this figure – if not readily available – by identifying what was paid and comparing it to market data.

Analysing qualitative data – some hints and tips

5.18 This requires you to take a more creative approach. The technique you adopt will depend on the type of data you have collected and **we cannot be prescriptive**.

Précis

5.19 If you are using an article, the most important thing you must do is **read it carefully**. For some articles, we can suggest that you do a **précis**. This forces you to read it thoroughly and gut it for the key points.

Example

Here is some data from a newspaper. Précis it into 100 words.

Financial Times	*Précis*
Halifax, the mortgage bank, yesterday agreed to pay £760m for a controlling stake in St James's Place Capital (SJPC), the holding company for J Rothschild Assurance, in a deal designed to pull the upmarket life assurer into the internet age.	
Halifax bought 17 per cent of the company from Prudential late on Tuesday at 300p a share, a premium of 70p to Tuesday's closing price. It will now extend the offer to up to 60 per cent of the shares, leaving SJPC with a separate listing.	
The bid is the latest move in Halifax's aggressive internet strategy, begun earlier this year when it poached Jim Spowart from Standard Life bank to set up Intelligent Finance (IF), an online bank due to launch this summer.	
It hopes to add £5bn of assets to IF by selling a St James's-branded private banking service, run by IF, through SJPC's 1,000-strong salesforce.	
'This is an absolutely cracking business,' said James Crosby, Halifax chief executive. 'It increases the scale of our distribution operation in long-term savings and will assist our drive for diversification (away from mortgages).'	
Sir Mark Weinberg, chairman of SJPC, said the company had decided last year to seek a strategic partner to help it use the internet to extend its product range, and began talks with Prudential, which then owned 29 per cent of the shares. 'It became clear that their vision and our vision were not parallel to the extent that there wasn't the opportunity for a value-creating partnership,' he said.	
Analysts said the deal, which is expected to be earnings-enhancing in the first year, would help IF as long as the product, still under wraps, is as exciting as the bank claims.	
The SJPC salesforce own about 8 per cent of the company and have options on another 8 per cent.	

Helping hand

Financial Times	*Précis*
Halifax, the mortgage bank, yesterday agreed to pay £760m for a controlling stake in St James's Place Capital, the holding company for J Rothschild Assurance, in a deal designed to pull the upmarket life assurer into the internet age.	Halifax, the mortgage bank, has spent £760m to control St James's Place Capital (SJPC), a life assurer with internet potential.
Halifax bought 17 per cent of the company from Prudential late on Tuesday at 300p a share, a premium of 70p to Tuesday's closing price. It will now extend the offer to up to 60 per cent of the shares, leaving SJPC with a separate listing.	Halifax acquired the controlling stake from Prudential Insurance in two stages.
The bid is the latest move in Halifax's aggressive internet strategy, begun earlier this year when it poached Jim Spowart from Standard Life bank to set up Intelligent Finance (IF), an online bank due to launch this summer.	The bid forms part of Halifax's strategy to develop internet businesses, such as Intelligent Finance (IF) an on-line bank.
It hopes to add £5bn of assets to IF by selling a St James's-branded private banking service, run by IF, through SJPC's 1,000-strong salesforce.	In addition, there will be cross-selling opportunities.
'This is an absolutely cracking business,' said James Crosby, Halifax chief executive. 'It increases the scale of our distribution operation in long-term savings and will assist our drive for diversification (away from mortgages).'	There are economies of scale in distribution and opportunities for diversification.
Sir Mark Weinberg, chairman of SJPC, said the company had decided last year to seek a strategic partner to help it use the internet to extend its product range, and began talks with Prudential, which then owned 29 per cent of the shares. 'It became clear that their vision and our vision were not parallel to the extent that there wasn't the opportunity for a value-creating partnership,' he said.	SJPC had been looking for a partner to develop its internet business for some time.
Analysts said the deal, which is expected to be earnings-enhancing in the first year, would help IF as long as the product, still under wraps, is as exciting as the bank claims.	The deal will help IF and it is expected to increase earnings
The SJPC salesforce own about 8 per cent of the company and have options on another 8 per cent.	

Précis (1)

Halifax, the mortgage bank, has paid £760m to Prudential Insurance to control St James's Place Capital (SJPC) a life assurer with internet potential. The bid forms part of Halifax's strategy to develop internet businesses, such as Intelligent Finance, an on-line bank. In addition, there will be cross selling opportunities, economies of scale in distribution and opportunities for diversification. SJPC had been looking for a partner to develop its internet business for some time. The deal will help IF as it will increase earnings.

What do you think? Could it be improved? It appears a bit unstructured.

Précis (2)

1   Halifax has paid £760m to Prudential to acquire St James's Place Capital.

2   Rationale

    (a)   Halifax and SJPC both want to develop an internet business and felt they would make good partners.

    (b)   Other benefits include cross selling opportunities, economies of scale in distribution, and diversification, and increased earnings

Answer 2 is probably too concise. It misses out the fact that Halifax is to launch an on-line bank, a key area of its strategy. However, it is clearer in terms of structure, because it adopts report format and has a heading.

5.20   Why is this technique useful?

(a)   It **forces you to read** the material thoroughly.

(b)   It forces you to **understand** the material – you have to understand it before you can summarise it.

Key words, phrases, themes and concepts

5.21   If you need to be more rigorous, instead of summarising each paragraph, as you go down the side, you can identify which **concepts apply**. Give each paragraph a number and note down in a short phrase what concepts are being discussed – based on your research questions and the project objective.

    Step 1.   Photocopy the article or type the transcript so that you have a **large** space in the margins either side.

    Step 2.   You may want to allocate simple **codes** for each theme or item relevant to the Project Topic.

    Step 3.   When this theme appears in a sentence, mark down the relevant code in the margin, at the same level.

5.22   You may decide that it is worthwhile **highlighting key words** or ideas with a colour highlighter pen – but this will make it harder if the same item can relate to two themes.

Example

Let us say that you have transcripts of tape recordings of interviews with sales personnel in an effort to understand how well they are motivated. Let us say that you want to reach sensible conclusions on what the data says.

Say that you want to ask certain questions of the data.

(1)   You can **search for key words** – ie the same word repeated as indication of certain topics being covered. This is perhaps a bit mechanistic but is used by some researchers in an attempt to convert qualitative into quantitative data.

(2)   You could use a **highlighter pen to colour code** areas dealing with each of the questions you are interested in. This also encourages close reading but it is less mechanistic. An area colour coded pink, for example, could deal with salary, areas coloured yellow could deal with salespeople's feelings about the job.

    However some items of data could relate to two themes, so you would be better off with the **coding approach** in 5.21 above.

Organisation

5.23   We have already suggested that you collect and organise your data in a way that is appropriate to how you intend to use it – don't just file things in chronological or

alphabetical order. By filing it in the order of how you intend to use it, you are, in effect, making a decision about its importance or use.

Visual aids

5.24 An aid you could use is a mind map or tree diagram – a visual aid. The advantages of this are that you are using the spatial relationships on paper to illustrate the connections between different concepts. The example below employs this approach.

Example

As part of **Project Topic 5: 'The identification of the effects of globalisation on an industry of your choice'**, you have chosen the aircraft manufacturing industry and have done widespread reading. You have obtained the following information about Airbus.

Airbus is going ahead to build a super-jumbo, seating between 550 and 650 people, challenging the Boeing 747. Development costs will be $12bn, and the first deliveries are expected in June 2005. The UK government has offered launch aid of £530m to get it started. This is a large plane, to be marketed at the major airlines. Airbus promises a 15% to 20% fall in aircraft operating costs. The terms of the launch aid are secret. (Many years ago, the EU and US agreed on a formula for assessing state aid to their relative industries. American aircraft makers enjoyed indirect support thanks to the demands of the arms industry. The US government is concerned that the launch aid breaches this agreement.)

There are relatively few aircraft makers in the world. Airbus's main competitor is Boeing. At time of writing Airbus is not a normal company. Each participant (Aerospatiale of France, BAe of the UK, DA of Germany and Casa of Spain) has the right to make part of the plane. Governments have a great interest in the aerospace manufacturing industry for defence reasons, and Aerospatiale is part owned by the French government. Aircraft engines are supplied by Rolls Royce, Pratt and Whitney and GE. Boeing is a principal competitor.

Below are some environmental factors, taken at random.

(a) Classify them as of high, medium, low importance to Airbus.

(b) Draw a mindmap of the general and competitive environment.

Factor

1	Better video conferencing
2	More working at home
3	Greater demand in rich countries for tailor-made holidays
4	Genetically modified food
5	EU-US disputes at the World Trade Organisation
6	Deregulation in air markets (in terms of destination served)
7	Ageing population in western world
8	Political instability in Asia (N Korea)
9	Air traffic is projected to rise 5% pa to 2030
10	Stricter asylum and immigration laws applied over Europe
11	Continued expansion of high speed train networks in Europe

Answer

(a) *Classification of importance*

You may well disagree with these – but you need a rationale.

High

5. May well affect financing of the project and Airbus's status as a company.

6. Firms can compete on different routes. This may restrain demand for jumbo jets: but this might be overridden by overall growth.

9. A huge increase. Airports cannot expand fast enough and there is only so much space: bigger aircraft are one solution.

11. High speed trains compete with aircraft for speed and are often more convenient; more relevant to short haul flights than long distance flights.

Medium

1. May reduce demand for business travel.

3. Affects destinations people want to fly to, and the market for scheduled and chartered flights: perhaps people will prefer smaller planes.

8. May slow demand for air traffic, or increase economic problems in the region.

Low

2. Affects other transport firms but not airlines, as this affects normal commuting not business trips.

4. Nothing to do with Airbus at all!

7. Demand can come from elsewhere; population is getting wealthier.

10. Affects airline operations but not overall demand.

Answer (b)

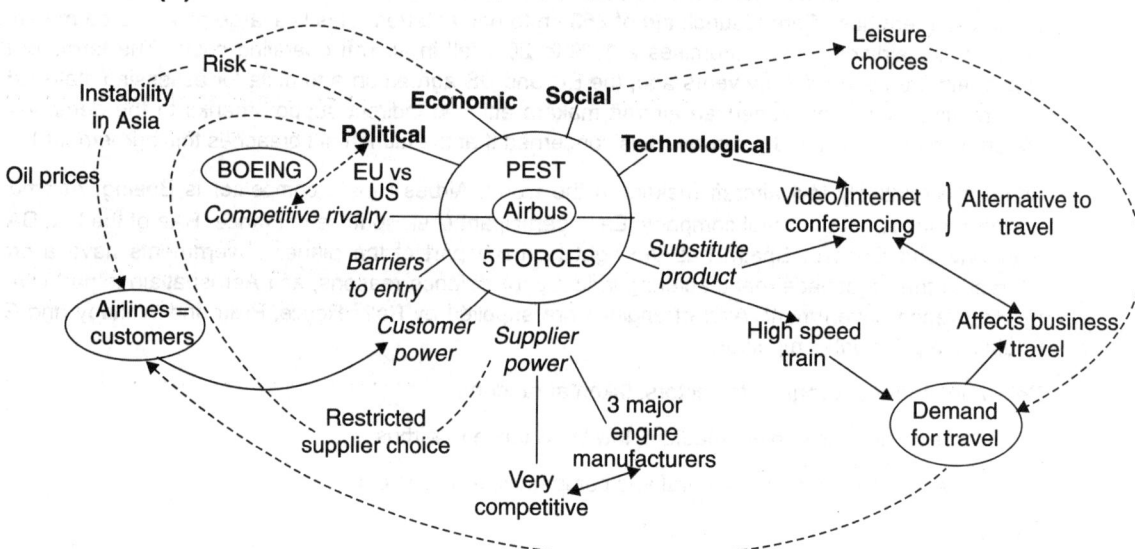

If you have sat paper 3.4 or 3.5, you will recognise that this diagram incorporates facts – about Airbus – and two theoretical models (PEST analysis and Porter's Five Forces Analysis) and shows how they are linked together. It both summarises and explains the interconnections between issues.

Chapter roundup

- Data has to be reviewed in the light of the project objective, regarding the scope, forms and context of the project.

- BPP suggest: Choose analytical tools, Look at the data, Organise the data, and Model the data.

- The ACCA's syllabus provides plenty of ideas as to the analytical frameworks you can adopt.

- Once you have collected data, you need to review it to ensure that it meets the project objective.

- Data should be organised in your file so that it supports the project objective.

- There are a number of techniques for modelling data, including spreadsheets, graphical approaches and textual analysis.

Chapter 8

SYNTHESIS

Chapter topic list

1   Concluding your work

2   Conclusions and the project objective

3   Unexpected results vs project failure

4   Before you start your report

5   Frequently asked questions

Introduction

This chapter very briefly covers the type of mental process you should go through after you have completed research and analysis but before you go into the nitty-gritty of writing up your Report and preparing your presentation underpinning the Key Skills Statement. Inevitably, this is a short chapter.

---

1   CONCLUDING YOUR WORK

How do you know you have finished?

1.1   Many research projects are open ended and take time to complete, simply because of the size and range of the subject matter. This is particularly true of postgraduate research in the UK, where a PhD requires original research and an original contribution to knowledge. Three years full time work is often given as an example.

1.2   At undergraduate level, this does not hold. The advantage of deadlines – whether at university or in doing ACCA exams – is that you are forced to come to a halt. With the Research and Analysis Project you can choose your own deadline.

1.3   But your Research and Analysis Project is in a different category of course. You do not face the deadline pressure of an undergraduate student, but there is a limit to the extent of your work, caused by the project objective.

1.4   If you have followed the advice of the earlier chapters you will have:

- Identified a precise project objective

- From the project objective, you will have identified the research and analytical work you need to do to find enough information to satisfy the project objective

Arguably, if this is what you have done and you have carried out your plans, you need go no further.

1.5 In practice, life might not be that simple.

(a) If you are unused to undergraduate work, you may lack **confidence** in what you have done.

(b) You may be unhappy with the work you have done, or feel that you need to do more.

1.6 Here is a checklist as a possible guide to taking this decision. How do you know you've finished? See if you can give a YES to **most** of these questions.

1	Have I done all the research and analysis activities I planned to do?	Yes/No	1	If yes, a good enough start – check with your mentor.
2	Do I already have ideas about what I want to say in my report from the work I have done?	Yes/No	2	If yes, write them down – this suggests you are drawing conclusions and can support them.
3	Although I'd really like to know more about the subject as it interests me, I don't think this is necessary for the Report.	Yes/No	3	If yes, you are brimming with enthusiasm but you have a clear head. Of course some extra reading might help and add extra points.
4	The project has proved to be much harder than I thought, but I have not given up.	Yes/No	4	You have not cut corners – IF your planning was good enough, and your research and analysis work covers the project objective, this indicates you have done enough.
5	I was unable to complete some of the research and analysis tasks that I had planned to do. However, I reviewed the project objective and found there were other ways of finding the same information and pursued these.	Yes/No	5	If yes, this implies you have kept sight of what you have tried to prove, although the road has been rockier than you thought.
6	Do the results of my research support the conclusions I expected to find	Don't answer!	6	If you **expected** an outcome and the results proved your original hunch as to what you'd find to be **incorrect**, so what? You have still researched and analysed data and drawn conclusions from it.

1.7 Even if you still do not know what you are going to say, if you've answered YES to most of the questions above, you are perhaps ready to start tying all the threads together.

2 CONCLUSIONS AND THE PROJECT OBJECTIVE

What if you still do not know what to conclude? Second mentor meeting

2.1 Your second mentor meeting is for you to discuss briefly how you have done, perhaps with a summary outline of what you are going to put in your report. Your second mentor meeting should cover your conclusions and initial plans for your report.

2.2 However, you may not feel ready or able to discuss this with your mentor, but you need to marshall your thoughts.

(a) Some people are able to keep everything in their heads, and plan what they are going to write before they start.

(b) Other people **think** as they write or speak. Often, the easiest way to start something is to talk to a friend, summarising in a brief sentence what you think your research and analysis has covered and what you think about it.

Help yourself come to conclusions

Step 1. Answer the questions in the project objective

2.3 Earlier on we suggested that two ways of looking at your research are to ask:

(a) What am I trying to prove or disprove?

(b) What am I trying to show?

In your own mind, can you begin to answer these questions?

Example

You have done **Project Topic 13: An analysis of personnel requirements under conditions of change** including employee development.

Your project objective has been to review and describe the effect of a company merger on the finance departments of the two merged companies.

If you ask 'What am I trying to show?' and can **describe** the following, you are in good position to draw a conclusion.

(a) Some theories of change management

(b) The effects of mergers on other companies, including problems such as systems incompatibility etc

(c) The training that staff felt they needed and what they actually received

(d) Managers' plans for the change, and how they responded to the new situation

(e) Details of human resource plans and procedures

(f) Operational and systems problems

(g) Notes from discussions

Your conclusion might be that the change was not properly prepared for. The firms' HRM planning systems were not effective in that there was mismatch between training delivered and actual needs, and that issues of productivity arising from the merger had not been dealt with effectively.

Example

Assume you are asking 'What am I trying to prove or disprove' and you have chosen **Project Topic 11: An analysis of the costs and benefits of internal audit/review activities within an organisation of your choice.**

Your project **objective** has been to prove that strengthening the internal audit department of Z Bank is of benefit. If you have the data below you should be able to come to conclusions, either way.

(a) Annual budget of internal audit department

(b) External audit fees

(c) Reliance placed by external auditors on internal audit

(d) Errors detected which would have been picked up by the department

(e) Background information about two major bank failures

(f) New controls introduced

(g) A new approach to risk management on internal audit advice

---

Still having difficulty?

2.4 If you are still having difficulty, we suggest you try to structure your thinking as below.

Force yourself to rewrite your findings and conclusions in terms of the project objective.

Example

For example, take **Project Topic 16: An analysis of the different sources of capital on investment decisions in an organisation of your choice.**

Your project is an analysis of the sources of capital used by Philibee Sdn Bhd, a Malaysian-owned fast food company, as it opens outlets over south east Asia, including the Philippines, Thailand and Singapore. The **project objective** seeks to address whether and why Philibee adopted different sources of capital for each market as opposed to the most theoretically efficient method overall.

Findings	Re-wording	Project objective
(1) Franchising is used in Thailand, owing to the difficulty of obtaining bank credit. The operation in Thailand has grown rapidly, but the local partner shares in the profits. (2) Philibee invested its own money in Singapore with no local partner (3) You did a spreadsheet model which identified how much Philibee had spent, and the return expected by shareholders and bondholders in Kuala Lumpur	A spreadsheet analysis would suggest that, ideally, the cheapest source of capital would have been **debt issuance overall.** In Thailand, Philbee expanded in the local **market** via franchise arrangements. This means of **sourcing capital** for expansion costs more and hence is **less efficient** than other sources overall.	Sources of capital for each **market** as opposed to the most efficient method **overall.**

Try again

2.5 Another way is to work **backwards from the project objective**, in a hierarchy.

Step 1. Start with the project objective.

Step 2. Identify key questions to be answered or points demonstrated.

Step 3. Slot in your points raised from your analysis in the 'boxes' identified in two.

2.6

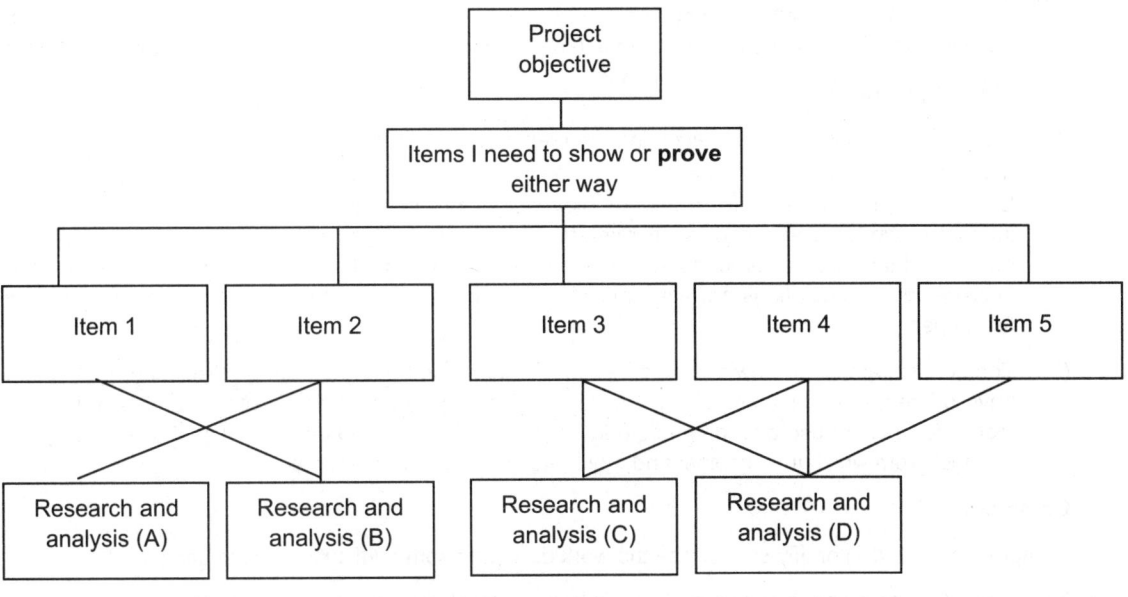

Example

An unpublished undergraduate dissertation came to the conclusions below.

(1) Demands for 'green' information from companies, are increasing. However, the way in which companies meet this demand is varied. Through an analysis of published environmental data and questionnaires it was found that this disclosure ranges in depth, format and distribution times and places. This is heightened because few environmental disclosure regulations are in existence. Differing information makes it hard for comparisons to be made between companies, which hinders decision making regarding environmental issues.

(2) The varying standards of environmental information raise questions as to who the intended audiences are and what are the companies' motivations for disclosing? An overwhelming hypothesis was that it is being treated only for publicity and corporate benefit purposes. A wider accountability and, therefore, the stakeholder view, is not high in companies' thoughts. This is all linked to the internal approach a company takes to environmental issues. The more dedication and resources applied internally, the better foundation for external reporting.

(3) **No standard methodology** is in place for environmental disclosure and, therefore, **no verification procedures**. This has questioned the credibility of this disclosure. **Environmental cost accounting** and **environmental reporting** both offer **solutions** to achieving standardisation. However, complex procedures, information requirements and audience readability make them not entirely fault-free. Equally, there is no common framework on how to interpret results.

Main findings

(4) How and why companies are disclosing environmental information is extremely varied at the current time. This is causing problems for both comparability purposes and the level of seriousness the business world is taking these issues.

(5) **Activity based costing** would increase accountability by correctly allocating environmental costs. However, the process is long, information requirements are high and understandability may be hindered for those with little accounting knowledge. Additionally, interpretation of environmental costs is perceived differently by individuals. **Environmental performance indicators (EPIs)**

Recommendations

(6) Clearly a form of standard methodology concerning disclosure of environmental data is required. This would then focus businesses on the seriousness of the issue and the audiences they need to aim at. It would also enable verification procedures to be put in place providing credibility to environmental information across the business world and enabling environmental issues to be incorporated within business decisions.

(7) A mixture of ABC and EPIs would aid communication, providing a balance of complexity and giving an even picture of environmental issues in both annual and environmental reports. However, environmental communication will never achieve all its objectives until a common framework for interpreting environmental figures is achieved.

The subject matter

(8) Environmental issues are becoming increasingly important as more natural resource are depleted. Companies can wait no longer to show accountability for their use of earth's gifts. Environmental disclosure is a way of expressing this to external parties whilst making their internal procedures aware of such matters. Within this field of writing the common census of opinion is that standard procedures need to be agreed upon. Guidelines, although voluntary, are in place but no regulations are available indicating that this topic is not as straightforward as may first appear.

(9) The benefits are clear, now it is time for more research to be carried out on disclosure methods. I have offered a combination. However, this has its limitations. Perhaps other formats with more testing for ease of use over different industries need to be carried out. This would offer a range of methods from which the simplest and most effective could implemented.

Comment

Paragraphs (1) and 2) briefly summarise the work done and some difficulties interpreting it.

Paragraph (2) continues a wider context, linked to an earlier chapter discussing how companies managed environmental issues.

Paragraph (3) and (4) should refer to work done earlier, largely summarising.

Findings of research and analysis of data. See paragraph 9 on the need for more research on disclosure methods.

---

3 UNEXPECTED RESULTS VS PROJECT FAILURE

Unexpected results

3.1 If you take the example in 2.4 above (Philibee), you might have found that your results did not answer your question either way. Let's see how the story develops.

Example

You had expected, for example, that the availability of sources of finance should make no difference to expansion plans in individual countries, but instead found wide variations. Area managers were under instructions to build the brand, and they chose the easiest ways to do so, such as franchising, rather than the most profitable.

You have come to the conclusion that in this case the sources of finance are not relevant to investment decisions, and capital rationing is not even thought of in Philibee.

3.2 Even if this is not the result you wanted, it is still a valid conclusion from the research you have done. You have carried out your investigation, and your result is clear. You may have wanted to prove that investment decisions were finely calibrated and that local managers calculated the best proportion of debt/equity, with allowance for risk.

What if I have identified areas for further research?

3.3 If your project identifies areas for further research, this is **not an unsuccessful** project. It is a statement of the limitations of scope and focus – nothing to be ashamed of.

Project failure

3.4 A failed project is different. This means that you are unable to come to any conclusion, that your research has proved impossible, to that you are unable to answer any of the questions you set yourself.

3.5 Effectively, you cannot even say – 'these are my findings, more work is needed'.

4 BEFORE YOU START YOUR REPORT

4.1 Remember the mentor meeting? You should prepare an outline on two sheets of A4 paper. This is a good opportunity to plan your report and summarise your main themes. This is covered in the next chapter.

5 FREQUENTLY ASKED QUESTIONS

5.1 In the Oxford Brookes Guidelines (paragragh 3.4, shown on page 11 of this book) there is a list of frequently asked questions, covering both the administration of the project and also some technical aspects. It would be worth looking through these at this stage in your work, to see if there is anything relevant to the way you start to write your report. You should also look at the checklist prior to submission, (paragragh 3.5) to make sure that you haven't over-looked anything.

Chapter roundup

- This chapter has covered how to draw conclusions from your data.

- Sometimes, the conclusions will be blindingly obvious.

- In other times you will have to force yourself to answer the questions suggested.

- An unexpected result does not necessarily indicate a failed project.

Part C
The Report

Chapter 9

WRITING THE REPORT

Chapter topic list

---

1 **Establishing the structure of the report**

2 **Planning the detailed contents**

3 **Format**

4 **Different audiences**

5 **Language**

6 **Example report**

7 **Referencing, citation and attribution of source material**

8 **Submission form**

Introduction

Having done all of your planning, research and analysis, you may now feel that you are facing the hardest task of all, which is to write the Report. You need not worry: once you have started (which is the hardest step of all) you should find that all your preparatory work will fall into place and you will produce the report with relative ease.

However, there are certain skills attached to report writing, and this chapter aims to familiarise you with them. They are critical, as one of the criteria for assessment set out in the Guidelines is a pass in communication skills which is achieved by:

- *A coherent and structured Report focused on the stated objectives and written in a lucid style.*
  (Module Guidelines Para 2.7)

The Guidelines specify the format of the report like this.

Introduction

- Topic chosen and its context
- Your reasons for choosing the topic
- Aims and objectives of the report

Information gathering

- Sources used, and reasons for their use (these must be secondary and may be primary)
- Description of methods used to gather information

Analysis

- Analysis of information

- Presentation of findings

Conclusions

- What the report has shown in relation to aims and objectives

BPP
PROFESSIONAL EDUCATION

1 ESTABLISHING THE STRUCTURE OF THE REPORT

1.1 The **structure** of your Report can make all the difference between passing and failing the Research and Analysis Project.

(a) A confidently presented, sensibly structured and well laid out report will attract the approval of the assessor, who will be far more likely to look favourably upon your efforts.

(b) A scrappy and ill thought out report, on the other hand, will mean that the assessor is more likely subconsciously to think that such poor presentation reflects poor preparation and confused thinking.

The external examiner has commented that candidates have failed the project because they have failed to follow the structure set out in the Guidelines. It is not sufficient just to describe the topic without the related analysis.

Overall design of the Report

1.2 The Guidelines set out the requirements.

(a) Overall structure for the main body of the report. This is as follows.

    (i)   Introduction and information gathering – up to 1,500 words
    (ii)   Analysis – up to 2,500 words
    (iii) Conclusions – up to 1,000 words

(b) Remember that the Guidelines impose an absolute maximum of 5,000 words for the whole project: if you exceed that number Oxford Brookes may well fail your project, regardless of the quality of the content. The figures given above are suggested word counts, not absolute requirements. The 5,000 word limit excludes the contents page, appendices and the bibliography. Appendices are not essential, and you should only produce them if they are strictly necessary although that is the obvious place to put your spreadsheet. If you do submit appendices there can be no more than five A4 pages, including your spreadsheet workings.

Remember to indicate your total word count on the title page of your report when you submit it to Oxford Brookes University. You must also fill it in on your submission form.

We suggest the following overall design for your report.

Page	Content
Page 1 – Title page	Who the report is for
	Who has written the report
	Date
	Title
	Word count
Page 2 – Contents	Table of contents
Pages 3 and 4	Terms of reference
	Executive summary
	Information gathering
Pages 5 to ?	The main content of the report
Page ? – Conclusions	Conclusions, drawn from the above
Page ?	Appendices (no more than five A4 pages)

(c) Note that the Guidelines state:

> 'The Research and Analysis Report and Key Skills Statement should be word processed on A4 paper and presented in a plastic folder/wallet.'

1.3 Page 1: Title page

Title
Author
Date
Word count

An example is shown below:

Oxford Brookes University

Research and analysis report

The effects of technological change on staffing costs

By: Paul Smith

March 2005

4,853 words

Page 2: Contents

1.4 Table of contents

Outline the contents of the report in numbered sections

Here is an example.

Contents	Page no.
Introduction	
1 Terms of reference	X
2 Executive summary	X
Information gathering	
3 Primary sources	X
4 Secondary sources	X
5 *Analysis*	X
6 *Conclusion*	X
Appendix A - questionnaire	
Appendix B - spreadsheet	

Pages 3 and 4: Introduction

1.5 You are limited to 1,500 words on the Introduction and Information gathering sections, and you must be quite rigorous in observing this. The Introduction will consist of two components: the **terms of reference** and **executive summary**.

1.6   Terms of reference set out the purpose for which the Report is written. They can be based around the proposition which you are examining, and the reason why you selected it.

Here is an example taken from a student dissertation on the communication of company environmental data and the use of environmental cost accounting and environmental performance indicators.

Example

Introduction

1.1   The extent of the subject area

This dissertation will focus on environmental impact disclosures made by companies to external audiences. I will achieve this by analysing the current state of environmental reporting which will then be taken one step further by introducing two methods of disclosing such information and the benefits they may achieve.

I chose to study the topic of environmental disclosure because I am aware of 'green' issues gaining increasing importance through media exposure and environmental events. This is filtering through to businesses where a rise in interest and concern about the environment has been reflected in new demands for information (Butler, 1992). The Advisory Committee on Business and the Environment (1996) explain:

'Deeper knowledge of a business's environmental performance would help analysts, fund managers and other key players to form more accurate judgements of its risk profile and worth.' (pp36). However, the 'Business and the Environment' journal (August 1997) indicates that this is not as straightforward as may first appear: 'In less than a generation, society will look back at the availability of environmental performance information today and be amazed at the gaps, clutter and noise.' (pp 4) This hints that a study in this area will provide several issues for discussion.

1.2   Aims and objectives of the dissertation

My dissertation will attempt to solve the following concerns.

- How and why companies currently disclose their environmental impact information, including a consideration of:

  (1)   The methods utilised
  (2)   The extent of the data content
  (3)   The vehicle of communication used for this distribution and its effectiveness
  (4)   The audience they are aiming at
  (5)   Their motivations for disclosing
  (6)   The influence wider accountability has on their motivations – if any

- Does the management cost accounting tool of activity based costing lend itself to be adapted to environmental cost disclosure and help external readers understand a company's environmental situation?

- Do environmental performance indicators, as a form of environmental reporting, help external readers understand a company's environmental situation?

- Which of ABC or EPIs offer a better foundation for company environmental disclosure?

- Is a standard environmental disclosure methodology possible? If so, what barriers will be incurred?

1.7   Note that this is just an example: terms of reference can be set out in a more tabular style, or could be a numbered list of points. Here is an example of a slightly more 'chatty' style, taken from a dissertation on the contribution of reward systems to company success.

Example

Introduction

This project evolved from a year's work in the statistics and finance department in Q Ltd. During the year I spent much of my time analysing sales and contribution figures for individual areas and for the whole company. The other half of my job was to calculate commission payments each month and to authorise bonuses.

I was particularly interested in how the accounting and control systems within Q Ltd influenced behaviour and in turn what result these changes in behaviour had on the firm. At the same time as this it was clear that Q Ltd was experiencing deteriorating sales and declining contribution.

Therefore I set myself the aim to explore how effective different reward systems (which require accounting and control systems to operate) have been and could be used in improving sales performance, contribution and ultimately the profit of the company. Conclusions are hard to prove but theory, opinion and logic can lead to some recommendations.

Structure of the report

Initially a chapter on the theory of reward systems will set the foundation for comments made throughout the text. Next, a short chapter on the structure and performance of Q Ltd should help the reader to understand and appreciate later references to the company in the main body of the project.

Rewards for salesmen will then be analysed in the next chapter. This will include a section on targets, due to their function as a basis for rewarding salesmen. Several pay schemes will be analysed in chapter 6 followed by a short chapter on competitions and incentives.

Chapter 8 will discuss how managers and executives are rewarded. After a short introduction, a section on the theory of truth inducing incentives will help reveal the behavioural problems which can arise in setting targets. Management pay schemes within Q Ltd will then be looked at followed by a longer section on executive incentives.

All these points will be brought together in the concluding chapter.

Executive summary

1.8 The executive summary should consist of just a few paragraphs summarising your main findings and recommendations. Although this appears early in the Report, forming part of the Introduction, you should not actually write it until the end. The purpose is to arm the reader with an idea of the conclusion you have reached, which will better enable him or her to appreciate what you say in your report.

Here is an example, which is taken from the dissertation on company environmental data.

Example: Executive summary

Demands for environmental information from companies are increasing. However, there are no standard methods for company disclosure of such data. This dissertation attempted to answer how and why companies are currently communicating environmental data, via an analysis of both environmental publications and a questionnaire I devised and sent to thirty companies.

It was found that methods and extent of data disclosure vary immensely between firms with little actual concrete information detailed. Environmental data is offered in both company annual reports and separate environmental publications. Both infer that environmental concern does not prevail over business benefits as the cause for such disclosure.

With a view to implementing standardisation, I constructed a set of activity based costing (ABC) environmental accounts and environmental performance indicators (EPIs) for the cereal manufacturer Weetabix Ltd, focusing on waste disposal costs.

Environmental disclosure can progress via implementing a standard disclosure methodology, together with independent verification procedures. These efforts will, hopefully, increase the seriousness of the issue and enable inter firm comparisons. However, success of standardisation revolves around the introduction, if possible, of a common interpretation framework for environmental costs and issues. Without this, environmental disclosure will never be placed on a level equal to other business concerns.

1.9 Again, it is common for executive summaries to be presented as a numbered list of points, and this is very much a case of personal preference. An example of this style is given here, drawn from the dissertation on reward systems.

Example

Summary of findings

(1) A change in a reward system will result in changed objectives for individuals and ultimately changed objectives for the organisation.

(2) The new pay scheme for salesmen changes their objective to maximising contribution rather than sales turnover.

(3) The new pay scheme for managers changes their objectives to maximising profit rather than contribution.

(4) Target setting is made very much more important by the introduction of the new pay scheme. For this reason more participation in the target setting process is required and the importance of truthful statements of sales managers' expectations needs to be stressed.

(5) To ensure the maximum benefit is gained from the new pay scheme more information needs to be given regarding the commission earned on different products; namely more information about margins.

(6) Other rewards, such as competitions, training, cars and promotion should not be forgotten, but instead should be integrated into the reward system so as to optimise motivation of the salesforce.

(7) Effectively planned and controlled reward systems do contribute to company success.

Page 5: Information gathering

1.10 This section will include the sources of information you used, and explain why you used them. It will explain the methods used to gather the information. It will explain where your conclusions have come from. The Guidelines include this because one of the purposes of the Research and Analysis Project is to demonstrate your ability to gather information and then apply that information.

1.11 It is possible to show how information has been gathered in a tabular format, if the subject matter warrants it. If, for example, your report is examining results or activities over a period of time, and your work is carried out alongside, it could be a time and word-effective way of explaining what you have done to present it as a chart.

Example

Monthly progress	Sept	Oct	Nov	Dec	Jan	Feb	Mar	Apr	May
Project proposal									
Preliminary research									
Exploratory interview									
Further interviews (× 4)									
Primary research									
Findings analysed									
Written report									

1.12 As you have seen in earlier chapters, there are two types of information: primary information and secondary information.

(a) Primary information is data which is collected specifically for a given project, for example the management accounts of the particular company you are writing about.

(b) Secondary information is that which can also be used for some purpose other than the specific task in hand, for example statistics for an industry in general. Secondary information can be regarded more as background information.

1.13 You need to consider in what order you will present the information you have obtained. If you need to set the scene and provide background information for the industry you are dealing with, and then move on to the precise results of the company under scrutiny, you should discuss your secondary information first. If, however, you are taking specific information relating to one company, and extrapolating or applying it elsewhere, then it may be better to present the primary information first.

We set out here an example, taken from a dissertation on performance measurement, which shows what information gathering techniques were used.

Example

Description of methods used to gather information

This describes in detail the procedure under which the research into this project was carried out. The research was broken down into two distinct sections – secondary research and primary research.

(a) **Secondary research**

The secondary research consisted of two different methods.

- **Conventional library research**. Reading through both books and journals, sorting out materials which covered operations management and management accounting areas, and following up references with various libraries. Facilities used for obtaining this data included: Oxford Brookes University, public libraries (ie Slough Central Library) and inter-library loan facilities (ie Thames Valley University).

- **Electronic research**. Searching through a variety of business related databases such as Searchbank, Financial Times, Economist and ABI. This initially proved to be a relatively quick way of finding and providing up-to-date information. However, it took considerable time to find articles with relevant data. The search yielded approximately fifty articles (1996-1999) drawn from journals in five disciplines: performance, measurement, dealer performance measurement (motor industry), forklift truck industry, balanced scorecard and customer satisfaction measurement. Once the information was found, this proved to be a very successful research method. Consequently, secondary research enabled the writer to achieve the project objectives in several ways.

  Firstly, it helped guide the writer in building up a good knowledge of the subject. An effective performance measurement model therefore could be devised.

  Secondly, it was also used as justification to evaluate the HDPMS critically in the Data Analysis section.

(b) **Primary research**

Primary data were obtained through the company's internal materials and interviews.

- **Internal materials**. Corporate literature and internal reports were kindly provided by a number of Z PLC departments such as Dealer Development, Finance, Marketing and Credit Control. The internal materials consisted of Z PLC Annual Reports, Z PLC Dealer Annual Business Plan, Z PLC European Project List Reviews, Customer Support Surveys and Monthly Awareness Reports.

  The internal data was utilised to examine the present HDPMS. This information was the foundation of the findings chapter (Chapter 4).

Page 6 onwards: information and analysis

1.14 This is the most important part of the Report, as it will contain the real meat of your argument.

1.15 The main content of the Report should follow numbered sections and numbered paragraphs, in the same sort of style as this textbook.

1.16 Each section should begin on a new sheet of paper. This makes it easier if you subsequently amend an early section at a later stage, as you will avoid having to repaginate the whole thing. Write on one the side of the paper only.

1.17 **Page ?: Conclusions**

In the conclusion you are asked to present your findings, and use your judgement as to what the data means. The conclusion should be supported by the arguments in your report. Paragraph 2.7 of the Guidelines says that a pass in the Analysis and Conclusions section of the Assessment Criteria will be achieved by:

> - A clear presentation of findings from the information gathered
> - Appropriate conclusions from the analysis related to the objectives of the report

To force yourself to ensure your conclusions are backed up by evidence, refer to relevant paragraph numbers in the main body of the report.

Example

Report

1 Meldarks Ltd ROCE has fallen from 15% to 10% in the past five years.

2 Net cash flows have switched from a net inflow of £3m to a net outflow of £0.5m.

3 Meldarks Ltd has kept buildings in the accounts at historical cost even though they are worth a lot more on a market value basis.

Conclusion

Meldarks' deteriorating ROCE (para 1) is made to look less obvious by low fixed asset valuations (para 3). This and the deteriorating cash flow (para 2) suggest that the company is in difficulties.

1.18 **Pages ? to ?: Appendices**

Put into the appendices anything the user does not have to know immediately to understand the contents of the Report. The most obvious item to put into an appendix is the spreadsheet. This is intended to 'analyse and present data in tabular and graphical form' according to the Guidelines, and is a compulsory component of your Report.

Appendices may also include:

- Calculations underpinning your narrative
- Facts of borderline relevance (but you should not have too many of those!)

Example

Text	Appendices
Over the past three years, reported ROCE has increased from X% to Y% largely as a result of the financial engineering: the continued use of fully depreciated fixed assets and a policy of non replacement (See Appendix A).	Here could go detailed calculations for the past three years, with workings to show how it is lower asset valuation rather than increased operating performance that has caused the improvement.

Remember that the appendices are limited to five pages, so you must be selective about their contents. Restrict yourself to the **spreadsheet** which you must produce, and maybe one other.

Make sure that your appendices make sense, and are not just jumbled workings with no logical structure. Otherwise their impact will be lost and you will derive no benefit from producing them.

1.19   **Back to page 3: Executive summary**

Write the executive summary at the front of the Report.

The executive summary is just this – a brief summary of the points raised in the Report. It goes at the front, but you write it after you have finished the body of the Report. It enables the reader of the Report to read the detail whilst already having read your conclusions and main comments. This structure means that the information, conclusions and overall thrust of the report can be absorbed more easily.

2   **PLANNING THE DETAILED CONTENTS**

2.1   This can be one of the most time-consuming tasks in producing a report such as this, but it is worth taking as much time as you need and not rushing. Much will depend on the extent to which you managed to organise your information at the information gathering and analysis stages. Once a detailed plan has been produced, the rest of the Report should slot into place.

Sometimes, you may be completely at a loss, so here are some rules of thumb.

Rule of thumb 1: look at the requirement

2.2   If you think that the **requirement** falls into **logical parts,** allocate separate sections for each requirement.

Rule of thumb 2: think of a structure

2.3   If you need to follow a line of reasoning, **identify the most logical way of making the data clear.**

2.4   **If you are at a loss for ideas,** then structure your requirements in a sensible and logical order based on, for example:

- Functions of the business (eg sales, marketing)
- Timescale
- Balanced scorecard categories
- Markets and customer bases
- Strategic business units

Rule of thumb 3: plan what you want to say

2.5   One approach is to jot down all the things you want to say as a series of headings, with perhaps a little expansion of some points. Then look at them together and, by experiment if necessary, put them into a logical order by putting numbers against each. Only if you are very certain that your thoughts are logical and coherent should you omit putting them on paper as a plan – apart from any other reason, you are likely to forget vital material if you do not have a plan.

You might try writing 'network' notes to present your headings visually (see the diagram).

A network note

```
                        ┌──────────────┐  →
                        │ INTRODUCTION │  →
                        └──────────────┘  →
                               │
   →  ┌──────────┐                          ┌──────────┐  →
   →  │ THEME A  │                          │ THEME B  │  →
   →  └──────────┘        ╭────────╮        └──────────┘  →
                          │ TOPIC  │
                          ╰────────╯
   →  ┌──────────┐                          ┌──────────┐  →
   →  │ THEME C  │                          │CONCLUSION│  →
   →  └──────────┘                          └──────────┘  →
```

Rule of thumb 4: separate pages for new sections

2.6   **Start each section on a separate piece of paper.** This means that you can alter some sections without having to repaginate all the other ones.

Rule of thumb 5: number every paragraph

2.7   **Give each section a number,** and number every paragraph in that section in a hierarchy, like the paragraph numbering in this textbook. This makes cross-referencing very easy.

3   FORMAT

3.1   The Research and Analysis Project will be assessed and graded as either a pass or a fail. Here is a table which shows the criteria on which presentation will be judged for a clear pass (which you will be intending to achieve) a marginal pass (which might therefore have to be the subject of some discussion) and a fail (which you are trying to avoid).

Clear pass	Precise, professional format and structure with	Format = look at any formal business report that you can find. Try your workplace.
	Good concise use of relevant appendices	Appendices are for supporting information, but remember – no more than 5 pages.
Marginal pass	Recognisable format and structure, although occasionally unclear	Overlap of topics
	Limited irrelevant used of appendices	Poor use of appendices – information which is not strictly necessary.
Marginal fail	Recognisable format, but ...poor use of structure	OK, it **looks** like a business report but this is not good enough.
	Difficult to navigate	You have not **organised** your material in a logical way.
		The marker finds it hard to find the way around your report; he/she has to jump to and fro to find relevant data.

Exercise 1

Here is a paragraph containing some facts about Carnelian Ltd, in no particular order. This paragraph illustrates two things.

- It will show you quite how irritating unstructured and unformatted data is to read and make sense of. The marker may be under time pressure, so don't annoy him or her.

- It introduces you to the concept of format and structure.

Carnelian Ltd was founded over a century ago. 50% of its sales are exports to Germany. It has two principal shareholders, Ms Underwood and Mr Mongrove, who each own 50% of the issued share capital. Net assets are £150,000. The company specialises in making artificial flowers for sale. The Finance Director is Mr Mace. There are 20 employees, of whom five are employed in marketing (reporting to Ms Underwood). The production department report to Mr Mongrove. Turnover per annum is £1m. Issued share capital is 1,000 ordinary shares of £1 each. The company used to market by mail order, but now mainly promotes itself through its website. The two people who work in accounts and the IT expert report to Mr Mace. The best selling flower is the silk orchid accounting for 30% of turnover. Profit before tax was £50,000 in 20X1. No one customer accounts for more than 1% of turnover.

Required

Produce a report about Carnelian Ltd incorporating all the data above.

Answer

You could have chosen a number of different formats. At the very least, you could have organised the data in logical order.

Report

To: The marker
From: A Candidate
Date:

Re Carnelian Ltd

Contents

1   Executive summary
2   Products and markets
3   Organisation and management
4   Financial position
Appendix A: customers
Appendix B: financial position

1   Executive summary

1.1   Carnelian Ltd is a long established, privately owned company specialising in the manufacture of artificial flowers for sale worldwide, employing a functional departmentation structure.

2   Customers and markets

2.1   Turnover from artificial flowers is £1m per annum.

2.2   £300,000 derives from one product, the silk orchid.

2.3   Exports to Germany account for 50% of turnover.

2.4   No one customer accounts for 1% of turnover. See Appendix A for a list of customers.

2.5   The main marketing activity is the website, which has replaced mail order.

3   Organisation and management

3.1   The company employs 23 people, including the directors.

3.2   The company is divided into three departments.

- Marketing – 5 personnel reporting to Ms Underwood.
- Production – 12 personnel reporting to Mr Mongrove.
- Finance and IT – three personnel reporting to Mr Mace.

4   Financial position and capital structure

4.1   The company makes a profit margin of 5% and a return of assets of 33%. See Appendix B for workings.

4.2   The sole shareholders are Ms Underwood and Mr Mongrove, each of whom own 500 of the issued share capital of 1000 ordinary shares of £1 each.

Appendix A

List of customers

Appendix B: financial position

B.1   Profit margin

Profit £50,000/turnover £1m = 5%

B.2   ROCE

£50,000/£150,000 =33%; Turnover: £1m
Net assets £150,000

Comment on the answer

You will note that the very requirement to produce a report structuring the data suggested some useful analysis such as calculating ROCE and profit margins. We are not saying that this is perfect by any means, but you can tell that the data about Carnelian Ltd is much easier to grasp than it was before. You may have chosen a different structure of course.

4 DIFFERENT AUDIENCES

4.1 Before you start to write the report itself, you should consider the **style and tone which you should adopt**. This may depend on the identity of the potential readers of the Report.

(a) The **main readers** will be the assessor and the members of the Oxford Brookes University Examination Board. The assessor will read the entire Research and Analysis Project in detail, while the members of the Examination Board are more likely to refer to it in part in order to get a general flavour or impression as to the standard of the material produced.

(b) You will also be required to make a presentation on your Report to your mentor, and probably also your peer group of other candidates, where your mentor has more than one student. Techniques for preparation and presentation to your mentor and peer group will be covered in a later chapter, but you should bear in mind that you may be **supplying your audience with extracts from your report, and consider this when writing it.**

The assessor

4.2 The assessor will be a member of the staff at Oxford Brookes University. You can assume that he or she will therefore have a wide range of technical knowledge, which means that **you will not need to explain general technical terms.**

However, you should think carefully about the subject matter of your report. You may have to provide more background material or explanation of terms if any of the following apply:

(a) Your report is about a **particular organisation**, because the assessor will not be familiar with it

(b) Your report is on a **particular industry**, because again it is unlikely that the assessor will have a detailed knowledge of it

(c) You have chosen, and received approval for, a topic which is not included on the list of **suggested topics published by Oxford Brookes University.** If this is the case, you may have to treat the assessor as an educated layman, and ensure that you define and explain any terminology which cannot be routinely understood

(d) You are an **overseas candidate** and you are discussing practices or procedures which are unique to your own country or your part of the world. In that case, you will have to provide sufficient information (still within your 5,000 word limit!) to enable the assessor to understand the points you make.

4.3 **The Oxford Brookes University Examination Board**

The Board will not be looking at the fine detail of your report. It is most likely that they will only look at it in any depth if you are marginal candidate and your project is hovering between a pass and a fail.

As a rule of thumb it is best to treat the Examination Board as your boss: pretend that the reader of your report is the managing director of the company which employs you, and that

197

a promotion depends on it. So use a suitably polite, but not unduly deferential style. Write as though you mean what you say and you believe in it!

If you can write reports at work, you can do so for the Research and Analysis Project.

4.4 Your mentor and peer group

This category is arguably the least important in terms of considering your audience, but you should not ignore them. They at least will have the opportunity to quiz you face to face if something is unclear, unlike the assessor and the Examination Board.

If you give out extracts from your report as part of your presentation, you may receive valuable feedback from your mentor and peer group as to the level at which you have pitched your report. If they (especially your mentor) find it unduly technical and impenetrable it is likely that the assessor will too. It would then be sensible to review your report again before submission.

There is no formal requirement for your mentor to read your report, and certainly there is no intention that the mentor should mark it or review it. However you may find it helpful if you ask your mentor to read it through to give you comments on the overall impression, style and structure.

5 LANGUAGE

5.1 When starting your research work and planning for your Report, you may feel that 5,000 words is a lot, and wonder how you will manage to produce that much. By the time you come to write it, you may wonder how you are going to manage to say everything you need to within only 5,000 words, especially given the breakdown given by the Guidelines. This allows you

(a) Up to 1,500 words for the introduction and information gathering sections
(b) Up to 2,500 words for the analysis section
(c) Up to 1,000 words for the conclusion

Remember that these figures are a maximum number allowed. If you consider that the word count so far for this chapter alone is 5,175, you will appreciate that 5,000 is not a very great number.

One way to keep your word count under tight control is to be as efficient as possible in your use of language. Practise the use of concise and precise language in all your written work, not just this report.

Stylistic requirements

5.2 There are certain stylistic requirements in the writing of reports, formal or informal.

5.3 Coupled with this, you may have time management problems with your writing. In the context of this Report, however, you do have the luxury of taking as much time as you need, unlike in your ACCA exams.

5.4 Consider the following actual extract from an exam script submitted for a past exam paper for the Chartered Institute of Marketing (Pearson, 1993). Note in particular the writing times.

> (a) Proposals for change in the organisational structure.
>
> (b) Creation of 'strategic business units' centred around each terminal
>
> This would allow each terminal to be represented at board level with each manager having his own operational and commercial staff beneath him. This will involve a huge restructuring of the organisation and individual job roles/responsibilities, however this move is necessary in order that commercial and operations staff work alongside each other and cooperate to solve problems in the most effective way, to the benefit of EAL in serving the needs of its customers. All commercial versus operations conflicts would be solved lower down the hierarchy which will in turn be flattened out as a result of restructuring. Each terminal general manager must have beneath him his appropriate support staff for his commercial and operations roles eg catering manager, retail operations manager, quality control engineers.'
>
> Total words = c 140   **Total writing time = 8 minutes**

5.5   Keeping the same heading we might change the section to read as follows.

> Each terminal to become an SBU under a general manager with his own support staff (catering, retail operations, quality control etc).
>
> BENEFIT
>
> Although requiring much restructuring and reformulation of job descriptions:
>
> (a) Commercial and operations staff would work together in meeting the needs of the customer
> (b) All commercial v operations conflicts would be solved lower down the hierarchy
> (c) Each terminal would be represented at board level
>
> Total words = c 70   **Total writing time = 4 minutes**

The re-wording cuts the original word length in half.

- It is **easier to understand and mark.**

- **It takes half the time to write, leaving you more time to think and to make extra points.**

- It takes up less of your precious ration of words.

Basic principle: 'Less is More'

5.6

	Example	
Rule	**No**	**Yes**
Keep words simple	Expenditure vs	Cost
	Aggregate vs	Total
Short words are quicker to write	Terminate vs	End
Avoid words you don't need to write	I would be grateful	Please
	Due to the fact that	Because
	In the not too distant future	Soon (better: give a time scale)
	At this point in time	Now (or currently)
	In the majority of instances	In most cases (or usually)
	It is recommended that A Ltd should consider	A Ltd should consider
	36 words (55 syllables)	14 words (18 syllables)

Jargon

5.7 Be **careful** of jargon: jargon is **technical language with a precise meaning** and therefore has its uses. Keep in mind the needs and likely response of your audience. Do not try to blind the assessor with technological jargon. If you do, the assessor may question whether you understand it yourself.

5.8 **Be precise.** Be careful of 'very' 'fairly' 'partly', unless you are unable to state facts.

5.9 **Avoid patronising language**

(a) There is a fine line between explaining technical vocabulary or situations which may not be familiar to the reader, and 'dumbing down'. By that we mean reducing the level of your writing to something well below the assumed competence of your audience.

(b) You do not need to explain routine technical terms. You can assume that your audience has a reasonable awareness of factors such as the current state of the domestic and international economy, the debate over the UK's adoption of the Euro, the advance of e-commerce, the now tempered enthusiasm for dot com start ups and so forth.

(c) Your meetings with your mentor and your peer group presentation could provide a suitable forum for you to discuss the style of language which you have adopted. You could receive some constructive feedback.

Spellcheckers

5.10 The Research and Analysis Project is designed to enable you to demonstrate your IT skills, among others. The main means of doing this is by the production of a spreadsheet, but you should remember that there are other IT tools which can help you, and which you will be expected to use.

5.11 The Criteria for Assessment of the report, set out in the Module Guidelines, paragraph 2.7, states that your IT skills will be assessed. As well as the production of a spreadsheet, a pass will be achieved by

> • Application of IT software to achieve a document with a clear layout and logical structure

5.12 The spellchecker is one of the most useful elements in a word processing package, and can help both the poor speller and the clumsy typist. It is similar in most packages. If you are working in Word, click on Tools and then Spelling, and Word will work right through your document seeing if the spelling matches the spelling of words in the computer's dictionary. If not, it will suggest alternatives from which you click on the best one to replace what you have typed.

For example, if you have typed 'drp' the choices you are offered include 'drip', 'drop', 'dry' and 'dip'. You also have the option to add what you have typed to the computer's dictionary, so that unusual technical or foreign words are not thrown up repeatedly.

5.13 You must bear in mind, however, that the **spellchecker will only pick up words which do not match an entry in the computer's dictionary**: it will not recognise the fact that you have merely typed in the wrong word, for example 'from' instead of 'form'. Take care also if you are an overseas candidate whose spellchecker is set to another language, including one of the nine variations of English included in many standard word processing packages. As the report must be written in English, you should set the spellchecker to UK English.

5.14 You still need to read through what you have written, for sense and correct language. Some people like to do this on the screen at the end of each section or paragraph, while others prefer to print out at intervals and read the hard copy. It really does not matter which you do, as long as you do one of them.

Grammar checkers

5.15 Having reached the stage you have in your academic and professional careers, your standard of grammar should be quite high. It is still worth running the grammar check over your report, however, as it enables you to stand back and see the wood from the trees.

5.16 The grammar check will perform tasks such as:

(a) Detecting sentences where you have omitted the verb

(b) Detecting sentences where you have used mixed singular and plural subject and verb (for example 'two of the main reasons for the development of the multinational company is ....'.)

(c) Indicating sentences which are unduly long or have too many clauses, potentially confusing the reader

You can specify in the grammar check what style of language you are using, such as 'casual' 'technical' and 'standard'. You can also use a grammar option that gives the readability statistics of your work. This is a useful tool in that it can indicate when your language is becoming over obscure.

5.17 **Thesaurus**

If you think your use of words is becoming repetitive, try the thesaurus. This will suggest alternatives and can also supply meanings.

6 EXAMPLE REPORT

6.1 This is an example of a report compiled from given data. It is obviously shorter than the one you will be expected to produce, and there is far less data to deal with, but it will give you a good illustration in miniature of the way in which information can be used to produce a report.

6.2 You are the management accountant of a company which specialises in producing dairy products for the slimming market. The results of your latest research have just been published.

6.3 **Data**

Market Research Results

This research was carried out from January to June 2002, using in-depth interviews in the respondents' homes, recorded on tape and interpreted by ourselves, 'The XYZ Research Agency', specialists in market research for the food industry.

Sample size: 500
Age range: 15-55
Socio-economic groups: ABC1*
Locations: Bristol, Manchester and Greater London
Sex: Males and Females

Three broad categories were tested and the results are as follows:

Motives for wanting to lose weight	*% of respondents with weight problems mentioning*
To feel good physically	68
For health reasons	67
To stay fit	43
Because I want to live longer	25
To stay mentally alert	23
To be more attractive	21
To be more popular	15

Methods for weight control	
Avoid certain foods, eat 'slimming items'	32
Eat and drink less	23
Play sports, keep 'fit'	22
'Have certain diet days'	7
Take medicines, stimulants	3

Food which people dislike giving up	*% of respondents with weight problems mentioning*
Cakes, pies, bakery products	31
Sweets, sugar	23
Beer, alcoholic beverages	17
Meat, sausages etc	15
Chocolate	13
Cream	9
Fruit juices	9
Potatoes	9
Pasta	9

In general, the comments also revealed that dieting means a loss of pleasure at mealtimes, causes problems when one can't eat the same as the family and also one is regarded as being 'ill' when dieting.

* Socio-economic groupings:

A   Higher managerial, Chief Executives etc.
B   Managerial, Executives etc
C1   Higher clerical, Supervisory etc

Required

Write a short formal report to the Marketing Director, Mr David Forsythe, highlighting the conclusions drawn from this research. Your recommendation will be used to help identify new products for possible development in this market

6.4 Suggested answer

To: Marketing Director
From: Management Accountant
Date:

REPORT ON NEW PRODUCT DEVELOPMENT

1   Executive summary
2   Methods of research
3   Findings

1   EXECUTIVE SUMMARY

This report highlights the conclusions drawn from market research into the 'slimming market' conducted by The XYZ Research Agency between January and June 2002. The report, to include recommendations for possible new product development and new promotion methods was requested by Mr David Forsythe, Marketing Director.

METHOD OF RESEARCH

This report has been compiled from research findings designed to show:

Respondents' motives for losing weight
Respondents' methods of weight control
Foods which respondents were reluctant to give up

Respondents were a sample group of 500 ABC1s aged 15-55 of both sexes in the Bristol, Manchester and Greater London areas. In-depth interviews were recorded in the respondents' homes, and analysed by XYZ Research: see Appendix A.

FINDINGS

Motives for losing weight (see Appendix A)

Most respondents expressed their motives for losing weight as the desire for physical well-being (68%), health (67%) and fitness (43%), with related concerns, such as longevity and mental alertness, also scoring over 20%.

Perhaps unexpectedly, the motives most commonly associated with 'slimming' – increased attractiveness and popularity – scored comparatively low, with 21% and 15% respectively.

Methods of weight control (see Appendix B)

The most frequently-stated method of weight control (32%) was based on food selection: consuming 'slimming items' and avoiding certain foods. Reduced consumption in general (23%) and increased physical activity (22%) featured strongly, however, compared to the use of medicines and stimulants, mentioned by only 3% of respondents.

Foods respondents disliked giving up (see Appendix C)

A significant proportion of respondents were reluctant to give up foods in the high-calorie 'snack' categories: cakes, pies and bakery products (31%), sweets and sugar (23%). Alcohol (17%), meat (15%) and chocolate (13%) also featured significantly, compared to the more 'healthy' food groups such as fruit juice, potatoes and pasta (9% each). Cream was the only dairy product mentioned, (9%)

General comments

Respondents experienced 'dieting' as a loss of pleasure, an inconvenience when it comes to family meals, and a social stigma.

APPENDIX A: MOTIVES FOR WEIGHT LOSS

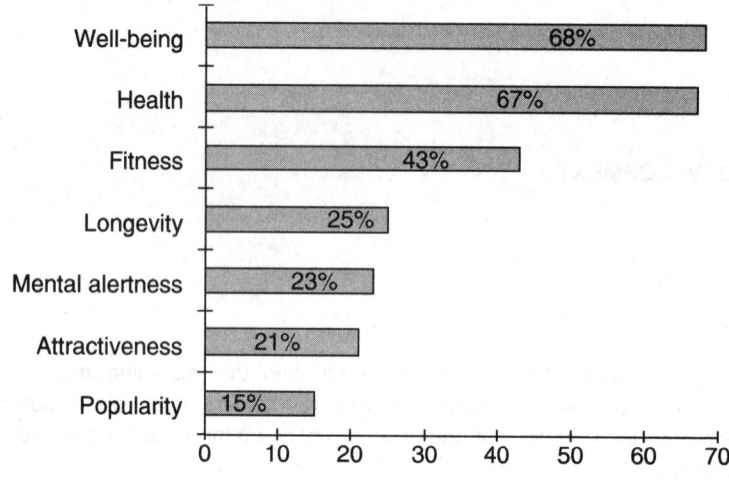

APPENDIX B: METHODS OF WEIGHT CONTROL

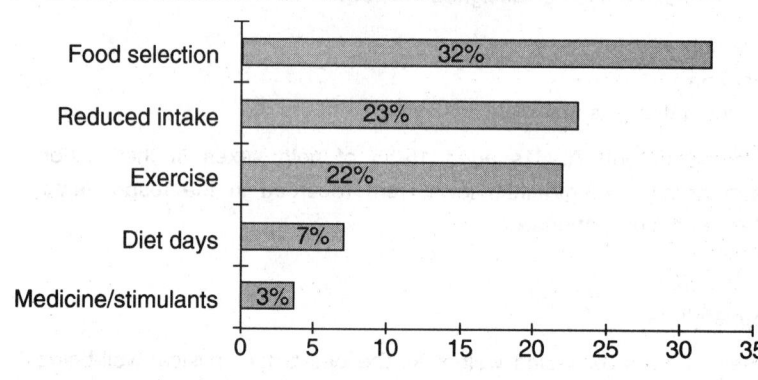

APPENDIX C: FOODS WHICH PEOPLE DISLIKE GIVING UP

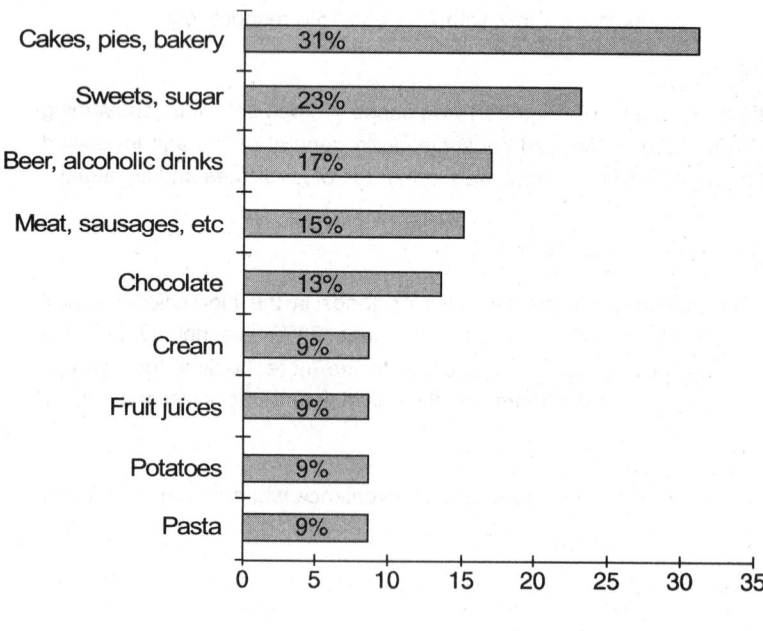

6.5 **Debrief.** What did you think of the report? Note that the report writer had constructed a graph of the data. You are required to submit a spreadsheet as part of your Report, but don't forget other ways of making your points clear, such as graphs and diagrams.

7 REFERENCING, CITATION AND ATTRIBUTION OF SOURCE MATERIAL

7.1 The Assessment Criteria in the Module Guidelines refer to referencing twice. In order to achieve a pass for your Communication Skills, you must demonstrate

- **Clear and accurate referencing**

Additionally, in order to achieve a pass under the heading of Information Gathering, you must have achieved

- **Referencing of appropriate sources of information**

Very clear guidance on references is provided in Appendix 1 to the Guidelines. The information is set out again here.

7.2 Extract from Guidelines

Appendix 1: HOW TO REFERENCE YOUR WORK

How to Reference Your Work and Construct a Bibliography

Referencing

Whenever you are directly quoting or referring to one of your sources of information, you should acknowledge this in the text as you go along. References should be clearly set out using the Harvard System. It is important to double check that all references in your text appear in the bibliography.

Bibliography

Your bibliography comes at the end of your Report. It is a list of all the sources you have used in compiling your Report eg books, articles, company publications, newspaper articles etc. The bibliography should be set out alphabetically using the Harvard System.

How to reference your work and construct a bibliography

Correctly referencing your work is simple, and compulsory. You must reference all your sources of information. We do advise you to reference as you go along, rather than leaving it until the end of your assignment. There is nothing more time consuming than constructing a bibliography retrospectively.

References within your text

In the Harvard system references within the text are set out as follows:

EXAMPLE

In any organisation made up of different interest groups some conflict over goals is inevitable (Needle, 1994).

In the bibliography the reference shown above would appear in this way:

EXAMPLE OF A BOOK REFERENCE

Needle, D. (1994) <u>Business in Context</u>. 2nd Edition, London, Chapman & Hall

NB: You only cite the edition if it is not the first. Please note that the title of the book is either underlined or emboldened.

EXAMPLE OF A JOURNAL OR NEWSPAPER REFERENCE

Buxton, J. (1998) Management: The Growing Business: Co-operative's Wheels of Fortune. <u>The Financial Times</u>, February 24

NB: It's the title of the journal or newspaper that is either underlined or emboldened.

EXAMPLE OF A JOURNAL ARTICLE WHERE NO AUTHOR IS GIVEN

<u>The Economist</u> (1997) 'New technology is no snap', October 11, p125

Citing Electronic Sources

No standard, agreed method has yet evolved for citing electronic sources. Electronic sources may include eftp sites, telnet addresses, WWW and gopher pages, newsgroups and e-mail messages. The following book should help:

Li, Xia and Crane, Nancy B. (1996**) Electronic styles, a handbook for citing electronic information** 2nd Edition, Medford, N.J., Information Today

---

There are also several guides you can view on the Internet.

A recommended example of a guide to citing Internet sources is accessible via:

http://cis.bournemouth.ac.uk/servicedepts/newlis/LIS_Gen/citation/harvardsystint.html

NB: This has a useful one-page summary as an appendix.

A simplified solution might be:

Author's last name, First name. Title of work. *Title of complete work if applicable in italics.* [protocol and address] [path] (date of message or visit).

EXAMPLE

Walker, Janice R. MLA-Style Citations of Electronic Sources.

http://www.cas.usf.edu/english/walker/mla.html 11 September 1996

7.3 You must observe these conventions, as the assessor will be looking for evidence of it. The logic is that in the main body of your report you refer to anyone whose work you are quoting or using, for example (Smith, 2002). Should the reader want to know more about that point, or read the book itself, they can turn to the bibliography to obtain full information about it. There it might be presented as

Smith, G. S. (2002) *Management Accounting Can Be Fun*, 3rd edition, London, Business Book Publishers.

7.4 If you have a variety of sources, you may want to split them into categories for your bibliography. A logical split might be:

(a) **References**: publications etc to which you have referred specifically in the text
(b) **Bibliography**: additional reading undertaken but not directly referred to in the text

7.5 Referencing correctly is also vital because it provides comfort that you have not plagiarised the work of anyone else. Whenever you mention thoughts or words of other people, you must attribute the source in the text and then give it in full in the bibliography. The external examiner has commented that in some cases students don't use enough external references, and in others they don't reference them properly. This can cause you to fail the project.

7.6 You may see in one book you are reading a reference to a source that the author has used and you may want to refer to that source yourself. In such a situation, you should make every effort to find a copy of the quoted source, so that you can quote it directly. If that is not possible (for example it is out of print or your library cannot locate a copy to borrow for you) you can refer to the book as follows:

Raimond, P. (1993) Management Projects. London, Chapman and Hall. Cited in Saunders, M., Lewis, P. and Thornhill, A. (2000) Research Methods for Business Students 2nd edition, Harlow, Financial Times Prentice Hall

This indicates clearly to the reader that you are citing something you have not read yourself, merely seen cited in another book. As far as possible you should try to obtain the original book and refer to it directly.

8 SUBMISSION FORM

8.1 Oxford Brookes University has produced a Submission form, two copies of which must accompany your work when it is submitted.

8.2   A copy of this is included here, but you should download two clean copies to submit with your project from the Oxford Brookes section of the ACCA website. The form changes from time to time, so submitting on a copy downloaded from the website will ensure that you are using the correct one.

8.3   See the form on the following page.

Note that this is not the same as the title page for your report, which will show your name, the title, the date and the word count, as discussed in section 1 of this chapter.

Submission Forms for Research and Analysis Project
INSTRUCTIONS

Sections A, B and C of this form should be completed by the student and Section D by the Mentor and accompany your work which must be sent **by some secure recorded means of delivery** to:

The ACCA Office, Oxford Brookes University, Wheatley Campus, Wheatley, OXFORD, OX33 1HX, United Kingdom

SECTION A (Student to complete)

Student Surname

Student First name

Student Address

Student Email address –
to receive project results via email. Please complete this only if you consent to receiving your results (and other correspondence) by email.

ACCA Student Registration number

Date of submission

I declare that the attached project is all my own work. I agree that I shall be bound by the regulations of Oxford Brookes University and the BSc (Applied Accounting Programme) regulations, which can be found on www.accaglobal.com/students/professionalscheme/degreepartnership/oxb_studyguide

Signature

Date   /   /

SECTION B (Payment Details)

A fee of £50 **sterling** must accompany this work which should be in the form of cheque, credit or UK debit card payment or bank draft. Cash is not acceptable.

Please choose **one** of the following options:

Option 1: Credit or UK Debit Card

Card Number   Start Date   Expiry Date   Issue No

Signature

Option 2: Cheque, or Bank Draft

You may opt to pay by cheque or bank draft (made payable to **OXFORD BROOKES UNIVERSITY**). **You must attach the cheques or Bank Draft to this form.**

FOR OFFICE USE ONLY

DATE RECEIVED ....   ACKNOWLEDGMENT SENT ....

PAYMENT RECEIVED ....   PAYMENT CLEARED ....

SENT TO MARKER ....   RECEIVED FROM MARKER ....

EXTERNAL EXAMINER ....   EXAM BOARD CONFIRMED ....

RESULT POSTED ....

Submission Forms for Research and Analysis Project
MARK SHEET

SECTION C (Student to complete)

Student Surname

Student First name

| | d | d | m | m | y | y |

ACCA Student Registration Number

Date of submission

Total Report word count:

Total Key Skills Statement word count:

Please note: this should not exceed 5,000 words, otherwise you risk failure

Please note: this should not exceed 1,500 words, otherwise you risk failure

SECTION D (Mentor to complete)

Mentor's Certification:

I certify that to the best of my knowledge the project is the student's own work and that it has been carried out in accordance with the University's regulations, (see Student Guide available on-line at www.acca.org.uk), and that three meetings have been held with the student in accordance with the guidelines contained in Section 2.3 of the Research and Analysis Project Guidelines.

Mentor's Name and Address (Please Print)

Capacity for acting as mentor:
(See 2.2 of the Research and Analysis Module Guidelines.)

Signature.. Date ....

SECTION E (For Office Use Only)

Marker's sheet

PROJECT	PASS	FAIL	COMMENTS
Communication Skills			
Information gathering			
Analysis and Conclusions			
IT Skills			
KEY SKILLS STATEMENT			
Preparing for meetings			
Questioning			
Listening			
The presentation			
Self-Assessment of Interaction			
OVERALL RESULT			

Marker's Code

Date

BPP
PROFESSIONAL EDUCATION

Chapter roundup

- Having completed this chapter, you should be able to establish the structure and form that your report will take.

- You are best advised to keep to the limits outlined by Oxford Brookes University as a guide to structure.

- You will have time to pay careful attention to language and structure.

Part D

Mentor meetings and the Key Skills Statement

Chapter 10

THE KEY SKILLS STATEMENT IN OUTLINE

Chapter topic list

1   Purpose and significance of the Key Skills Statement

2   Format and length

3   The communication process in outline

4   Potential problems in communication

5   Barriers to communication

6   Oral communication

7   Learning from communication

Introduction

The Key Skills Statement is the second element of the Research and Analysis Project, and is as vital as the Report. Do not give in to the temptation of overlooking its importance, assuming that you do not need to do much work on it and treating it as an afterthought. The requirements for the Statement are very precise, and you may find it quite challenging to include all of the required components in the limited number of words permitted.

The Key Skills Statement also requires you to describe and then reflect upon the meetings with your mentor, and it will provide evidence to the University of your skills of communication and self-analysis. The Guidelines describe it as an 'opportunity to demonstrate your personal learning that has occurred through interaction with your mentor...' and you should therefore view it as an opportunity, which could well be of value in your future career, rather than an additional chore.

---

1   PURPOSE AND SIGNIFICANCE OF THE KEY SKILLS STATEMENT

1.1   The Guidelines give a page of guidance on the preparation of the Key Skills Statement. The guidance is set out here.

> The Key Skills Statement is your opportunity to demonstrate your personal learning that has occurred through interaction with your mentor and peer discussion group if applicable.
>
> The Statement should concentrate on skills of communication and working with others and focus on your meetings with your mentor as the vehicle for your evidence.
>
> You should draw on the meetings with your mentor and, if applicable your peer group, to analyse your ability to communicate and work with others using the framework below.
>
> **PREPARING FOR MEETINGS**
>
> Describe how you prepared for the three meetings. Assess the importance of planning and organising in relation to the effectiveness of your meetings and of meetings in general.

> **QUESTIONING**
>
> Consider and explain the role of questioning in ensuring productive discussions with your mentor, in particular the use of appropriate questioning techniques.
>
> **LISTENING**
>
> Explain the importance of listening in ensuring that communication with your mentor was effective. Consider active listening techniques, sources of error and distortion in communication.
>
> **THE PRESENTATION**
>
> Assess the presentation identifying what went well and what could have been improved.
>
> You should attach 2 sides of A4 to your key skills statement showing an outline of your presentation.
>
> **SELF ASSESSMENT OF INTERACTION**
>
> Using an appropriate model of communication analyse and evaluate interaction with your mentor and if applicable with your peer discussion group, in relation to the key elements of successful communication.
>
> Reflect on IT skills used.
>
> For each of the above areas illustrate your self-analysis with examples taken from the discussions and by referring to appropriate literature on communication. Where appropriate consider what you would do differently in the future in similar circumstances.
>
> As a guide each section should be approximately 300 words. However, the overall total of 1,500 words, excluding your presentation outline, should not be exceeded for the key skills statement.

Purpose

1.2 The requirement to produce a Key Skills Statement is included to ensure that you extract the maximum value from the preparation of the Report and from the Research and Analysis Project as a whole. Although the end requirement is a structured piece of writing, it encompasses evidence of skills such as preparation, questioning, listening, responding to questions, public presentation and self assessment.

1.3 Demonstration of these skills will show that you have not just the ability to write, but also to **communicate** in a variety of ways.

1.4 The University makes it clear that the production of the Key Skills Statement is to be a **learning process**. Much of the Statement you produce will consist of reflection on the process for the production of the Report. There is scope for identifying how you could have improved on aspects of this, for example what could have been improved in your presentation. You are required to carry out a self assessment of your abilities to

- Listen
- Ask questions
- Respond to others

It is important to note that you are not expected to have achieved perfection in these skills, but rather to recognise their importance and consider the extent to which you have tried to exercise them.

1.5 When covering each of the topic headings, you are actively encouraged to consider what you might do differently in the future sin similar circumstances. The process of giving such thought to these key skills in the required depth is an essential part of the Research and Analysis Project as a whole and the University believes that you will derive great benefit from doing so.

1.6   As part of the self-assessment process, you will be expected to exercise **honesty and integrity**, and identify your weak areas as well as your areas of strength. This critical self-evaluation is one of the essential procedures in gaining your degree.

Assessment

1.7   The Key Skills Statement, like the Report, will be marked in terms of a pass or a fail. A pass will be demonstrated by an analysis of your ability to communicate and work with others by providing:

(a)   Reflection on the nature and structure of your meeting with your mentor through the identification of relevant and influencing factors

(b)   Reflection on the meetings with your mentor examining the nature of the interactions which took place and showing an understanding of the key elements of successful face to face communication, in particular questioning and listening techniques

(c)   A clear outline for the presentation made at the third meeting, including identification of what went well and what could have been improved

(d)   A self assessment, drawing on evidence from meetings with your mentor, of your abilities to listen actively, ask appropriate questions, respond to others and achieve satisfactory outcomes.

2   FORMAT AND LENGTH

Format

2.1   The Key Skills Statement should be presented in the same format as the Research and Analysis Report. It should be word processed on A4 paper and presented in a plastic wallet with the Report. The Oxford Brookes Guidelines imply that you should submit a second submission with your Key Skills Statement.

2.2   The word count for the Key Skills Statement must be indicated on the front page, as was the case for the Report, and also on the Submission Form.

2.3   The Guidelines give a framework around which the Statement should be written. This includes five specific headings which must be covered.

(a)   Preparing for meetings
(b)   Questioning
(c)   Listening
(d)   The presentation
(e)   Self assessment of interaction

As well as the Key Skills Statement, you must produce two sides of A4 showing an outline of your presentation.

Length

2.4   The total word count for the Statement, not including the outline of your presentation, must not exceed 1,500. The Guidelines suggest that each section should be about 300 words long, although that is a guide, and you do not have to produce exactly that number for each section. You will find, however, that your ability to write cogently and concisely will be tested to the limit in trying to keep to only 300 words for some of the headings.

2.5 The Guidelines state that not only do you have to discuss the headings as described in Guidelines Section 2.5 on the Key Skills Statement, but you must also illustrate your self-analysis. You can do this with examples:

(a) Taken from the discussions

(b) By reference to the appropriate literature on communication set out in Appendix 2 to the Guidelines.

Where appropriate you are required to consider what you would do differently in the future in different circumstances.

2.6 You will find that covering all of that within the constraint of 300 words will be quite a difficult task, especially when you consider that this section alone, from the beginning of 2.1, is almost 300 words long! It will call for very disciplined writing, focusing precisely on what you have to say.

Style

2.7 **The style of writing in the Key Skills Statement will be different from that in the Report.** In the latter, your style will be quite formal. The purpose is to convey information, analyse that information and come to a conclusion based upon it. Much of the language used is likely to be technical and complex, and apart from the Introduction where you set out what you have tried to achieve in writing the Report, it will largely be written in the third person.

This means that you will not refer to yourself as such, but rather to the Report and its results.

Example

First person: I discovered that 67% of the finance directors who responded to my questionnaire felt that their company accounting procedures had benefited from the existence of internal audit.

Third person: It was noted that 67% of the finance directors who responded to the questionnaire felt that their company accounting procedures had benefited from the existence of internal audit.

2.8 The Key Skills Statement demands a different approach. You will be setting out **your own assessment of your own abilities,** and in some cases you will have to be fairly critical. You will be expected to recognise weaknesses which you have identified and consider how they can be remedied or improved. Such self-evaluation and criticism can often be a difficult experience, and writing about it even more so. There is a risk that you will lack confidence in carrying out this exercise, and that this will be reflected in your style of writing.

2.9 You will be writing in the first person (ie using 'I' and referring specifically to your own experiences) and this in itself can cause you to feel vulnerable, as it is often easier to immerse oneself in anonymity. You must maintain your confidence in doing this, and ensure that you highlight the good points. **Where you identify weaknesses, counter them by saying how you will improve upon them.**

2.10 Imagine yourself in this scenario

Exercise 1

1   Your presentation to your mentor and a peer group of eight other Research and Analysis Project students has not gone well.

2   Just before delivering your presentation, you discovered that three of the other students had chosen exactly the same research topic as you, an analysis of the financial position of Marks and Spencer plc and the impact of its trading decisions on its suppliers. This made you feel nervous and exposed, as you would be faced with a highly knowledgeable audience.

3   Once the presentation started, you had too much to say, and had to bring proceedings to a fairly abrupt halt after 20 minutes, when the mentor indicated that you had taken up too much time. This meant that your conclusions remained largely unsaid.

4   During the brief period for questions allowed at the end, you were completely floored by a question on a complex accounting ratio from one of the other students researching Marks and Spencer, and became flustered and confused, unable to come up with an answer.

5   You feel that the presentation has been an unmitigated disaster, and wonder how you can possibly reflect this in the relevant section of your Key Skills Statement.

Spend five minutes thinking of how you can accentuate the positive things to come out of this experience.

Answer

The section of your Key Skills Statement dealing with the presentation could look something like this.

PRESENTATION

1   I delivered my presentation to my mentor and a group of eight fellow students on 30 November 2004.

2   Three of my audience were also engaged in research on the position of Marks and Spencer. This provided a stimulating challenge for me, as it meant that I was delivering to a knowledgeable audience. It generated both advantages and disadvantages.

Advantage

3   There would be more scope for discussion and debate, and my presentation would not be limited to my speaking to the audience with limited feedback

Disadvantages

4   The fact that there were others present with a detailed knowledge dented my confidence and made me feel exposed on certain complex aspects of my presentation. This made me unduly nervous during my opening remarks, and detracted from the content of the presentation. During questions, I was asked a very unexpected question to which I had no prepared response.

5   I realise that I should have prepared for my presentation in greater depth, as I had assumed that no one would have a detailed knowledge of my subject matter. When asked the difficult question, I should have taken the opportunity to open up debate and canvas the opinions of my fellow students, rather than react negatively because I could not answer the question.

Timing

6   Once I had established the flow, the presentation went well and I felt confident. However, I had to stop short, as my notes were too detailed and I exceeded the time limit. On another occasion, I will practise the whole presentation and amend it as necessary to ensure that the timing is better organised.

Conclusion

7   I have learned from this exercise that planning is of paramount importance in preparing for a presentation. That would give me greater confidence to deal with the unexpected and thus make the presentation more effective.

(298 words)

2.11 The word count falls just within the recommended 300 for each section of the Key Skills Statement, and with some thought it could be reduced.

   (a) The solution illustrates a style which presents the facts of what happened.

   (b) It also tries to portray them in as positive a light as possible.

   (c) It stresses what has been learned for the future.

   (d) It implied that the giving of the presentation has been a beneficial learning experience.

3 THE COMMUNICATION PROCESS IN OUTLINE

3.1 Effective communication is a **two-way process**, perhaps best expressed as a **cycle**. Signals or 'messages' are '**sent**' by the communicator and '**received**' by the other party. He 'sends' back some form of confirmation that the 'message' has been received and understood: this is called '**feedback**'.

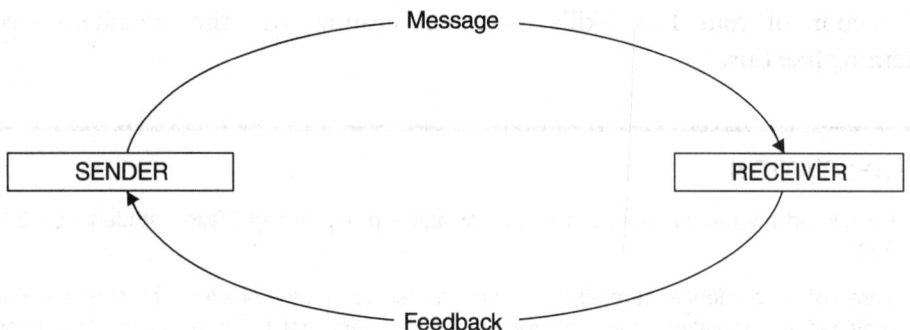

If you send a letter and receive an acknowledgement back, it corresponds to a **single cycle** of communication.

3.2 In more detail, the communication cycle can be set out as follows.

IMPULSE TO COMMUNICATE

ENCODING OF MESSAGE   } sender activity
RELAY OF MESSAGE

DECODING OF MESSAGE   } receiver activity
FEEDBACK

3.3 **Impulse to communicate**

   Deciding to communicate and deciding **what** to communicate is the first stage of the process. For example, you might:

   (a) Conceive an **idea,** chew over it for a while, and then decide to set it out for someone else in a logical way

   (b) **See or feel** something which causes you to send an involuntary message – a cry for help, a groan, an exclamation of delight

   (c) '**Blurt out**' something you feel without thinking too much about it.

3.4 Messages should ideally be **reviewed** and put into some working order in the brain **before** mouth, body or machinery are used to articulate and present the idea for someone else's

benefit. You may sometimes have **time** to organise and reorganise your message (editing or rewriting a letter or essay, for example) but in many cases you will not (face to face or on the telephone). **Planning** – as far as possible – is essential to **efficient and effective** communication.

3.5 Encoding the message

Words, numbers, pictures and gestures turn the idea in the brain into a message for communication. The idea/feeling/opinion has to be put into a **form** which can be **transmitted**: a form which the sender and receiver must both **understand**, if the sender's message is to be correctly interpreted by the receiver.

3.6 This is like a 'code', because the words, numbers, pictures and gestures we use are only symbols representing our ideas: in communicating we must translate our ideas into a code which we think the receiver will be able to 'decipher' or translate **back** into the idea which we will then both share.

3.7 We have to bear in mind that a symbol that we use and understand may be ambiguous (have more than one possible meaning) or mean something different to a person of different age, nationality, experience or beliefs. Just because we understand what we mean, it does not necessarily follow that someone else will.

Exercise 2

Give three examples of each of the following.

(a) Words that you use with your friends that other people may not understand. (What are the 'in' expressions in your age group or circle?)

(b) Words that you use in your job or studies that 'lay' people would not understand.

(c) Symbols that are commonly used, of which you have had to learn the meaning. (Think about road signs, for example.)

(d) Situations where you have been 'accused' of saying something you didn't mean, because of an expression, gesture or tone of voice.

Answer

This will vary, depending on your age group, and where you live. Examples might include 'cool', 'no worries', 'wicked' and some of the internet and texting abbreviations which are now becoming a common form of language. Work examples could include 'the P & L ' for profit and loss account. People usually tailor their message to the recipient as an automatic response. Jargon is usually used in a work context: you would not discuss variance analysis or transfer pricing with your children!

3.8 Relaying the message

Once the idea has been **encoded** as a message, the sender needs to choose how to **transmit**, or get it across to the receiver. The particular route or path via which the message is sent, connecting the sender and receiver, is called the **channel** of communication. (Examples would include a notice board or house journal, postal, telecommunication or computer systems.)

3.9 The tool or instrument which is used is the **medium** (plural 'media'). The selected medium or media will usually come under one of the broad headings of:

(a) **Visual** communication – such as a gesture, chart, picture, or screen display

(b) **Written** communication – such as a letter, memorandum, note, report, or list

(c) **Oral** communication ('by mouth'), which includes both face-to-face and remote communication, such as by telephone or television

3.10 Choice of medium

The choice of medium will depend on such factors as:

(a) The **time** necessary to prepare and transmit the message, considering its urgency

(b) The **complexity** of the message: what communication channel will enable it to be most readily understood

(c) The **distance** the message is required to travel and in what condition it must arrive

(d) The need for a **written** record, for example to confirm transactions or for legal documents

(e) The need for **'interaction'**, **immediate exchange** (for example, question and answer), or instant **'feedback'**

(f) The need for **confidentiality** or, conversely, the spreading or dissemination of information widely and quickly

(g) **Sensitivity** to the effect of the message on the recipient: the need for tact, persuasive power, personal involvement, or an impersonal, purely business approach

(h) **Cost,** considered in relation to all the above, for the best possible result at the least possible expense

---

Exercise 3

What medium might you choose if your message:

(a) Needed to be delivered to a large number of people, quickly, over a short distance, and with interactive questions and answers?

(b) Contained urgent bad news for just one person whom you know well, over a long distance?

(c) Was to explain a complex process with many stages, which would have to be carried out by a group of people?

(d) Was requesting payment from a large number of people, geographically scattered?

Answer

(a) A meeting or presentation

(b) A telephone call – if privacy could be obtained for the recipient

(c) Written sets of instructions, ideally with a flowchart or diagram, for reference; perhaps supporting a verbal presentation

(d) Written statements – for information, checking and economy

---

3.11 Decoding the message

The first step in communication from the receiver's point of view is the **decoding** of the message: understanding what it says.

(a) The receiver must **grasp the meaning of the words or symbols** used by the sender: the 'key' to the code is, as we have said, not always shared by the receiver.

(b) The receiver must **interpret the message as a whole**. What it 'says' is not necessarily what it 'means', and 'reading between the lines' may be necessary to establish the underlying meaning of the message.

(i) The meaning may be **disguised** if a sender is being sarcastic or deliberately ambiguous.

(ii) Both sender and receiver will have to be aware that meaning may be interpreted according to factors such as the **context** in which the words are said, the relationship between the communicators and the tone of the voice used.

Exercise 4

Take a simple sentence like 'You've been really helpful' and see how many different meanings those words could have, depending on how they are said and the circumstances in which they are said.

3.12 Giving feedback

Feedback is the reaction of the **receiver** which indicates to the **sender** that the message has (or has not) been **successfully received, understood and interpreted**.

It may be:

Positive

- Action taken as requested
- A letter/note/memo sent confirming receipt of message, or replying to question/invitation etc.

- Accurate reading back of message
- Smile, nod, murmur of agreement, thumbs up

Negative

- No action, or wrong action taken
- No written response at all, or written request for more information, clarification of message, repetition etc.
- Failure to repeat message correctly
- Silence, gesture or sound of protest, blank look, shrug

Feedback is **vital** to success in communication precisely because there are so many **potential barriers** and breakdowns to guard against.

3.13 Summary of the communication cycle

Adding what we have now covered, briefly, we can illustrate the communication process as a more complex cycle, as follows.

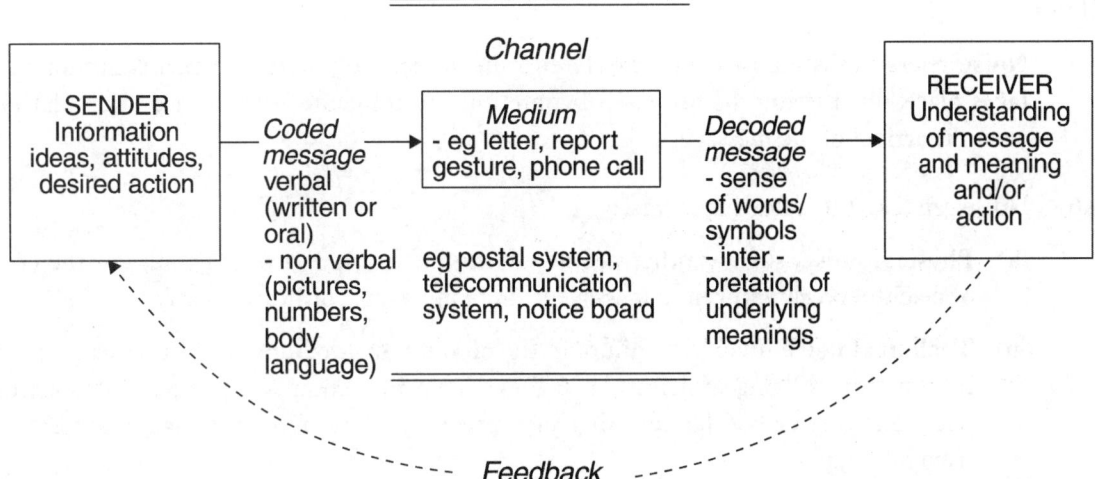

4 POTENTIAL PROBLEMS IN COMMUNICATION

4.1 Two technical terms used to describe problems or breakdowns which occur in communication are:

(a) **Distortion**

(b) **Noise**

Distortion

4.2 **Distortion** refers to the way in which the **meaning** of a communication is lost in 'handling'.

4.3 It occurs largely at the encoding and decoding stages of communication, where:

(a) The precise **intention** of the sender (what he wants to communicate) is not **translated** accurately into language, so that the 'wrong' message is sent

(b) The language used is not properly **understood** by the receiver, so that the 'wrong' message is received

4.4 Foreign or regionally-specific language, incorrect use of a word, technical or otherwise obscure terms (jargon), unfamiliar and unexplained pictures or diagrams, or words/pictures with more than one possible interpretation: these can all be sources of distortion, even when both parties are **trying** to understand and make themselves understood. Each party may simply have failed to take into account (a) **who** they were talking to, and (b) the **context or situation** within which they were talking.

In addition, **differing** opinions and attitudes, lack of concentration or co-operation can set up **barriers** to understanding: either party may **deliberately** make a meaning unclear, or choose to understand only what they want the message to say.

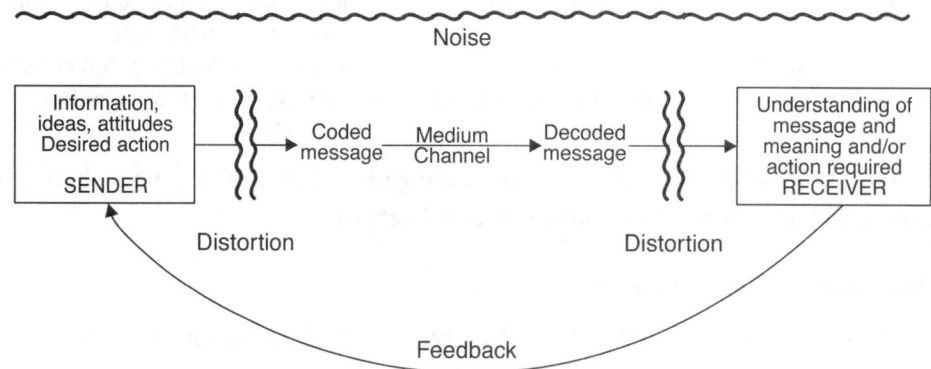

Noise

4.5 **Noise** refers to distractions and interference in the environment in which communication takes place, obstructing the **process** of communication by affecting the accuracy, clarity or even the arrival of the message.

4.6 Noise can take the following forms.

(a) **Physical noise,** such as other people talking in the room, passing traffic or the clatter of machinery, can prevent a message from being heard, or heard clearly.

(b) **Technical noise** involves a failure in the **channel or medium** of communication while information is being transmitted. A breakdown in a computer printer, a crackle on a telephone line or bad handwriting may prevent an effective exchange of information from taking place.

(c) **Social noise** is interference created by differences in the personality, culture or outlook of the sender and recipient. It includes difficulties in communication experienced by members of different social classes, old and young, male and female, boss and subordinate.

(d) **Psychological noise**, such as excessive emotion (say, anger or fear), prejudice or nervousness, can also interfere with the effective transmission of a message: the meaning may get clouded by irrelevant expressions of emotion or attitude, or the message may reach the recipient in a garbled state (because of a nervous stammer or angry spluttering, perhaps).

4.7 The problem of noise can be reduced by **redundancy**: using more than one channel of communication, so that if a message fails to get through by one channel, it may succeed by another. A spoken comment might be **confirmed** by an appropriate gesture, an agreement or decision made by telephone or at a meeting can be backed up by issuing a letter, or minutes.

4.8 Communicators must, however, be aware of possible sources of noise in their situation: a bustling office is not the place for a confidential discussion; a computer printer which produces poor quality graphics should not be used for important presentation diagrams; a hot-tempered person with known racial and sexual prejudices should not be appointed to conduct job interviews.

Personal differences

4.9 There are many factors in an individual's personality, mentality, experience and environment which make him unique – and can therefore cause distortion or noise in the communication process. Here are just a few of them.

(a) Racial, ethnic or regional **origins**: there are cultural and linguistic implications, but also 'political' implications for the status and perception of 'alien' or minority groups.

(b) Religious **beliefs** and **traditions**.

(c) **Social class** and socio-economic groupings, with their different values, opportunities and therefore expectations.

(d) **Education and training** – to different levels, and in different specialisms.

(e) **Age** – with its physiological implications (for hearing, sight, mobility etc) as well as differences in experience, and therefore in values and attitudes, language and culture, skills (eg in new technology) and so on.

(f) **Gender** – as well as physiological and psychological differences, there are social factors and customs (such as sexual discrimination and harassment, family rôle expectations and so on).

(g) **Health and fitness** – affecting the efficiency of the senses, psychological well-being and ability to cope with stress and change, capacity for certain types of work or recreational activity, and social factors (the perception of disability, obesity etc).

(h) **Personality traits and types** – a wide range of characteristics which shape attitudes and behaviour: introvert/extrovert, stable/neurotic, active/passive etc.

(i) **Intelligence** – in terms of mental ability and understanding, linguistic or numerical ability. Like education, there are different levels and different areas of intelligence, both of which may create barriers to communication.

(j) **Occupation or profession** – offering different opportunities for experience and knowledge, different motivations and different degrees of perceived social standing and value.

(k)   **Interests.** Like occupations, interests or hobbies offer (and reflect) experience and knowledge, and also have social/cultural values attached to them (Think about your perception of people who are interested in hang-gliding, knitting, opera and football.)

5   BARRIERS TO COMMUNICATION

5.1   The communication model seen in the previous section can be criticised on the grounds that it is too idealistic. In a perfect world it would be fine, but in reality we are usually not in a perfect world. There are many things which can go wrong when people are trying to communicate, and these can be summed up under the heading barriers to communication.

5.2   **General faults in the communication process**

(a)   **Distortion** or omission of information by the sender.

(b)   **Misunderstanding** due to lack of clarity or technical jargon.

(c)   **Non-verbal signs** (gesture, posture, facial expression) contradicting the verbal message, so that its meaning is in doubt.

(d)   **'Overload'** – a person being given too much information to digest in the time available.

(e)   **People** hearing **only what they want** to hear in a message.

(f)   **Differences** in social, racial or educational **background**, compounded by age and personality differences, creating barriers to understanding and co-operation.

5.3   **Communication difficulties at work**

(a)   **Status** (of the sender and receiver of information)

(i)   A senior manager's words are listened to closely and a colleague's perhaps discounted.

(ii)   A subordinate might mistrust his or her superior believing that he or she might look for 'hidden meanings' in a message.

(b)   **Jargon.** People from different job or specialist backgrounds (eg accountants, personnel managers, IT experts) can have difficulty in talking on a non-specialist's wavelength.

(c)   **Suspicion.** People discount information from those not recognised as having expert power.

(d)   **Priorities.** People or departments have different priorities or perspectives so that one person places more or less emphasis on a situation than another.

(e)   **Selective reporting.** Subordinates giving superiors incorrect or incomplete information (eg to protect a colleague, to avoid 'bothering' the superior); also a senior manager may only be able to handle edited information because he does not have time to sift through details.

(f)   **Use.** Managers who are prepared to make decisions on a 'hunch' without proper regard to the communications they may or may not have received.

(g)   **Timing.** Information which has **no immediate** use tending to be forgotten.

(h)   **Opportunity.** No opportunity, formal or informal, for people to say what they think may be lacking.

(i)   **Conflict.** Where there is conflict between individuals or departments, communications will be withdrawn and information withheld.

(j) **Personal differences,** such as age, educational/social background or personality mean that people have different views as to what is important or different ways of expressing those views. Sometimes individuals' views may be discounted because of who they are, not what they say.

(k) **Culture**

   (i) **Secrecy.** Information might be given on a need-to-know basis, rather than be considered as a potential resource for everyone to use.

   (ii) **Can't handle bad news.** The culture of some organisations may prevent the communication of certain messages. Organisations with a 'can-do' philosophy may not want to hear that certain tasks are impossible.

Exercise 5

Before reading on, what problems are suggested by the following?

(a) [On the noticeboard] 'P Brown. Your complaint about the behaviour of your colleague S Simms is being looked into. Manager.'

(b) 'Prima facie, I would postulate statutory negligence, as per para 22 Sec three et seq. Nil desperandum.' 'Eh?'

(c) 'I don't care if you're the Queen of Sheba. I've always done my job my way, and always will!'

(d) 'Smith – you've been scratching your head and frowning like mad ever since I started the briefing half an hour ago. I've tried to ignore it but – have you got fleas or something?'

(e) 'Sorry, this line's terrible – *how* many? *how* much? – what was that? NO, it's OK: I'll remember it all. We'll deliver on Monday – no, MONDAY: no, MONday ...'

(f) Date: 11 March. Report on communication for staff meeting 12 March. 463 pages.

(g) 'Look. Nobody pays you to think: leave that to us professionals. Just do your job.'

Answer

(a) Lack of confidentiality. Likely to cause friction between employees and embarrassment. Insensitive to both the complainant and the subject of the complaint. Means that people are unlikely to complain in future.

(b) Too much jargon; confusing. Lack of comprehension on the part of the listener.

(c) Communication at risk due to stubborn approach. Patronising, hostile attitude. Resistant to change.

(d) Likely to cause embarrassment to the subject. Frivolous approach to mention fleas. Likely to impede communication as the 'victim' will feel diminished.

(e) A classic case of distortion.

(f) Too brief. Not clear what it's demanding. Demanding too much

(g) A response that does not encourage further communication

Types of problems

5.4 The scenario set above suggests that communication problems fall into three broad categories.

(a) **System.** There may be a bad formal communication system.

(b) **Misunderstanding.** There may be misunderstanding about the actual content of a message.

(c) **Personality.** Inter-personal difficulties.

5.5 **Improving the communications system**

(a) **Establish better communication links** in all 'directions'.

(i) **Standing instructions** should be recorded in easily accessible manuals which are kept fully up-to-date.

(ii) Management **decisions** should be sent to all people affected by them, preferably in writing.

(iii) Regular **staff meetings,** or formal consultation with trade union representatives should be held.

(iv) **A house journal** should be issued regularly.

(v) **'Appraisal' interviews** should be held between a manager and his subordinates, to discuss the job performance and career prospects of the subordinates.

(vi) **New technology** such as e-mail should be used but not so as to overload everybody with messages of no importance.

(b) Use the **informal organisation** to supplement this increased freedom of communication.

5.6 **Clearing up misunderstandings** about message content.

(a) **Confirmation** – issuing a message in more than one form (eg by word of mouth at a meeting, confirmed later in minutes).

(b) **Reporting by exception** should operate to prevent **information overload** on managers.

(c) **Train** managers who do not express themselves clearly and concisely. Necessary jargon should be taught in some degree to people new to the organisation or unfamiliar with the terminology of the specialists.

5.7 Communication between superiors and subordinates will be improved when **interpersonal trust** exists. Exactly how this is achieved will depend on the management style of the manager, the attitudes and personality of the individuals involved, and other environmental variables. Management authors. Peters and Waterman advocate 'management by walking around' (MBWA), and informality in superior/subordinate relationships as a means of establishing closer links.

6 ORAL COMMUNICATION

6.1 Oral communication means communication **by speech, or word of mouth.** In the context of your Research and Analysis Project and the writing of the Key Skills Statement, you will mainly be involved in two different types of oral communication:

(i) Meetings with your mentor to discuss your Report and progress to date
(ii) Your presentation to your mentor and peer group

6.2 You may also experience different forms of oral communication, for example if part of your research involves verbal questioning or discussion, or the distribution and explanation of a questionnaire.

6.3 A later chapter will deal in depth with the presentation you are required to make, so this section covers oral communication in more general terms.

6.4   Face-to-face oral media include:

- Conversations
- Interviews
- Meetings
- Public addresses or briefings

6.5   Oral communication can also take place when sender and receiver are not physically face-to-face, through:

- Telephone calls
- Intercom
- Audio/video tape recordings
- Video conferencing

6.6   Oral communication is the most basic and generally used way of sending a message to another person.

Advantages and disadvantages of oral communication

6.7   **Advantages of oral communication**

(a)   It is a **swift and direct medium**. There is little or no time lapse between the sending and receiving of the message.

(b)   It is therefore suitable for 'interactive' communication: the exchange of ideas, opinions, attitudes on the spot. Decisions can be arrived at and action taken more swiftly than is possible through lengthy correspondence. All parties present are able to contribute.

(c)   This creates **greater flexibility**: circumstances and attitudes can be changed more easily, especially since the personality, voice and manner of the parties involved can be employed in persuasion and motivation.

(d)   **Instant feedback** is obtainable to overcome doubts or misunderstandings. The sender will be able to ascertain immediately whether his message has been received and correctly interpreted.

(e)   In face-to-face oral communication, there is the added advantage of being able to *see* as well as hear the other party. Verbal meaning may be reinforced and feedback given by non-verbal cues.

(f)   Face-to-face communication allows for the **sensitive handling of personal messages**, such as bad news, reprimand or conflict resolution. Parties can respond flexibly to the situation, offering support, sympathy, encouragement or directness as required.

6.8   **Disadvantages of oral communication**

(a)   **Technical noise**, such as background sounds or bad telephone lines, can interfere with effective transmission.

(b)   **Memory is untrustworthy, and perceptions differ**. A written confirmation and record of an oral event will be required, so that both parties can check that they agree on what has been decided, can recall the details later, and can produce evidence if necessary.

(c)   **Less time is usually available for planning** the message's general content, let alone the exact wording. Inferior decisions may be made, because they had to be thought through on the spot in a meeting or on the phone, without sufficient planning or

BPP PROFESSIONAL EDUCATION

information. Time may be wasted and misinterpretation caused by ill-conceived or thoughtless utterances, 'putting one's foot in it'.

(d) Face to face, **strong personalities** may 'swamp' and overrule weaker ones, however valid their respective ideas. A louder voice on the telephone may hinder the two-way process. Clash of personalities may become a crippling barrier to effective communication.

(e) Where a large number of people is involved, it is even more **difficult to control** the process, and ensure that it is effective.

6.9 Skills in oral communication

You spend much of your time in oral communication of some sort, either speaking or listening. You probably take it very much **for granted**: it is something you have always done, and got by with. Think, however, of the consequences of **failure** in oral communication.

(a) If you do not speak with **precision and clarity**, you will not be understood correctly.
(b) If you do not speak with **tact and sensitivity**, you will not get a positive response.
(c) If you do not speak with **persuasiveness**, you will not get your desired response.
(d) If you do not **listen attentively**, you will not get feedback, messages etc.

6.10 Here are some basic communication skills

(a) Defining the **purpose** of the communication

(b) Anticipating factors likely to affect the reception of the message by the **audience**

(c) Judging how much to say, and **structuring** your message so that it reinforces your main idea

(d) Adapting your **style** – vocabulary, sentence structure and tone – to your purpose and the needs of the recipient

(e) **Listening** attentively when you are on the receiving end of communication, and using **non-verbal cues** to aid understanding

(f) Seeking and offering **feedback**

(g) Anticipating potential **barriers** to communication

(h) Appreciating the **roles**, relationships and constraints particular to business communication

These all apply equally to spoken communication.

6.11 The same stages apply in oral communication as in written: a message is conceived, encoded, transmitted, decoded, interpreted and acknowledged. In face-to-face oral communication, however, you are sending and receiving messages at the same time, or very close together. You **switch rapidly** between speaking and listening, and all the time your relationship with the other person, your tone of voice, your expressions and gestures, are modifying, qualifying or confirming the messages you are sending and your response to messages received.

Words at work

6.12 Some communications experts argue that using phrases like 'no problem', 'no worries' in a conversation sets the other person thinking that there **might** be problems or worries that you are keeping quiet about.

Here's a list of words and phrases that are thought to be very persuasive.

Delighted	Certainly
Assured	Yes
Confident	Please
Peace of mind	Thank you
Enjoy	You
Pleasure	Help
Satisfied	Look after
Appeal	Straightforward
Happy	Situation
Special	Position
Valued	Recommended
Normal	Easier for you
However	Better for you
Good	Quicker for you
Popular	Significant
Substantial	I will organise that for you
You're welcome	Glad I could help
You'll be pleased to hear	

6.13 Articulation

We learn to speak **instinctively**. Babies imitate their parents; children pick up words wherever they hear them; adults enlarge their vocabulary and absorb the styles of speech that they are used to hearing. Our speech patterns become **deeply ingrained**, and although we may notice (and admire or dislike) the way others speak, we rarely pay attention to our **own articulation** and pronunciation until we have encountered a real problem. (You know you have a problem when someone has to ask you to repeat your message several times, and then spell it out.)

6.14 **Listen to other people speaking.** Do they speak clearly, so that you never have trouble understanding them? Do they speak with a strong regional or foreign accent which makes it difficult to understand them sometimes? Do they speak exaggeratedly, in a would-be 'posh' style, which sounds false and affected and distracts from what they say?

Exercise 6

Dictate the following sentences to someone else, allowing them time to write each sentence down, but speaking at your normal pace, and reading each item only once. (Alternatively, record yourself reading, and come back later and try to transcribe the sentences yourself.)

What a little pop, pet.
Jo gave George a rum for his money.
That stuff isn't it.
You have an aim and a dress.
They are having pea stalks.
He grows great vines.
Why choose 'Glow in the dark'?
You'll hear the waiter speak.
Will we have passed her at dinner?

Write in the alternative ways of hearing these sentences. What did you have to do in the way of articulation, pronunciation and intonation to make yourself clear?

6.15   People tend to have a certain image about **patterns of speech** and accents: the mode of speech is a **badge** of belonging to a like-speaking group with which the individual can **identify**. This can be an almost exclusive identification, based on the assumption that 'people who speak differently, think differently'. In most countries of the world hostility between groups is perpetuated by accent and speech mannerisms.

6.16   The important thing is that you **desire to communicate effectively**.

(a)   Clear articulation is vital, not because it is associated with a particular region, section of society or level of education, but because you want to be understood immediately and unambiguously by **any other person**, in order to get a response that you require.

(b)   A dialect or accent may be attractive to listen to and perfectly comprehensible within a certain community, but unless the speaker can make himself readily understood by someone who does not share it (over a long-distance telephone line, say, or in a gathering of people from various countries and regions) it will prevent him from communicating effectively to those outside his own community.

(c)   Be considerate to the recipient of your message: don't use or pronounce words in a way that he will not understand.

(d)   If you are satisfied that your speech is clear, unambiguous and not mannered just for the sake of it: fine.

Delivery

6.17   **Volume and pitch**. If you are articulating clearly, you will be much more audible, but you will also have to consider how to **project** your voice. Speaking softly or even at a normal level will be ineffective in a large room with a high ceiling and heavy curtains: the sound of your voice will be absorbed by everything except the person x yards away whom you are trying to inform or persuade, and whose attention you want to grab and hold. Stand or sit straight, keep your chin up and pitch your voice to travel to the **furthest** listener. Try not to shout, grate or squeak: find your own best pitch. You project your image when you project your voice: get it right.

One to one or in a small group, particularly if in an intimate or informal context, you will not create a good impression by aggressive voice projection. The same is true in small rooms. You do not want to appear brash, insensitive, rude or deaf. Look for **feedback** indicating that you are clearly but not painfully audible, and stick to that pitch and volume.

6.18   **Intonation and pace** affect how your message reaches its recipient, as much as volume affects whether it does.

(a)   Be aware of how the placing of **emphasis** on different words alters the meaning of a sentence: the stress **implies** something to the listener.

(b)   Likewise, notice how **inflexion** and **tone** alter meaning, when you raise or lower your voice, lift at the end of a question, lift and drop in an exclamation etc.

(c)   How do you make your voice sound cheery, gloomy, disapproving, encouraging, affectionate, enthusiastic, indifferent, hostile?

Exercise 7

Experiment with the simple sentence: 'Nobody is available to see you.'

(a)   Try stressing each word in turn, and consider the implications of each change.

(b)   Try each as a statement, and as a question (not all combinations will work).

(c) Try making the statement with each of the emotional overtones mentioned in Paragraph 6.18 (c) above.

6.19 **Pace and pauses** are further elements in fluent but clear delivery. Don't garble your words or string together long breathless sentences.

6.20 You do **not** have to pause frequently and at length: if you do, your audience may not stay with you. If you need time in which to frame your next idea, there are phrases and expressions you can use almost without thought, to preserve the fluency of your message. Notice how your vocabulary consists not only of single words, but of blocks of words which have become associated in your mind. Here are some examples.

'Of course it's really a matter of'
'I wonder if I might just'
'On the other hand, it wouldn't surprise me if'
'in fact', 'not at all', 'thank you very much'
etc.

Don't: use blocks of words that are so firmly established as to be clichéd: 'to coin a phrase' 'to err is human'.	**Don't:** resort to 'stabilisers' like 'um', 'ah', 'you know', or 'sort of like', 'you know what I mean?'

6.21 Here are the **possible** results of a survey to ask people how they felt about others' **talking habits**. How many of these habits do you have or do you notice in other people?

	Extremely annoyed %	*Not annoyed* %	*Don't know* %
Interrupting while others are talking	88	11	1
Swearing	84	15	1
Mumbling or talking too softly	80	20	0
Talking too loudly	73	26	1
Monotonous, boring voice	73	26	1
Using filler words such as 'and um', 'like um' and 'you know'	69	29	2
A nasal whine	67	29	4
Talking too fast	66	34	0
Using poor grammar or mispronouncing words	63	36	1
A high-pitched voice	61	37	2
A foreign accent or a regional dialect	24	75	1

7 LEARNING FROM COMMUNICATION

7.1 Learning can be defined in very broad terms as the process of acquiring knowledge or skills which will be drawn upon and used at some future point. Most authorities acknowledge that learning is a lifelong process, starting from the moment of birth and continuing from that point, whether consciously, as at school or university, or subconsciously for the rest of one's life.

Control loops

7.2 For many basic skills, a simple control loop shows how something is learned. When learning to swim, you may try various different movements. If a movement causes you to go under water, you will learn quickly (almost instantaneously!) and you will not do that again. If a movement or sequence of movements causes you to continue to move or float on the top of the water, you will carry on doing that in future. You are learning by the experiences you have, but you may not necessarily think about or understand what you are doing: it may well be a reflex action.

A more complex way of learning includes analysis and reflection, enabling the individual to adapt his learning in one situation to a different situation. This needs understanding of the learning which is happening, so that it can be applied elsewhere.

Kolb's learning model

7.3 The theorist D.A. Kolb, along with others, has published a model showing how experience and ideas are integrated together, so that learning becomes an ongoing circular process rather than a one-off process specific to a given very precise situation. It can be summarised like this.

The Kolb experiential learning model (Kolb, 1973)

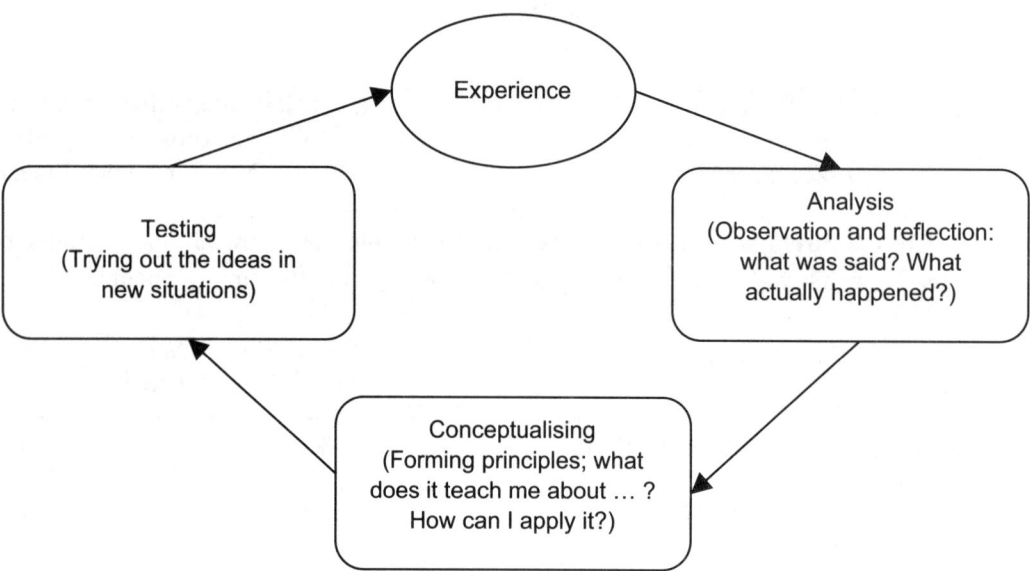

7.4 This introduces different stages to the learning cycle. The individual goes through the cycle:

(a) Has an experience
(b) Analyses what happened
(c) Conceptualises what that might mean in terms of the future
(d) Tests the theory next time a similar situation arises

7.5 In the context of the individual learning to swim, therefore, the stages in the learning cycle would proceed like this.

(a) Stops kicking legs and sinks under water

(b) Considers why he sank under the water and links it with the fact that he stopped kicking

(c) Recognises principle that if he carries on kicking his legs he will stay on the surface

(d) Applies the principle next time he tries to swim, and is successful.

Learning from the Research and Analysis Project

7.6   As we have already said, the preparation of the Research and Analysis Project is designed to be a learning exercise. You report on this exercise in the Key Skills Statement, recognise where your communication skills are lacking and take steps to improve them.

This is an ongoing learning process. By applying the stages in Kolb's experiential learning model, as shown in the diagram, you should find that your listening, questioning and presentation skills are enhanced.

7.7   This will be directly relevant to you in the production of your Research and Analysis Project, as these skills are assessed by you, and you must consider how they may be improved in the light of what you have learned. It will also be relevant in the wider context, as in virtually all professional working environments, listening, questioning and presentation skills are vital, and will enable you to carry out your job more efficiently and effectively.

Chapter roundup

- The Key Skills Statement is a critical part of your Research and Analysis Project.

- It requires you to reflect on the communication process, considering especially noise, feedback and barriers.

- Oral communication, in the form of meetings with your mentor, is as important as written communication.

Chapter 11

MENTOR MEETINGS

Chapter topic list

1   The role of the mentor

2   The sequence of meetings

3   The first mentor meeting

4   The second mentor meeting

5   The third mentor meeting

6   Questioning

7   Feedback

8   Listening

9   Recording the meeting

10   Reflecting on the meeting

11   The mentor's certification

Introduction

It has already been explained that the role of your mentor is to monitor your progress throughout the Research and Analysis Project. He or she will be asked to verify your participation in the three meetings that are compulsory within the module. Your mentor will also be asked to confirm that your project has been carried out in accordance with the University's regulations.

This chapter will tell you how to plan, participate in and record each meeting properly, and how to extract the maximum benefit so that your experience of the meetings can be utilised efficiently in preparing your Key Skills Statement.

1   THE ROLE OF THE MENTOR

1.1   It is important that you recognise and understand the role of the mentor and bear it in mind while you are planning your meetings. The Guidelines set out in Appendix 3 some notes on the mentor/student relationship.

You should remind yourself of this now.

Your mentor will also be required to sign a form declaring that to the best of their knowledge your work is entirely your own.

> **MENTOR GUIDELINES**
>
> The mentor is primarily interested in the progress of your Project but is not your tutor. They will need to hear about your plans and will ask questions to help you reflect on the clarity of your thinking and the focus of your Report.

It is important to realise that your mentor is not your assessor but, as already stated, will be asked to provide confirmation that you participated in three meetings with him/her, provided a satisfactory

A mentor need not have expert knowledge of the field of your research or in research methods. You should not expect them to give you direction regarding the content, relevant references or design of your research for the Research and Analysis Report or Key Skills Statement.

1.2   The mentor, therefore, will be taking an overview of your report, rather than becoming embroiled in the fine detail and technical content.

1.3   Some business texts deal with the role of the mentor. One authority regarded mentoring as a process whereby mentor and student work together to discover and develop the student's latent abilities (Shea, 1992). The relationship is one in which the mentor is described as '...counsellor, friend and foil...' enabling you the student to sharpen your skills and hone your thinking.

Mentors often gain great satisfaction from passing on the fruits of their experience, and can find that the 'coaching' aspect helps their own development.

1.4   Oxford Brookes University has provided clarification to the effect that your mentor should not be a close relative, as it could make it more difficult to achieve a balanced relationship leading to the appropriate interaction and feedback required for completion of the Key Skills Statement.

2   THE SEQUENCE OF MEETINGS

2.1   The Guidelines give guidance as to the purpose of the meetings in section 2.3. The guidance is set out here.

MEETINGS WITH YOUR MENTOR

The three meetings with your mentor, each of which would normally be about half an hour long, should follow the framework set out below.

MEETING 1 – AT THE OUTSET

To prepare for this you should have some idea about your choice of topic and have embarked on preliminary investigation into the research areas and methods you may want to use. Following this meeting you should be able to set out a clear proposal of your choice of topic, research method and draft aims and objectives for your report.

MEETING 2 – MIDWAY THROUGH YOUR REPORT

At this stage you should have completed the gathering of information on your topic and have some initial views as to your findings. An interim update on your progress in the form of a word-processed document should be presented to your mentor. This will then provide the framework for your discussion.

MEETING 3 – TOWARDS COMPLETION OF YOUR REPORT

You are required to prepare and deliver a fifteen minute presentation on your report to your mentor, and if applicable your peer group. You should use appropriate presentation techniques in conjunction with your talk. You should be prepared to answer questions and provide explanations when requested.

Your mentor will be asked to provide confirmation that the three meetings took place in accordance with the guidelines above.

NB. It may be useful for you to keep a personal diary of reflections on your meetings to help you when writing up your Key Skills Statement.

You may, if your mentor is happy to participate, arrange for further appointments in addition to the three compulsory meetings outlined in the above diagram.

2.2   The Guidelines also supply a process model, which is a diagram showing the interaction of work stages and meetings. You have already seen this but there is no harm in seeing it again.

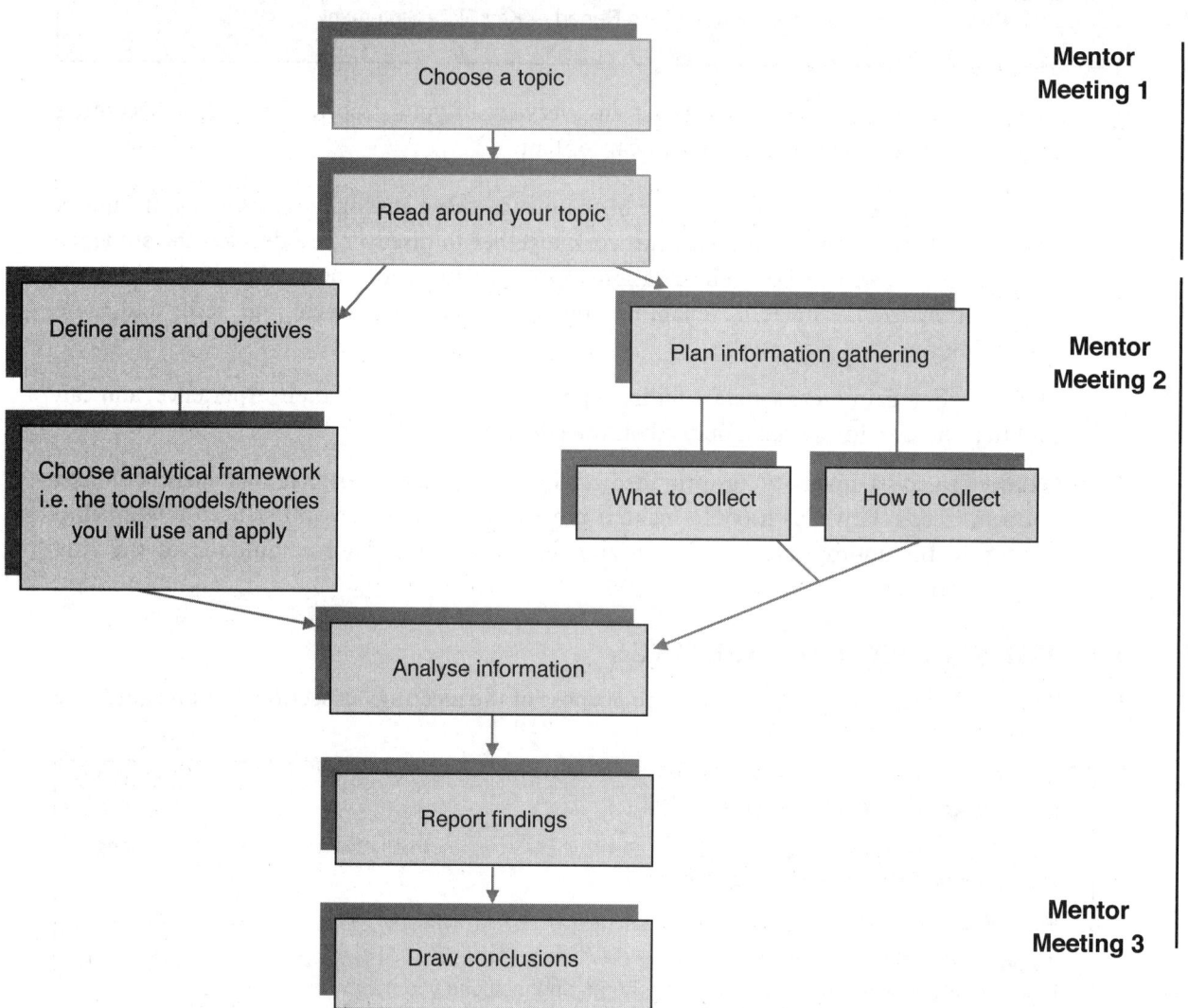

2.3   Although the Guidelines require three compulsory meetings, following a set format, there may well be scope for other meetings with your mentor. This may hinge on:

(a)   The topic you have chosen

(b)   Your relationship with your mentor

(c)   The number of other students involved.

2.4   The examiner has said that additional meetings with your mentor are to be positively encouraged. They are likely to happen if you are encountering problems or you just feel that you need to chat something through. They will demonstrate that you are taking the project very seriously. If you do have additional meetings with your mentor, you should **plan** for them, **record** them and then **reflect** upon them in the same way as for the three 'formal' meetings. In fact it would be advisable to treat any additional meetings as being a formal part of your project structure and refer to them in your Key Skills Statement. Therefore you should arrange an appointment with your mentor for an additional meeting and ensure that both of you document it.

Do not ask your mentor questions in passing, on a 'by the way' basis when you happen to see him or her, as you may then lose track of what has been said and what advice offered. Results obtained in a casual *ad hoc* way will be of less value in the construction of your Report and Key Skills Statement.

The advantages of meetings

2.5 At the start of your Project work, you may wonder why you have to go through such a clearly defined structure of meetings and give a presentation. You may think that it would be more straightforward for you to submit your Report and Key Skills Statement, and that you are capable of doing that without having to undergo any consultation process.

2.6 It is important that you appreciate that the Research and Analysis Project as a whole, and specifically the production of the Key Skills Statement, is an exercise in communication. Your meetings with your mentor are the vehicle by which you demonstrate your ability to communicate.

Face to face discussion

2.7 Face to face discussion is particularly effective as it:

(a) Allows **non-verbal cues**, both **audible and visual**, to be used to enhance understanding and persuasion.

(b) Allows immediate **exchange and feedback**.

(c) Allows communication **between** or with a number of people.

(d) Humanises the **context** of communication by opening the parties to each other's direct scrutiny and to personality factors.

2.8 These qualities make it particularly suitable for the following **applications**.

(a) Generating and **developing new ideas**, since each party may be encouraged and prompted by the others.

(b) **Feedback, constructive criticism and exchanges of views**, where necessary to resolve problems or conflicts.

(c) **Decision-making**, since each party may contribute a necessary viewpoint or piece of information.

(d) Using **personal charisma and logic** (especially with the opportunity to invite and answer questions) to persuade.

(e) Encouraging **co-operation**, information-sharing and sensitivity to others.

(f) Dealing with difficult or **personal issues** (such as discipline, grievance, counselling, bad news etc) honestly and sensitively.

(g) Encouraging **honest, open and spontaneous** communication – since it is much more difficult to give a dishonest or prepared answer or opinion face-to-face than in writing or on the phone.

2.9 Due to the fact that face to face discussion is perceived as being particularly effective, Oxford Brookes have clarified that it is not acceptable for you to hold meetings with your mentor by video-conferencing. Additionally, all meetings with your mentor, and the project itself, must be in English.

3   THE FIRST MENTOR MEETING

3.1   The objective of this meeting is to reach a final decision on your choice of topic, and to have clearly identified your research method and the draft aims and objectives for your report.

Before the first meeting, you should establish some basic 'terms of reference':

Location

3.2   It is most likely that the meeting will be held in the mentor's office at work or at your college. You should consider whether you are happy with this, or whether you would prefer to meet on neutral ground or indeed your own 'home territory'.

Given that your relationship with your mentor should be amicable and supportive, you are unlikely to feel that the mentor's office is a hostile environment, but it is a factor worth considering.

Date, time and likely duration

3.3   The date and time must be agreed with the mentor in advance. Make sure that you will have enough time before the meeting to do the basic groundwork and preliminary investigations and give sufficient thought to your likely topic and how you will work on your Report.

3.4   The Guidelines suggest that each meeting will be about half an hour long, although you should appreciate that this is just a guideline. Bear in mind, however, whether you will be able to cover the matters you want to discuss in half an hour, and ensure that you do not have to rush off elsewhere should the meeting exceed half an hour.

Outline agenda

3.5   It would be helpful to send this to your mentor in advance, so that he or she can be adequately prepared for the meeting too. If you have supplied your proposed title, or even a list of possible topics to the mentor, they will be far better placed to use the time in the meeting constructively.

3.6   An outline agenda for the first mentor meeting could look something like this.

Example

OXFORD BROOKES RESEARCH AND ANALYSIS PROJECT

MENTOR MEETING 1

15th January 2005

Offices of A,B,C & Co., Chartered Certified Accountants

Student: Paul Smith

Mentor: Rosie Barker

AGENDA

1   Proposed topic: an analysis of the impact of e-business on the UK personal banking industry

2   Methods of research: primary and secondary

3   Potential problems with finding information

4   Proposed timetable:

- Mentor Meeting 2
- Mentor meeting 3 (and presentation)
- Submission of Project

From this, the mentor knows the likely topic, the fact that you want to discuss finding information and that you will probably suggest dates.

Likely questions

3.7   The discussion will in reality consist of a series of questions and answers, probably starting with your mentor asking how you are getting on.

To this end, the Guidelines set out some example questions which may be asked by the student or the mentor. You may want to use these to start to structure your first meeting, and to anticipate what your mentor is likely to ask you. Remember, **planning and anticipation** are the two key tools for making a meeting effective.

These are the examples of questions to be asked at the first meeting:

MENTOR	STUDENT
What is your report going to be about?	I have considered the following alternatives; can I talk them through with you?
How do you plan to do the report?	
Why are you doing it in this way?	This is my plan; what do you think?
What problems do you envisage?	
When will you do x, y and z?	

There are also some examples of questions which the student should not expect the mentor to answer. These relate to any of the three meetings, not just the first one.

The examples provided in the Guidelines are:

What do I have to do to pass?
What do I do next?
What shall I read on this topic?
What do you know about this topic?
Will you structure my project for me?

3.8   This is an extract from a first meeting between mentor and student. Do you think that the meeting is being conducted within the spirit of the Guidelines?

Exercise 1

M: So, S., have you had any thoughts about the topic for your Research and Analysis Project?

S: No, not really. I read through the list of suggestions supplied by Oxford Brookes, but none of them appealed to me. I thought I might do something about the brewing industry. What do you think?

M: I think that you need to be more specific. Several of the topics let you discuss an industry of your choice, so perhaps you should narrow the list down to those, for example the effects of globalisation on the industry, the impact of e-business, the motivation of employees, and so on. You could also select a specific brewer you know about and build the Report around that.

S: Yes, maybe. But can't I choose a topic I want to do?

M: You can, but you have to put details in writing to Oxford Brookes and ask them to confirm whether it is acceptable. You must give them a month to reply, and there's no point in starting work until you've received confirmation. That means you've wasted a month if you want to submit by the April deadline, and it also means that this meeting is a bit of a non-event.

S: OK, let's forget about that: I'll do the effect of globalisation on the brewing industry. So what shall I do next? Can you suggest some good web sites I can get information from?

M: I don't really have much knowledge of brewing, and in any event you should be doing this basic research for yourself as a forerunner to the detailed research you will need to do later. I think that you need to go away and do some basic research into sources of information, the type of research you are going to do and the basic structure of your report, and then we should have another initial meeting to establish these facts before you go on. But you need to think seriously whether you will be able to submit by April: it might be wiser to submit in October, which will give you more time to really get to grips with the work involved.

Answer

In this example, S. has not done anything approaching the necessary amount of basic research, and the meeting is really a waste of everybody's time. S. is trying to get M. to tell him what to do, and the Guidelines make it clear that the mentor is not a tutor or supervisor in this context.

S would have done better to have chosen the types of project prior to the meeting, or at least to have identified a short list. That would have given focus and structure to the meeting. Additionally, S clearly has not researched the necessary timing issues. On balance, a poor start, and this would not demonstrate the skills of communication and business acumen which are expected.

---

4 THE SECOND MENTOR MEETING

4.1 The second mentor meeting should take place mid way through the production of the Report (although you will not necessarily have started writing yet). You should have completed the gathering of information, and should be en route to reaching some initial conclusions.

4.2 You should present to your mentor a word-processed interim update on progress achieved to date, and this will then form the basis for your discussion. The Guidelines do not specify how long this should be. Rather than word counting, you should take the view that this should contain adequate information so that the reader knows where you have got to. If your mentor agrees, you may want to supply this in advance of the meeting, so that your mentor has good background knowledge. It will also then provide the structure for your meeting.

Again the meeting should take about half an hour.

The interim report

4.3 Your interim report should be structured around a number of headings. This will effectively create the plan for the meeting. Here are some suggestions.

(a) Summary of the title and objectives of the Report (so you can assess whether you are achieving them)

(b) Background reading carried out (in general terms)

(c) Primary research done: list what you have read

(d) Problems encountered, for example in accessing source material, and impact on the Report

(e) Initial conclusions reached

(f) Further work to do and likely impact on conclusions

4.4 As well as these subjects, you are likely to discuss

(a) How you are managing to stick to your timetable

(b) Any potential word processing problems, such as tricky diagrams or tables of statistics

(c) Generally how you are feeling about the Project as a whole.

Likely questions

4.5 The Module Guidelines contain some examples of the questions which might be asked by the student and the mentor at the second meeting.

MENTOR	STUDENT
What difficulties have you had? How will you/have you overcome them? What are you going to do next? Are you on schedule/do you need to reschedule?	I have had this problem; could you offer some advice?

4.6 You should notice that these questions are **constructive**, and their terminology implies that the student and the mentor between them will try to resolve the issues. For example, the mentor asks how a problem can be resolved, and the student has the opportunity to ask for advice as to how to solve the problem.

The potential need to reschedule can be raised and discussed, and the mentor would be in a good position to recognise whether the student is now setting too tight a deadline.

4.7 It is this second stage which highlights the benefits of the mentor-student relationship.

4.8 As in the first stage, however, the mentor is not expected to tell the student what to do next or to write the Report for them. He or she must still stay one step removed from the process of producing the Report.

4.9 If you and the mentor are to schedule additional meetings, they could well occur between the second and third meetings. This is likely to be the case if the second meeting did not go very well or you had not completed the information gathering stage.

Such meetings should be **planned for and documented** just like the three scheduled meetings. The most appropriate method of planning for an additional meeting would be to produce another interim report, focusing on the headings listed earlier.

5 THE THIRD MENTOR MEETING

5.1 The third meeting should be held towards completion of your Report. It is the most formal and arguably the most nerve wracking of the three meetings, as you are required to give a presentation, fifteen minutes, to your mentor and also, if appropriate, to your peer group.

5.2 Your peer group consists of any other students with whom your mentor is working. This is most likely to be the case where your mentor is your college tutor or your employer in a location where there are other students studying for the ACCA qualification.

5.3 As well as giving the presentation, you should also be prepared to answer questions and provide explanations when requested.

Timing

5.4 The process model shown in section 2 of this chapter shows meeting 3 at the end of the Report production process, at the stage when you are drawing your conclusions. You should certainly not plan to hold the third meeting prior to that, as you will not have completed the necessary thought and writing processes. Since you are expected to answer questions and explain your comments and findings, you must have all the necessary information when preparing your presentation.

5.5 If you are working alone, and your mentor has no other students, you will probably be able to set the date of the third meeting to suit you. You should bear in mind, however, that Oxford Brookes envisages two Research and Analysis Project assessment periods each year, with the two deadlines in April and October. If you miss the deadline you are aiming for, your Project will be held over for another six months, until the next assessment period.

If you have a peer group, the date of the third meeting will be less flexible, as it is likely that the students in the peer group will all give their presentations at the same session.

Likely questions

5.6 The procedure for planning and giving the presentation will be discussed in detail in the next chapter. There will be some opportunity at the third meeting for a discussion between you and your mentor, as well as the open forum of discussion after your presentation.

5.7 Here are some examples of the questions your mentor may ask you when reviewing your project.

  (a) What went well or badly?
  (b) Does the Report meet its objectives?
  (c) Does the Report make sense?

5.8 As you can see, these are very broad and general questions, reflecting the **summarising and concluding** nature of the third meeting with your mentor. At this stage you should not be discussing the fine detail of the contents of your Report and the research you undertook, but should be considering **wider issues such as the conclusion reached and whether or not your Report can be regarded as a success.**

This is reflected in the fact that the Guidelines do not suggest any examples of questions which you might ask your mentor at the third meeting: the assumption is that you have virtually finished.

6 QUESTIONING

6.1 Questioning and listening are the elements that the three mentor meetings have in common. The mentor will be asking you about the progress you are making at each stage, and you are able to ask the mentor for a limited amount of help and advice.

The principal questioner, however, will be the mentor, and it is your answers, and the discussions which ensue, which will enable the mentor to confirm to Oxford Brookes that the correct procedures have been observed.

6.2 In any questioning situations, there is a simple recipe for the right procedure:

  (a) **Ask** the right questions.
  (b) **Listen** to the answers.

6.3 Questions should be paced and put carefully. The mentor should not be trying to confuse the student, plunging immediately into demanding questions or picking on isolated points. Nor, however, should the mentor allow the student to digress, or gloss over important points. The mentor must **retain control** over the information-gathering process.

A variety of **questioning styles** may be used to achieve different purposes.

Open questions

6.4 These are open-ended questions of the type 'Who...? What...? Where...? When...? Why...?'.

(a) They force you to put together responses in **complete sentences.**

(b) They **encourage** you to talk.

(c) They keep the interview **flowing**.

(d) They are much more **revealing** than allowing the student to 'get away with' 'yes' or 'no' answers.

For example: 'Why do you want to write about CVP analysis?' is more effective than 'So you want to write about CVP analysis, do you?'

Closed questions

6.5 These only offer a **choice** of responses, such as 'yes' or 'no'. They have several drawbacks, compared to the open question.

(a) They elicit answers only to the **question asked** by the mentor: there may be other questions and issues that he has not anticipated – but will **emerge** if the student is given the chance to express himself freely.

(b) They do not allow the student to **express** his personality so that interaction can take place on a deeper level.

(c) They make it easier for students to **conceal** things ('You never *asked* me....').

(d) They make the mentor **work** very hard to get information.

However, a closed question can be useful for **pinning down** an item of information that the student seems reluctant to give, or is being long-winded about. 'Will you finish the work on 1 April?' will get the required information more quickly than 'How long will it take you to finish?'

Probing questions

6.6 These are similar to open questions in their phrasing but aim to discover the **deeper significance** of an answer. ('But what was it about **the motor industry** that particularly appealed to you?')

Such questions provide a **clearer focus** to too short or too generalised answers. Some mentors too often let a general and fairly uninformative answer pass without a probe, simply because they are working through a list of prepared open questions.

Multiple questions

6.7 These are just that: two or more questions asked at once. ('Tell me about your topic. How did your knowledge of Just In Time procedures help you there, and do you think you are up-to-date or will you need to spend time researching?')

This type of question can be used to encourage the student to talk at some **length, without straying** too far from the point. It might also test the student's ability to listen and handle large amounts of information, but should be used judiciously in this case: it can be rather intimidating and that is not the purpose of the Research and Analysis Project.

Leading questions

6.8 These suggest a certain reply to the student, for example 'Don't you agree that...?'. 'Surely...?')

The danger with this type of question is that the student will simply give the answer that **he thinks** the mentor **wants to hear.** It might, however, be used to deal with a highly reticent or nervous student, simply to encourage him to talk, or to test a student's ability to stand up for his own views.

Exercise 2

Identify the type of question used in these examples, and consider the effect they might have on you if you are the student who is responding to them.

1   'So you're interested in researching the effect of conditions of change on future personnel requirements, are you , Mark?'

2   Surely you're not interested in personnel issues, Mark?'

3   'How about doing something really interesting, like the impact of changing conditions on personnel requirements, Mark? Would you consider researching that?'

4   'Why are you interested in personnel issues, Mark?'

5   'Why particularly personnel issues, Mark?'

Answers

1   A closed question: it expects a yes or no answer, and would not give the student enough scope for expanding the discussion.

2   This is a leading question expressed in negative terms. The student could be intimidated into immediately dropping the idea of researching personnel issues.

3   This is another form of leading question, although this time it is couched in positive terms. The questioner is inviting the student to agree with the questioner's view of personnel as a research topic, and the implication is that the questioner will disapprove should the student disagree.

4   This is an open question which enables the student to expand the discussion and put forward his own viewpoint. It would enable the student to demonstrate the thought processes behind the decision.

5   This is also an open question but rather more specific. It invites the student to home in on the precise topic under discussion and explain why other alternatives were discarded.

---

7   FEEDBACK

7.1 One of the most useful features of each of the three meetings with your mentor is the feedback you will receive. At the third meeting you will receive a lot of feedback from your peer group, but this will be on your presentation and Report as a whole.

7.2 At the two earlier meetings, you will receive valuable feedback from your mentor on the progress of your work. Receiving feedback is a recognised skill, and using it constructively can improve your prospects of success.

7.3 **Guidelines on feedback**

(a) listen carefully to what is said: active listening skills are covered in the next section.

(b) be appreciative of the feedback: the giver will then probably give you more feedback, which may be useful, if he is confident that you appreciate it.

(c) ask for clarification if you don't understand the point that is being made.

(d) don't take criticism too personally: negative feedback does not mean that the giver does not like you. It just means that one aspect or idea can be improved.

(e) try to take positive steps to improve on the basis of feedback received.

8 LISTENING

8.1 During your meetings with your mentor you will be **talking**, but also, just as importantly, **listening**. This is often regarded as a passive activity, but you will find that if you **engage in 'active listening'** it will pay dividends in terms of what you gain.

8.2 The Research and Analysis Project tests your communication skills, and the ability to listen, along with the ability to talk and question, provide the basis of communication.

Listening is about decoding and receiving information. Effective listening helps

(a) The sender of the message to **listen effectively** in turn to the receiver's reply

(b) Reduce the effect of **'noise'**

(c) **Resolve problems** by encouraging understanding from someone else's viewpoint.

8.3 In the last chapter, we discussed the communication model, which contains the key elements of sender, message, means of communication and receiver. If someone is talking to you, no matter how clearly and lucidly, but you are not listening properly, the communication process will fail.

8.4 **Definition of listening**

The assumption tends to be that listening is not so much an ability or skill as a physical attribute of human beings: we all have ears, so we can all listen – barring a physical hearing deficiency. Listening is simply equated with **hearing**. However, tests show that the average person remembers only half of what he has heard immediately afterwards.

By consciously engaging in the process of active listening, we can improve the effectiveness of our listening, and develop listening skills.

Why is it important to listen effectively?

8.5 Many benefits are available from effective listening.

(a) It is a **quick, direct** source of information, which you may be interested in, or need in order to make decisions.

(b) It offers the opportunity to use the speaker's **tone** of voice, to help you interpret underlying messages.

(c) It is **interactive** and flexible, so you can:

(i) Make sure the information is **adapted** to your needs and that you understand it

(ii) **Add** information of your own, to stimulate new ideas and solve problems.

(d) It builds **relationships**, encourages understanding of the other person's feelings and point of view, and establishes a personal element to the discussion.

(e) It encourages **further** and more spontaneous communication, which deepens relationships. It also encourages honesty because the speaker has less time to plan ahead, is less likely to withhold information, and will find it more difficult to disguise his feelings.

8.6 Try this exercise for size.

Exercise 3

Applying these benefits to the business context, why do you think listening might be particularly useful for a marketer or salesperson?

Answer

(a) *It is a quick, direct source of information* – say, for getting an initial feel for customers' receptivity to a new product.

(b) *It is interactive and flexible.* The marketer can ensure that he has got and understood the information he requires. If creative thinking is required, active listening can stimulate ideas. Active listening is vital for handling and overcoming customers' objections.

(c) *It contributes to relationships.*

(i) A salesperson who listens shows respect for his customers' expertise, experience and opinions in a more direct and personal way than one who asks for written feedback.

(ii) Listening also allows the salesperson to use his personality: say, for greater effectiveness in making the customer feel important.

(iii) Human relationships are a prime factor in customer satisfaction (or dissatisfaction): customer loyalty may be enhanced by a communication style based on interpersonal communication and a degree of informality.

(d) *It encourages communication.* The perception that the salesperson is interested and willing to listen motivates customers to offer information and ideas which may be commercially useful for the organisation. Writing down ideas can be time consuming (or even intimidating for those who are not confident about their writing skills): the opportunity to speak informally to a sales rep is both more convenient and encouraging.

Ways of listening

8.7 Like reading, listening may have a number of purposes, which should be borne in mind as you listen.

Listening for content

8.8 If you trust the source of the message to be correct and objective, or you only want to know what the source's viewpoint is (in which case it doesn't matter if it is incorrect or subjective), listening for content will be a straightforward receiving activity – but still requires skilful listening in order to:

(a) **Receive** physically as much as possible of what is said (ensuring that it is audible, and that your attention doesn't wander).

(b) **Interpret** as much as possible of what is said, in the way the speaker intends (understanding the message).

(c) Give appropriate **feedback** to achieve both of the above (asking for repetition or louder delivery, asking questions, encouraging the speaker to continue and so on).

8.9 In addition, you may want to make an effort to **remember** the content of the message. The surest way is to write down the important points, but the way you listen – noticing key words, for example, or listening just as hard to repetitions and summaries – will make recall easier.

Critical listening

8.10 If you require an objective viewpoint or accurate information, and you do not have absolute confidence that the source is able and intending to give it to you, you will need to listen critically. This is essentially like evaluating a piece of writing.

(a) Be **alert** to things you know to be factually false, and reappraise the source's credibility.

(b) Appraise the speaker's **vocabulary** and way of speaking for attempts to distract or persuade you. Tone of voice and **body-language** – if you can see the speaker – will be an additional source of guidance in this.

(c) Question the speaker's **assumptions** and logic (if only to yourself). Consider whether an illogical argument is the product of muddled thinking or an attempt at manipulation – and whether the conclusion is therefore invalid, or may still be true.

(d) Look for **balance** – or bias – in the argument. It may or may not be conveniently signalled verbally ('On the one hand ... On the other hand ...').

(e) Appraise the **supporting evidence** given, if any.

(f) Consider the source's **credibility** and purpose in communicating.

(g) Bear in mind your own biased **perceptions** as you respond critically to the message and to the speaker: don't dismiss the message because you dislike the voice!

Listening to the tone of voice of the speaker adds an extra dimension to the process of interpreting (is he being ironic, for example, or serious?) and evaluating (is he carried away by emotion, or trying to be persuasive?).

Empathetic listening

8.11 'Empathy' is defined as 'the power of understanding and imaginatively entering into another person's feelings'.

Empathetic listening is a highly active form of listening, which goes a step beyond critical listening in the attempt fully to understand the message and what lies behind it. In effect, the listener must engage with the speaker, interpreting in the content and style of the message both the surface and underlying meanings and the feelings and motives which prompted them: a third, unspoken 'message' in its own right. Questions to ask yourself when listening empathetically include the following.

(a) **What** do the speaker's vocabulary, tone, manner and selection of content say over and above the surface message?

(b) **Why** is the speaker saying this, and in this way (vocabulary/tone of voice)?

(c) How does the speaker **feel** about this – whether or not it is actually said?

   (d) How would **I** feel in the same situation?

   (e) How might this idea/information **apply to me**, to my life?

   (f) What **feedback** can I give that would be helpful to the speaker, both to improve and encourage communication (say, asking a question) and to meet the underlying motives and needs (for encouragement, respect, friendliness, comfort or whatever)?

Attentive listening

8.12 Here are some brief hints to being a good listener, whether it be in one-to-one discussions, lectures, meetings or telephone conversations. In the context of your Research and Analysis Project, you will listen listen mainly to your mentor and your peer group.

   (a) **Be ready.** Get your attitude right at the start, and decide to listen. You might even be should have done some background research for the meeting or discussion so that you have established a context for the message you intend to receive.

   (b) **Be interested.** Don't try to soak up a message like a sponge, and then complain that you found it dull. Make it interesting for yourself by asking questions: how is this information relevant to me and how can I use it?

   (c) **Be patient.** Try to hold yourself back from interrupting if you disagree with someone, and don't compete to get your view in before the previous speaker has properly finished. Wait until a suitable opening (while your point is still relevant to the immediate discussion, but not while the speaker is just drawing a breath between phrases). Don't be so preoccupied with how you're going to respond that you forget to listen to what is said in the meantime.

   (d) **Keep your mind open.** Be aware of your negative reactions to the speaker's message, delivery or appearance. Control them, and don't jump to conclusions: you may miss something.

   (e) **Keep your mind going.** Being open-minded does not mean accepting everything blindly. Use your critical faculties: test the speaker's assumptions, logic and evidence. Also test your own interpretation of words and ideas, making sure they make sense in their context.

   (f) **Keep your mind on the job.** Concentrate. It is very easy to switch off as attention wanders or you get tired. Don't be distracted by details of the speaker or the room. Don't get side-tracked by irrelevancies in the message: co-operate with the speaker in getting to the point of what he is trying to say. Listen for main points, and the summary or conclusion.

   (g) **Give feedback.** You can encourage the speaker and ensure your own understanding by sending feedback signals, particularly during pauses in the speech or message. For example, try an interested and attentive look, a nod, a murmur of agreement or query ('Yes... Really?'). If there are opportunities, use some verbal means of checking that you have understood the message correctly. Ask questions, referring to the speaker's words in a way that demonstrates your interpretation of them ('You said earlier that...' 'You implied that..'): the speaker can then correct you if you have missed or misinterpreted something. Remember, you're not trying to score points for cleverness or clairvoyancy: co-operate with the speaker, and if you don't understand something, or you think you've got something wrong, say so.

   (h) **Use non-verbal cues (if available).** Be aware of the messages given by gestures, factual expression, tone of voice and so on.

(i) **Avoid interruptions**: if you interrupt it will disturb the speaker's flow, and can cause the conversation to go right off the rails. There are different reasons for interruptions:

    (i)   boredom

    (ii)   failure to understand

    (iii) a burning desire to state your own case and not hear out the other person

but they can all cause communication to break down completely.

(j) **Allow silence**: many people are embarrassed by silence and think that it is a sign of weakness or conversation drying up. In a complex, technical conversation, however, nothing could be further from the truth. Participants must have time to formulate their thoughts, mentally come to a conclusion and prepare what they are going to say, and this cannot happen instantaneously.

Try to indicate that you are happy with silence when it does occur, by looking relaxed and not pre-empting the speaker's next remarks.

Exercise 4

James, a mentor, and Pat, a student, are about to conduct the second meeting to discuss the progress of Pat's Research and Analysis Project on the financial position of Barclays Bank. Pat is quite nervous about the meeting and lacking self-confidence, as he feels that things are not progressing very well. He is wondering how to extract the maximum benefit from the meeting.

J: So, Pat, how have you been getting on?

P: Well, not too badly, but I've...

J: Sorry, I completely forgot to offer you a coffee. Would you like one?

P: Yes, thank you, that would be lovely. I've got to the stage where I've done the basic background reading and quite a lot of information gathering, but I seem to have come to a bit of a grinding halt.

J: I see. Milk and sugar?

P: Milk, please, no sugar.

    James gets up, goes out of the room and reappears five minutes later with the coffee. While James is out of the room, Pat can hear him chatting in the corridor outside

J: There we are. So, you've done the background reading and finished the information gathering, have you? Well that's excellent progress. You are doing well. I must congratulate you.

P: Well, yes, thank you, I have done those stages, I suppose, but I don't think it's going all that well.

J: Oh come on, don't do yourself down: it sounds as though you're bang on schedule.

P: It's just that whenever I start to try to plan the Report itself I can't ......

    Pat's mobile phone, buried in the depths of his briefcase, starts to play the Star Wars theme tune

P: Sorry, do you mind if I get that, it might be about my holiday flights. I'm expecting the travel agent to ring me.

    Hello. Yes, that's fine. So you'll charge my credit card today? Thanks. Bye.

J: Where are you going? Somewhere nice?

P: Just Majorca. I can't wait though. I love the sunshine.

J: So where were we? Oh yes, you can't get down to work and write the Report. Well I suggest we look at the headings you've got.....

Can you identify the features within this conversation which indicate that poor listening skills are being displayed? What rules do you think you could set for yourself to avoid these pitfalls?

Answer

(a) Immediately after the key question 'how are you getting on?' James **interrupts** Pat's response. Had James been listening, he would have heard the 'but' at the end of Pat's opening phrase, which should have alerted him to potential problems.

Rule: don't interrupt straight after a key question.

Rule: listen out for words like 'but', 'and' and 'because' tailing off at the end of a sentence. They can be indicative of the other person having a problem

(b) James puts a stop on the conversation completely by **changing the subject** (and Pat's thought processes) to coffee.

Rule: arrange the social aspects of the meeting (drinks, who sits where, take coats etc.) before you start. Then you can focus on listening.

(c) James goes out of the room to make the coffee and obviously **holds another conversation.** This means that he is less likely to retain the previous conversation in his head.

Rule: concentrate on the conversation in hand and don't start another one.

(d) When James resumes the conversation, he **summarises inaccurately**. He has obviously not listened to Pat's comment that he has come to a grinding halt. James has heard what he wants to hear, that is that the Project is going well. When Pat tries to tone down James' praise, James brushes Pat's protests aside.

Rule: when you summarise a conversation inaccurately, let the other person correct you.

(e) Pat's mobile phone rings just as Pat is trying to express his concerns. The fact that Pat is expecting a call means that he could have been half waiting for the phone to ring, rather than concentrating on the conversation.

Rule: turn off mobile phones and pagers completely before any situation where you are required to listen carefully. Even if you just turn it off instead of answering, it will interrupt your train of thought. Do not engage in a complex or more interesting conversation until you have finished the first one.

(f) James tries to get the conversation back on track, but again summarises inaccurately, and suggests an inappropriate course of action.

Rule: if you have been interrupted in a conversation and are not exactly sure what has been said, ask the other person to summarise and see how well their memory of the conversation matches yours.

---

9 RECORDING THE MEETING

9.1 Section 2.3 of the Module Guidelines, on meetings with your mentor, suggests that

> 'It may be useful for you to keep a personal diary of reflections on your meetings to help you when writing up your Key Skills Statement'.

This is valuable advice, as the meetings are likely to take place over a period of some months and you could easily forget, or even misinterpret, what has been said. We cannot stress enough the importance of making notes at your meetings. It is almost impossible to remember what was said at a meeting which happened months ago.

Means of recording

9.2 The Guidelines suggest a personal diary, but there are various ways of recording the meetings.

9.3   **Tape recorder**

This will provide a totally accurate record, but you should request permission from your mentor before you tape your conversations. Some people do not like having their conversations recorded as it detracts from the spontaneity and means that the discussion is less likely to be free-ranging. You may also find that having a verbatim recording makes it more difficult to reflect on the conversations, as you may be tempted just to write down what is said rather than think about it.

However, recording the meetings means that you need not worry about missing or forgetting anything, and it means that you can concentrate on listening to and participating in the conversation, only writing key points down.

9.4   **Minutes**

You would take minutes during the course of the meetings and then write them up afterwards. You could ask your mentor to read the minutes and confirm whether your understanding of proceedings is correct. The mentor may find this helpful as he or she has to provide confirmation to Oxford Brookes that the meetings have happened in accordance with the Guidelines, and a structured set of minutes could serve as useful evidence.

The drawback is that you might become so engrossed in taking minutes at the meeting that you don't participate fully in the discussions and miss the opportunity to raise important points.

9.5   **Brief notes**

Where a critical point is made during the meeting, or some piece of factual information is passed on by your mentor, you would just jot it down in the course of the meeting. It would then be sensible to write up the notes immediately after the meeting, so that you do not lose the thought processes while they are fresh.

You must make the time to write up the notes, or at the very least to write a comprehensive summary of the conversation held. Some authorities say that for a traditional lecture, you should spend at least twice the time again as the lecture time in writing up and ensuring that you understand your notes. This may be slightly over the top for writing up the notes of a meeting, but you should think in terms of at least spending as much time again as the time of the meeting.

10   **REFLECTING ON THE MEETING**

10.1   Notice that the Guidelines use the word 'reflections'. One definition of the verb 'to reflect' is **'to meditate, to consider attentively'**, while a reflection can also be described as a **thought which generates further thinking.**

10.2   Your reflections will be discussed in your Key Skills Statement. This contains much self-analysis and should contain examples taken from your discussions. You need to consider how **successful and relevant** your discussions were, and how they could have been more **effective.**

Comparison of meeting process with meeting outcome

10.3   The Guidelines provide you with detailed guidance of the objective and probable subject matter of each mentor meeting. They can be summarised like this:

Meeting 1	• Finalise the topic
	• Agree the research method
	• Set out draft aims and objectives
Meeting 2	• Report that information gathering is complete
	• Formulate initial view of findings
	• Present interim report
Meeting 3	• Give presentation to mentor and peer group
	• Review completion of Report

10.4 If you regard those as a checklist of what should be achieved at each meeting, you can then consider whether they have been achieved and tick them off once done.

10.5 If at the end of a meeting you think that the objectives have not been achieved, try to identify why that is the case, and think what you would have done differently. This will tell you whether the meeting has been successful or not, and you should be realistic in your assessment of this in the Key Skills Statement.

Documenting your thoughts

10.6 You must document (or record) your thoughts so that they provide an adequate framework for the self-analysis which is a critical part of the Key Skills Statement.

Since you will be writing up your Key Skills Statement some time after the event, the notes must contain sufficient detail for you to remember what you felt at the time. It might be helpful to structure your notes for each meeting around these headings.

(a) **Title of meeting**

1,2,3 or an additional meeting?

(b) **Planning**

- Was a plan prepared?
- Did the meeting follow the plan?
- If not, how did it diverge from the plan?
- What could I have done to keep to the plan?
- Should I concentrate more on the plan for the next meeting?

(c) **Questions**

- Were they open or closed?
- Did they generate further discussion?
- Could the mentor and I answer them?
- Could any questions have been phrased better (by either student or mentor)?
- Were any key questions left out?
- I think after the meeting 'I wish I'd asked X'?

(d) **Listening**

- Achieved satisfactorily?
- Conscious attempt to use listening techniques/avoid interruptions etc.?
- Any errors/distortions/noise?

(e) **Interaction**

- Consider a model of communication (eg in Chapter 10)

Mentor meetings:

- Was it a two-way conversation with participation from both?

- Did I extract the most from the discussion?

- Did I act upon suggestions made by the mentor?

- Do I need to do anything specific before the next meeting as a result of the mentor's comments?

- Does the mentor think that I am doing OK?

- What shall I do with the feedback?

Peer group presentation:

- Was their reaction positive or negative?

- Did I respond well to questions?

- Was I sufficiently well prepared?

(f) **Presentation**

- Could I have done the presentation better?
- Was I sufficiently well-prepared?
- What general comments emerge from the feedback?
- What will I do about those comments?
- Did I feel confident?
- Did I learn anything from the other presentations I saw?

(g) **Overall**

- Was the meeting useful?
- Did it achieve its objectives?
- Did it contribute to the production of my Project?

When you are formulating and answering these questions, you must be scrupulously honest. In the Key Skills Statement you are expected to recognise your strengths and your weaknesses, and identify ways in which you can improve.

11 THE MENTOR'S CERTIFICATION

11.1 Once the project is complete, the mentor must fill in and sign section D of the Submission Form (there is a copy at the back of this book).

11.2 The external examiner has commented that in some instances candidates have failed to ensure that the qualification of the mentor was recorded and certified, and so could not be awarded the degree until the section was satisfactorily completed.

11.3 Staff at Oxford Brookes University regularly carry out an audit of the authenticity of the mentor's certification. For example, if the mentor says that they are qualified to act by virtue of being a member of the ACCA, that will probably be checked by reference to the ACCA's list of members. Oxford Brookes also write to some mentors, asking them for confirmation of their identity.

Chapter roundup

- The mentor is the person who will monitor the progress of your work through the Project but they will not be regarded as your tutor.

- The three meetings with your mentor are a fundamental part of the project.

- The Key Skills Statement requires you to reflect upon your meetings with your mentor and consider ways in which they could have been more effective.

- Questioning, feedback and listening are essential elements in every meeting with your mentor.

- It is important that you record the events at your mentor meetings adequately.

Chapter 12

DELIVERING YOUR PRESENTATION

Chapter topic list

1 The requirement for a presentation

2 Presenting to your mentor

3 Presenting to your peer group

4 Planning your presentation

5 Planning the content

6 Communication aids

7 Delivery

8 Taking questions

9 Feedback

Introduction

This chapter is devoted to the presentation which you must make to your mentor, and probably also to your peer group, in the third meeting.

You may find this prospect, especially if you are presenting to a group, absolutely terrifying. You need not feel this. The cardinal rule when preparing for a presentation is:

PREPARATION
PREPARATION
PREPARATION

If you prepare and practise sufficiently before the event, you will be confident and therefore successful.

---

1 THE REQUIREMENT FOR A PRESENTATION

1.1 The Guidelines state

You are required to prepare and deliver a fifteen minute presentation on your report to your mentor, and if applicable your peer group. You should use appropriate presentation techniques in conjunction with your talk. You should be prepared to answer questions and provide explanations when requested.

The Guidelines then say of the peer group option

Where your mentor is working with more than one student, presentations in meeting 3 can take place in a group. This will enable you to deliver your presentation to an audience, receive feedback from your peers and in turn, critically review the work of others.

1.2   The presentation is one of the topics which must be specifically incorporated into the Key Skills Statement. You must identify what went well and what could have been improved. You must attach an outline of your presentation, on two sides of A4 paper, to the Key Skills Statement.

1.3   You can deduce from these requirements that Oxford Brookes University attach great importance to the presentation, and it is a critical part of the assessment procedure which will grant your degree.

2   PRESENTING TO YOUR MENTOR

2.1   If you are a student working alone (ie not in a college environment) or your mentor does not act in that capacity to other students, you will deliver your presentation solely to your mentor. This may feel like a slightly artificial situation, as in many ways it is more difficult to present formally to one person than it is to a large group.

Preparation

2.2   If you are delivering your presentation just to your mentor, you should prepare for it in exactly the same way as you would if presenting to a group, as covered in detail in later sections of this chapter. You should be standing, treat the mentor as if he or she were an 'audience' and use visual aids and handouts.

2.3   You may find it easier to pre-empt the questions you will have to field after your presentation. The Guidelines make it clear that the main purpose of the third mentor meeting is the presentation, but they also suggest the questions that are likely to be asked by the mentor.

(a)   What went **well or badly**?
(b)   Does the report meet its **objectives**?
(c)   Does the report make **sense**?

2.4   These questions reflect the fact that this is the **review stage**, and they are expressed in very general terms. Of course, it is highly likely that you will be asked additional questions on some aspects of the technical content of your report, but if you have prepared adequately and covered your material in an appropriate way, as discussed later, this should not present problems.

2.5   One critical factor to remember is that the mentor **is on your side**. Your mentor wants you to pass the Research and Analysis Project and be awarded your degree, so you should not regard him or her as a hostile audience trying to trip you up. It is not an 'us and them' situation' rather it is an 'us and us' situation, as you are both working towards the same end.

3   PRESENTING TO YOUR PEER GROUP

3.1   Your peer group may consist of only one or two other students, or there may be a large number, depending on the other responsibilities of your mentor. You may never have met any of them before, or you may know them all well from studying for the ACCA exams together.

3.2   A peer group is exactly as its name implies: it is a group of your peers, or equals. They will be at various different stages in their ACCA studies, as some will have done the minimum number of exams necessary prior to submitting the Research and Analysis Project, while

others may have completed the ACCA qualification. The common feature is that you are all at the point of submitting the Project, so you will have almost written the Report, and be embarking on the Key Skills Statement.

3.3 You may find that being part of a group provides a refreshing change. If you have been working alone on your Research and Analysis Project, and have only discussed it with your mentor, the comments and views of other people could be enlightening.

3.4 Many authorities believe that learning in a group is beneficial, and most degree courses adopt it to some extent, usually by means of seminars and discussion groups.

Discussion helps you:

(a) To think
(b) To develop your ideas
(c) To see things from a different perspective
(d) To unravel problems where previously you had met a dead end
(e) To realise you are not the only person with the problems you have

3.5 An advantage of presenting to a peer group is that you will see other people's presentations and be able to participate in question and answer sessions yourself. This may help you in putting the final touches to your Report and in preparing to write your Key Skills Statement.

4 PLANNING YOUR PRESENTATION

4.1 The aspects of planning considered here are relevant for a presentation both to your mentor or to your peer group.

There are three key elements to consider when planning a presentation:

(a) The audience
(b) The logistic arrangements
(c) The content

In later sections of this chapter we will look at communication aids, dealing with questions and coping with feedback.

The audience

4.2 In the case of this presentation, you will be faced with a captive audience, in that they are there because the mentor is hearing all the presentations at the same time. They are likely to be a receptive and responsive audience, because they will know that they can learn from the experience.

4.3 You should consider these points:

(a) **Will they be interested in the topic of the presentation?**

The audience may have a general expectation that they will learn something new, interesting, or useful on a topic that they are pre-disposed to **gather information** about: it is up to the speaker to hold their attention by satisfying the desire for relevant information. They may also have some **prior knowledge**, on which the speaker can build: there will be a fine line to tread between boring the audience by telling them what they already know, and losing them by assuming more knowledge than they possess.

(b) **Do they need specific information from the presentation?**

An audience which is deliberately seeking information, and intending to use it to further their own objectives, is highly motivated. If their objectives match the speaker's (which should certainly be the case among the peer group: you all want to pass the Research and Analysis Project), this motivation aids the speaker. It is therefore important to gauge, as far as possible, what this highly-motivated group **want** to hear from you, and **why**.

4.4 Taking into account audience needs and expectations, your message needs to have the following qualities.

(a) **Interest.** It should be lively/entertaining/varied or relevant to the audience's needs and interests, or preferably both.

(b) **Congeniality.** This usually means positive, supportive or helpful in some way (eg in making a difficult decision easier, or satisfying a need). Avoid:

(i) **Sensitive** comments on which your listeners may have strong beliefs or feelings contrary to your own.

(ii) Language or suggestions that might be **offensive**, threatening or detrimental to their interests (involving competition, cost, danger, risk and so on).

(c) **Credibility.** It should be **consistent** in itself, and with known **facts**; apparently **objective**; and from a source perceived to be **trustworthy**.

(d) **Accessibility.** This means both:

(i) **Audible/visible.** (Do you need to be closer to the audience? Do you need a microphone? Enlarged visual aids? Clearer articulation and projection).

(ii) **Understandable.** (What is the audience's level of knowledge/education/ experience in general? and of the topic at hand? What technical terms or **jargon** will need to be avoided or explained? What concepts or ideas will need to be explained?).

The logistics

4.5 At the planning stage, you might also consider **physical factors** which will affect the audience's concentration: their ability and willingness to **keep** listening **attentively and positively** to your message. Some of the these may not be in your control, as you will probably not have any choice over the location but as far as possible, give attention to the following.

(a) **Listening conditions.** Try and **cut out background noise** – conversations outside the room, traffic, loud air conditioning or rattling slide projector, say. (There may be a trade-off between peace and quiet, and good ventilation, also required for alertness: be sensible about the need to open a door or window or switch on a fan.)

(b) **Freedom from interruption and distraction.** Do not let the **focus shift** from you and your message to outside views of people passing by and so on. Arrange not to be disturbed by others entering the room. Announce that questions and comments will be invited at the end of the session.

(c) **Ventilation, heating and lighting.** A room that is too stuffy, or draughty, too hot or cold, too bright or too dim to see properly, can create physical malaise, and shifts attention from the speaker and his message to the listener and his discomfort.

(d) **Seating and desking**. Excessive comfort can impair alertness – but uncomfortable seating is a distraction. Combined with inadequate arrangements for writing (since many people may wish or need to take notes), it can cause severe strain over a lengthy talk.

(e) **Audibility and visibility**. Inadequate speaking volume or amplification is a distraction and a strain, even if it does not render the message completely inaccessible. Excessive volume and electronic noise is equally irritating. Visibility requires planning not just of effective visual aids (clear projection in suitable light, adequately enlarged etc) but also of seating plans, allowing unobstructed 'sight lines' for each participant.

(f) **Seating layout**. Depending on the purpose and style of your presentation, you may choose formal classroom-like rows of seating, with the speaker in front behind a podium, or informal group seating in a circle or cluster in which the speaker is included. The formal layout enhances the speaker's credibility, and may encourage attention to information, while the informal layout may be more congenial, encouraging involvement and input from the whole group. You may have little choice about this.

(g) **Time**. Listeners get tired over time – however interesting the presentation: their **concentration span is limited**, and they will not be able to listen effectively for a long period without a break. Although your presentation is only 15 minutes long, the cumulative effect of a number of presentations may make the audience tired when it comes to you. Bear in mind, too, that the **time of day** will affect your listeners' concentration, even if your presentation is a brief one: you will have to work harder if your talk is first thing in the morning, late in the day (or week), or approaching lunch-time.

(h) **The speaker's appearance**. We will talk more about this under **delivery**, below – but it should already be obvious that the appearance of the speaker may sabotage his efforts if it is uncongenial or unappealing, lacks credibility or the authority expected by the audience, is distracting in some way, and so on.

Planning the structure

4.6 Structure is all-important in a presentation. If your presentation is not well-structured and your audience loses the thread, it can be difficult to continue to hold their interest. This in turn means that you can feel vulnerable, if you feel that the presentation is not going well, so your performance deteriorates.

4.7 Remember that a presentation differs from private reading. If you are reading a book or an article and do not understand something, you can go back and read through it again. or take a break and go back to it later. The audience at a presentation does not have that luxury, so you the speaker must get it right first time.

4.8 The classic advice on delivering a presentation is:

(a) Tell them what you are going to say
(b) Say it
(c) Tell them what you've said

4.9 This means that your presentation can be split into three broad sections:

(a) The introduction
(b) The presentation itself, and
(c) The conclusion

4.10 Armed with your clearly-stated objectives and audience profile, you can plan the **content** of your presentation. This can be quite a daunting prospect as you need to remember the information, put it in the right order and state it clearly, all in one fluid movement.

4.11 One approach which may help to clarify your thinking is as follows.

(a) **Make a mindmap (or brainstorm)**. Write down all the thoughts and points that come to you on the subject in hand. Do not worry at this stage about the **order or relevance** of the ideas – just keep them coming, until your brain 'dries up' on the subject.

(b) **Prioritise**. Using the techniques of **classifying/clustering ideas** or the hierarchy of objectives approach, select the **key points** of the subject, and a **storyline** or theme that gives your argument a unified sense of 'direction'.

The **fewer** points you make (with the most emphasis) and the clearer the **direction** in which your thoughts are heading, the easier it will be for the audience to grasp and retain your message. Discard – or de-emphasise – all points which do not further your simple design.

(c) **Structure**. Make notes for your presentation which show your selected main points and how they **link** to each other. In other words, **illustrate** simply the **logical order** or pattern of your speech as a whole. Ideally this will follow the structure of your Report.

(d) **Outline**. Following your structured notes, **flesh out** your message. The outline should include an **introduction**; **supporting evidence**, **examples and illustrations**; **notes** of where (and what) **visual aids** will be required; signals of **logical progressions** and a **conclusion**. These points are developed later.

(e) **Practise**. Learn the **basic outline**, or sequence of ideas, rather than a word-for-word 'script': if you repeat a speech by rote, it can sound stilted, unspontaneous and mechanical. Practice runs, or rehearsals, will help you to remember your storyline, and will give you confidence that you **can** find the words to put it across, once you get going. (You may, however, choose to polish and learn by heart certain important elements of the outline: introduction, supporting facts/quotes/anecdotes, and conclusion, say.)

Your **rehearsals** should **indicate** difficult logical leaps, dull patches, unexplained terms and other potential barriers to understanding, which you can then eliminate or minimise by adjusting your outline or style. They will also help you gauge and adjust the **length** of your presentation. You should attempt **at least** one full, timed 'dress' rehearsal. You may choose to rehearse in front of a mirror, to a mock audience of family/friends, or on audio or video-tape, in order to assess the full effect. This will also help you get the timing right.

(f) **Cue**. Your outline may be ideal for rehearsal, but may be too unwieldy to act as a cue or **aide-memoire** for the talk itself. You should be now be fairly familiar with your material: memory 'joggers' are all you require, and help you to avoid the tendency, when nervous, of trying to read word-for-word from a script, instead of getting involved in communicating spontaneously and directly with the audience.

Small cards, which fit into the palm of the hand, are ideal. (If you are using an overhead projector, slides may be used in a similar fashion to guide you – and also the audience.) They should contain very brief, clear notes (verbal or pictorial – whatever works for you), which give you:

(i) **Key words** for each topic, and the logical links between them
(ii) Reminders for when to use **visual aids**
(iii) The **full text** of any detailed information you need to quote

Exercise 1: Planning for a presentation

You have been asked by your manager to give a brief talk to the junior staff on the subject of: 'The tidy office: efficiency, safety and image'.

You know this issue is a bit sensitive at the moment, having recently had to tell people off about the state of the Sales Administration Department offices. The staff are on the defensive, and have been complaining loudly about the cleaning lady. However, several files have been mislaid, others turning up in wastepaper bins or marked by rings from the bottom of coffee cups. It seems as if, every time a visitor is due in the Department, you have to make people interrupt their duties to have a swift 'spring clean': they sulk. Unfortunately you do not always get enough warning of visits – and morale suffers again, because the staff are as aware of the mess as you are. Most recently, you have lost two of your assistants through illness, one suffering asthmatic attacks caused by dust (which you know *is* the cleaning lady's fault), and another having strained his back picking up a stack of loose files which he had accidentally knocked off the edge of his desk.

You are going to have to do something about the tidiness problem. The staff's habits will have to be corrected firmly – but tactfully, because of the atmosphere of hostility that is creeping into the issue. Stress positive aspects of a tidy office, in line with the title of your talk. Make *helpful* notes for your talk.

Answer

TIDY OFFICE

Efficiency	Safety	Image

Files etc easily traced and secure	Dust etc – x's asthma	Coffee-stained, crumpled files
[*NB – don't criticise specific ...*]	[*NB = 'appreciate = not down to you', but ... all responsible for safety ...*]	Impression to visitors
Easier use of desk surface	Accidents; tripping over, knocking things off desk	
Easier movement round office		
No interruptions for Spring cleaning!		

CO-OPERATION

We've all been guilty of
lapses
We all hate the   inconvenience
              danger
              embarrassment
Together – let's make this a

TIDY OFFICE: FOR EFFICIENCY, SAFETY + IMAGE

5 PLANNING THE CONTENT

5.1 Some authorities think that the best approach is to plan the introduction and the conclusion more or less together (tell them what you're going to say and tell them what you've said) and then plan for the chunk that goes in the middle. This is not compulsory, however, and you may prefer to plan just by going through the structure of your Report.

Introduction

5.2 This is a **vital part** of your presentation, because if you do not establish your credibility and gain the audience's interest at this stage, when their concentration is at its peak, it will be very difficult to win them back later. It is also useful for the audience to get an overview of the **shape** of your presentation, to guide them through it: a bit like the scanning process in reading. The **introduction** should therefore do the following.

   (a) Make an **initial impact** which focuses the audience's attention on your presentation. Establish – quickly – the **relevance** of the topic to the audience: set up the problem they need solved, the question they need answered, the threat or opportunity facing them. Use curiosity, or surprise.

   (b) Establish the **speaker's (that means your!) credibility** (and congeniality, if appropriate). Establish – quickly – your authority to speak on the subject, the clarity of your thinking and the supporting evidence you have available. Establish a rapport with the audience – through anecdote, humour or identification with them (in solving the problem, facing the threat etc).

   (c) Give them a **taste** of the subject and the **style** in which you intend to address it, to arouse their curiosity or interest, and **focus** their thoughts on the matter in hand.

   (d) **Prepare** the audience for the content and structure of your presentation.

The conclusion

5.3 Again, this is an important stage of the talk, because people tend to rally their concentration when they realise the end of a talk is approaching. The **conclusion** should be used to accomplish the following.

   (a) **Clarify and draw together** the points you have made into the single main idea or story: use an example, or anecdote, review, summary or conclusion – but do **not** introduce any new ideas at this stage.

   (b) **State, reinforce or imply** what you want/expect your audience to do (or know, believe, feel, agree to etc) following your presentation. As in a letter, leave the audience with the seed of response or action in their minds, particularly if your purpose is persuasive.

   (c) **Reinforce** the audience's recall of the content of your talk, and the response they are expected to make as a result. Again, you may use repetition, or something more theatrical (a joke or anecdote, quotation or surprising statistic) to make your main message **memorable**.

Title

5.4 This may be devised after you have planned your talk, to reflect its content and style, or may be given to you. The title is **part of the message**, and – as a first impression – an important part. It should be:

   (a) **Brief**

   (b) **Meaningful** – preferably a clear indication of what your talk is about

   (c) **Interesting**, curiosity-arousing (though not obscure), motivating to the audience

   (d) **Honest**, so that the audience do not feel cheated when they hear the talk itself. (Do not title your talk 'How to make a million pounds' if you are not going to tell the audience how … .)

For example:

(i) An analysis of the financial situation of Microsoft

(ii) Implementation of information systems: avoiding the pitfalls

(iii) Internal audit for X plc: What are the costs and benefits?

5.5 Clarifying the message

Your structured notes and outline should contain cues which clarify the **logical order**, shape or progression of your information or argument. This is helpful for you, because it keeps you 'on track', but it is primarily intended to guide your audience, in order to:

(a) Maintain a **sense of purpose**, which keeps up their motivation to listen

(b) Help them to **follow you** at each stage of your argument, so that they arrive with you at the conclusion

5.6 Logical cues indicate the **links** between one topic or statement and the next. Here are some examples.

(a) You can simply begin each point with **linking words or phrases** like:

This has led to ...

Therefore ...
So ...   [conclusion, result or effect, arising from previous point]
As a result ...

However ...
But ...   [contradiction or alternative to previous point]
On the other hand ...

Similarly ...   [confirmation or additional example of previous point]
Again ...

Moreover ...   [building on the previous point]

b) You can set up a **framework** for the whole argument, giving the audience an overview and then filling in the detail. For example:

'There are three main reasons why ... Firstly ... Secondly ... Thirdly ... .'

'So what's the answer? You could take two sides, here. On the one hand ... . On the other hand ... .'

'Let's trace how this came about. On Monday 17th ... . Then on Tuesday ... .'

'Of course, this isn't a perfect solution. It has the advantages of ... . But there are also disadvantages, in that ... .'

'You might like to think of communication in terms of the 5 C's. That's: concise, clear, correct, complete, courteous. Let's look at each of these in turn'.

(c) You can use more elaborate devices which **summarise** or repeat the previous point and lead the audience to the next. These also have the advantage of giving you, and the listener, a 'breather' in which to gather your thoughts. They are particularly effective in **persuasive** communication, since they can set up a logical progression, or contrast, in a dramatic way.

'So we've seen some of the effects of poor communication in the banking industry. We probably agree that they are something! So what can we do? How can we improve our communications? Let's look at some ideas ... .'

'As we've seen, the competition's Brand X has the advantage of price, and a popular brand image. It looks good, doesn't it? They're reaching a lot of people with a clear message: Brand X is cheaper. But – does Brand X represent *value* for money? Let's look at the facts ... .'

5.7 Other ways in which **content** can be used to **clarify** the message include the following.

    (a) **Examples** and illustrations – showing how an idea works in practice.

    (b) **Anecdotes** – inviting the audience to relate an idea to a real-life situation.

    (c) **Questions** – rhetorical, or requiring the audience to answer, raising particular points that may need clarification.

    (d) **Explanation** – showing how or why something has happened or is so, to help the audience understand the principles behind your point.

    (e) **Description** – helping the audience to visualise the person, object or setting you are describing.

    (f) **Definition** – explaining the precise meaning of terms that may not be shared or understood by the audience.

    (g) The use of **facts,** quotations or statistics – to 'prove' your point.

5.8 Your **vocabulary and style** in general should contribute to the clarity of the message. Remember to use short, simple sentences and non-technical words (unless the audience is sure to know them): **avoid** jargon, clichés, unexplained acronyms, colloquialisms, double meanings and vague expressions (like 'rather', 'good'). Remember, too, that this is **oral** communication, not written: use words and grammatical forms that you would normally use in speaking to someone – bearing in mind the audience's ability to understand you, the formality of the occasion and so on.

5.9 **Visual aids** will also be an important aspect of content used to clarify meaning. We discuss them specifically later in this chapter.

Adding emphasis

5.10 **Emphasis** is the 'weight', importance or impact given to particular words or ideas. This can largely be achieved through **delivery** – the tone and volume of your voice, strong eye contact, emphatic gestures and so on – but can be **reinforced** in the content and wording of your speech. Emphasis can be achieved by a number of means.

    (a) **Repetition:**   'If value for money is what the market wants, then value for money is what this company must deliver.'

                                 'One in five customers has had a quality complaint. That's right: one in five.'

    (b) **Rhetorical questions:** 'Do you know how many of the customers had a quality complaint? One in five. Do you think that's acceptable?'

    (c) **Quotation:**   '"Product quality is the number one issue in customer care in the early 21st century." That's the conclusion of our survey report.'

    (d) **Statistical evidence:** 'One in five of our customers this year have had a quality complaint: that's 10% more complaints than last year. If the trend continues, we will have one complaint for every two satisfied customers – next year!'

    (e) **Exaggeration:**   'We have to look at the quality control system of X Ltd. Because if the current trend continues, the company will end up without any customers at all.'

Adding interest

5.11 Simple, clear information often **lacks impact,** and will only be interesting to those already motivated by the desire for the information you will need to **balance** the need for your clarity with the need to make his message vivid, attention-grabbing and memorable. All the devices discussed so far can be used for impact.

Here are some further suggestions.

(a) **Analogy, metaphor, simile** etc – **comparing** something to something else which is in itself more colourful or interesting.

'Customer relations is like planting a seed. You may not see anything happening for a while. But you keep watering the soil. And one day – without your having done anything special – there's a shoot there, with deep roots. And that plant will keep growing and – with a bit more care – bear lots of fruit.'

(b) **Anecdote or narrative** – telling a **story** which illustrates or makes the point, using suspense, humour or a more human context.

(c) **Curiosity or surprise** – from incongruity, anticlimax or controversy.

'I'm going to tell you how you can read twice as fast, *and* understand more – not less – of what you've read.'

'If you put all the widgets we've sold this year end to end, they would stretch twice around the equator.'

'Improving communication is a complete waste of time ... Is that what you think?'

6 COMMUNICATION AIDS

6.1 We will now look at how visual aids can be introduced into presentations. There are several suggestions here, but you do not have to use them all. Don't overdo it.

6.2 **They act as an aid to communication.** This may seem obvious, but it is important to remember that visual aids are not supposed to be impressive or clever for their own sake, but to support the message and speaker in achieving their purpose. They should 'add value' to some extent to what you are saying.

Slides

6.3 **Slides** are usually **still photographs,** but may include text and diagrams, projected onto a screen or other surface. Slides have several useful features.

(a) They allow the use of **photography,** including **colour,** which can be very powerful in creating a **mood or impression,** and can also – being perceived as an image of reality – be used to prove a point.

(b) They are **pre-prepared** – ie not generated by writing or drawing during the presentation. This allows careful **planning** and execution, and slides can be finished to a very high degree of style, quality and 'professionalism' you.

(c) The **sequence and timing** of slides is controlled by the presenter, allowing you to synchronise the images with relevant points in the talk. Slides are therefore flexible in keeping pace with the presenter and audience.

(d) The swiftness with which one image follows another is particularly suited to messages of **contrast** or comparison: two products, say, or before and after scenarios.

6.4 The **drawbacks** to slides are as follows.

(a) They require a **darkened room** for effective projection, which may hinder the taking of notes by the audience.

(b) **Malfunctions** or incompetent use of the slide projector are frustrating and distracting. (You may well have been to a slide presentation where images were upside down, or wrongly sequenced, or the presenter had to keep 'clicking' backwards and forwards.)

(c) There is a temptation to base a presentation **around a sequence** of slides, once the projector and conditions are set up: often, only a small proportion of the images shown are actually necessary to fulfil their purpose.

Overhead projector

6.5 An **overhead projector** allows the presenter to place sheets of clear film, on which any form of message can be drawn or printed, on a light box which projects the image onto a screen behind and above the presenter. This is commonly used as a tuition medium in lecture halls.

6.6 The films or **acetates** can be pre-prepared, by hand or printing or using a photocopier or PC (see below), or can be written on by the presenter during the presentation. They are versatile, therefore, for text or line drawings, in black or colour. Use of the photocopier allows copies of documents to be shown much more cheaply than by photographing onto slide format; the same is true of professionally-prepared text which can be generated on a computer or word processor and printed out on acetate. Because the acetates themselves are clear, this medium is particularly useful for **building up** images and diagrams, adding extra layers for each new stage, or degree of complexity, or to demonstrate similarities of line and layout.

6.7 **Disadvantages** of overhead projection are mainly due to the need for physical handling, which can be distracting for the audience and the presenter, unless handled very smoothly. There is, too, always a risk of technical breakdown, which renders the aid useless: the format is not readily adaptable.

Presentation software

6.8 **Programs for presentations** allow the user to build up a series of graphical displays or images which can be used for presentation. With additional hardware, this type of software can be used to produce 35 mm slides for an on-screen slideshow or storyboard (which can be synchronised with a sound track). The slides that your lecturer uses on the overhead projector may well be produced by similar means using, for example, the Microsoft PowerPoint package. You have also no doubt seen PowerPoint-type presentations running continuously on computers in shops, telling you about the features of the computer itself or of a software package.

6.9 Quite commonly now lecture halls and conference theatres are equipped with a large VDU type screen and the person giving the presentation simply has to plug his or her laptop PC into the hall's system to give a computerised display of their slides, allowing a certain amount of **animation** (the slides 'build', point by point, as you watch) and professional looking transitions between slides, so that one can dissolve into the next, or fold into itself to reveal the next and so on. If you are presenting to a large peer group, you may find that you use a hall or lecture room with these facilities.

6.10 Here is an example of a set of slides produced using Microsoft PowerPoint. Note that professional looking **design templates** can be applied at the click of a mouse button. You would simply need to specify matters such as font type and size and colours wanted.

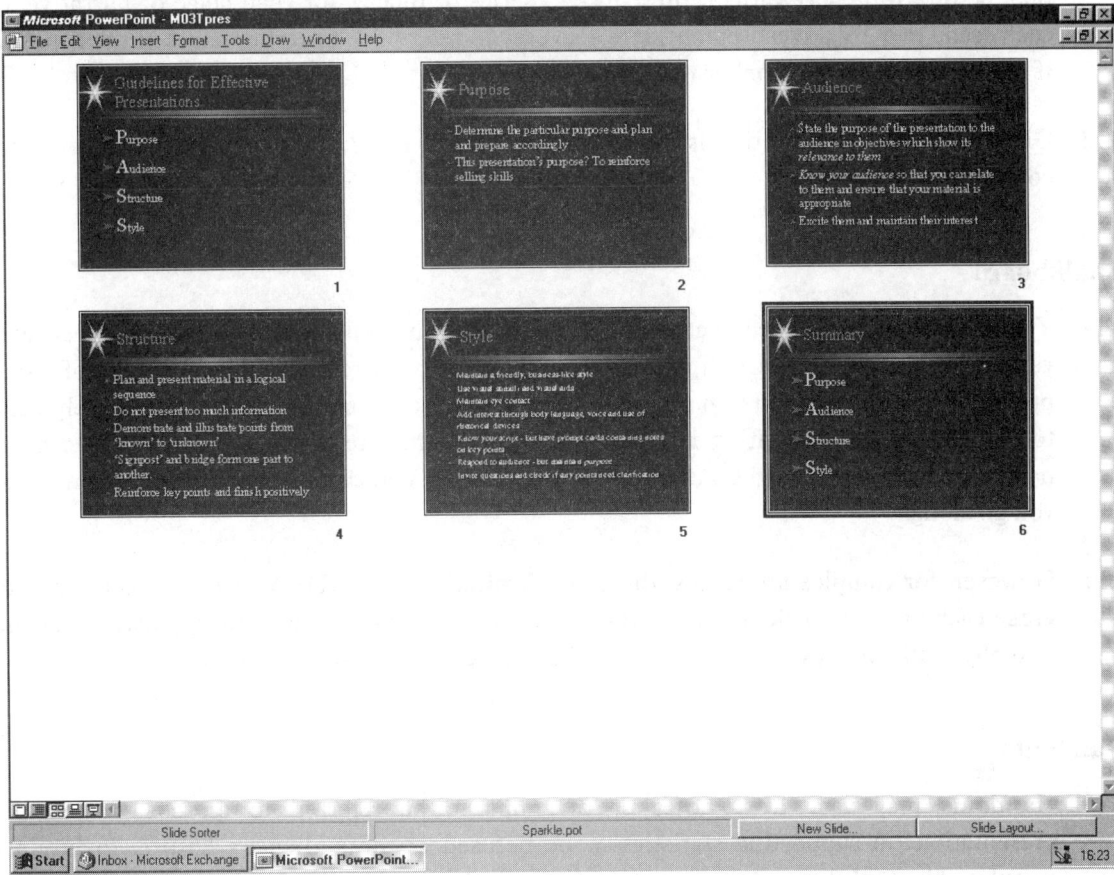

6.11 Flipcharts

If you intend to **write your notes** or draw your diagrams himself, in the course of the presentation, a **flipchart** may be used as a cheaper and less risky alternative to the overhead projector. A flipchart is simply a large pad of paper mounted on an easel-style frame. As each sheet of notes/images is finished with, it is 'flipped' over to the back, revealing the next sheet.

6.12 Compared to the overhead, the flipchart presents a **smaller** and less impactful image, which may be a problem for a larger audience or room. It does not allow layering of pre-prepared

images – but this can be overcome by simply adding words or drawings to the existing ones as you go along. A flipchart can be pre-prepared for time-saving, clarity and added sophistication: the **story boards** used by advertising designers and film/animation makers may be of a flip chart variety, presenting a series of images for each stage of narrative, or each scene in a TV advertisement. It is also easy to refer back to earlier pages of the flipchart if required for a conclusion, or to answer questions.

6.13 Given that your presentation is likely to be in a small room, a flipchart could be your best communication aid.

Chalkboard

6.14 You probably came into contact with the **chalkboard**, blackboard or its modern 'wipe-clean' variants, at school. Unlike a flipchart, you cannot pre-prepare a complete sequence of visual presentations: only the first, perhaps an overview of your presentation. If you merely need to confirm points by writing key words, or to confirm the spelling of difficult terms or names, a chalkboard may be sufficient for your needs. You can add to a diagram or notes as you go along.

6.15 However, for complex sequences, the major **limitation** of the board is the need to clear or **erase** each visual to make room for the next. This can be **time-consuming**, distracting and also physically messy (as anyone who has had to clean a blackboard will know).

Handouts

6.16 **Handouts** may vary from notes or diagrams to be referred to on cue during the presentation, to supporting statistics to be perused at the audience's leisure, to product samples. They fulfil much the same function as other pre-prepared aids, with the following added advantages.

(a) The audience can take them **away** as a reminder .

(b) The audience is relieved of the requirement to take notes, which may eliminate some **distractions** (although note-taking is a part of active listening and need not generally be discouraged).

(c) The presenter does not have to **do anything** to produce or activate the aid during the talk – merely to draw the audience's attention to it.

(d) Handouts can be produced to a highly-planned and **professional quality**, if the purpose of the presentation warrants it and the resources are available.

Props and demonstrations

6.17 **Objects** (eg products) **and processes** (eg the operation of a product) can be displayed or demonstrated to the audience. This, being the evidence of their own eyes, can lend enhanced credibility to the message, and also added interest. **Demonstrations** are particularly effective to illustrate – or 'prove' – how efficient a process is, how easy a device is to operate, and so on. A **display** gives a physical reality to an object: its colour, feel and 'look' all contribute to its perceived value and quality.

Using visual aids

6.18 Whatever medium or device you are using, visual aids are **versatile** with regard to content. On any of the above formats, you might use maps, diagrams, flowcharts, verbal notes, drawings, photographs and so on.

In general you need to consider the following.

(a) Visual aids are **simplified and concrete**: they are easier to grasp than the spoken word, giving the audience both motivation and time to absorb complex relationships and information.

(b) They are **stimulating** to the imagination and emotions, and therefore useful in gaining attention and recall. They can be 'worth a thousand words' in time-saving on lengthy explanation and description.

(c) Visual aids can also be **distracting** for the audience – and for the presenter, who has to draw/write/organise/operate them. They can add complexity and ambiguity to the presentation, if not carefully designed for relevance and clarity.

(d) Visual aids impose **practical requirements**.

   (i) The medium you choose must be **suitable** for the size of your **audience and venue**. (Demonstrations, or handing round a small number of samples, is not going to work for a large audience; a flipchart will not be visible at the back of a large room; a slide projector can be overwhelming in a small room.)

   (ii) **Skill, time and resources** must be available for any pre-preparation of aids that may be required in advance of the presentation.

   (iii) **The equipment, materials and facilities** you require must be available in the venue, and you must **know** how to **use** them. (No good turning up with a slide projector if there is no power source, or film when there is no overhead projector, or without proper pens for a particular type of board.)

Guidelines for effective use of visual aids

6.19 (a) Ensure that the aid is:

   (i) **Appropriate** to your message, in content and 'style' or mood
   (ii) **Easy to see** and understand
   (iii) Only used when there is **support** to be gained from it

(b) Ensure that all **equipment** and materials are **available and working** and that you can (and do) operate them efficiently and confidently. This includes having all your slides/acetates/notes with you, in the right order, the right way up and so on.

(c) Ensure that the aid does not become a **distraction**.

   (i) Show each image **long enough** to be absorbed and noted, but not so long as to merge with following idea.

   (ii) Maintain **voice and eye contact** with your audience, so they know that it is you who are the communicator, not the machine.

   (iii) **Introduce** your aids and what they are for, placing the focus on the verbal presentation.

   (iv) Hand out **supporting material** either well before the presentation (to allow reading beforehand) or at the relevant point: if you hand it out just before, it will distract or daunt the audience with information they do not yet understand.

(v)   **Write or draw,** if you need to do so during the presentation, as quickly and efficiently as possible (given the need for legibility and neatness).

7   DELIVERY

7.1   **Delivery** of a presentation is equivalent to 'style' and 'presentation' in writing.

Here we will look briefly at some of the dynamics of communication between a speaker and audience.

Pre-presentation nerves

7.2   **Stage-fright** can be experienced before making a phone call, going into an interview or meeting, or even writing a letter, but it is considerably more acute, for most people, before standing up to talk in front of a group or crowd of people. Common fears are to do with **making a fool of oneself,** forgetting one's **lines,** being unable to answer **questions,** or being faced by blank incomprehension or **lack of response.** Fear can make vocal delivery hesitant or stilted and **body language** stiff and unconvincing: this may give the audience the impression that you are lying, or uninterested, or unsure of what you are saying. (Or worse: fainting, incoherence, memory lapse and physical fumbling can be caused by fear, in what is called a **self-fulfilling prophecy:** because you **think** the worst is going to happen, fear creates conditions which **make** it happen.)

7.3   A **controlled amount of fear,** or stress, is actually **good for you:** it stimulates the production of **adrenaline,** which can contribute to alertness and dynamic action. Only at excessive levels is stress harmful, degenerating into **strain.** If you can **manage your stress** or stagefright, it will help you to be **alert** to feedback from your audience, to think 'on your feet' in response to questions, and to project vitality and enthusiasm.

7.4   Some people are simply **more prone** to strain than others. If you tend to be crippled by nerves, you need to learn to relax, using techniques such as breathing exercises, physical exercise, visualisation of positive outcomes and so on. By and large, however, you can **control** your nervousness by the following simple means.

(a)   **Reduce uncertainty and risk.** This means:

(i)   **Preparing thoroughly** for your presentation, including rehearsal, and anticipating questions.

(ii)   **Checking** that equipment, seating, conditions and so on are as required and expected.

(iii)   **Preparing** whatever is necessary for your own confidence and comfort (hayfever medication, glass of water, handkerchief, note cards etc).

(iv)   **Ensuring** that you – and the audience – have the correct venue details and start time.

(v)   **Keeping your notes to hand,** and in order, during your presentation. Keep a marker (say, your finger) on the point you've reached, so you need not fear losing your place.

(b)   **Ensure that you look and feel your best:** presentable appearance, sleep the night before, no hangover and so on.

(c)   **Have confidence in your message.** Forget fear of failure, and concentrate on the desired outcome: that is why you are there. Believe in what you are saying. It will also make it easier to project enthusiasm and energy.

(d) **Control physical symptoms.** Breathe deeply and evenly. Control your gestures and body movements. Put down a piece of paper that is visibly shaking in your hand. Pause to collect your thoughts if necessary. Smile, and maintain eye contact with members of the audience. If you **act** as if you are calm, the calm will **follow**.

The presenter's appearance

7.5 The dress and mannerisms of the presenter are part of the delivery of his speech, and are often the first and most readily-judged aspects of the presentation as a whole. There are two major pitfalls.

(a) **You may lose credibility if your dress and general appearance are untidy or careless.** Dress and grooming are a **reflection** of individual personality, and it is important for the speaker to feel comfortable and at ease in whatever he is wearing. However, poor grooming can be distracting to the audience, and may convey a **negative impression** of the speaker's taste, attitude to the presentation and audience, and organisational culture. The important thing is to show that you care about your appearance and the impression it will make on others, no matter what your personal style.

(b) **Your non-verbal signals may convey unease or lack of confidence.** Again, exaggerated or repeated mannerisms may simply be distracting or irritating to the audience, but non-verbal cues are also **interpreted** to imply attitudes, as discussed below.

7.6 Any number of factors may contribute to a speaker **looking** confident and relaxed, or nervous, shifty and uncertain. **Cues** which indicate confidence – without arrogance – may be as follows.

(a) An upright – but not stiff – **posture**: slouching gives an impression of shyness or carelessness.

(b) **Movement** that is purposeful and dynamic, used sparingly: not constant or aimless pacing, which looks nervous.

(c) **Gestures** that are relevant, purposeful and flowing: not indecisive, aggressive, incomplete or compulsive. Use gestures **deliberately** to reinforce your message, and if possible keep your hands up so that gestures do not distract the audience from watching your face. Watch out for habitual, irrelevant gestures you may tend to make such as rubbing your nose or taking off your glasses.

(d) **Eye-contact** with the audience. This is vital, not just to maintain credibility, giving an impression of honesty and sincerity, but to maintain the involvement of the audience. Eye-contact should be **established immediately**, when you stand up to speak or acknowledge any introduction you may have been given. It should be **re-established** immediately after periods when you have had to look away, to consult notes or use visual aids.

Staring at a single individual or group can make them uncomfortable, but a fixed gaze on 'space', or a wandering gaze avoiding the audience's eyes, makes you look shifty, dishonest or as if you are trying to make up your message as you go along. The most effective technique is to meet the eyes of **each person** in the audience, one by one.

Your gaze is thus wandering – but **purposefully** – across the whole audience, **involving** them all, without intimidating anybody: establish eye-contact long enough for it to be registered, to accompany a point you are making, and then move on. Eye-contact is also a way of inviting and seeking feedback: an important guide to how the audience is receiving and responding to your message.

Delivery techniques

7.7 In chapter 11 we considered oral communication and the ability to speak to other people in general terms. You should refer back to that chapter to refresh your memory on the main points.

7.8 In addition, there are some tips which can help you in the specific context of giving presentations, so do not overlook these:

(a) Relate to the audience: look at people, ask if they can hear you at the back

(b) Speak clearly and avoid the temptation to speak too quickly. Remember that although you may feel that you know your script backwards, the audience may be grappling with the concepts you are introducing for the first time. You must give them time to absorb what you are saying.

(c) Don't turn your back on the audience unless to write on a flipchart. If that is necessary, stop talking while you are doing it, as your voice will become muffled and indistinct

(d) Don't walk through or stand in the beam of an overhead projector while it is switched on: your shadow will be projected onto the screen, and it is not usually flattering

(e) Don't read your notes out loud: if you think that you are likely to do that, make small cards instead with the key points, and use them as an aide memoire

(f) Try to respond to your audience: if their expressions are becoming glazed, try to vary the speed of your delivery and the intonation, or ask a question in general terms to stimulate interest

8 TAKING QUESTIONS

8.1 The Guidelines make specific reference to the fact that you should be prepared to answer questions and provide explanations when requested. If you do not want to be interrupted during the presentation (which does create a risk that you will be put off your flow) you should say at the beginning that you will be happy to take questions at the end.

8.2 **Inviting or accepting questions** can be a helpful – if slightly nerve-wracking – part of a presentation.

(a) In informative presentations, questions offer an opportunity to **clarify** any misunderstandings, **or gaps** that the audience may have perceived.

(b) In persuasive presentations, questions offer an opportunity to **address and overcome** specific doubts or resistance that the audience may have, which the speaker may not have been able to anticipate.

Tackling questions

8.3 The manner in which you **field questions** may be crucial to your credibility. Everyone knows you have prepared your **presentation** carefully: ignorance, bluster or hesitation in the face of a question may cast doubt on your expertise, or sincerity, or both. Moreover, this is usually the last stage of the presentation, and so leaves a **lasting impression**.

The only way to tackle questions effectively is to **anticipate** them. Put yourself in your audience's shoes, or, more specifically, in the shoes of an ignorant member of the audience and a hostile member of the audience and a member of the audience with a particular axe to grind: what questions might **they** ask and why? When questions arise, listen to them carefully, assess the questioner's manner, and draw the questioner out if necessary, in order to ascertain exactly **what** is being asked, and **why**. People might ask questions:

(a) To **seek additional information** of particular interest to them, or to the group – if you have left it out of your talk

(b) To **seek clarification** of a point that is not clear

(c) To **add information** of their own, which may be relevant, helpful and accurate – or not

(d) To **lead the discussion** into another area (or away from an uncomfortable one)

(e) To **display** their own knowledge or cleverness

(f) To **undermine** the speaker's authority or argument, to 'catch him out'

If you have anticipated questions of the first two kinds (a) and (b) in the planning of your talk, they should not arise: incorporate the answers in your outline.

How to answer

8.4 The important points about answering questions are as follows.

(a) You may seek **feedback** throughout your talk, as to whether your message is getting across clearly – and it is common to **invite the audience** to let you know if anything is unclear – but by and large, you should encourage questions only at the **end** of your presentation. That way, disruptive, rambling, hostile and attention-seeking questions will not be allowed to **disrupt** your message to the audience as a whole.

(b) You should **add or clarify information** if required to achieve your purpose. An honest query deserves a co-operative answer.

(c) You need to maintain your **credibility and authority** as the speaker. **Strong tactics** may be required for you to stay in control, without in any way ridiculing or 'putting down' the questioner.

    (i) If a question is based on a false premise or incorrect information, **correct it**. An answer may, or may not, then be required.

    (ii) If a question is **rambling: interrupt,** clarify what the question, or main question (if it is a multiple query) is, and answer that. If it is completely irrelevant, say politely that it is outside the scope of the presentation: you may or may not offer to deal with it informally afterwards.

    (iii) If a question is **hostile** or argumentative, you may wish to show understanding of how the questioner has reached his conclusion, or why he feels as he does. However, you then need to reinforce, repeat or **explain your own view**.

    (iv) If a question tries to **pin you down** or 'corner' you on an area in which you do not wish to be specific, be **straightforward** about it.

    (v) If a question **exposes an area** in which you do not know the answer, **admit** your limitations with honesty and dignity, and invite help from members of the audience, if appropriate.

(vi) Try and answer **all questions** with points **already made** in your presentation, or related to them. This reinforces the impression that your speech was in fact **complete and correct**.

(d) **Repeat** any question that you think might not have been audible to everyone in the room.

(e) **Clarify** any question that you think is lengthy, complex, ambiguous or uses jargon not shared by the audience as a whole.

(f) Answer **briefly,** keeping strictly to the point of the question (while relating it, if possible, to what you have already said). If your answer needs to be lengthy, structure it as you would a **small talk**: introduce what you are going to say, say it, then confirm what you have said!

(g) Keep an eye on the overall **time-limit** for your talk or for the question-and-answer session. **Move on** if a questioner is taking up too much time, and call a halt, courteously, when required.

'I'll take one more question ... ' or 'I'm afraid that's all we have time for' is standard practice which offends few listeners. Indeed, leaving an audience wishing there was time for more is a sign of their interest and your success: unanswered questions tend to be taken away with the listener, which may increase the impact of your message.

Exercise 2

When you have time, watch a television programme such as the BBC's Question Time or an equivalent political discussion programme in your own country. See how questions are fielded and dealt with. Politicians are very skilled in dealing with questions, but also look at how the host deals with both audience and guests. The whole show is based on questions. This is a very useful exercise for you.

Exercise 3

Here are two examples of questions and how they can be handled. Which response do you think is the more effective?

Example 1

Questioner:	So do you think that there is no future for any of the dotcom start-ups?
Presenter:	(*Laughing*) No, no, of course I don't think that's the case: that's a ridiculous suggestion. Of course some of them will survive, but......
Questioner:	But what criteria would you apply for a successful start-up?
Presenter:	Well the problem with all start-ups is that there is a long-term cash outflow, so of course the banks wonder when they'll start to see any return on their investment.

Example 2

Questioner:	So do you think that there is no future for any of the dotcom start-ups?
Presenter:	Of course that's the question which worries a lot of people at the moment, and it receives a lot of coverage in the press. I don't think that there is no future at all: rather I think that only the better ones will survive.
Questioner:	But what criteria would you apply for a successful start-up?
Presenter:	I think there are several criteria: A clear feasible cashflow forecast Realistic assumptions in the production of budgets Definite clearcut financing agreements Motivated management

Answer

In Example 1, the presenter makes the unforgivable mistake of patronising and ridiculing the questioner. The likely effect of this is to make the rest of the audience hostile and to detract from the overall impression given by the presentation. The presenter also fails to answer the question, and instead turns it back to his particular hobbyhorse.

In Example 2, the presenter manages to appear to compliment the questioner on the question, which will go down well with the audience, and also clearly answers the second question by producing a list of points.

---

9 FEEDBACK

9.1 Many people find it very difficult to respond to feedback and make the best use of it, because it is usually viewed as a form of criticism. This is especially so when the feedback relates to a presentation as opposed to written work, as:

(a) It is more immediate, coming as it does straight after the presentation

(b) It seems more personal, because you will have put a great deal of highly personal effort into your presentation, which will have involved you standing alone in front of an audience

Feedback from the mentor

9.2 Remember that it is part of the role of the mentor to question you on the work done, and it is a critical part of his role to report to Oxford Brookes University that you have delivered a presentation and answered questions on it.

9.3 You should try to accept his comments in that very positive light, and take the view that they are helping you to achieve your ultimate goal, which is your degree in Applied Accounting.

9.4 If your mentor gives you constructive criticism, he or she is not saying that you are wrong in what you have said, or that your ideas are no good. The criticism is designed to help you to improve your presentational skills and it will be invaluable when drafting your Key Skills Statement, as you have to state what went well and what could have been improved.

9.5 If your mentor provides you with detailed suggestions as to how to do some aspect differently in the future, it will precisely fulfil one of the precise purposes of the Key Skills Statement. Your mentor will tell you whether your ideas have not come across properly, whether the sequence is not easy to follow or where the train of logical thought breaks down. It may be that you cannot see the wood for the trees, and have not realised that your arguments do not hang together. Without the mentor, you would not necessarily realise this, and you would not then achieve your full potential in the Research and Analysis Project.

Feedback from your peer group

9.6 The emphasis within the feedback from your peer group is likely to be different from that received from your mentor. Your peer group does not have a specific responsibility to report that you have completed the stages of the Research and Analysis Project. To put it at its most basic, the members of it are listening to your presentation because you will then be listening to theirs.

9.7 Whereas your mentor will be familiar with your thought processes and the content of your Report from the two previous meetings, your peer group will have had no prior knowledge of it. This will mean that their feedback will probably concentrate on the mechanics of your presentation (audibility, confidence, effective use of visual aids) rather than the technical content.

9.8 This can be as useful as the more measured feedback from your mentor. When writing up your Key Skills Statement, you must consider all aspects of the presentation and scope for improvement. Members of the peer group are likely to reflect upon the quality of your presentation in the light of their own, so that they come up with more practical points.

When receiving peer group feedback, bear in mind that they are learning from the process too, as you will learn from watching their presentation and providing feedback on it to them.

Chapter roundup

- You are required to prepare and deliver a fifteen minute presentation as part of your Research and Analysis Project.

- The key to a successful presentation is planning, of both the content and also the physical logistics of delivering the presentation.

- Various communication aids are available, such as slides, presentation software, flipcharts and handouts.

- The way in which you deliver your presentation can be almost as important as what you actually say.

- Taking questions and responding to feedback are an important part of the procedure.

Chapter 13

WRITING THE KEY SKILLS STATEMENT

Chapter topic list

1   The contents of the Key Skills Statement

2   Preparing for meetings

3   Questioning

4   Listening

5   Assessment of the presentation

6   Self-assessment of interaction

7   Frequently asked questions and checklist

Introduction

In chapter 10, we discussed the purpose and significance of the Key Skills Statement in outline, and also covered its format and content. The chapter also contained some general information on the communication process and oral communication in particular. We then discussed listening and questioning in some detail in chapters 11 and 12.

This chapter will cover the writing of the Key Skills Statement itself. Remember that it is quite a short document consisting of five specific sections of approximately 300 words each, and you will need to be very disciplined over your writing style.

1   THE CONTENTS OF THE KEY SKILLS STATEMENT

1.1   The Guidelines are extremely precise in setting out the required contents of the Key Skills Statement. This is the required framework.

Preparing for meetings

Describe how you prepared for the three meetings. Assess the importance of planning and organising in relation to the effectiveness of your meetings, and meetings in general.

Questioning

Consider and explain the role of questioning in ensuring productive discussions with your mentor, in particular the use of appropriate questioning techniques.

Listening

Explain the importance of listening in ensuring that communication with your mentor was effective. Consider active listening techniques, sources of error and distortion in communication.

> **The presentation**
>
> Assess the presentation identifying what went well and what could have been improved. You should attach two sides of A4 to your key skills statement showing an outline of your presentation.
>
> **Self-assessment of interaction**
>
> Using an appropriate model of communication, analyse and evaluate interaction with your mentor and if applicable with your peer discussion group, in relation to the key elements of successful communication.
>
> Reflect on IT skills used.

1.2 In each of these areas, you are required to illustrate your self-analysis with examples taken from your discussions with your mentor, and by referring to recommended reading on communication. The recommended reading consists of the books set out in the reading list in Appendix 2 of the Research and Analysis Project Guidelines, including this book.

1.3 You are also required in each case, if it is appropriate, to consider what you would do differently in the future in similar circumstances.

1.4 The mark sheet that must be submitted with your Research and Analysis Project lists these five headings and you will be given a straightforward pass or fail for each of them. It is essential therefore that you address them all in equal depth.

The main difficulty

1.5 Arguably the most difficult aspect of writing the Key Skills Statement will be covering all of the requirements in **sufficient depth but with the necessary brevity**. You are only permitted 1,500 words in total.

(a) The best way to overcome this difficulty is to ensure that you **allow yourself enough time to prepare the statement.** If you rush, you will find it very difficult to produce a statement which fulfils the requirements of the Guidelines, and that could easily cause you to fail the Research and Analysis Project as a whole, regardless of the merits of your Report.

(b) Use the time to **plan the Key Skills Statement in as much detail as possible.** Decide precisely what you are going to say under each of the headings and what examples you are going to use from your discussions and your presentation. If you have a choice of examples of equal relevance, choose the one which you will be able to describe in fewer words, so that you have some flexibility in your word count.

(c) You will probably need to **prepare at least three drafts of the Statement** to hone it down to its most concise and cogent form. Make sure that you allow yourself enough time to do this, and do not be frustrated at the seemingly slow progress in doing this. Each draft you prepare will improve the Statement immeasurably and will make you more familiar with its contents, making the next draft much easier to write.

Assessment criteria

1.6 In conjunction with indicating a pass or fail for each of the required headings, the marker will also consider whether you have fulfilled the required criteria in your key skills statement.

The Guidelines state that:

> 'A pass will be demonstrated by an analysis of your ability to communicate and work with others by providing:
>
> - Reflection on the nature and structure of the meetings with your mentor through the identification of relevant and influencing factors (Criterion 1)
>
> - Reflection on the meetings with your mentor examining the nature of the interactions which took place and showing an understanding of the key elements of successful face to face communication, in particular questioning and listening techniques (Criterion 2)
>
> - A clear outline for the presentation made at Meeting 3 including identification of what went well and what could have been improved (Criterion 3)
>
> - A self-assessment, drawing on evidence from meetings with your mentor, of your abilities to actively listen, ask appropriate questions, respond to others and achieve satisfactory outcomes. (Criterion 4)

1.7 These criteria tie in closely with the headings required in the statement.

Criterion 2 will be addressed under the Questioning and Listening headings of the statement.

Criterion 3 will be addressed under the Presentation heading.

Criterion 4 will be addressed under the Self-assessment of interaction heading.

The only criterion which does not have an obvious match in terms of a heading in the statement is **Criterion 1**. This, however, will be addressed throughout the Key Skills Statement in rather more general terms.

In the next sections of this chapter, we shall discuss each of the headings in turn.

2 PREPARING FOR MEETINGS

2.1 The requirements under this heading are threefold. You must discuss

- **How** you prepared for the three meetings

- The importance of planning and organising in relation to the effectiveness of **your** meetings, and

- The importance of planning and organising in relation to meetings **in general**

The order in which you cover these is up to you, and you may want to deal with them in the precise order set out in the Guidelines. However, it may seem more logical to start with some general comments about the importance of planning and then move on to apply those observations to your own experiences in particular.

Planning generally

2.2 The importance of planning has already been stressed in this book in the context of planning your research and overall plan of attack, and also in the context of writing your report. The key factors to remember and to highlight in your Key Skills Statement are that:

(a) Planning is a **means to an end**

(b) It enables tasks to be achieved with the maximum **efficiency and effectiveness**

(c) It establishes **what needs to be done**

(d) It works out **how to do it**

(e) It highlights **potential problems** before they become significant and means that they can be more easily avoided

2.3 Planning for meetings has the same purposes. It will encompass factors such as

(a) **Practicalities**: date, time, location

(b) **Attendance**: whose attendance is vital, whose would be beneficial, whether the participants are drawn from internal or external sources or both

(c) An **agenda,** which lists the topics for discussion, possibly also incorporating briefing notes for participants

(d) **Notifying** those expected to attend, and providing them with all necessary **information** in advance

Planning techniques

2.4 Planning is the stage in a project when you should be totally immersed in the subject matter and the desired outcome of the project. It can be a fairly intense experience, and because of this, different people favour different techniques.

Here are some suggestions.

(a) **Planning charts**, produced on a day by day or week by week basis (ie time charts)

(b) **Mind maps,** setting down all relevant thoughts as they come into your head, so that they can then be sorted into order

(c) **Flowcharts** of a proposed sequence of events

(d) **Networks** and critical path analysis

Whichever of these is chosen, it will have the same outcome in that it will enable the planner to view the project both as a whole and its component parts, and start to **put the whole thing into perspective**.

2.5 Successful planning for a meeting means that the overall structure of the meeting will be established in advance, so that the meeting, when it happens, achieves its purpose in as efficient a way as possible.

Planning your meetings

2.6 The Guidelines require you to describe how you prepared for **your** meetings in particular. Section 2.3 sets out the purpose of the three meetings, and your description of your planning should focus on that.

2.7 **Planning for the first meeting**

(a) Likely topic areas
(b) Where the information will come from
(c) Research methods
(d) Possible timing of work
(e) Proposed submission date of project

2.8 **Planning for the second meeting**

(a) Production of the progress report

(b) Decide whether you will supply the report to your mentor in advance or provide it to be read at the meeting

(c) Word processing of the progress report (if you are not doing it yourself)

(d) Are you coming to a conclusion of some sort?

(e) Questions to ask or problems to raise with your mentor

(f) Any need to re-schedule final production of the Project

2.9 Planning for the third meeting

This is the meeting that requires the most detailed planning as it will include your presentation, which will require careful preparation. You will also need to plan for:

(a) Taking questions
(b) Reviewing the success of your presentation
(c) Timing the meeting to enable your peer group to be present (where appropriate)

The importance of planning in relation to the effectiveness of *your* meetings

2.10 In the light of what you have said about planning generally and your description of the planning processes you adopted for your three mentor meetings, conclude whether your own planning was adequate and effective, and in what ways it could have been improved.

In order to do this, you will need to carry out a critical evaluation of the effectiveness of your meetings. This can be done by reference to the purposes of the meetings set out in section 2.3 of the Guidelines. The key question to ask is whether the meetings achieved their expected objectives. If they did not, the planning, or lack of it, may have been a contributory factor.

Writing the section on planning

2.11 Each section of the Key Skills Statement should be about 300 words. It is important to keep to this if you are not to exceed the overall total of 1,500 words, although you may have a little flexibility in the word count between sections.

In this section, you need to draw together the points you have considered under the three headings above.

2.12 Here is an example.

Example

Preparing For Meetings

Planning is essential (Cameron, 1999). It has four complementary elements:

- Establishing what needs to be done
- Working out how to do it
- Determining how much you can get done
- Predicting and interpreting the outcome

(Luck, 1999)

In the context of meetings, effective planning enables the business of the meeting to be conducted efficiently, so that the objectives of the meeting are fulfilled.

I planned for the three meetings with Mr. James Smith, my mentor, by doing the following:

Meeting 1

Mr. Smith and I agreed that the meeting should be at his office on 1st March 2005 at 10.00 am.

I reviewed the list of possible project topics and narrowed it down to a shortlist of three which interested me.

I identified that in the case of each of them I would be able to access background information from the college library and the Internet, but would need to design and circulate a questionnaire on the procedures adopted by the relevant organisations.

Meeting 2

Mr. Smith and I agreed that the meeting should be at his office on 1st June 2005 at 10.00 am.

Ten days before the date of the meeting, I started to write my interim report, but I then realised that I had not received back all the questionnaires I had sent out, so my information was incomplete.

Meeting 3

The date for the meeting was fixed by Mr. Smith as 14th July 2005, as several students would be involved. I prepared a detailed timetable of what I needed to do before then.

I wrote an outline of my presentation by 1st July.

I prepared OHP slides and handouts by 8th July.

I rehearsed my presentation each day from 11th to 13th July, to check the timing.

Overall I think that my planning was effective. At the end of Meeting 1 I had decided on the topic and work required. I should have planned my time more carefully before Meeting 2, and chased up outstanding questionnaires, as I could not be sufficiently precise about my initial conclusions. In future I would certainly ensure that I had all relevant information before the meeting. The timetable for the presentation work paid dividends as I was confident about the task well in advance.

This first draft of the first section of the statement contains 379 words which is obviously far too many.

Exercise 1

Read through it again and see how many words you can knock out or rearrange so that the word count becomes more acceptable.

Answer

Planning is essential (Cameron, 1999) and it includes these elements:

- Establishing necessary actions
- Working out actions
- Assessing feasibility
- Predicting and interpreting the outcome

(Luck, 1999)

Effective planning of meetings enables:

- Efficient conduct of the meeting
- Fulfilment of objectives

I planned for the three meetings with Mr. James Smith, my mentor, like this:

Meeting 1

We agreed that the meeting should be at his office on 1st March 2005 at 10.00 am.

Before then I:

- Reviewed the list of topics supplied

- Wrote a shortlist of three which interested me

- Identified that in each case background information was available from the college library and the Internet, but that I would need to design and circulate a questionnaire on the procedures adopted by the relevant organisations.

Meeting 2

We agreed that the meeting should be at his office on 1st June 2005 at 10.00 am.

On 22nd May I began my interim report, but I then realised that I had not received back all the questionnaires, so my information was incomplete.

Meeting 3

The date for the meeting was fixed by Mr. Smith as 14th July 2005, as several students would be involved. My preparation timetable was:

- Outline presentation   1st July
- OHP slides, handouts   8th July
- Rehearsals of timing and content   11th to 13th July

Overall I think that my planning was effective.

At the end of Meeting 1 I had decided on the topic and work required.

More careful planning and review of results was needed before Meeting 2, as my initial conclusions were unsubstantiated. In future, I would ensure that I did this.

The presentation timetable paid dividends: I felt confident and fully-prepared.

2.13 After redrafting, the word count has now been reduced to 285. This would give you scope for rephrasing some of the section if you feel that you have cut it too much, and allows you a little flexibility to go over 300 words if necessary in another section.

3 QUESTIONING

3.1 The requirement for this section is again both general and specific. In general terms, you have to **consider and explain the role of questioning in ensuring productive discussions with your mentor** (with specific mention of questioning techniques) and you must also provide illustrations from your **own** experience and examples from the **recommended reading.** Remember that this book appears on the recommended reading list, so you could use examples from here.

3.2 Again the order in which you tackle this section is entirely up to you, but it may be logical to cover it like this:

(a) The role and value of questioning generally

(b) Examples of questioning techniques

(c) Illustrations of questions asked and their value in your own discussions with your mentor.

The role and value of questioning generally

3.3 The significance of questioning as a communication tool has been discussed in some detail in chapters 11 and 12. It is important that you appreciate that questioning is important as it gives rise to feedback, which, when used constructively, is a fundamental feature of self-evaluation.

In short, questions are designed to:

(a) Generate answers
(b) Stimulate discussion
(c) Iron out problems
(d) Encourage progress

3.4 During the course of your meetings, you will encounter different types of question.

(a) Questions from the mentor on your proposal and rate of progress
(b) Questions you ask your mentor, mainly for opinions or advice
(c) Questions from your mentor asking you to assess or evaluate yourself
(d) Questions from your peer group on aspects of your presentation

Examples of questioning techniques

3.5 The two main types of questioning are **open** and **closed**.

(a) Remember that **open questions** are open-ended and aim to encourage the recipient of the question to talk, while closed questions only offer a choice of responses.

(b) **Closed questions** can be quite useful in terms of pinning down specific pieces of information (for example 'Do you think that you will submit your Project on time?').

3.6 In your discussions with your mentor, you will probably have seen many examples of open questioning. You have only to look at the list of example questions for student/mentor meetings set out in Appendix 3 of the Guidelines to see that the majority of questions are open.

3.7 Here are some examples.

> 'What is your Report going to be about?'
>
> 'Why are you doing it in this particular way?'
>
> 'What difficulties have you had?'
>
> 'What went well in your presentation and what went badly?'

3.8 The above are questions which you are likely to be asked by the mentor. They will hopefully **stimulate you to talk candidly about ideas and progress,** and they will not allow you to get away with a mere 'yes' or 'no' answer. They will generate a genuine discussion and allow ideas to flow, so that you really have to think about your answers. This will help in turn to clarify things in your own mind and put problems and issues into perspective.

3.9 However, closed questioning will be of value too. The Guidelines give some general examples:

> 'Are you on schedule/do you need to reschedule?'
>
> 'Does the Report meet its objectives?'

The value of these questions is that **they may make you face up to something unpalatable.** If you are behind schedule, but trying to pretend that you are not, you may only face that reality on being asked a blunt question requiring a yes or no answer.

3.10 You will also face questions during and/or after your presentation, from your mentor and, if applicable, from members of your peer group. These can fall into a number of categories:

(a) **Probing questions,** which aim to discover the deeper significance of an answer:

'So why were you interested in the motivation of employees and the impact of salaries in particular?'

These can provide a clearer focus to too short or too generalised answers. They can be helpful when an open question has not detailed a satisfactory answer.

284

(b) **Multiple questions,** where two or more questions are asked at once.

'Do you think that Xerxes plc is a good example of a company which observes all International Accounting Standards rigorously, or can you think of a better example?'

The value of this type of question is that it can encourage a person to talk at some length, but still within the parameters of the topic area, without straying too far from it.

However the drawback can be that the respondent chooses to answer one part of the question only and the questioner thinks that all aspects have been covered. They only discover that they have not after the event.

(c) **Leading questions,** which have the disadvantage of suggesting a certain reply.

'Surely you don't think that calculating working capital ratios would be relevant here?'

The drawback here is that it is only the totally confident or strong-willed person who might be brave enough to give a negative response.

3.11 In writing the section of the statement on questioning, you should outline possible questioning techniques, but restrict yourself to the techniques you experienced in the course of your own discussions, so that the examples you then provide follow on logically.

Your own illustrations

3.12 In this part of the section, you should include some examples of the value of questioning in the context of the production of your own Research and Analysis Project. Bear in mind also that this part should give you scope to fulfil the requirement of the Guidelines to consider what you would do differently in the future in similar circumstances.

Example

Lucy, a student, and Peter, her mentor, are conducting their first meeting. Here is an extract from their conversation.

Peter: So, Lucy, what thoughts have you had about a topic for your report?

Lucy: I was thinking about taking topic number 3 from the Oxford Brookes list, which is 'An examination of the impact of an aspect of existing or impending legislation on an organisation'.

Peter: What legislation would you choose, and what organisation?

Lucy: The effect of the Insolvency Act 1986 and the provisions under that for a company to enter a scheme of voluntary arrangement with its creditors. Because it can do that it can sometimes avoid formal insolvency procedures like liquidation.

Peter: That's a very interesting area, but potentially quite a sensitive one. Which organisation would you plan to discuss?

Lucy: Well my uncle's company has been having all sorts of problems recently. He's the managing director and they were hoping to go for a Stock Exchange listing next year, but they're concentrating on just staying afloat at the moment.

Peter: Have you discussed it with your uncle yet?

Lucy: No, but he knows I'm taking the ACCA qualification, and is always happy to discuss business issues with me.

Peter: What do you think his views will be about discussing the problems of his own company?

Lucy: Come to think of it, I suppose he might be a bit sensitive, especially with the public profile of the company at the moment. I know I can research the relevant sections of the Insolvency

Act and cases where creditors' voluntary arrangements have come to Court, but maybe he won't discuss the fine detail with me about his own company.....? Do you think he's likely to?

Peter: I can't really speak for him, but in his position I wouldn't, and there might be the issue of price-sensitive information too.

Lucy: I think you're right. I hadn't really thought it through properly. Perhaps I'd better go for my second choice topic.

Peter: That's a good idea. Tell me what it is.

Exercise 2

On the basis of the information about Lucy and Peter's conversation, write a suggested paragraph by Lucy on the value of questioning at her first meeting with Peter.

Answer

At my first mentor meeting, I outlined my proposal to consider the impact of various aspects of the Insolvency Act 1986 on my uncle's manufacturing company. By asking open questions which made me think carefully through my answer, Peter caused me to realise that this was potentially a very sensitive issue, and that I may find it difficult to obtain all the necessary information. Questioning was of great value in the process of deciding what topic to choose, and caused me to choose one far more suitable.

You should appreciate that this is just a suggested solution, and there are many different ways in which the main point could be communicated.

4   LISTENING

4.1   Under this heading you are required to:

(a) Explain the importance of listening in ensuring that communication with your mentor was effective

(b) Consider active listening techniques, sources of error and distortion in communication

(c) Illustrate your self-analysis with examples taken from your discussions

(d) Refer to appropriate literature on communication

(e) Consider what you might do differently in the future in similar circumstances.

The list as set out above would be a logical order in which to cover the information, with the exception that the references to appropriate literature on communication should probably be covered with active listening techniques, before you move on to the specific examples relevant to your own discussions.

The importance of listening for effective communication with your mentor

4.2   The skills needed for active listening were discussed in detail in chapter 11. It is important that you appreciate that **listening is a critical part of the communication process.** It is all about **decoding and receiving information.** It helps to

(a) Enable the sender of the message to **listen effectively** to the reply given by the receiver
(b) **Reduce the effect of 'noise'** as a barrier to communication
(c) **Resolve problems** by encouraging understanding from someone else's viewpoint

If the recipient of a message is not listening properly, the message will fail.

4.3   You can consider the importance of listening within your mentor relationship in the same way as you consider the importance of questioning. As we have seen, your mentor is likely

to be asking you open, thought-provoking questions, and you will be asking open questions in return, such as 'What do you think of this as a proposal for a topic?'

It is important that both you and your mentor listen, if the communication is to be a two-way process. You can appreciate the value of this if you re-read the example above involving Lucy and Peter and consider what might have been the outcome had Lucy refused or failed to listen to the points arising from Peter's questioning.

Active listening techniques

4.4 Many of the books on the recommended reading list contain material on the value of listening, but there is a very good section on active listening in Cameron (1999).

This provides a list of things which you should try to do if you are to acquire good listening skills, for example:

(a) Concentrate on the speaker
(b) Show your interest
(c) Avoid interruptions
(d) Allow silence

4.5 You could consider in this section whether any of the techniques were relevant in the context of your relationship with your mentor. Ask yourself whether you did concentrate on what your mentor was saying, or whether you avoided interrupting.

4.6 Sources of error and distortion in the communication process are considered in chapter 10 of this book. The main potential problem in communication is **noise**, which can be

(a) **Physical** (such as other people talking, external noises)

(b) **Technical** (such as a failure in the means of communication, even as basic as poor handwriting)

(c) **Social** (such as personality, culture or outlook differences between sender and recipient)

(d) **Psychological** (such as emotions like anger or fear, causing a stammer, for example)

You could consider in this section, for example, whether you suffered from undue nerves in giving your presentation, which therefore caused a barrier to communication between you and your audience.

Self analysis and scope for improvement

4.7 You must **critically evaluate the use of listening skills** in meetings with your mentor and in your presentation. These could be **your** listening skills, as used in

(a) Meetings with your mentor
(b) Your taking of questions after your presentation

Or they could be the **listening skills of others,** for example those of your audience at your presentation, as evidenced by the nature of the questions they asked you.

Exercise 3

You have completed your presentation on the use of management accounting to support decision-making in an organisation. During the presentation a number of things happened.

1   A fire engine went past with its siren sounding. You were very nervous during the presentation, and because of this decided to press on and not to stop.

2   At the end of the presentation, Alex asked you a question. She was sitting right next to the projector and was very softly spoken. As you talked to her, other members of the peer group began to talk amongst themselves.

3   Your next question was from Bernard. His question was very long and consisted of several parts and sub questions, and seemed to indicate that he might have missed the point of one of the main arguments of your presentation. However, you tried your best to answer what you believed to be his question.

How would you comment on these events in the listening section of your key skills statement?

Answer

You should be honest with yourself, and use situations like these as illustrations of the fact that you appreciate the importance of listening skills, and that you have realised how to improve in the future.

If you are citing these as practical examples, you might draft something like this.

1   My presentation was interrupted by a passing fire engine, but I decided not to stop speaking. On reflection, this was a mistake, as the members of the audience were unable to hear for a short time, and consequently lost the thread of my remarks. On a similar future occasion, I would pause to let the noise die down, and then continue.

2   While taking questions, I answered a question which was not heard clearly by the rest of the audience, and addressed my answer directly to the questioner, not to the audience as a whole, with the result that other members of the audience lost interest. On reflection, I would have repeated the question so that others would have felt that they were participating, and would have addressed my answer to the whole audience, not just one member.

3   While taking questions, one questioner asked an unduly long question, which indicated that he had not fully understood one of the themes of my presentation. I found that answering the question took a long time, and the interest of other members of the audience was lost. On reflection, I should have told him that I would deal with his question and discuss the issues separately with him at the end of the session.

5   ASSESSMENT OF THE PRESENTATION

5.1   Under this heading, you are required to assess your presentation, identifying what went well and what could have been improved. Additionally, you must attach two sides of A4 to your key skills statement, showing an outline of your presentation. This outline is additional to the suggested total of 300 words for this section of the key skills statement.

5.2   As with the other areas of the statement, you should illustrate your self-analysis with examples taken from your own experience and by reference to the recommended reading in the Oxford Brookes University reading list. You should consider what you would do differently in the future in similar circumstances.

Outline of the presentation

5.3   The reason for including this as a submission with your Key Skills Statement is to enable the assessor of your Research and Analysis Project to have the full picture as to what you said at the presentation, as well as your thoughts as to how it went.

It may be sensible to prepare this outline first, as this will focus your mind on your presentation and how it went, so that writing the section on problems encountered will flow more easily.

5.4 You should be able to use a slimmed-down version of the notes that you prepared prior to your presentation, as long as the final presentation itself did not deviate from those. Obviously you can also use the Report itself, but do not fall into the trap of becoming bogged down in too much detail and effectively trying to cram all of it into what is meant to be a summary of your presentation about it.

5.5 The two page outline should have five main sections (although this is not mandatory, and you could well have more) and should also refer to communication aids used in the presentation, such as slides and handouts. An example is shown here, but you should appreciate that it is not particularly specific or technical, and is intended as a guide only.

Example

Outline of Presentation
Delivered 1st March 2005
At Anytown College

Introduction

Title of Report:	The effects of globalisation on the brewing industry
Reasons for choice of title:	Previous work experience in the industry
	Interest in international issues
	Wide variety of sources of information
Project proposed:	That globalisation of the brewing industry has led to increased competition and a greater necessity for effective marketing techniques, but has opened up vast new markets to all brewers, especially the smaller niche brewers.

Slide 1: showing title, reasons and proposal

Research carried out

Review of available methods:	Literature, including industry journals, business journals and company press releases
	Internet material on the industry
	Direct contact with companies in the UK and overseas
	Review of relevant company accounts over a period of years for specific references to globalisation
Methods adopted:	Reading of journals for background information, including Brewers' Monthly, The Economist, The American Master Brewers' Digest
	Reference to numerous different websites, including those of all the brewers selected as part of the sample contacted directly
	Letters of enquiry sent to a sample of 20 UK brewers of differing sizes and to 30 brewers overseas
	Requests for interview with senior personnel in five UK brewing companies
	Review of published accounts for the period 1995 to 2000 for the sample of 50 brewers to search for reference in the notes to the impact of globalisation

Problems encountered

Response rate: 77% non-response rate from the sample of 50 UK and overseas brewers
60% refusal rate from the 5 UK brewers asked for interviews
Consideration of impact on validity of results and conclusions

Slide 2: chart of response rates

Results logged   Comments arising in responses to letters of enquiry
Issues identified in responses to letter of enquiry
Issues raised in discussions with the two brewers who allowed an interview

Slide 3:bar chart of frequency of issues raised generally

Slide 4: bar chart of issues raised by large multi-national brewers

Slide 5: bar chart of issues raised by small independent brewers

Commentary on whether issues and results were expected or unexpected
Commentary on the distinctions in feedback from the two different categories

Conclusions reached

Main conclusion: Globalisation is having far-reaching results in the industry, especially with regard to:
- Increased competition
- Wider availability of untapped markets
- Greater need for sophisticated marketing techniques and public awareness education

Greatest impact is for the small independent brewers
Greatest risk is for the small independent brewers

Slide 6: summarised list of conclusions

An outline such as this will enable the assessor at Oxford Brookes University to understand the content of your presentation while considering what you have said in the main section of the Key Skills Statement about how it actually went.

Assessment of the presentation

5.6 As we have already discussed in the context of preparing for the presentation, you may have found this element of the entire Research and Analysis Project the most daunting, and it could be the part of the Project where you feel there was the greatest scope for improvement on your part.

5.7 You must therefore try to be **honest** in your assessment of your presentation. Remember that one of the main purposes of the Research and Analysis Project is for you to assess and evaluate your communication skills with a view to learning what can be improved in the future.

5.8 However, **don't forget to accentuate the positive!** If you think that your presentation went extremely well and there was nothing much that could be improved on a future occasion, say so! You are still fulfilling the requirement for self assessment and evaluation.

5.9 You can consider your presentation from two angles

   (a) The **technical content,** ie the research and work you carried out

   (b) Your **presentation technique,** ie how you spoke and communicated with your audience

   The **technical content** will probably have gone quite well: after all you will have been immersed in the subject for some time and you should feel happy and confident handling it. The parts of this section dealing with the technical content are likely to be those which emphasise what went well, and where you can bring out the skills which you have displayed.

   It is more likely that you will feel that your **presentation skills** show room for improvement, and it is in this area that your self analysis and evaluation are likely to come up with ways in which you might present things differently in the future.

Referring to the recommended reading

5.10 Many of the recommended texts set out in Appendix 2 of the Guidelines (including this book) contain material on preparing for and delivering presentations, and you should seek to refer to at least one of them in this section of the Key Skills Statement. You will probably not be able to refer specifically to the recommended texts when discussing the merits of the technical content of your presentation.

5.11 The one element which appears consistently in all of the texts is the need to **plan** for a presentation as thoroughly as you possibly can. Thorough preparation enhances **confidence**, which in turn contributes to the overall impression conveyed by your presentation.

5.12 Cameron (1999) devotes some time to delivery technique. These are the main things which she thinks you should remember

   (a) Relate to your audience
   (b) Make it easy for people to hear
   (c) Try to be interesting
   (d) Beware of becoming bogged down in detail
   (e) Avoid giving handouts while you speak
   (f) Keep your notes brief
   (g) Watch your audience
   (h) Be honest
   (i) Manage your time

5.13 When you are considering how well your presentation went, you could do worse than consider these points and whether you observed them, quote Cameron in your Key Skills Statement, and identify in which of these areas you feel you could improve in the future.

5.14 Don't forget that the presentation also includes the question and answer session at the end, and you should consider your effectiveness in that. Guirdham (1995) includes a section on handling the question and answer session. In the light of what she says, think about how well you performed and identify what improvements could be made on future occasions.

Example

We include here a hypothetical example of this section of the Key Skills Statement.

Presentation

Title: Recent investment decisions by X Ltd. and the impact on them of different methods of risk and uncertainty analysis (Project Topic 14)

I delivered my presentation to my mentor and a group of five fellow students on 1st June 2005.

Overall impression

Overall, I think that my presentation went well. I had spent two weeks preparing for it and this level of preparation and attention to detail paid off, as I felt confident and at ease throughout. Adequate planning of a presentation is essential (Guirdham, 1995). I had also invested some time in preparing slides, and gave out handouts of these beforehand, so that the audience could refer to and annotate them throughout the presentation. They seemed to appreciate this, as it meant that the figures shown on the slides were then available throughout.

Strong points

I think that the following were particularly strong points arising:

- I maintained my audience's interest throughout (Cameron, 1999)
- I kept to the allocated time of exactly 15 minutes, including answering questions
- I handled questions well and was not thrown by any of them

Areas which could have been improved

There was only one significant area which I would have handled differently with the benefit of hindsight. I would have included less detailed and complex information on my slides, as I noticed that my audience wanted more time to study the figures shown than I could give them. However, this was alleviated to a certain extent by the fact that I had supplied handouts, and therefore the material could be referred to later.

Conclusion

I felt that the presentation was an extremely valid part of the Project as a whole. The fact that I would have to deliver a presentation was invaluable in focussing my mind on the central issues of my Project, as I knew that I would have to distil the information gathered to a presentable format.

5.15 That extract is 295 words long excluding the heading. Notice the fact that it is itself set out under the headings:

- Overall impression
- Strong points
- Areas for improvement
- Conclusion

By using headings like these, you are clearly seen to be addressing the requirements of the Guidelines.

6 SELF-ASSESSMENT OF INTERACTION

6.1 In this final section of the Key Skills Statement, you are required to use **an appropriate model of communication** to analyse and evaluate your interaction with your mentor, and if applicable with your peer discussion group, in relation to the key elements of successful communication. Again, you are required to refer to the appropriate recommended reading and illustrate your self-analysis with examples taken from your discussions.

6.2 This is the section of the Key Skills Statement which will contain the most theory, although you will of course be applying it in the context of your own experiences.

6.3 You should notice that the requirement has several components:

   (a) Use of a communication model

   (b) Identification of the key elements of successful communication

   (c) Reference to the recommended reading

   (d) Evaluation of your own communication with your mentor and peer group.

6.4 As with all of the previous sections of the Key Skills Statement, you are limited to about 300 words. Before you start this section, it is worth carrying out a word count so far, so you know how many words you have available. If you have written 310 words on each of the previous four sections, for example, you will only have 260 available for this section. If this is likely to present a problem and you think that it will be difficult to come in at under that figure, spend a little while pruning the foregoing sections, so that you have more scope here. Remember that it is vital that you do not exceed the total of 1,500 for the Key Skills Statement as a whole.

Use of a communication model

6.5 This diagram shows the classic *communication model*, as discussed in an earlier chapter.

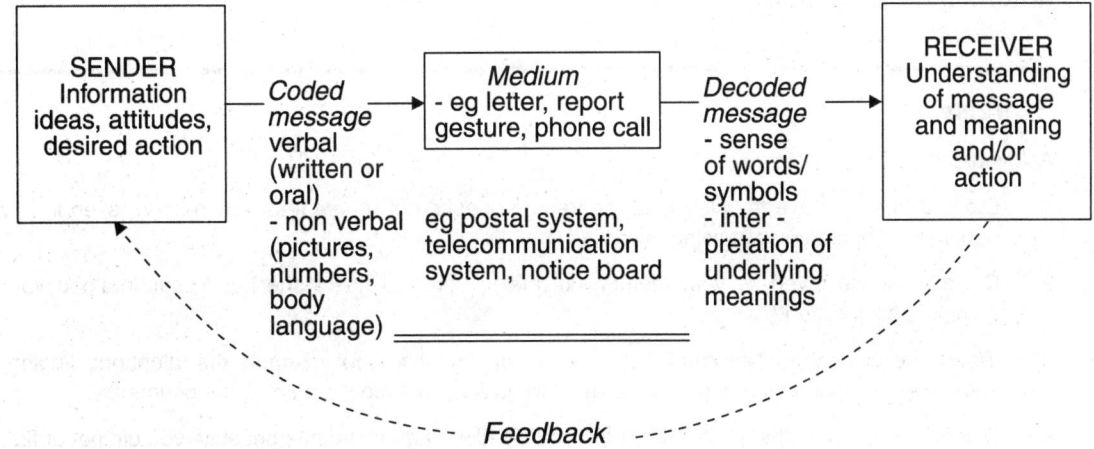

6.6 In the context of this diagram:

   (a) You the student are the **sender**

   (b) Your mentor is the **receiver** (although of course these two roles can be reversed)

   (c) The **coded message** is both verbal (what you actually say) and non-verbal (your body language)

   (d) The **medium** is the meeting (or presentation in Meeting 3)

   (e) The **decoded message** is your mentor's (or your) interpretation of the message

(f) **Feedback** will come from your mentor to you (and vice versa when the roles are reversed)

6.7 However, the process of communication is not always as simple as that. There are barriers to communication, as we discussed in chapter 10, and this diagram (BPP, 1998) shows how they can affect the process.

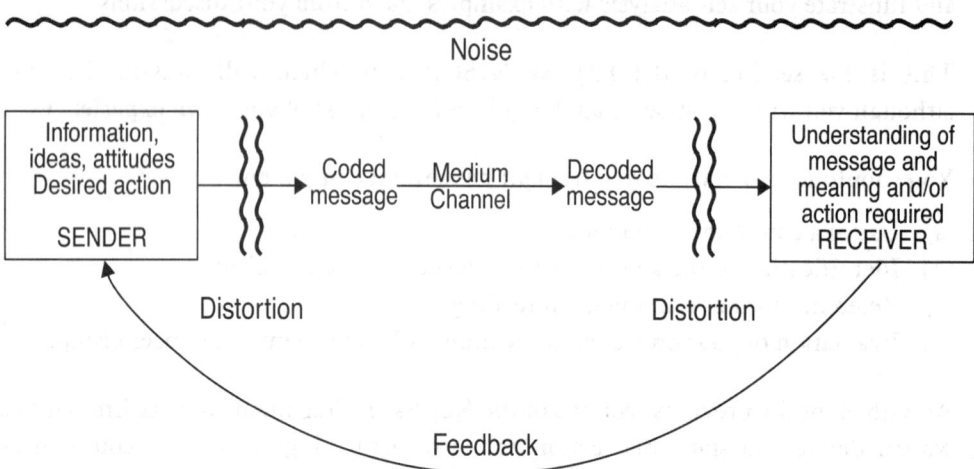

6.8 You should review your notes and records of your mentor meetings in the light of these two diagrams. You may prefer to use one of the diagrams of the communication model in one of the recommended texts, so that you can refer specifically to it, for example that in Guirdham (1995). You can of course use the models set out in this text, which are equally valid.

6.9 Do you think that your communication with your mentor is accurately summarised by these two models? Problems are most likely to have occurred in the decoding of the message and in the receiver's understanding of the message, although there is also the risk of distortion at the input stage.

Exercise 4

Ask yourself these questions:

1   Did your mentor have to ask you to rephrase a question or repeat it for any reason (even if only because an aircraft was passing overhead)?

2   Did a response given by your mentor indicate to you that he or she had misunderstood your comment or question?

3   Was there any form of interruption to any of your meetings, for example the telephone ringing, knocks at the door, external noise, the need to go and photocopy one of your documents?

4   Did you have to ask the mentor for further clarification of a point made because you did not at first understand it?

6.10 If the answer to any of those is 'yes' and you and your mentor could have done something to prevent it (for example done the photocopying beforehand, diverted phone calls etc) you should identify it as a factor which could have caused your communication to falter or fail. Where appropriate you can indicate what you would differently in the future.

6.11 If you honestly believe that none of these potential problems arose, you can be very positive in your self-evaluation, and show that your communication skills are good.

Key elements of successful communication

6.12 If communication is to be successful, the message must be:

(a) **Credible** (inspiring trust and/or belief)

(b) **Congenial** (appearing pleasant or compatible with the recipient)

(c) **Of the correct length** (not overloaded, but still with sufficient depth)

(d) **Relevant** (so that it is the 'correct' message)

(e) Sent via a **suitable medium**

(f) **Correctly interpreted**

(g) Capable of **acknowledging the needs and expectations** of the receiver.

Do you think that those descriptions could be used to describe the communication process in **your** meetings with **your** mentor?

6.13 If your mentor or members of your peer group question the comments you make, or seem to disagree with them or require further clarification, it is arguable that the interaction between you does not correspond with the key elements of successful communication. If this is the case, you need to acknowledge this in your self-evaluation and recognise it as a potential problem.

Example

All of these strands could be brought together into the one section required like this.

Self-assessment of interaction

Recognition of the importance of communication is an essential part of this research project. The basic communication model is well-documented by a number of authorities, for example Guirdham (1995). The critical elements are the sender and receiver, the message itself and the way in which it is encoded and decoded, and the medium. The main potential barriers are noise and distortion of the message.

In my meetings with my mentor, communication and the interaction between us was generally successful. At all three meetings, the communication fulfilled the essential criteria of being credible, congenial, relevant and of appropriate length. There were no instances of complete misunderstanding on either side, and the stated purposes of the meetings were met without difficulty.

Only one problem of communication with my mentor was encountered. At the second meeting we briefly found ourselves talking at cross-purposes when discussing rescheduling. I was referring to one submission date, while my mentor was referring to another. This became apparent after some minutes of discussion, but in future it would be advisable when discussing dates or times to spell them out to ensure that all parties have correct information.

When dealing with my peer group, some aspects of communication became a little more difficult. It became clear to me that holding discussions with a group (in this case 7) requires more careful handling than dealing with one individual. The message can become distorted by interruptions, as happened in my case when a question from one person side-tracked me away from the main theme of the presentation, and the rest of the group did not realise that this was the case. On future occasions, it would be more effective to deal with anything other than central questions as a separate issue at the end of the presentation.

(Word count: 296)

IT skills

6.14 Oxford Brookes has recently introduced a requirement that the self assessment of interaction section of the Key Skills Statement should include 'a reflection on IT skills used.' The reason for this was to ensure that students give thought to their use of IT skills, as it is a requirement for all universities that students can demonstrate competent use of IT, including, for example, the production of a spreadsheet. This requirement does not appear anywhere in the ACCA papers themselves (which provide the 'technical content' of the degree) so clear evidence must be demonstrated in the project. Students are therefore now required to add a short paragraph in the Key Skills Statement.

6.15 In this part of the self assessment, you should clearly state where you used a spreadsheet in the project, and where and how you found it helpful. You could explain for example how you used it to collate replies to a questionnaire, or even explain how you used IT to assist in the planning of your project, by means of drawing up a Gantt chart or similar. You can also comment if you did not find the use of a spreadsheet particular helpful. For example, if you are doing one of the more 'wordy' topics (such as Topic 3, on an aspect of legislation) you may be hard pressed to find a way to use a spreadsheet (although remember you must produce one) . Use your Key Skills Statement to explain that difficulty and to reflect if you would do anything differently in the future.

6.16 The only drawback to this addition to the Guidelines is that it makes it even more difficult to say what you need to in the appropriate number of words.

7 FREQUENTLY ASKED QUESTIONS AND CHECKLIST

7.1 In paragragh 3.4 of the Oxford Brookes Guidelines (on page 11 of this book) you will find a list of frequently asked questions, covering both the administration and content of the project. It would be worth looking at this now, before you submit your project, to make sure that you have not overlooked anything. The same applies to the checklist at paragraph 3.5, which aims to ensure that you haven't forgotten anything before you submit your project. It was drawn up as an attempt to reduce the number of students who were unnecessarily delayed or penalised because they forgot routine items!

Chapter roundup

- The Key Skills Statement must be structured following the Guidelines.

- You must describe how you prepared for meetings and the importance of planning.

- Questioning must be included, both as a general subject and also in the context of your own experience.

- The importance of listening must be stressed with examples from your own experience.

- You must supply a two sided outline of your presentation.

- You must conclude how well you performed as a communicator.

Appendices

REFERENCING

It is essential that you reference your sources throughout your Report, and also construct a bibliography.

Referencing techniques using the Harvard system are explained in Chapter 9 of this book, and are also covered in Appendix 1 of the Project Guidelines.

Note that Appendix 1 states that you must double check that all references in your text appear in the bibliography.

The bibliography must indicate all the sources you have used, including newspaper articles, company publications and Internet resources.

In order to give you some practice at these techniques, we set out in this appendix an exercise in referencing, which will help you to make the connection between writing the text and constructing the bibliography.

The extracts which follow are from a book about Walt Disney. [1]

The bibliography included at the end of the book is also reproduced.

From the pages of text, **attempt these activities.**

1   List the authors to whom Bryman refers.

2   Check these in the bibliography and make a list of the different type of resources that Bryman used.

3   Did he read all the material he quotes?

4   From the bibliography, identify:

(a) An 'Introduction'
(b) Articles written by unknown authors. Why are they unknown?

---

[1] Bryman, A. (1995) <u>Disney and his Worlds</u>, Routledge

Extract 1

However, one of the issues with which Weber was especially concerned was how charismatic leadership can be transformed into a relatively stable force. Weber recognized that charismatic leadership was inherently transitory and that it needed to be placed on a stable footing for it to persist beyond the specific circumstances that give rise to the charismatic leader's ascendancy or beyond the leader's lifetime. Weber employed the term 'routinization of charisma' to describe the process by which charismatic leadership becomes an enduring force, arguing that a failure to routinize a leader's charisma will almost inevitably result in the dissipation of that charisma. In fact, the issue of the routinization of charisma occupied Weber's attentions more than the nature and genesis of charismatic leadership as such because he recognized that without routinization charisma is bound to be ephemeral. There are two main aspects to the routinization of charisma in Weber's writings (Bryman, 1992, 1993). One is that charismatic leaders have to create a structure which incorporates and enshrines their charisma. This will establish continuity for the visions of charismatic leaders and provide a sense of security for their followers. Thus, the *development of structure* is one aspect of the process whereby permanence can be given to charismatic leadership. Second, there is the issue of the *succession* to the charismatic leader. In other words, what will happen when the charismatic leader dies or leaves the organization or movement? Weber delineated a number of different ways whereby succession might take place: the charismatic leader designates a successor; charisma becomes associated with a bloodline; the successor is 'revealed'; or charisma becomes associated with an 'office' or position. Weber recognized that charisma is changed by the process of routinization, since it becomes something that can be transferred and as such no longer attaches to a special person by dint of his or her extraordinary qualities.

Weber's notion of charismatic leadership was developed out of the religious context where charisma means 'gift of grace'. He applied it to a variety of religious leaders and then broadened it further to encompass political figures as well. In recent years, a number of writers have sought to explore the notion within business organizations (for example, Bass, 1985; Biggart, 1989; Bryman, 1992, 1993; Conger, 1989, 1993; Gaines, 1993). It was suggested in Chapter 1 that Walt Disney fits fairly well the image of a charismatic leader in the business sphere, but how successfully was his charisma routinized? Of course, in the first of the two senses of the idea of routinization, Walt did routinize his charisma in that he created an organization and a culture that embodied his visions. In fact, it is hard to envision a charismatic leader in the business context for whom at least the creation of an organization does not apply. As to the second aspect of routinization, it is clear that Walt did not specifically nominate a successor. When founders of organizations, such as Steve Jobs of Apple Computer, leave (or die) there is a profound sense of loss among those left behind (Rose, 1989), and it is apparent that Walt's passing engendered a similar sense of despair. While Roy was an obvious successor, it has to be remembered that he was over eight years older than his brother and that he had been considering retirement at the time of Walt's death. He was able to continue as part of the Disney troika and it seems that, for the five years of their reign, this triumvirate successfully routinized Walt's charisma, in large part due to the continued presence of a Disney in the leadership. The troika also had the advantage of a stream of activities that Walt had set in motion so that they were to a significant extent executing his visions.

Roy's death in 1971 ushered in a period in which there was no longer a Disney at the helm. It is also clear that neither Tatum nor Walker enjoyed charisma of office, in that they were not able to bathe in the glow of positions which were viewed as emblematic of Walt's charisma. To make matters worse, as Potts and Behr (1987), have observed, Walt's successors were trapped by a 'strong culture'. In the early 1980s, a number of management writers pointed to the advantages to organizations of having a strong culture and the importance of having leaders who foster such a culture (for example, Deal and Kennedy, 1982; Peters and Waterman, 1982), although later evidence suggests the need for a much more cautious assessment of the advantages of strong culture s (for example, Kotter and Heskett, 1992). In the case of Disney, it is easy to see why greater caution might be necessary. The company had developed a strong culture which was an extension of Walt's vision for the company – a preoccupation with quality, perfectionism, and a commitment to providing family entertainment. To this was harnessed a belief in customer satisfaction which would be particularly relevant to the operation of the theme parks, while the Disney University became the vehicle

Extract 2

opened, the visitor was able to purchase a block of tickets for rides and attractions, which had been graded according to their popularity. Each block would have a certain number of tickets for each grade of ride. Even this approach was dropped when in 1982 the passes which are still used today were introduced and allowed unlimited access to the rides in any park. At Disney World, visitors typically purchase multi-park tickets which allow access to all the rides in all the parks (and the minor parks depending on the type of pass) over a set number of days. Findlay (1992) suggests that the continuous exchange of money in the early Disneyland years gave the impression of a visit being expensive. It may be that one of the concerns was that this 'psychologically bad situation', as one of the Disney Imagineers called it (Bright, 1987: 109), inhibited people's preparedness to spend money on merchandise. While the significance of the consumption of merchandise and food at the parks has grown greatly since 1955, it is likely that Walt and his associates were profoundly aware of its profitable nature, particularly in the light of its importance in the studio's early years (see Chapter 1).

A second register of consumerism at the Disney theme parks revolves around an observation that has been made in a number of guises previously, namely, that some of the corporate-sponsored attractions in the parks relate to the goods and services that they sell. In presenting to us pictures of past and future revolving around electrical goods (Carousel of Progress) and cars (World of Motion), the good life is construed in terms of our identities as consumers – we are what we buy. The new Innoventions buildings at Disney World can be viewed more appropriately as showcases for the electronics, information technology and computer products of companies such as IBM, Sega and AT&T. Kuenz (1993) suggests that a major reason for the frequent allusion to the family in the parks is that it is the chief locus of consumption. Stimulating this image acts as a prompt to remind the visitor of his/her identity as consumer of both the corporation's products and the Disney merchandise itself, though this is not to suggest that visitors are unreflective automata who rush to buy character dolls and tee-shirts as soon as they can, but that the image is a convenient, self-serving one.

The third context of consumerism relates to consumption at the parks themselves. Some commentators have written as though the parks are simply shopping milieux. Yoshimoto (1994) suggests that the point of providing guests with narratives to mould their experiences of the parks is to naturalize consumption, so that people consume without being aware of what they are doing. By making consumption part of the experience itself, its nature as consumption is not fully revealed. In Yoshimoto's view, the 'ingenuity of Disney magic lies in its attempt to integrate shopping as part of the attractions without destroying the autonomy of the latter' (1994: 187). It is not surprising, therefore, that more and more shopping malls are adopting a Disney approach to retailing, so that shopping takes place in themed environments. Increasingly, it is difficult to distinguish large malls with themed environments from theme parks. The most frequently cited illustration of this trend is the West Edmonton Mall in Alberta, Canada; to all intents and purposes it is a shopping mall which increasingly resembles a theme park (Crawford, 1992; Shields, 1989). In fact, West Edmonton Mall's publicity tries to give the impression that it provides a great deal more than a Disney theme park:

> Imagine visiting Disneyland, Malibu Beach, Bourbon Street, the San Diego Zoo, Rodeo Drive in Beverly Hills and Australia's Great Barrier Reef . . . in one weekend – and under one roof. . . . Billed as the world's greatest shopping complex of its kind, the Mall covers 110 acres and features 828 stores, 110 restaurants, 19 theaters . . . a five-acre water park and a glass dome that is over 19 storeys high. . . . Contemplate the Mall's indoor lake complete with four submarines from which you can view sharks, octopi, tropical marine life, and a replica of the Great Barrier Reef. . . . Fantasyland Hotel has given its rooms a number of themes.
> (Travel Alberta publicity material, quoted in Urry, 1990: 147)

However, even less extreme cases than this, such as the Metro Centre in Gateshead, sometimes exhibit this tendency to narrativize shopping by creating themed locations, such as a Mediterranean Village (Chaney, 1990). In large part, of course, the aim of theming the experience of shopping is to keep the shopper in that role for as long as possible and for shopping to become an attraction in its own right. Crawford (1992) argues that the advantage of theming is that mundane goods reap the benefit of 'adjacent attraction', whereby their display in exotic contexts renders them more glamorous and interesting. This is especially

Bibliography

Abercrombie, N., Hill, S., and Turner, B.S. (1980) *The Dominant Ideology Thesis*, London: Allen & Unwin.

Adamson, J. (1975) *Tex Avery: King of Cartoons*, New York: Da Capo.

Adler, S. (1983) 'Snow White for the defense: why Disney doesn't lose', *American Lawyer*, March: 32–5.

Aldridge, A. (1994) 'The construction of rational consumption in *Which?* magazine: the more blobs the better?' *Sociology*, 28: 899–912.

Alexander, G. (1994) 'Power play in the magic kingdom', *The Sunday Times* (Section 3), 28 August: 5.

Alexander, J. (1953a) 'The amazing story of Walt Disney: Part 1', *Saturday Evening Post*, 31 October: 24–5, 80, 84–6, 90, 92.

—— (1953b) 'The amazing story of Walt Disney: Part 2', *Saturday Evening Post*, 7 November: 26–7, 99–100.

Allan, R. (1985) 'Alice in Disneyland', *Sight and Sound*, Spring: 136–8.

Allen, H. and Denning, M. (1993) 'The cartoonists' front', *South Atlantic Quarterly*, 92: 89–117.

Alvesson, M. (1990) 'Organization: from substance to image?', *Organization Studies*, 11: 373–94.

Andrae, T. (1988) 'Of mouse and the man', in *Walt Disney's Mickey Mouse in Color*, New York: Pantheon.

Ang, I. (1990) 'Culture and communication: toward an ethnographic critique of media consumption in the transnational media system', *European Journal of Communication*, 5: 239–60.

Anon. (1932) 'Mickey Mouse's fourth birthday finds organization world-wide', *Motion Picture Herald*, 1 October: 42–3, 51.

—— (1934) 'The big bad wolf', *Fortune*, November: 88–95, 142–8.

—— (1948) 'The mighty mouse', *Time*, 25 October: 33.

—— (1950) 'Money from mice', *Newsweek*, 13 February: 84–9.

—— (1954) 'Father Goose', *Time*, 27 December: 30–4.

—— (1962) 'The wide world of Disney', *Newsweek*, 31 December: 48–51.

—— (1965) 'Disney's live-action profits', *Business Week*, 2 July: 78–82.

—— (1967) 'Disney without Walt', *Forbes*, 1 July: 39–40.

Apple, M. (1983) 'Uncle Walt', *Esquire*, December: 164–8.

Arlidge, J. (1992) 'Disney casts recruits for European venture', *Independent*, 7 January: 3.

Bailey, A. (1982) *Walt Disney's World of Fantasy*, New York: Everest House.

Barker, M. (1989) *Comics: Ideology, Power and the Critics*, Manchester: Manchester University Press.

—— (1993) 'Seeing how far you can see: on being a "fan" of 2,000AD', in D. Buckingham (ed.), *Reading Audiences: Young People and the Media*, Manchester: Manchester University Press.

Barley, S.R., Meyer, G.W., and Gash, D.C. (1988) 'Cultures of culture: practitioners and the pragmatics of normative control', *Administrative Science Quarterly*, 33: 24–60.

Barrier, M. (1974) 'Of mice, wabbits, ducks and men: the Hollywood cartoon', *AFI Report*, 5: 18–26.

—— (1979) '"Building a better mouse": fifty years of Disney animation', *Funnyworld*, 20: 6–15.

Bass, B.M. (1985) *Leadership and Performance Beyond Expectations*, New York: Free Press.

Baudrillard, J. (1983) *Simulations*, New York: Semiotext(e).

—— (1993a) 'I don't belong to the club, to the Seraglio: interview with Mike Gane and Monique Arnaud', in M. Gane (ed.), *Baudrillard Live: Selected Interviews*, London: Routledge.

—— (1993b) 'Hyperreal America', *Economy and Society*, 22: 243–52.

Bauman, Z. (1992) *Intimations of Postmodernity*, London: Routledge.

Beard, R. (1982) *Walt Disney's Epcot Center*, New York: Harry N. Abrams.

Bendazzi, G. (1994) *Cartoons: One Hundred Years of Cinema Animation*, London: John Libbey.

Bierman, J.H. (1976) 'The Walt Disney robot dramas', *Yale Review*, 66: 223–36.

—— (1979) 'Disneyland and the "Los Angelization" of the arts', in M. Matlaw (ed.), *American Popular Entertainment*, Westport, Conn.: Greenwood Press.

Biggart, N.W. (1989) *Charismatic Capitalism: Direct Selling Organizations in America*, Chicago: University of Chicago Press.

Billig, M. (1994) 'Sod Baudrillard! Or ideology critique in Disney World', in H.W. Simons and M. Billig (eds), *After Postmodernism: Reconstructing Ideology Critique*, London: Sage.

Birmingham, S. (1964) 'The greatest one-man show on earth: Walt Disney', *McCall's*, 91: 98–101, 121.

Birnbaum, S. (1989) *Walt Disney World: The Official Guide*, New York: Avon Books.

Blake, P. (1972) 'Walt Disney World', *Architectural Forum*, 136: 24–41.

Blocklyn, P.L. (1988) 'Making magic: the Disney approach to people management', *Personnel*, 65: 28–35.

Boehme, L.R. (1975) 'The Magic Kingdom: is it really magic?', *American Opinion*, May: 13–20, 85–90.

Boorstin, D.J. (1961) *The Image: A Guide to Pseudo-events in America*, New York: Harper & Row.

Boyer, P.J. (1991) 'Katzenberg's seven-year itch', *Vanity Fair*, November: 64–79.

Bragdon, C. (1934) 'Mickey Mouse and what he means', *Scribner's*, July: 40–3.

Bright, R. (1987) *Disneyland: Inside Story*, New York: Harry N. Abrams.

Bristol, G.T. (1938) 'Snow White: inanimate characters become a new force in merchandising', *Dun's Review*, April: 13–17.

Brophy, P. (1991) 'The animation of sound', in A. Cholodenko (ed.), *The Illusion of Life: Essays on Animation*, Sydney: Power.

Bryman, A. (1992) *Charisma and Leadership in Organizations*, London: Sage.

—— (1993) 'Charismatic leadership in business organizations', *Leadership Quarterly*, 4: 289–304.

Bryson, B. (1993) 'Of mice and millions', *Observer Magazine*, 28 March: 16–23.

Budd, M., Entman, R.M., and Steinman, C. (1990) 'The affirmative character of U.S. cultural studies', *Critical Studies in Mass Communication*, 7: 169–84.

Bukatman, S. (1991) 'There's always Tomorrowland: Disney and the hypercinematic experience', *October*, 57: 55–78.

Cabarga, L. (1988) *The Fleischer Story*, New York: DaCapo.

Calás, M.B. (1993) 'Deconstructing charismatic leadership', *Leadership Quarterly*, 4: 305–28.

Carlzon, J. (1987) *Moments of Truth*, New York: Ballinger.

Carr, H. (1931) 'The only unpaid movie star', *American*, March: 55–7, 122–5.

Chamberlain, M. (1981) 'How the world of Disney is building for the future', *Marketing Week*, 11 December: 28–37.

Chaney, D. (1990) 'Subtopia in Gateshead: the MetroCentre as a cultural form', *Theory, Culture and Society*, 7: 49–68.

—— (1993) *Fictions of Collective Life: Public Drama in Late Modern Culture*, London: Routledge.

Chase, M. and Shaw, C. (1989) 'The dimensions of nostalgia', in C. Shaw and M. Chase (eds), *The Imagined Past: History and Nostalgia*, Manchester: Manchester University Press.

Churchill, D.W. (1934) 'Now Mickey Mouse enters art's temple', *New York Times Magazine*, 3 June: 13, 21.

—— (1938) 'Disney's philosophy', *New York Times Magazine*, 6 March: 9, 23.

Clegg, S. (1990) *Modern Organizations: Organization Studies in the Post-modern World*, London: Sage.

Cohen, E. (1979) 'A phenomenology of tourist experiences', *Sociology*, 13: 179–201.

—— (1988) 'Traditions in the qualitative sociology of tourism', *Annals of Tourism Research*, 15: 29–46.

Condit, C.M. (1989) 'The rhetorical limits of polysemy', *Critical Studies in Mass Communication*, 6: 103–22.

Conger, J.A. (1989) *The Charismatic Leader: Beyond the Mystique of Exceptional Leadership*, San Francisco: Jossey-Bass.

—— (1993) 'Max Weber's conceptualization of charismatic authority: its influence on organizational research', *Leadership Quarterly*, 4: 277–88.

Cooke, P. (1990) *Back to the Future: Modernity, Postmodernity, and Locality*, London: Unwin Hyman.

Corner, J., Richardson, K., and Fenton, N. (1990) *Nuclear Reactions: Form and Response in Public Issue Television*, London: John Libbey.

Cox, G.D. (1989) 'Don't mess with the Mouse', *National Law Journal*, 11, 31 July: 1, 26–7.

Crafton, D. (1982) *Before Mickey: The Animated Film, 1989–1928*, Cambridge, Mass.: MIT Press.

Crawford, M. (1992) 'The world in a shopping mall', in M. Sorkin (ed.), *Variations on a Theme Park: The New American City and the End of Public Space*, New York: Noonday.

Culhane, J. (1976) 'The old Disney magic', *New York Times Magazine*, 1 August: 11, 32–6.

Culhane, S. (1986) *Talking Animals and Other People*, New York: St Martin's Press.

Curran, J. (1990) 'The new revisionism in mass communication research: a reappraisal', *European Journal of Communication*, 5: 135–64.

Custen, G.F. (1992) *Bio/Pics: How Hollywood Constructed Public History*, New Brunswick, N.J.: Rutgers University Press.

Davidson, B. (1964) 'The fantastic Walt Disney', *Saturday Evening Post*, 7 November: 66–74.

Davis, S.O. (1980) 'Wish upon a falling star at Disney', *New York Times Magazine*, 16 November: 144–52.

Deal, T.E. and Kennedy, A.A. (1982) *Corporate Cultures*, Reading, Mass.: Addison-Wesley.

Debord, G. (1994) *The Society of the Spectacle* (1967), New York: Zone Books.

deCordova, R. (1994) 'The Mickey in Macy's window: childhood, consumerism, and Disney animation', in E. Smoodin (ed.), *Disney Discourse*, New York: Routledge.

Dennett, A.S. (1989) 'A postmodern look at EPCOT's American Adventure', *Journal of American Culture*, 12: 47–53.

De Roos, R. (1963) 'The magic worlds of Walt Disney', *National Geographic*, August: 159–207.

Dickson, E.J. (1993) 'Who's afraid of the big bad mouse?', *The Sunday Times Magazine*, 28 March: 30–4.

Disney, R. (1969) 'My unforgettable brother, Walt Disney', *Reader's Digest*, March: 133–9.

Disney, W. (1931) 'Mickey Mouse: how he was born', *Windsor Magazine*, October: 641–5.

—— (1934) 'The life story of Mickey Mouse', *Windsor Magazine*, January: 259–63.

—— (1941) 'Growing pains', *American Cinematographer*, March: 106–7, 139–42.

Doctorow, E.L. (1972) *The Book of Daniel*, London: Macmillan.

Dorfman, A. and Mattelart, A. (1975) *How to Read Donald Duck: Imperialist Ideology in the Disney Comic*, New York: International General.

Eckert, C. (1978) 'The Carole Lombard in Macy's window', *Quarterly Review of Film Studies*, 3: 1–22.

Eco, U. (1986) *Travels in Hyperreality*, London: Pan.

Eddy, D. (1955) 'The amazing secret of Walt Disney', *American*, August: 28–9, 110–15.

Edwards, R. (1979) *Contested Terrain: The Transformation of the Workplace in the Twentieth Century*, London: Heinemann.

Eisen, A. (1975) 'Two Disney artists', *Crimmer's: The Harvard Journal of Pictorial Fiction*, Winter: 35–44.

Eisman, R. (1993) 'Disney magic', *Incentive*, September: 45–56.

Eliot, M. (1993) *Walt Disney: Hollywood's Dark Prince*, New York: Birch Lane.

Elliott, H. (1994) 'Disney goes for older generation', *The Times*, 3 May: 5.

Ewen, S. (1988) *All Consuming Images: The Politics of Style in Contemporary Culture*, New York: Basic Books.

Eyssartel, A.-M. and Rochette, B. (n.d.) *Des mondes inventés: les parcs à thèmes*, Paris: Les Éditions de la Villette.

Featherstone, M. (1991) *Consumer Culture and Postmodernism*, London: Sage.

Feifer, M. (1985) *Going Places*, London: Macmillan.

Feild, R.D. (1942) *The Art of Walt Disney*, New York: Macmillan.

Fessier, M. (1967) 'Legacy of a last tycoon', *Los Angeles Times West*, 12 November: 16–23.

Fielding, H. (1992) 'Teach yourself post-modernism', *Independent on Sunday*, 15 November: 21.

Finch, C. (1973) *The Art of Walt Disney: From Mickey Mouse to the Magic Kingdoms*, New York: Harry N. Abrams.

Findlay, J.M. (1992) *Magic Lands: Western Cityscapes and American Culture after 1940*, Bekeley, Cal.: University of California Press.

Fiske, J. (1989) *Understanding Popular Culture*, London: Unwin Hyman.

Fjellman, S.M. (1992) *Vinyl Leaves: Walt Disney World and America*, Boulder, Col.: Westview Press.

Fleischer, R. (1993) *Just Tell Me When to Cry: Encounters with the Greats, Near-Greats and Ingrates of Hollywood*, New York: Carroll & Graf.

Flower, J. (1991) *Prince of the Magic Kingdom: Michael Eisner and the Re-making of Disney*, New York: John Wiley.

Ford, B. (1989) *Walt Disney*, New York: Walker.

Ford, G. (1975) 'Warner Brothers', *Film Comment*, 11: 10–16, 93, 96.

Forgacs, D. (1992) 'Disney animation and the business of childhood', *Screen*, 33: 361–74.

Francaviglia, R.V. (1981) 'Main Street USA: a comparison/contrast of streetscapes in Disneyland and Walt Disney World', *Journal of Popular Culture*, 15: 141–56.

France, V.A. (1991) *Window on Main Street*, Nashua, N.H.: Laughter Publications.

Freedland, J. (1994) 'Mighty mouse in magic kingdom', *Guardian*, 31 January: 8–9.

Fushaho, A. (1988) 'Disneyland's dreamlike success', *Japan Quarterly*, 35: 58–62.

Gaines, J. (1993) '"You don't necessarily have to be charismatic . . .": an interview with Anita Roddick and reflections on charismatic processes in The Body Shop International', *Leadership Quarterly*, 4: 347–59.

Galbraith, J.K. (1992) *The Culture of Contentment*, New York: Houghton Mifflin.

Garfield, B. (1991) 'How I spent (and spent and spent) my Disney vacation', *Washington Post*, 7 July: B5.

Gergen, K.J. (1992) 'Organization theory in the postmodern era', in M. Reed and M. Hughes (eds), *Rethinking Organization: New Directions in Organization Theory and Analysis*, London: Sage.

Gindin, R. (1984) 'The mystique of training at Disney World', *Restaurant Business*, 10 February: 242.

Giroux, H.A. (1994) 'Beyond the politics of innocence: memory and pedagogy in the "Wonderful World of Disney"', *Socialist Review*, 23: 79–107.

Goff, N. (1979) 'Disney: all gassed up and ready to go', *Financial World*, 1 September: 14–18.

Goldberger, P. (1972) 'Mickey Mouse teaches the architects', *New York Times Magazine*, 22 October: 40–1, 92–9.

Gomery, D. (1994) 'Disney's business history: a reinterpretation', in E. Smoodin (ed.), *Disney Discourse*, New York: Routledge.

Gordon, M. (1958) 'Walt's profit formula: dream, diversify – and never miss an angle', *Wall Street Journal*, 4 February: 1, 12.

Gottdiener, M. (1982) 'Disneyland: a Utopian urban space', *Urban Life*, 11: 139–62.

——— (1986) 'Recapturing the center: a semiotic analysis of shopping malls', in M. Gottdiener and A.P. Lagopolous (eds), *The City and the Sign*, New York: Columbia University Press.

Gottlieb, A. (1982) 'Americans' vacations', *Annals of Tourism Research*, 9: 165–87.

Gould, S.J. (1979) 'Mickey Mouse meets Konrad Lorenz', *Natural History*, 88: 30–6.

Greene, K. and Greene, R. (1991) *The Man Behind the Magic: The Story of Walt Disney*, New York: Viking.

Grossman, C.L. (1993) 'Vegas deals new hand of family fun', *USA Today* (International Edition), 11 August: 5A.

Grover, R. (1991) *The Disney Touch: How a Daring Management Team Revived an Entertainment Empire*, Homewood, Ill.: Irwin.

——— (1994) 'Jeffrey Katzenberg: no more Mr Tough Guy?', *Business Week*, 31 January: 46–7.

Haden-Guest, A. (1973) *The Paradise Program: Travels through Muzak, Hilton, Coca-Cola, Texaco, Walt Disney and other World Empires*, New York: Morrow.

Halas, J. and Manvell, R. (1959), *The Technique of Film Animation*, London: Focal Press.

Halevy, J. (1958) 'Disneyland and Las Vegas', *The Nation*, 7 June: 510–13.

Hall, S. (1980) 'Encoding/decoding', in S. Hall, D. Hobson, A. Lowe, and P. Willis (eds), *Culture, Media, Language*, London: Hutchinson.

Hand, D.D. (n.d.) *Memoirs: David Dodd Hand*, privately printed.

Harmetz, A. (1985) 'The man re-animating Disney', *New York Times Magazine*, 29 December: 13–18, 3, 37, 42–3.

Harrington, M. (1979) 'To the Disney station: corporate socialism in the Magic Kingdom', *Harper's*, January: 35–44, 86.

Harvey, D. (1989) *The Condition of Postmodernity*, London: Basil Blackwell.

Hayes, T.C. (1984) 'Trouble stalks the Magic Kingdom', *New York Times*, 17 June: 1, 12.

Heydebrand, W.V. (1989) 'New organizational forms', *Work and Occupations*, 16: 323–57.

Holleran, A. (1992) 'The mouse and the virgin', in *Fodor's 93: Walt Disney World*, New York: Fodor's.

Holliss, R. and Sibley, B. (1988) *The Disney Studio Story*, New York: Crown.

Hollister, P. (1940) 'Genius at work: Walt Disney', *Atlantic Monthly*, December: 689–701.

Horton, J.O. and Crew, S.R. (1989) 'Afro-Americans and museums: towards a policy of inclusion', in W. Leon and R. Rosenzweig (eds), *History Museums in the United States*, Urbana, Ill.: University of Illinois Press.

Howell, J.M. and Avolio, B.J. (1992) 'The ethics of charismatic leadership: submission or liberation?', *The Executive*, 6: 43–54.

Hulett, S. (1992) 'Walt Disney's *Pinnochio*', in *1992 Screen Cartoonists Annual*.

Hunt, P. and Frankenberg, R. (1990) 'It's a small world: Disneyland, the family and the multiple re-presentations of American childhood', in A. James and A. Prout (eds), *Constructing and Reconstructing Childhood: Contemporary Issues in the Sociological Study of Childhood*, London: Falmer.

Iacocca, L. (1984) *Iacocca: An Autobiography*, New York: Bantam.

Jackson, K.M. (1993) *Walt Disney: A Bio-bibliography*, Westport, Conn.: Greenwood.

Jackson, T. (1994) 'Disney seeks solutions to the park's midlife and identity crises', *Tampa Tribune* (Business and Finance section), 8 August: 8–9.

Jacobs, L. (1939) *The Rise of the American Film: A Critical History*, New York: Harcourt, Brace.

Jacobson, G. and Hillkirk, J. (1986) *Xerox: American Samurai*, New York: Collier.

Jameson, F. (1991) *Postmodernism, or, The Cultural Logic of Late Capitalism*, London: Verso.

Jenkins, I. (1992) 'French turn on "fascism" at Disney', *The Sunday Times* (section 3), 16 February: 6.

Jermier, J.M. (1993) 'Introduction – charismatic leadership: neo-Weberian perspectives', *Leadership Quarterly*, 4: 217–33.

Johnson, D.M. (1981) 'Disney World as structure and symbol: re-creation of the American experience', *Journal of Popular Culture*, 15: 157–65.

Jones, C. (1991) 'What's up, down under?', in A. Cholodenko (ed.), *The Illusion of Life: Essays in Animation*, Sydney: Power.

Kapsis, R.E. (1989) 'Reputation building and the film art world: the case of Alfred Hitchcock', *Sociological Quarterly*, 30: 15–35.

Kasindorf, J. (1991) 'Mickey Mouse time at Disney', *New York*, 7 October: 32–42.

Kasson, J.F. (1978) *Amusing the Million: Coney Island at the Turn of the Century*, New York: Hill & Wang.

Keat, R., Whiteley, N. and Abercrombie, N. (1994) 'Introduction', in R. Keat, N. Whiteley, and N. Abercrombie (eds), *The Authority of the Consumer*, London: Routledge.

King, M.J. (1981) 'Disneyland and Walt Disney World: traditional values in futuristic form', *Journal of Popular Culture*, 15: 116–40.

—— (1983) 'McDonald's and Disney', in M. Fishwick (ed.), *Ronald Revisited: The World of Ronald McDonald*, Bowling Green, Ohio: Bowling Green University Popular Press.

—— (1991) 'The theme park experience: what museums can learn from Mickey Mouse', *The Futurist*, November-December: 24–31.

King, P. (1986) 'The marketing challenge: backstage at Walt Disney World', *Food Management*, July: 74–8, 142–8.

Kinney, J. (1988) *Walt Disney and Assorted Other Characters: An Unauthorized Account of the Early Years at Disney's*, New York: Harmony.

Klein, N.M. (1993) *Seven Minutes: The Life and Death of the American Animated Cartoon*, London: Verso.

Kottak, C.P. (1982) 'Anthropological analysis of mass enculturation', in C.P. Kottak (ed.), *Researching American Culture*, Ann Arbor, Mich.: University of Michigan Press.

Kotter, J. and Heskett, J.L. (1992) *Corporate Culture and Performance*, New York: Free Press.

Kuenz, J. (1993) 'It's a small world after all: Disney and the pleasures of identification', *South Atlantic Quarterly*, 92: 63–88.

Lang, G.E. and Lang, K. (1988) 'Recognition and renown', *American Journal of Sociology*, 94: 79–109.

Langer, M. (1992) 'The Disney–Fleischer dilemma: product differentiation and technological innovation', *Screen*, 33: 343–60.

Langley, W. (1993) 'Euro-dismal', *The Sunday Times*, 22 August: 9.

Lash, S. (1990) *Sociology of Postmodernism*, London: Routledge.

Lawrence, E.A. (1986) 'In the Mick of time: reflections on Disney's ageless mouse', *Journal of Popular Culture*, 20: 65–72.

Leerhsen, C. (1989) 'How Disney does it', *Newsweek*, 3 April: 14–20.

Lenburg, J. (1993) *The Great Cartoon Directors*, New York: Da Capo.

Lennon, P. (1993) 'Priest who took Mickey for a ride', *Guardian* (section 2), 25 October: 2–3.

Leyda, J. (1942) 'The dimensions of Disney', *Saturday Review*, 6 June: 5.

Lloyd, C. (1994) 'Airport rides ready for take-off', *The Sunday Times* (section 3), 10 July: 10.

Long, K.H. (1994) 'Quiet region debates value of theme park', *Tampa Tribune* (Travel section), 31 July: 1.

Lowenthal, D. (1985) *The Past is a Foreign Country*, Cambridge: Cambridge University Press.

—— (1989) 'Nostalgia tells it like it wasn't', in C. Shaw and M. Chase (eds), *The Imagined Past: History and Nostalgia*, Manchester: Manchester University Press.

Lowenthal, L. (1944) 'Biographies in popular magazines', in P.F. Lazarsfeld and F. Stanton (eds), *Radio Research: 1942–1943*, New York: Duell, Sloan & Pearce.

Lutz, E.G. (1920) *Animated Cartoons: How They Are Made, Their Origin and Development*, New York: Scribner.

Lyotard, J.-F. (1984) *The Postmodern Condition: A Report on Knowledge*, Manchester: Manchester University Press.

MacCannell, D. (1976) *The Tourist: A New Theory of the Leisure Class*, New York: Schocken.

—— (1992) *Empty Meeting Grounds: The Tourist Papers*, London: Routledge.

McDonald, J. (1966) 'Now the bankers come to Disney', *Fortune*, May: 138–41, 223–4.

McGuigan, J. (1992) *Cultural Populism*, London: Routledge.

Maltin, L. (1973) *The Disney Films*, New York: Crown.

—— (1987) *Of Mice and Magic: A History of American Animated Cartoons*, revised edition, New York: Plume.

Mann, A. (1934) 'Mickey Mouse's financial career', *Harper's*, 168: 714–21.

Marin, L. (1984) *Utopics: Spatial Play*, London: Macmillan.

Marling, S. (1993) *American Affair*, London: Boxtree.

Martin, J. (1992) *Cultures in Organizations: Three Perspectives*, New York: Oxford University Press.

Massie, J. (1992) 'How we got here', *1992 Screen Cartoonists Annual*.

Masters, K. (1994) 'A house divided', *Vanity Fair*, 57 (November): 122–8, 156–60.

Mechling, E.W. and Mechling, J. (1981) 'The sale of two cities: a semiotic comparison of Disneyland with Marriott's Great Adventure', *Journal of Popular Culture*, 15: 166–79.

Medved, M. (1993) 'Still wishing on a star', *The Sunday Times*, 8 August: 24–5.

Merritt, R. and Kaufman, J.B. (1992) *Walt in Wonderland: The Silent Films of Walt Disney*, Perdenone: Edizioni Biblioteca dell'Imagine.

Meyer, M. (1994) 'Of mice and men', *Newsweek*, 5 September: 40–7.

Miller, D. Disney (1956) *The Story of Walt Disney*, New York: Dell.

Mills, S.F. (1990) 'Disney and the promotion of synthetic worlds', *American Studies International*, 28: 66–79.

Mintzberg, H. (1991) 'The entrepreneurial organization', in H. Mintzberg and J.B. Quine (eds), *The Strategy Process: Concepts, Contexts, Cases*, Englewood Cliffs, N.J.: Prentice-Hall.

Mooney, J. (1994) 'Disney on the edge?', *Empire*, November: 78–84.

Moore, A. (1980) 'Walt Disney World: bounded ritual space and the playful pilgrimage center', *Anthropological Quarterly*, 53: 207–18.

Morison, E.E. (1983) 'What went wrong with Disney's world's fair', *American Heritage*, 35: 70–9.

Morley, D. (1980) *The 'Nationwide' Audience*, London: British Film Institute.

—— (1993) 'Active audience theory', *Journal of Communication*, 43: 13–19.

Mosley, L. (1986) *The Real Walt Disney: A Biography*, London: Grafton.

Mulkay, M. and Chaplin, E. (1982) 'Aesthetics and artistic career', *Sociological Quarterly*, 23: 117–38.

Murdock, G. (1989a) 'Cultural studies: missing links', *Critical Studies in Mass Communication*, 6: 436–40.

—— (1989b) 'Critical inquiry and audience activity', in R. Dervin, L. Grossberg, B.J. O'Keefe, and E. Wartella, *Rethinking Communication, vol. 2: Paradigm Exemplars*, Newbury Park, Cal.: Sage.

Nadler, D.A. and Tushman, M.L. (1990) 'Beyond the charismatic leader: leadership and organizational change', *California Management Review*, 32: 77–97.

Natale, R. (1986) 'Prince of the Magic Kingdom: Michael Eisner re-animates Disney', *California Business*, December: 18–23.

Neff, R. (1990) 'In Japan, they're Goofy about Disney', *Business Week*, 12 March: 39.

Nelson, S. (1986) 'Walt Disney's EPCOT and the world's fair performance tradition', *Drama Review*, 30: 106–46.

—— (1990) 'Reel life performance: the Disney–MGM Studios', *Drama Review*, 24: 60–78.

Nye, R.B. (1981) 'Eight ways of looking at an amusement park', *Journal of Popular Culture*, 15: 63–75.

Olins, R. (1993) 'Dynamic duos – or terrible twins?', *The Sunday Times* (section 3), 30 May: 8.

Peary, D. and Peary, G. (eds) (1980) *The American Animated Cartoon: A Critical Anthology*, New York: Dutton.

Peters, T. and Austin, N. (1985) *A Passion for Excellence*, New York: Random House.

Peters, T. and Waterman, R. (1982) *In Search of Excellence: Lessons from America's Best-run Companies*, New York: Harper & Row.

Potts, M. and Behr, P. (1987) *The Leading Edge: CEOs who Turned Their Companies Around*, New York: McGraw-Hill.

Reader, I. (1993a) 'Introduction', in I. Reader and T. Walter (eds), *Pilgrimage in Popular Culture*, London: Macmillan.

Reader, I. (1993b) 'Conclusions', in I. Reader and T. Walter (eds), *Pilgrimage in Popular Culture*, London: Macmillan.

Real, M.R. (1977) *Mass-mediated Culture*, Englewood Cliffs, N.J.: Prentice-Hall.

Relph, E. (1976) *Place and Placelessness*, London: Pion.

Ritzer, G. (1993) *The McDonaldization of Society*, Thousand Oaks, Cal.: Pine Forge.

Roberts, E.A. (1994) 'History is different from Disneyhistory', *Tampa Tribune* (Commentary section), 31 July: 1.

Robertson, R. (1990) 'After nostalgia? Wilful nostalgia and the phases of globalization', in B.S. Turner (ed.), *Theories of Modernity and Postmodernity*, London: Sage.

Rojek, C. (1993a) 'Disney culture', *Leisure Studies*, 12: 121–35.

—— (1993b) *Ways of Escape: Modern Transformations in Leisure and Travel*, London: Macmillan.

Rose, F. (1989) *West of Eden: The End of Innocence at Apple Computer*, London: Business Books.

—— (1990) 'Taking care of business', *Premiere*, November: 104–12.

Rosenau, P.M. (1992) *Post-modernism and the Social Sciences: Insights, Inroads, and Intrusions*, Princeton, N.J.: Princeton University Press.

Ross, I. (1982) 'Disney gambles on tomorrow', *Fortune*, 4 October: 62–8.

Rowe, C. and Koetter, F. (1978) *Collage City*, Cambridge, Mass.: MIT Press.

Rugare, S. (1991) 'The advent of America at EPCOT Center', in R. Diprose and R. Ferrell (eds), *Cartographies: Structuralism and the Mapping of Bodies and Spaces*, North Sydney, Australia: Allen & Unwin.

Sayers, F.C. (1965) 'Walt Disney accused', *Horn Book*, December: 602–11.

Sayle, M. (1983) 'Of mice and yen', *Harper's*, August: 36–45.

Schein, E.H. (1985) *Organizational Culture and Leadership*, San Francisco: Jossey-Bass.

Schickel, R. (1986) *The Disney Version: The Life, Times, Art and Commerce of Walt Disney*, revised edition, London: Pavilion.

Schiller, H.I. (1973) *The Mind Managers*, Boston, Mass.: Beacon.

—— (1989) *Culture, Inc.: The Corporate Takeover of Public Expression*, New York: Oxford University Press.

Schudson, M. (1979) 'Review essay: On tourism and modern culture', *American Journal of Sociology*, 84: 1249–58.

Schultz, J. (1988) 'The fabulous presumption of Disney World: Magic Kingdom in the wilderness', *Georgia Review*, 42: 275–312.

Sehlinger, B. (1994) *The Unofficial Guide to Walt Disney World*, New York: Prentice Hall.

Seldes, G. (1931) 'Mickey Mouse maker', *New Yorker*, 19 December: 23–7.

—— (1937) 'No art, Mr Disney?', *Esquire*, September: 91, 171–2.

Sertl, W.J. (1989) 'Hollywood divine: Disney–MGM Studios in Orlando', *Travel and Leisure*, 19: 140–6, 192–6.

Shearer, L. (1972) 'How Disney sells happiness', *Parade*, March 26: 4–6.

Shields, R. (1989) 'Social spacialization and the built environment: the West Edmonton Mall', *Environment and Planning D: Society and Space*, 7: 147–64.

—— (1991) *Places on the Margin: Alternative Geographies of Modernity*, London: Routledge.

—— (1992) 'The individual, consumption cultures and the fate of community', in R. Shields (ed.), *Lifestyle Shopping: The Subject of Consumption*, London: Routledge.

Simons, C. (1990) 'Business and leisure', *Landscape Architecture*, 80: 42–5.

Smith, R.C. and Eisenberg, E.M. (1987) 'Conflict at Disneyland: a root-metaphor analysis', *Communication Monographs*, 54: 367–80.

Smoodin, E. (1993) *Animating Culture: Hollywood Cartoons from the Sound Era*, Oxford: Roundhouse.

Snyder, N.H., Dowd, J.J., and Houghton, D.M. (1994) *Vision, Values and Courage: Leadership for Quality Management*, New York: Free Press.

Solomon, C. (1989) *Enchanted Drawings: The History of Animation*, New York: Alfred A. Knopf.

—— (1990) 'The new toon boom', *Los Angeles Times Calendar*, 19 August: 8–9, 94–5.

—— (1993) 'Disney's daughter attacks book', *Los Angeles Times*, 17 July: F14.

Sorkin, M. (1992) 'See you in Disneyland', in M. Sorkin (ed.), *Variations on a Theme Park: The New American City and the End of Public Space*, New York: Noonday.

Spanier, D. (1994) 'Poker with the plastic pirates', *The Financial Times*, 22 January: xi.

Stanley, L. (1993) 'On auto/biography in sociology', *Sociology*, 27: 41–52.

Starobinski, J. (1966) 'The idea of nostalgia', *Diogenes*, 54: 81–103.

Stephanson, A. (1987) 'Regarding postmodernism – a conversation with Fredric Jameson', *Social Text*, 17: 29–54.

Susman, W. (1989) 'Did success spoil the United States?: dual representations on postwar America', in L. May (ed.), *America: Culture and Politics in the Age of Cold War*, Chicago: University of Chicago Press.

Sutton, R.I. (1992) 'Feelings about a Disneyland visit: photography and the reconstruction of bygone emotions', *Journal of Management Inquiry*, 1: 278–87.

Taylor, J. (1987) *Storming the Magic Kingdom: Wall Street, the Raiders and the Battle for Disney*, New York: Viking.

Terrell, J. (1991) 'Disneyland and the future of museum anthropology', *American Anthropologist*, 93: 149–53.

Tester, K. (1993) *The Life and Times of Post-modernity*, London: Routledge.

Thomas, B. (1976) *Walt Disney: An American Original*, New York: Simon & Schuster.

—— (1991) *Disney's Art of Animation from Mickey Mouse to Beauty and the Beast*, New York: Hyperion.

Thomas, F. and Johnston, O. (1981) *Disney Animation: The Illusion of Life*, New York: Abbeville.

Thomas, M. (1969) 'The men who followed Mickey Mouse', *Dun's Review*, 94: 34–8.

Tichy, N.M. and Devanna, M.A. (1986) *The Transformational Leader*, New York: John Wiley.

Tietyen, D. (1990) *The Musical World of Walt Disney*, Milwaukee, Wis.: Hal Leonard.

Toth, M.A. (1981) *The Theory of the Two Charismas*, Washington D.C.: University Press of America.

Toufexis, A. (1985) 'No Mickey Mousing around', *Time*, 11 March: 40.

Turner, B.S. (1987) 'A note on nostalgia', *Theory, Culture and Society*, 4: 147–56.

Turner, R. (1991) 'Hollywood blues as Disney stumbles', *The Sunday Times*, 17 November: 7.

Turner, V. and Turner, E. (1978) *Image and Pilgrimage in Christian Culture*, New York: Columbia University Press.

Urry, J. (1990) *The Tourist Gaze: Leisure and Travel in Contemporary Societies*, London: Sage.

Van Maanen, J. (1991) 'The smile factory: work at Disneyland', in P.J. Frost, L.F. Moore, M.R. Louis, C.C. Lundberg and J. Martin (eds), *Reframing Organizational Culture*, Newbury Park, Cal.: Sage.

—— and Kunda, G. (1989) '"Real feelings": emotional expression and organizational culture', *Research in Organizational Behavior*, 11: 43–103.

Wakefield, N. (1990) *Postmodernism: The Twilight of the Real*, London: Pluto.

Waldrep, S. (1993) 'The contemporary future of tomorrow', *South Atlantic Quarterly*, 92: 139–55.

Wallace, I. (1949) 'Mickey Mouse and how he grew', *Collier's*, 9 April: 20–36.

Wallace, K. (1963) 'The engineering of ease', *New Yorker*, 7 September: 104–29.

Wallace, M. (1981) 'Visiting the past: history museums in the United States', *Radical History Review*, 25: 63–96.

—— (1985) 'Mickey Mouse history: portraying the past at Disney World', *Radical History Review*, 32: 33–57.

Waller, G.A. (1980) 'Mickey, Walt and film criticism from *Steamboat Willie to Bambi*', in D. Peary and G. Peary (eds), *The American Animated Cartoon: A Critical Anthology*, New York: Dutton.

Walsh, K. (1992) *The Representation of the Past: Museums and Heritage in the Post-modern World*, London: Routledge.

Wanger, W. (1943) 'Mickey Icarus, 1943', *Saturday Review*, 4 September: 18–19.

Warde, A. (1994) 'Consumers, identity and belonging: reflections on some theses of Zygmunt Bauman', in R. Keat, N. Whiteley, and N. Abercrombie (eds), *The Authority of the Consumer*, London: Routledge.

Warren, S. (1994) 'Disneyfication of the metropolis: popular resistance in Seattle', *Journal of Urban Affairs*, 16: 89–107.

Wasko, J., Phillips, M., and Purdie, C. (1993) 'Hollywood meets Madison Avenue: the commercialization of US films', *Media, Culture and Society*, 15: 271–93.

Wasserman, A. (1983) 'Un and loathing at EPCOT', *Industrial Design Magazine*, March/April: 34–9.

Weber, B. (1969) 'The Disney troika', *California Business*, 20 October: 7, 18–19.

Weber, M. (1968) *Economy and Society* (1925), 3 vols, eds G. Roth and C. Wittich, New York: Bedminster.

Weinstein, R.M. (1992) 'Disneyland and Coney Island: reflections on the evolution of the modern amusement park', *Journal of Popular Culture*, 26: 131–64.

Welsh, T. (1994) 'Best and worst corporate reputations', *Fortune*, 7 February: 32–6.

Westley, F.R. and Mintzberg, H, (1989) 'Visionary leadership and strategic management', *Strategic Management Journal*, 10: 17–32.

Wiener, J. (1993) 'Murdered ink', *The Nation*, 256: 743–50.

Willis, S. (1993) 'Disney World: public use/private state', *South Atlantic Quarterly*, 92: 119–37.

Wilson, A. (1992) *The Culture of Nature: North American Landscape from Disney to the Exxon Valdez*, Cambridge, Mass.: Basil Blackwell.

Wolf, J.C. (1979) 'Disney World: America's vision of Utopia', *Alternative Futures*, 2: 72–7.

Yoshimoto, M. (1994) 'Images of empire: Tokyo Disneyland and Japanese cultural imperialism', in E. Smoodin (ed.), *Disney Discourse*, New York: Routledge.

Zehnder, L.E. (1975) *Florida's Disney World*, Tallahassee, Fla.: Peninsular Publishing.

Zukin, S. (1990) 'Socio-spatial prototypes of a new organization of consumption: the role of real cultural capital', *Sociology*, 24: 37–56.

—— (1991) *Landscapes of Power: From Detroit to Disney World*, Berkeley, Cal.: University of California Press.

Study Guide

Relevant to: **All registered students, Global**

1. INTRODUCTION

Students must be registered with Oxford Brookes University in order to be eligible for the Oxford Brookes University degree of BSc (Honours) in Applied Accounting.

Registration takes place automatically for those students who have indicated to ACCA that they wish to be opted in to the degree scheme.

Students not indicating on their initial registration form that they wish to be part of the scheme can opt in any time prior to attempting 2.4 + or 2.5 + or 2.6. Eligible students can write to the Admissions Administration requesting to be opted in or can enter their details via the E-business facility.

2. GRADUATE PROFILE
2.1 ENTRY REQUIREMENTS

Students holding recognised university entrance qualifications (two A Levels plus three GCSEs in five separate subjects including Maths and English or equivalent) will enter the degree at Part 1. Except for students graduating through the transitional arrangements (see Section 3.9), students with relevant and semi-relevant degrees will be able to claim exemptions from some of the papers of Part 1 and Part 2 up to a maximum of six papers, and provided the papers do not include any of the new papers 2.4, 2.5 or 2.6. Students studying for the ACCA qualification via the Mature Student Entry Route (MSER) are also eligible for the degree.

2.2 AIMS

One of the principle aims of the degree is to widen access to Oxford Brookes degrees enabling more students worldwide to work towards an Oxford Brookes degree.

Oxford Brookes University believes that the subject matter of accounting requires a vocational component which focuses specifically on those elements of knowledge, skills and attitudes necessary for effective job performance in this important area, and this degree aims to meet those needs.

A further aim of this degree is to ensure that Oxford Brookes University has an input into developing the professionally competent accountants and business advisors of the future.

2.3 GENERIC LEARNING OUTCOMES

On completing their course of study students will have demonstrated an ability to:

in the area of knowledge and understanding

> i. describe and apply fundamental accounting concepts and principles to a range of business transactions and situations;

> ii. critically evaluate accounting concepts and principles and their application in solutions to practical accounting problems;

> iii. understand and apply the techniques, processes and procedures which are required to ensure the efficient and effective use and deployment of human resources;

> iv. understand and apply the principles of corporate and business law, and the area of revenue law relating to businesses and their employees;

> v. evaluate the audit process and its application for both external regulation and for business control and development for a range of organisations.

in the area of disciplinary and professional skills:

> i. record financial information using double-entry bookkeeping techniques;

> ii. prepare financial statements using a wide range of appropriate accounting techniques;

> iii. appraise the performance and financial situation of organisations using a range of interpretative techniques; discuss the limitations of those techniques;

> iv. select and apply appropriate management accounting and quantitative techniques to business planning, decision making and control;

> v. communicate financial information to a variety of different audiences.

in the area of transferable skills:

> i. analyse problems, identify critical factors, construct and select appropriate solutions;

> ii. communicate logically and clearly verbal and numerical data in writing;

> iii. apply study and time-management skills;

> iv. produce an independently researched academic account of a business problem or question;

> v. use (or understand the use of) information technology to record, manipulate and analyse financial data, and solve accounting problems.

3. COURSE REGULATIONS
3.1 CONDITIONS FOR ADMISSION
Applicants who meet the entry requirements and are registered with ACCA will be eligible for registration for the award of the Oxford Brookes BSc (Hons) in Applied Accounting.

Students currently registered with ACCA will be eligible for registration with Oxford Brookes University for the BSc (Hons) in Applied Accounting subject to the transition arrangements (see 3.9).

Students registering for the Oxford Brookes University degree may study in a variety of ways for the ACCA/Oxford Brookes University modules and for the Oxford Brookes University Research and Analysis Project. These study methods may include:

1. Colleges offering ACCA courses leading to the Oxford Brookes University award.

2. Correspondence or distance learning material which teaches to the ACCA syllabus and the Oxford Brookes University award.

No responsibility is taken by Oxford Brookes University for any of these study methods unless they are specifically recommended or approved by Oxford Brookes University.

A list of delivery centres and materials specifically recommended or approved by Oxford Brookes University will be available on the ACCA website, as this information becomes available.

3.2 ADMISSION WITH CREDIT
Subject to ACCA's Exemption regulations, applicants will be admitted with credit, or awarded exemption from a maximum of 240 credits.

3.3 EXAMINATION PROCEDURES
Examination procedures and Committees will be conducted by ACCA in accordance with its regulations.

3.4 EXTERNAL EXAMINERS
External Examiners will be appointed by Oxford Brookes and will attend ACCA Examination Review Board meetings. The duties and powers of the External Examiners will be in accordance with their rights and responsibilities as laid down for the time being by the Academic Regulations of the University

3.5 OXFORD BROOKES EXAMINATION BOARD
Examination Board meetings, chaired by the Head of the Oxford Brookes Business School or his/her nominee, will be held to consider the award of BSc (Honours) in Applied Accounting. The Examination Board meetings will be attended by a minimum of two additional members of the Business School, normally including the Liaison Manager, and a minimum of one of the External Examiners.

3.6 CONDITIONS FOR PROGRESSION
ACCA's regulations in relation to progression will apply.

3.7 CONDITIONS FOR THE AWARD OF BSc (Hons) IN APPLIED ACCOUNTING
3.7.1 BASIC PRINCIPLES
To qualify for the award of BSc (Hons) in Applied Accounting, the candidate must, within 10 years of first registering, have:

- Passed the required papers in the ACCA/Brookes examinations (see 3.7.2.) or 3.9 for transition students

- Passed the Research and Analysis Project

- Candidates must have been registered with the ACCA throughout that period. Exceptionally, a student may be permitted to suspend registration for a determined period. However, to be eligible for the degree the required papers and the Research and Analysis Project must still be passed within 10 years of the initial registration for the Professional Examinations.

3.7.2 REQUIRED PAPERS
In determining the papers that need to be taken, three factors are taken into account:

- The learning covered by the paper

- The volume of study undertaken

- A requirement that at least one third of the degree-level study must be on an ACCA/Oxford Brookes scheme. This means that at least three papers under the Quality Control Procedures of Oxford Brookes University must be taken after May 2000.

For a student taking their first examination after September 2001, the papers required are Papers 1.1 to 1.3 and papers 2.1 to 2.6 of the new scheme. Papers 1.1, 1.2, 1.3, 2.1, 2.2 and 2.3 may be credited by ACCA/Oxford Brookes, but not papers 2.4, 2.5 or 2.6

3.7.3 EXISTING STUDENTS AND MEMBERS AND NEW STUDENTS SITTING EXAMINATIONS BEFORE SEPTEMBER 2001
For students who take their first papers before September 2001, transitional arrangements apply (see Section 3.9).

3.8 Honours classification
Apart from students graduating under the transitional arrangements, all students taking their first examinations after September 2001 will be awarded an Honours classification based on the average mark achieved in all ACCA papers passed in Parts 1 and 2 examinations, according to the following table:

Average ACCA mark	Degree Classification	Oxford Brookes Average Mark
66% or above	First Class	70% and above
58% - 65%	Second Class, first division	60% - 69%
54% - 57%	Second Class, second division	50% - 59%
50% - 53%	Third Class	40% - 49%
Below 50%	Fail	Below 40%

3.9 Transition arrangements

Transition arrangements apply to students who have taken and passed existing scheme papers to September 2001. The arrangements cover eligibility for an Oxford Brookes Degree and classification of the degree:

The regulations below relate to a student's situation prior to the June 2000 examinations session and assume subsequent completion of the Research and Analysis Project

Students at Foundation Stage Students who prior to June 2000 have not completed ACCA examinations beyond the Foundation stage will be eligible for the degree	**Requirements** Need to Pass: • Existing paper 6 or new scheme paper 2.6 AND • Existing paper 8 or new scheme paper 2.4 AND • Existing paper 10 or new scheme paper 2.5 AND • Pass or hold a valid exemption from all other papers in the first two parts of either the existing or new scheme

Classification - Based on the average of the marks from paper 6 (or 2.6), paper 8 (or 2.4), paper 10 (or 2.5) and any new scheme papers needed to complete the first two parts of either scheme.

Students at Certificate Stage Students who, prior to June 2000, have no passes at the Certificate stage or who have not passed papers 6 and 8 and have no conditional passes at Module E will be eligible for the degree.	**Requirements** Need to pass: • Existing paper 6 or new scheme paper 2.6 AND • Existing paper 8 or new scheme paper 2.4 AND • Existing paper 10 or new scheme paper 2.5 AND • Pass or hold a valid exemption from all other papers in the first two parts of either the existing or new scheme

Classification - Based on the average of the marks from paper 6 (or 2.6), paper 8 (or 2.4), paper 10 (or 2.5) and any new scheme papers needed to complete the first two parts of either scheme.

Students who, prior to June 2000, have passed paper 6, but not paper 8 and who have no conditional passes at Module E will be eligible for the degree.	**Requirements** Need to pass: • Module E at or by the June 2001 sitting **(NB: If not passed by this date eligibility will be lost)** AND • Existing paper 8 or new scheme paper 2.4 AND • Pass or hold a valid exemption from all other papers in the first two parts of either the existing or new scheme

Classification - Based on the average of the marks from the three papers of Module E, paper 8 (or 2.4) and any new scheme papers needed to complete the first two parts of either scheme.

Students who, prior to June 2000, have passed paper 8 but not paper 6 and have no conditional passes at Module E will be eligible for the degree	**Requirements** Need to pass: • Module E at or by the June 2001 sitting **(NB: If not passed by this date, eligibility will be lost)** AND • Existing paper 6 or new scheme paper 2.6 AND • Pass or hold a valid exemption from all other papers in the first two parts of either the existing or new scheme

Classification - Based on the average of the marks from the three papers of module E, paper 6 (or 2.6) and any new scheme papers needed to complete the first two parts of either scheme.

Students who, prior to June 2000, have passes in papers 6 and 8 and have no conditional passes at Module E will be eligible for the degree	**Requirements** Need to pass: • Module E at or by the June 2001 sitting **(NB: If not passed by this date eligibility will be lost)** AND • Pass or hold a valid exemption from all other papers in the first two parts of either the existing or new scheme

Classification - Based on the average of the marks from the three papers of module E and any new scheme papers needed to complete the first two parts of either scheme.

Students at Professional Stage Students who, prior to June 2000, have not completed Module E and have no conditional passes in this Module will be eligible for the degree.	Requirements Need to pass: • Module E at or by the June 2001 sitting AND **(NB: If not passed by this date eligibility will be lost)** • Pass any outstanding paper in the first two parts of either the existing or new scheme

Classification - Based on the average of the marks for the three papers of Module E and either any new scheme paper or paper 6 or 8 (passed at or after June 2000) which is needed to complete the first two parts of either scheme.

Any student who prior to the June 2000 examination session held conditional passes or exemptions at Module E or had completed Module E is not eligible to be awarded the degree.

The table shown in 3.8 will be used to convert the average mark calculated from the above into a degree classification.

3.10 EXCEPTIONAL CIRCUMSTANCES IN RELATION TO THE OXFORD BROOKES UNIVERSITY RESEARCH PROJECT

The University's Regulations for the review of and appeals against decisions of an Examination Committee will apply to students taking the Research and Analysis Project. Details of the regulations are available on the ACCA website.

Candidates may not ask for a review of the Examination Committee's decision based on a disagreement with the academic judgement of the Examiners.

Students in exceptional circumstances, e.g. illness, should delay submitting their projects until they are sure that their work is of an appropriate standard.

3.11 TERMINATION OF THE ACCA/OXFORD BROOKES AGREEMENT

The initial agreement will be valid for five years following signature. After this time, it will be renewed annually, for one-year periods, subject to either party giving one years' written notice to the other of an intention not to renew the agreement.

In the event of termination, both ACCA and the University will make every effort to ensure that the interests of all students enrolled on the programme are protected. In particular, ACCA, where requested by the University, shall continue to offer the programme to existing students enrolled at the date of termination, to the same standards as determined by and in accordance with the signed agreement, until the completion of their programme, including any additional periods required for extensions.

3.12 ALUMNI

All Oxford Brookes University graduates will be invited to join the Oxford Brookes University Alumni Society.

3.13 CHEATING

WARNING

Oxford Brookes University has very strict rules regarding cheating, plagiarism and syndication. These rules are designed to ensure that all students' work for assessment is actually the result of their individual effort, skills and knowledge and has not been produced by means that will give an unfair advantage over other students. These rules apply to both the examinations and the project.

All assessments are intended to determine the skills, abilities, understanding and knowledge of each of the individual students undertaking the assessment. Cheating is defined as obtaining an unfair academic advantage and any student found using any form of cheating, attempting to cheat or assisting someone else to cheat may be subject to disciplinary action in accordance with the University's Disciplinary Procedure. The University takes this issue very seriously and students have been expelled or had their degrees withheld for cheating in assessments. If you are having difficulty with your work it is important to seek help from your tutor rather than be tempted to use unfair means to gain marks. Do not risk losing your degree and all the work you have done.

The University's regulations define a number of different forms of cheating, although any form of cheating is strictly forbidden. These are:

- Submitting other people's work as your own - either with or without their knowledge. This includes copying in examinations; using notes or unauthorised materials in examinations

- Impersonation - taking an assessment on behalf of or pretending to be another student, or allowing another person to take an assessment on your behalf or pretend to be you

- Plagiarism - taking or using another person's thoughts, writings or inventions as your own. To avoid plagiarism you must make sure that quotations from whatever source must be clearly identified and attributed at the point where they occur in the text of your work by using one of the standard conventions for referencing. The Library has a leaflet about how to reference your work correctly and your tutor can also help you. It is not enough just to list sources in a bibliography at the end of your essay or dissertation if you do not acknowledge the actual quotations in the text. Neither is it acceptable to change some of the words or the order of sentences if, by failing to acknowledge the source properly, you give the impression that it is your own work

- Collusion - except where written instructions specify that work for assessment may be produced jointly and submitted as the work of more than one student, you must not collude with others to produce a piece of work jointly, copy or share another student's work or lend your work to another student in the reasonable knowledge that some or all of it will be copied

- Duplication - submitting work for assessment that is the same as, or broadly similar to, work submitted earlier for academic credit, without acknowledgement of the previous submission

- Falsification - the invention of data, its alteration, its copying from any other source, or otherwise obtaining it by unfair means, or inventing quotations and/or references.

Index and Bibliography

BIBLIOGRAPHY

Cameron, S. (2002) <u>Business Students' Handbook: learning skills for study and employment</u>. 2nd Edition, Harlow, Financial Times/Prentice Hall

Guirdham, M. (2002) <u>Interpersonal Skills at Work</u>, 2nd Edition, London, Prentice Hall

Hayes, J. (2002) <u>Interpersonal Skills at Work</u>. 2nd Edition, Hove, Routledge

Honey, P. (1988) <u>Face to Face: A Practical Guide to Interactive Skills</u> 2nd Edition, Aldershot, Gower

Hussey, J. Hussey, R. (1997) <u>Business Research</u>. Basingstoke, Macmillan

Kolb, D. A., I. M. Rubin and J. M. McIntyre (1973) <u>Organisational Psychology: An Experiential Approach</u>. Englewood Cliffs, NJ, Prentice Hall

Luck, M. (1999) <u>Your Student Research Project</u>. Aldershot, Gower

Northedge, A. (1990) <u>The Good Study Guide</u>. Milton Keynes, Open University

Pearson, D. (1993) <u>Strategic Marketing Management: Analysis and Decision</u>. London, BPP Publishing

Pedler, M. Burgoyne, J. Boydell, T. (1994) <u>A Manager's Guide to Self Development</u>. Maidenhead, McGraw Hill

Saunders, M. Lewis, P. Thornhill, A. (2003) <u>Research Methods for Business Students</u>. 3rd Edition, Harlow, Financial Times/Prentice Hall

Shea, G. F. (1992) <u>Mentoring: A guide to the basics</u>. London, Kogan Page

ACCA Order

To BPP Professional Education, Aldine Place, London W12 8AW
Tel: 020 8740 2211　　Fax: 020 8740 1184
email: publishing@bpp.com　　website: www.bpp.com
Order online www.bpp.com/mybpp

Mr/Mrs/Ms (Full name)
Daytime delivery address

Postcode

Daytime Tel

Date of exam (month/year)　　Scots law variant　Y / N

Occasionally we may wish to email you relevant offers and information about courses and products. Please tick to opt into this service. ☐

POSTAGE & PACKING

Study Texts/Kits

	First	Each extra	Online
UK	£5.00	£2.00	£2.00
EU*	£6.00	£4.00	£4.00
Non EU	£20.00	£10.00	£10.00

Passcards/Success CDs/i-Learn/i-Pass

	First	Each extra	Online
UK	£2.00	£1.00	£1.00
EU*	£3.00	£2.00	£2.00
Non EU	£8.00	£8.00	£8.00

Learning to Learn Accountancy/Business Maths and English

	Each	Online
UK	£3.00	£2.00
EU*	£6.00	£4.00
Non EU	£20.00	£10.00

Grand Total (incl. Postage) £ ☐☐☐☐☐

I enclose a cheque for (Cheques to *BPP Professional Education*)
Or charge to Visa/Mastercard/Switch
Card Number
Expiry date　　Start Date
Issue Number (Switch Only)
Signature

Course	6/05 Texts	1/05 Kits	1/05 Passcards	Success CDs	7/05 i-Learn	7/05 i-Pass	Learn Online
PART 1							
1.1 Preparing Financial Statements (UK)	£26.00	£12.95	£9.95	£14.95	£40.00	£30.00	£100
1.2 Financial Information for Management	£26.00	£12.95	£9.95	£14.95	£40.00	£30.00	£100
1.3 Managing People	£26.00	£12.95	£9.95	£14.95	£40.00	£30.00	£100
PART 2							
2.1 Information Systems	£26.00	£12.95	£9.95	£14.95	£40.00	£30.00	£100
2.2 Corporate and Business Law (UK)**	£26.00	£12.95	£9.95	£14.95	£40.00	£30.00	£100
2.3 Business Taxation FA2004 (12/05 exams)	£24.95 (8/04)	£12.95	£9.95	£14.95	£34.95 (8/04)	£24.95 (8/04)	£100
2.3 Business Taxation FA2005	£26.00 †	£12.95	£9.95	£14.95	£40.00 (9/05)	£30.00 (9/05)	£100
2.4 Financial Management and Control	£26.00	£12.95	£9.95	£14.95	£40.00	£30.00	£100
2.5 Financial Reporting (UK)	£26.00 (7/05)	£12.95	£9.95	£14.95	£40.00	£30.00	£100
2.6 Audit and Internal Review (UK)	£26.00	£12.95	£9.95	£14.95	£40.00	£30.00	£100
PART 3						8/04	
3.1 Audit and Assurance Services (UK)	£26.00	£12.95	£9.95	£14.95		£30.00 (4/05)	£60
3.2 Advanced Taxation FA2004 (12/05 exams)	£24.95 †	£12.95	£9.95	£14.95		£24.95	£60
3.2 Advanced Taxation FA2005	£26.00 †	£12.95	£9.95	£14.95		£30.00 (9/05)	£60
3.3 Performance Management	£26.00	£12.95	£9.95	£14.95		£24.95	£60
3.4 Business Information Management	£26.00	£12.95	£9.95	£14.95		£24.95	£60
3.5 Strategic Business Planning and Devt	£26.00	£12.95	£9.95	£14.95		£24.95	£60
3.6 Advanced Corporate Reporting (UK)	£26.00 (7/05)	£12.95	£9.95	£14.95		£24.95	£60
3.7 Strategic Financial Management	£26.00	£12.95	£9.95	£14.95		£24.95	£60
INTERNATIONAL STREAM						7/05	
1.1 Preparing Financial Statements (Int'l)	£26.00	£12.95	£9.95	£14.95	£40.00	£30.00	£100
2.2 Corporate and Business Law (Global)	£26.00	£12.95	£9.95	£14.95			
2.5 Financial Reporting (Int'l)	£26.00	£12.95	£9.95	£14.95	£40.00	£30.00	£100
2.6 Audit and Internal Review (Int'l)	£26.00	£12.95	£9.95	£14.95	£40.00	£30.00	£100
3.1 Audit and Assurance Services (Int'l)	£26.00	£12.95	£9.95	£14.95		£30.00	£60
3.6 Advanced Corporate Reporting (Int'l)	£26.00	£12.95	£9.95	£14.95	£40.00 (12/05)	£30.00	£60
Success in Your Research and Analysis Project - Tutorial Text (10/05)	£26.00						
Learning to Learn Accountancy (7/02)	£9.95						
Business Maths and English (6/04)	£9.95						

SUBTOTAL £

† 8/05 for 6/06 & 12/06 exams. New edition Kit, Passcard, i-Learn and i-Pass available in 2006)

We aim to deliver to all UK addresses inside 5 working days; a signature will be required. Orders to all EU addresses should be delivered within 6 working days. All other orders to overseas addresses should be delivered within 8 working days. *EU includes the Republic of Ireland and the Channel Islands. **For Scots law variant students, a free **Scots Law Supplement** is available with the 2.2 Text. Please indicate in the name and address section if this applies to you.

ACCA Order

To BPP Professional Education, Aldine Place, London W12 8AW
Tel: 020 8740 2211
Fax: 020 8740 1184
email: publishing@bpp.com
website: www.bpp.com
Order online www.bpp.com/mybpp

Mr/Mrs/Ms (Full name)

Daytime delivery address

Postcode

Daytime Tel

Date of exam (month/year)

Scots law variant   Y / N

Occasionally we may wish to email you relevant offers and information about courses and products. Please tick to opt into this service. ☐

POSTAGE & PACKING

Home Study Packages

	First	Each extra	Each
UK**	£6.00	£6.00	-
EU**	-	-	£15.00
Non EU	-	-	£50.00

Success CDs/i-Learn

	First	Each extra	Online
UK	£2.00	£1.00	£1.00
EU**	£3.00	£2.00	£2.00
Non EU	£8.00	£8.00	£8.00

Learning to Learn Accountancy/Business Maths and English/Success in Your Research and Analysis Project

	Each	Online
UK	£3.00†	£2.00
EU**	£6.00	£4.00
Non EU	£20.00	£10.00

(†£5.00 Success in Your Research and Analysis Project)

Postage and packing not charged on free copy ordered with Home Study Course.

Grand Total (incl. Postage)   £ ☐

I enclose a cheque for ☐ (Cheques to *BPP Professional Education*)

Or charge to Visa/Mastercard/Switch ☐

Card Number

Expiry date   Start Date

Issue Number (Switch Only)

Signature

	Home Study Package*	Home Study PLUS*	Success CDs	7/05 i-Learn	Learn Online
PART 1					
1.1 Preparing Financial Statements UK	£115.00	£180.00	£14.95	£40.00	£100.00
1.2 Financial Information for Management	£115.00	£180.00	£14.95	£40.00	£100.00
1.3 Managing People	£115.00	£180.00	£14.95	£40.00	£100.00
PART 2					
2.1 Information Systems	£115.00	£180.00	£14.95	£40.00	£100.00
2.2 Corporate and Business Law UK***	£115.00	£180.00	£14.95	£34.95 (8/04)	£100.00
2.3 Business Taxation FA2004 (12/05 exams)	£115.00	£180.00	£14.95	£40.00 (9/05)	£100.00
2.3 Business Taxation FA2005 (2006 exams)	£115.00	£180.00	£14.95	£40.00	£100.00
2.4 Financial Management and Control	£115.00	£180.00	£14.95	£40.00	£100.00
2.5 Financial Reporting UK	£115.00	£180.00	£14.95	£40.00	£100.00
2.6 Audit and Internal Review UK	£115.00	£180.00	£14.95	£40.00	£100.00
PART 3					
3.1 Audit and Assurance Services UK	£115.00	£150.00	£14.95		£60.00
3.2 Advanced Taxation FA2004 (12/05 exams)	£115.00	£150.00	£14.95		£60.00
3.2 Advanced Taxation FA2005 (2006 exams)	£115.00	£150.00	£14.95		£60.00
3.3 Performance Management	£115.00	£150.00	£14.95		£60.00
3.4 Business Information Management	£115.00	£150.00	£14.95		£60.00
3.5 Strategic Business Planning and Development	£115.00	£150.00	£14.95		£60.00
3.6 Advanced Corporate Reporting UK	£115.00	£150.00	£14.95		£60.00
3.7 Strategic Financial Management	£115.00	£150.00	£14.95		£60.00
INTERNATIONAL STREAM					
1.1 Preparing Financial Statements (Int'l)	£115.00	£180.00		£40.00	£100.00
2.2 Corporate and Business Law (Global)	£115.00	£180.00			
2.5 Financial Reporting (Int'l)	£115.00	£180.00		£40.00	£100.00
2.6 Audit and Internal Review (Int'l)	£115.00	£180.00		£40.00	£100.00
3.1 Audit and Assurance Services (Int'l)	£115.00	£150.00			£60.00
3.6 Advanced Corporate Reporting (Int'l)	£115.00	£150.00		£40.00 (12/05)	£60.00

Success in Your Research and Analysis		
Project - Tutorial Text (10/05)	£26.00	
Learning to Learn Accountancy (7/02)	Free/£9.95	
Business Maths and English (6/04)	Free/£9.95	

SUBTOTAL   £ ☐

We aim to deliver to all UK addresses inside 5 working days; a signature will be required. Orders to all EU addresses should be delivered within 6 working days. All other orders should be delivered within 8 working days. *Home Study Courses include Texts, Kits, Passcards and i-Pass (i-Pass not available for 2.2 Global and 3.1 International). You can also order one free copy of either Learning to Learn Accountancy or Business Maths and English per person. **EU includes the Republic of Ireland and the Channel Islands. ***For Scots law variant students, a free **Scots Law Supplement** is available with the 2.2 Text.

REVIEW FORM & FREE PRIZE DRAW

All original review forms from the entire BPP range, completed with genuine comments, will be entered into one of two draws on 31 January 2006 and 31 July 2006. The names on the first four forms picked out on each occasion will be sent a cheque for £50.

Name: _____   Address: _____

_____

_____

How have you used this Tutorial Text?
(Tick one box only)

☐ Home study (book only)

☐ On a course: college _____

☐ Other _____

Why did you decide to purchase this Text?
(Tick one box only)

☐ Have used BPP Texts in the past

☐ Recommendation by friend/colleague

☐ Recommendation by a lecturer at college

☐ Saw advertising

☐ Other _____

During the past six months do you recall seeing/receiving any of the following?
(Tick as many boxes as are relevant)

☐ Our advertisement in *Student Accountant*

☐ Our advertisement in *Pass*

☐ Our brochure with a letter through the post

Which (if any) aspects of our advertising do you find useful?
(Tick as many boxes as are relevant)

☐ Prices and publication dates of new editions

☐ Information on Text content

☐ Facility to order books off-the-page

☐ None of the above

Your ratings, comments and suggestions would be appreciated on the following areas and features of this book

	Very useful	Useful	Not useful
Self assessment (Chapter 2))	☐	☐	☐
Overview (Chapter 3)	☐	☐	☐
Project definition (Chapter 4)	☐	☐	☐
Project management (Chapter 5)	☐	☐	☐
Research and analysis (Chapters 6 and 7)	☐	☐	☐
Synthesis (Chapter 8)	☐	☐	☐
Report writing (Chapter 9)	☐	☐	☐
Mentor meetings (Chapters 10 and 11)	☐	☐	☐
Presentation (Chapter 12)	☐	☐	☐
Key Skills Statement (Chapter 13)	☐	☐	☐
Examples	☐	☐	☐
Exercises	☐	☐	☐
Proforma forms	☐	☐	☐
Checklists	☐	☐	☐

	Excellent	Good	Adequate	Poor
Overall opinion of this Tutorial Text	☐	☐	☐	☐

Do you intend to continue using BPP Study Texts/Kits?   ☐ Yes   ☐ No

Please note any further comments and suggestions on the reverse of this page.

Please return to: Stella Dinenis, BPP Professional Education, FREEPOST, London, W12 8BR or email your comments to stelladinenis@bpp.com

REVIEW FORM & FREE PRIZE DRAW (continued)

Please note any further comments and suggestions below

FREE PRIZE DRAW RULES

1. Closing date for 31 January 2006 draw is 31 December 2005. Closing date for 31 July 2006 draw is 30 June 2006.

2. Restricted to entries with UK and Eire addresses only. BPP employees, their families and business associates are excluded.

3. No purchase necessary. Entry forms are available upon request from BPP Professional Education. No more than one entry per title, per person. Draw restricted to persons aged 16 and over.

4. Winners will be notified by post and receive their cheques not later than 6 weeks after the relevant draw date.

5. The decision of the promoter in all matters is final and binding. No correspondence will be entered into.

Submission Forms for Research and Analysis Project

INSTRUCTIONS:

Sections A, B and C of this form should be completed by the student and Section D by the Mentor and accompany your work which must be sent **by some secure recorded means of delivery** to:

The ACCA Office, Business School, Oxford Brookes University, Wheatley Campus, Wheatley, OXFORD, OX33 1HX, United Kingdom

SECTION A (Student to complete in Block Capitals)

Student Surname
Student First name
Student Address

Student Email Address – to receive project results via email. Please complete this only if you consent to receiving your results (and other correspondence) by email. Your business email is preferable.

ACCA Student Registration Number

Date of submission

Project topic number chosen

Alternative project topic '99' must be approved and signed by Oxford Brookes in advance of submission (acca@brookes.ac.uk)

I declare that the attached project is all my own work. I agree that I shall be bound by the regulations of Oxford Brookes University and the BSc (Applied Accounting Programme) regulations, which can be found on www.accaglobal.com/students/professionalscheme/degreepartnership/oxb_studyguide

Signature (for regulations)   date ....

Date on front of Research and Analysis Project Guidelines used

SECTION B (Payment Details)

A fee of £50 **sterling** must accompany this work, which should be in the form of cheque, credit or UK debit card payment or bank draft made **payable to Oxford Brookes University**. Cash is not acceptable.

Please tick **one** of the following options:

Option 1: Credit or UK Debit Card (We cannot accept American Express)

Card Number   Start Date   Expiry Date   Issue No

Signature (for payment)   date ....

Option 2 to tick:	Cheque		Bank Draft	

FOR OFFICE USE ONLY
DATE RECEIVED...

Submission Forms for Research and Analysis Project

MARK SHEET

SECTION C (Student to complete in Block Capitals)

Student Surname

Student First name

ACCA Student Registration Number [   ]   Date of submission [   ]

Total Report word count:
Please note: this should not exceed 5000 words, otherwise you risk failure

Total Key Skills Statement word count:
Please note: this should not exceed 1500 words, otherwise you risk failure

SECTION D (Mentor to complete and sign)

Mentor's Certification:

I certify that to the best of my knowledge the project is the student's own work and that it has been carried out in accordance with the University's regulations, (see Student Guide available on-line at www.accaglobal.com), and that three meetings have been held with the student in accordance with the guidelines contained in Section 2.3 of the Research and Analysis Project Guidelines.

Mentor's Name	Address (Block capitals)

Capacity for acting as mentor: (tick choice) *(See 2.2 of the Research and Analysis Project Guidelines.)*	Employer Tutor/lecturer Qualified Chartered Certified Accountant	

Signature...   Date...............................

SECTION E (For Office Use Only)

Markers sheet

PROJECT	PASS	FAIL	
Communication Skills			Please refer to the attached sheet for full feedback comments.
Information gathering			
Analysis and Conclusions			
IT Skills			
KEY SKILLS STATEMENT			
Preparing for meetings			You are required to undertake the mentoring again.(Moderator to delete as appropriate).
Questioning			
Listening			
The presentation			
Self-Assessment of Interaction			
OVERALL RESULT			

Yes
No

Marker code		Date...................	Moderator code		Date ....